Cancel
The Apocalypse

The New Path to Prosperity

ANDREW SIMMS

Little, Brown

LITTLE, BROWN

First published in Great Britain in 2013 by Little, Brown

Copyright © Andrew Simms 2013

A CIP catalogue record for this book
is available from the British Library.

ISBN 978-1-40870-236-9

Typeset in Caslon by M Rules
Printed and bound in Great Britain by Clays Ltd, St Ives plc

Papers used by Little, Brown are from well-managed forests
and other responsible sources.

MIX
Paper from
responsible sources
FSC® C104740

Little, Brown
An imprint of
Little, Brown Book Group
100 Victoria Embankment
London EC4Y 0DY

An Hachette UK Company
www.hachette.co.uk

www.littlebrown.co.uk

To the Pathfinders
(and Scarlett, of course)

Traveller, you jumped . . .
For the pilot Joseph Kittinger, who did

A silver balloon
moonward bound

the cold and lack of air
the view, the view
that took you there

a space suit
and that parachute

you meant to pack
for when you jumped
to journey back

rising, falling
did you learn, what
it means, standing firm?

                              Anon.

Acknowledgements

First I want to acknowledge that many of these chapters grew from and draw upon countless other pieces of work: reports, talks, lectures and conversations that I have had over recent years with a wide range of marvellous friends and colleagues. By definition many of these have been joint enterprises (talking to oneself occasionally can be gratifying, but done too much has certain collateral dangers). I thank and admire all of you, and you know who you are. The material included, though, is my own, so no one else can be blamed. In one chapter, for example, I've drawn on reports on growth written for nef (the new economics foundation), in another the starting point was a lecture given to the Schumacher Society. It would be long-winded to trace all such evolutions, but for the interested there are endnotes you can follow. Thank you to Richard Beswick, my editor, for his extraordinary combination of tireless civility, extreme patience and straight talking.

And thank you to Scarlett Simms, for allowing me to use the computer in between her sessions creating remarkable fantasy worlds. Thanks to the people I know, in no particular order, who, in their different ways, give me strength, and who throw themselves heart, head and soul at the great challenges of our time: June Simms, my brother and sister Richard and Caroline, David Boyle, Nick Robins, Neal Lawson, James Marriott, Kevin Anderson, Ruth Potts, Pete Myers, George Hornby, Tony Greenham, Lindsay Mackie, Joe Smith, Richard Murphy, Molly Conisbee, Viki Johnson, Fred Pearce, Victoria Chick, Jayati Ghosh, Anna Coote, Ann Pettifor, Stewart Wallis, Gus Speth, Tim Jenkins, Dan Vockins, Etienne Pataut, Helen Kersely, Andy Fryers, Stephen Reid, Dannie Paffard, Jenny Scholfield, Pat Conaty,

Andrew Kelly, Richard Murphy, Caroline Lucas, Saamah Abdallah, Sue Mayer, John Christenson, John Sauven, Webster Wickham, Stan Allen, John Jackson, Ed Mayo, Philip Pullman, Frannie Armstrong, Paul Moss, Richard Black, Bevis Gillett, Jeremy Leggett, Tim Lang, George McRobie, Colin Hines, Adair Turner, Nick Hildyard, George Monbiot, Jonathon Porritt, John Magrath, Juliet Michaelson, Richard Savage, Di Bligh, Lemn Sissay, Saci Lloyd, Naomi Klein, Bill McKibben, Rob Hopkins, Felicity Neilsen, Leo Murray and Nicky Saunter. I am indebted in ways that even I, let alone they, will never know to the entire staff of nef, past and present, and my colleagues in the Green New Deal group. Also to my colleagues with whom over years I shared many experiences on the board of Greenpeace UK, and fellow judges of the Ashden Awards for Sustainable Energy.

Charles Dickens once described my old home town of Chelmsford as 'the dullest and most stupid spot on the face of the earth'. Nevertheless, it's the place where I grew up, and I was shaped in reaction to it. Also, I still have family, mother, sister, nephews and nieces who live there, so I owe it too odd gratitude. Finally, I'm grateful to my small corner of London, Rachel Maybank and everyone who makes it a community, Rina Hossain, and all at the Lavish Habit, Trinity Stores and The Fat Delicatessen who sustained me while I wrote.

Contents

To be truly radical is to make hope possible rather than despair convincing.

Raymond Williams

All great and beautiful work has come of first gazing without shrinking into the darkness.

John Ruskin

1

The Motive

Some reputational risks of predicting the apocalypse

Prophecies of doom are nothing new.

> Edward Teller, theoretical physicist

If the Apocalypse comes, beep me.

> Buffy the Vampire Slayer

The world should be ending about now. It has been foretold. Global warming, economic collapse or a comet – stepping outside your front door seems more hazardous than ever. If a new climate-borne disease doesn't get you, the nanobots will. But we're all waiting, and it isn't quite happening. When is *now*? As I write or perhaps the moment you read this book? In reality, the exact time seems not to matter, and that is the point.

If you believe all the warnings, humanity has been on the edge of obliteration for at least as long as people have been able to write down their intimations of apocalypse. But the warnings are wearing thin. Permanent threat, like perpetual war, is tiring. It raises suspicion of a hidden agenda or becomes the subject of justified ridicule. And, in one sense, I become less concerned. Should I be?

Fears bring forth a parade of sober-suited government spokespeople on news programmes. For example, unsolved problems stemming from the international banking crisis of 2008 left the global economy teetering, threatening the continued existence of the European single currency zone. This, and not the related slashing of public spending – money for schools, hospitals and public transport – excused by the debt crisis, caused apocalyptic newspaper headlines.

'"DESCENT INTO CHAOS" BEGINS' could be the title of a children's edition of Orpheus' journey into the Underworld. But it shouted from the front page of the London *Evening Standard*, and was a fairly typical newspaper headline in 2011 and 2012. The satirical magazine *Private Eye* deliberately confused the opening of an exhibition of apocalyptic art with the economy. Through it all, and regardless, the pay and bonuses of the bankers who caused the crisis either remained relatively unchanged or went up.

Separately, all hell was then meant to froth as Earth passed through a 'photon belt'. Sounds serious, and you might think so, but to be surrounded by a photon belt you would most likely have to be standing in the middle of a black hole, and therefore past caring, flattened by immense gravitational forces. As good news is no news, the media focused instead on another random reading of numbers from the Bible that were said to predict the end of everything. History carried on.

These were some of the apocalyptic tides due at the time of writing. Hundreds and hundreds of others were already meant to have happened. In fact, civilisation was supposed to be over before it had barely begun.

The freelance researcher Chris Nelson, infuriated by a cacophony of Christian fundamentalist warnings about the rapture and encroaching 'end times', combed the growing literature[1] of doomsday warnings to produce a list of destructions avoided by humanity. It covers millennia, providing a potted history of the non-arrival of the apocalypse.[2] But it raises an important question, which is the springboard for this book. Because we've been wrong so many times before, and continue to be, does that mean we can consider ourselves safe in perpetuity?

The ingenuity and imagination poured into picturing our downfall is impressive.[3] Around 4800 years ago Assyrians thought that the world might end due to human 'degeneracy'. They committed their fears to clay tablets that lasted, deviously, to disprove the words impressed upon them.

Doom-laden millenarians were common throughout history,
but this contemporary woodcut of the great flood in the Bristol Channel
in 1607 was a reminder that bad things really could happen.

An orgy of frightful anticipation accompanied the approaching second millennium in AD 1000, more recently dubbed Y1K. When that moment passed, it became Y1K+, a thousand years plus the lifetime of Christ. They hadn't been wrong, there was still thirty-three years to the end of time. That date too came and went. Yet even these self-reinventing millenarians were amateurs of flexible interpretation. Joachim of Fiore, a thirteenth-century Italian mystic, and his followers the Joachites spread the date of disaster over more than a century between 1260 and 1378, then seemingly tired of being wrong. Followers of William Miller, who set up the Second Adventists, later to become the Seventh Day Adventists, never grew bored of miscalculation. They thought that the day of reckoning was at least due in: 1843, 1845, 1846, 1849, 1851, 1874 and 1999. When Thomas Malthus, founder of the Statistical Society and a professor of history and political economy, published 'An Essay on the Principle of Population' in 1798, which warned of a demographic time-bomb triggering global starvation, he made it possible to be both wrong and respectable. The American political scientist Francis Fukuyama repeated this feat with his 1992 book *The End of History and the Last Man*, published after the Cold War, just as history was starting up again.

For the year 2000 – Y2K – there was an apocalyptic queue with everything from AIDS to nuclear war, alien invasion, terror, rapture, and ice unbalancing the Earth waiting in line. Enter the modern era without cause for complacency. We've survived Earth's encounter with the photon belt, the Mayan calendar allegedly predicting bad things in the year 2012 (confusion surrounded the correct interpretation), and the threatened collision with a 'trans-dimensional object'. Keep predicting for long enough, and either the law of averages or our ageing Sun will indeed finally finish us off. But for now, that's it, case closed. We've been wrong so many times before that there can't be anything truly to worry about. Can there?

Brighter than the dinosaurs?

Love . . . bears it out, even to the edge of doom.

William Shakespeare

Humanity has an ambiguous attitude towards the dinosaurs, fascinated and terrified in equal measure. Just watch people tiptoe nervously around the animatronic Tyrannosaurus rex in London's Natural History Museum (it can't walk, so if it did turn nasty even a baby could crawl away). Dinosaurs inform any amount of myth and folklore – from ancient dragons to incarnations of very modern fears, like Godzilla, born of Japan's twentieth-century nuclear nightmare.

But we also think of them as unintelligent. Partly for having relatively small brains, and partly for being stupid enough to become extinct. To be called a dinosaur implies you are consigned to history for failing to adapt. The experts will tell you, of course, that this isn't strictly true: several life forms from the time of the dinosaurs survive. There's the coelacanth, for example, a fishy contemporary that swam among them and is often referred to as a 'dinosaur' fish. And there is strong evidence that birds are direct descendants of dinosaurs.

Yet, like several rock and movie stars, it was how they left the world that made their reputation. It's not often that history is so definitive, yet every child is imprinted with the fireball that struck Earth off the coast of what is now Mexico sixty-five million years ago.

It changed the climate, massively reduced plant growth by blotting out the sun, and signalled the end of the dinosaurs. How silly of them not to see that coming.

This was the end-Cretaceous mass-extinction event. It left the land empty of large animals. Plant and marine life was shattered too. The planet was much warmer, with sea levels reaching an astonishing three hundred metres higher than today.

Homo sapiens has been around for about three hundred thousand years. Yet dinosaurs, big and stupid, survived and thrived for about 165 million years, and only came to a sudden brutal end because of that unlucky chance encounter with a large meteorite. Put another way, we've got about another 164.7 million years longer to hang around before we even match them. Given our larger brains, and all the false alarms to date, how lucky do we feel that we might catch and exceed the dinosaurs for longevity?

With that record it seems grossly unfair that the term 'Dinosaur' ever became a term of abuse. But they are a useful reminder that being a splendour of evolution is no guarantee of survival. Unnervingly, their virtual extinction is not the only warning from history. It's all a question of time frames. Five thousand years of false alarms might seem to us sufficient cause for a little smugness, self-confidence and a sense of untouchability.

At a seminar I gave in 2011 at the home of the Science and Technology Policy Research Unit at the University of Sussex, I talked about approaching a climate crossroads where one turning takes us past a threshold of potentially irreversible global warming. But I added that it was within our power to affect a large-scale, rapid transition that would avert such a terrifying prospect. When it came to questions, one academic, whose career was long enough to remember the original 1970s debate around the first *Limits to Growth* report, questioned whether we really did face such a choice. Hadn't humanity always 'muddled through'? Wouldn't and shouldn't we continue to do so?

It's worth looking at other great upheavals in geological history, and comparing them with our current circumstances.

Take, for example, the gloriously named Paleocene–Eocene Thermal Maximum (PETM). It oversaw one of Earth's more recent extinction events just fifty-five million years ago. It wasn't the worst, we'll get to that, but it casts our present predicament in an interesting light.

Over several millennia, temperatures rose during the PETM by an amount that overlaps with current projections for human-driven global warming. The difference is, according to the NASA climate scientist James Hansen, that we are likely to achieve similar degrees of warming in a fraction of that time.

One way of measuring climate change is to track how fast climatic zones shift, and that is done by studying the migration of plant and animal species. Those adapted to live at a particular range of temperature and rainfall will tend, if they can, to migrate, to keep up with it – to stay, as it were, in their comfort zone.

That means you can observe how fast such zones have moved across the surface of the Earth in past phases of cooling and warming. The evidence for different types of plants and animals can be found locked in layers of sediment in the fossil record. Today we can observe these movements in real time. Hansen notes that such climate zones, dramatically, are moving about ten times faster than they did during the PETM extinction event. One calculation suggests that to keep in step with the speed of temperature change, and therefore keep up with the climatic conditions to which they are adapted, plant and animal species will need to migrate by thirty feet per day.[4]

The PETM waved goodbye to countless life forms, but as with the end-Cretaceous event, Earth's history shows that things can get a lot worse. There were four previous mass-extinction events before the reign of the dinosaurs.

The first happened at the end of the Ordovician period around 430 million years ago. Of all the varieties of life that occupied the land and sea, six out of every ten died out. In the Devonian period ocean reefs were the early home to a great diversity of life. Late in the period, around 360 million years ago, climatic conditions changed and another mass extinction occurred. Leap forward another 110 million years to the end of the Permian period and the Earth experienced an extinction event of extraordinary scale. About 250 million years ago an estimated 80–95 per cent of all marine species perished; those great nurseries of life, the reefs, didn't reappear for about ten million years.

It is a constant refrain of those who would downplay the seriousness of long-term environmental change that the planet often experiences change, the climate often varies. What is often forgotten is the period of time it can take to reset itself and find a new equilibrium. It's not like waiting for a particularly hot or cold front to pass over in a few days. Cycles last for tens, hundreds of thousands and even millions of years, providing little comfort for those of us with mere human lifespans.

During the late Triassic, just over two hundred million years ago, another great convulsion led to mass extinction. Around half of all marine invertebrate species and eight out of ten of all four-limbed creatures on land died out.

There's something perversely comforting about reading of the horrors of the past from the comfort of the present. These events were rare and separated by millions of years. The last one was a very, very long time ago.

Given such great sweeps of geological history, you'd have to be either very unlucky or very stupid to witness a mass-extinction event. It could be either, or both, because we are living through one right now. In newspapers or on television news, you are more likely to read about the movement of interest rates, political, financial or sex scandals. But larger than all of those, a mass-extinction event is happening, let's call it what it is: an apocalypse of our own making.

Environmental change and habitat destruction, the result of human actions, has greatly accelerated the normal background rate of species becoming extinct. By exactly how much it has done so is the subject of debate. But the fact that we are driving, and living through another great die-off, with hugely unpredictable but overwhelmingly negative consequences, is not.

Humanity's impact is accepted even by figures such as the self-styled 'skeptical environmentalist', the Danish statistician Bjørn Lomborg.[5] Precise estimates for the accelerated extinction rates are complicated by the fact that many species still remain to be discovered. But by measuring the loss of known species through the decline of habitats, current rates are thought to be anything from one hundred to one thousand times faster than the background rate.

Encouragingly, these may be revised downward, not because humanity is destroying less habitat, but because improved methods for calculating loss may give a more accurate picture. The actual range may be only half that previously thought, according to two scientists from the Universities of California in the United States and Sun Yat-sen in Guangzhou, China. Even so, the message from the scientists Stephen Hubble and Fangliang He does not represent a rescue ship for the diversity of life on Earth. 'Mass extinction may already be upon us,' they say.[6] A study conducted by the Earth Institute at Columbia University and funded by the US National Science Foundation concluded that the world's oceans are probably acidifying much faster today, through absorbing carbon, than during the four major mass-extinction events of the last three hundred to four hundred million years. The PETM saw slower acidification, and was the only mass extinction 'remotely as fast as today'. Decisions taken now could have 'significant implications on a geologic timescale' according to Richard Feely of the US National Oceanic and Atmospheric Administration.[7]

Yet, however well grounded, or even conservative, are messages like this, they tend to go down badly, or be ignored altogether.

Incontrovertible evidence of the need to shape up and live differently on planet Earth seems to bring out the squirming teenager in us all. The failure to tidy a room and clear out month-old, half-eaten food from beneath a bed may breed whole new malign life forms, but we'll deny to the point of forcible eviction by health and safety inspectors that it is i) a problem, and ii) our problem.

It is not as if we lack scientific insight. The basic chemistry of climate change has been understood for over two centuries, and the particular link to the economic exploitation of fossil fuels for more than one hundred years, since it was spelt out by the Swedish Nobel Prize-winning chemist Svante Arrenhuis. More recently NASA's Hansen and colleagues described how we are consigning to history the climatic conditions in which human civilisation developed.[8]

Working with an atmospheric physicist colleague, I decided to find out how much time is left before meaningful climate thresholds are crossed. We erred, perhaps too much so, on the side of trusting to more optimistic outcomes, and asked a fairly simple question. When would the accumulation of greenhouse gases, based on recent trends, make it 'likely' (a term carefully defined by the Intergovernmental Panel on Climate Change to describe a particular balance of probability) that planet Earth will warm at the surface by an average of 2°C? We were conservative in the sense that many people think this represents too much warming to be safely allowed, and because we picked from the bottom end of the spectrum of risk that an environmental domino effect would happen – that is to say, that one environmental trend, such as glaciers melting, will accelerate another, such as the release of methane from land or sea beds.

Still, when the sums were done, it turned out that if nothing much changed, this point would be passed one hundred months from August 2008, taking us to the end of the year 2016. We didn't say that this meant that people would wake up on the morning of 1 January 2017 to witness fire in the sky and emaciated polar bears roaming the streets of London. We merely said that from that point on, the dice would be unfavourably loaded towards the likelihood of long-term, potentially irreversible global warming. An unpleasant thought, awkward, undesirable, but just what the numbers said. With slightly different assumptions, more or less generously applied, the period might be a bit longer or shorter. But this dynamic, a function of physics and chemistry and earth science, cannot be argued away with political assertions or ideological posturing. We might not like it, but we have to deal with it. Which brings us, full circle, to the reputational risk of predicting the apocalypse.

Visions and creative readings of esoteric religious texts (like the Bible) produce numerous flawed yet confident predictions of disaster. Because these haven't happened some conclude, by extension, that *any* warning of destructive upheaval must be wrong, regardless of the discipline it comes from. This is to place on an equal footing theory derived from verifiable scientific experiment, with gobbledygook floating up from patterns of words and numbers dimly discerned in books about faith and belief. But even pointing out the logical conclusions of human action, based on empirical observation and allowing for uncertainties, can still prove too uncomfortable for some.

Hence one blogger, writing for the *Daily Telegraph* website,[9] questioned why people should pay any more attention to our observation than they should to the apocalyptic predictions of someone like the Christian preacher of the apocalypse Harold Camping, who said that millions would be killed by earthquakes set to happen at 6 p.m. on Saturday 21 May 2011, rumbling consecutively in each global time zone.

If nothing else it must have comforted the writer, allowing wriggle room for those who prefer to believe that there is no fundamental problem, no need to change how we treat the biosphere.

Not all warnings of apocalypse are equal, however. That spiritual and religiously inspired predictions prove false does not change the fact that bad things do happen to life on Earth. It is precarious. In terms of mass extinctions due to environmental change, they have happened before and, objectively, measurably, something of this nature is happening again.

The difference this time is human consciousness and the ability to know and make choices. This book is about those choices. Something with potentially massive and tragic consequences is happening around us. Yet we are still in a situation where we can choose to take a different path.

Confusingly, in recent years the world does seem to have entered into a period of 'superdisasters', and not all apparently climate-related. This trend was predicted by the World Disasters Report 1999, a publication of the International Federation of Red Cross and Red Crescent Societies. Some, like mega-tsunamis (2004 and 2011) and earthquakes, are events in which the initial incident, if not entirely the impact and aftermath, is hard, if not impossible, to ascribe to human influence. Others, such as vast floods, droughts, hurricanes, cyclones and tornadoes, linked to extremes of climate, are not. Yet a changing climate is not the only thing to threaten the fabric of modern civilisation.

Even in the wealthiest countries, recent years reveal us to be vulnerable to a number of systemic threats. From the collapse of banks to threats to our food chains, the way we live and organise our economies has come to threaten, well . . . the way we live and organise our economies.

As the road sign says, there are hazards ahead. Which should we really worry about? Which do we have control over? Which do we just need to learn to live with? This book is not exhaustive. For example, it will not speculate about how best to tackle the threat of collision with a comet, or the likelihood of a particle accelerator accidentally producing a black hole that consumes the planet, fascinating as those conundrums are. But it will examine a range of profound challenges, examples of systemic threats, look at how we got into the mess in the first place, and then ask what can be done to 'cancel the apocalypse'.

Because, whatever counsels of doom and helplessness you hear, there are many, many things that can be done. One of the worst consequences of the financial crash of 2008 was the view expressed by politicians like the UK chancellor of the Exchequer, George Osborne, that economies in the grip of austerity could not afford to be distracted by worrying about the environment. In effect, tackling one crisis, badly, was used as an excuse for not tackling a bigger one. This book argues, on the contrary, that the solutions to these crises are not only related, but positively self-reinforcing. A reformed banking system, for example, one that is servant, not master, to wider society and not interested in profit alone, makes it much easier to invest in a green economy.

In the face of the scale of these problems, some solutions might appear small and piecemeal. What difference does it make if one community becomes a Transition Town, with a planned reduction in its fossil-fuel dependence, or if by looking at how individuals use transport, energy, buy and grow food, we seek to reduce their greenhouse gas emissions? Isn't it trivial that some people might club together to share tools or cars, or the skills needed to make and mend clothes or other household items?

Without doubt, very large-scale changes are needed that call for national and global action, for the deep re-engineering of infrastructure and changes in the motivations and obligations of multinational companies. This book will touch on all of those. But just as important as changes in energy, transport and farming systems, corporate governance and the design of cities and buildings is a shift in values and outlook, a change in the way we see ourselves in the world and in relation to each other. In this regard mainstream economics, with its brutally reductive and flawed assumptions about self-interested human gratification, has a lot to answer for.

The reason that a myriad small-scale, more sustainable initiatives matter is that they reject economic norms, showing that change can happen, and they represent the threat of good examples that in a conducive framework can be multiplied. They're also expressions of a different set of values, which, as they diffuse in society, insights from psychology and behavioural economics tell us can change social norms. Do that, and peaceful revolutions become possible. Initiatives from below can create the conditions for large changes from above. Governments often follow people, leading from behind, not the other way around. The sudden appearance of the Occupy movement in the aftermath of the bank crisis, to challenge the power and privilege of finance in several countries, crystallised and catalysed growing disquiet about inequality and 'affluenza'. Without it, the issue would not have risen up the political agenda so dramatically, changing opinions on executive high pay.

Change, too, can be messy, unpredictable and throw up unexpected consequences. In this light, social experimentation and innovation can be as important as technological innovation. Later in the book there'll be historical examples to demonstrate this.

Now, though, the horsemen are galloping, and there are more than four of them. Climate change, financial meltdown, the global peak and decline of oil production, a mass-extinction event of plant and animal species, over-use of fresh water supplies, soil loss, economic infrastructure increasingly vulnerable to external shocks – it's the age of the complex superdisaster.

These threats are not just the products of excitable newspaper headline writers. They are real. Any one of them could pull the rug from under lifestyles we have come to take for granted. Combinations of them working together threaten system collapse.

But lost in the hail of potential catastrophes is the simple, historical, fact that human beings have an amazing ability to change and adapt. The new question is whether we have become so locked in – culturally, ideologically, economically and in our built environment – that we will not be able to change in time. All the trends say that a rapid transition of some description is non-negotiable if we are to avoid catastrophe. Throughout this book are chapters that broadly alternate between looking at big threats and big opportunities, to which there can be answers equally effective, both big and small.

But this is not a finished blueprint. There can be none, because paths are made by walking, and in doing so we change the map of the world we live in. Neither is it a technical manual – that would be dull. If anything, it offers an attitude, a belief that while problems are real, not only can they be solved, but we will be better for beginning to do so. This sense is grounded in observation, experience, a lot of research, a ferocious optimism that we can enjoy the world and that there is space for everyone to lead good lives without ruining it. It is, however, only a book, with limits on its space. I have organised it, with the help of a little irresistible alliteration, around my interests and the issues I have been actively involved with.

Why, then, do I think we can 'cancel the apocalypse'? I will list the reasons in chapter order:

The motive. Explained above. The lure of a world in which we and our loved ones may continue to flourish seems to me quite strong.

The model. The economy we have is visibly flawed in theory and practice and there is no shortage of alternatives.

The measures. Finding a new path needs a better compass that can point in the right direction. In this case we have an embarrassment of riches.

The myth. Every society is guided by deep cultural stories to help avoid major mistakes. I explore the ***Icarus Complex***, which I think is helpful.

Meaning and imagination. Beyond the point that our basic needs are met, materialism reveals itself as the key to an empty room. A fuller understanding of human well-being sets us free from the chains of consumerism and opens the door to fuller lives.

The money. A great lie of modern politics and economics is that we cannot afford to do the things we need to do. This chapter says why and how we have the resources to cancel the apocalypse.

The memories. Living history is full of examples that can steer us away from danger and towards successful rapid transition. It shows that change is not only possible, but that we've done it before.

The mechanisms. A look at just two major issues, food and energy, makes it clear that we can feed and power the world, and do so without having to resort to controversial technologies.

The message. The marketing and advertising industries created a world in which we are defined primarily as passive consumers. Ironically, the rhetoric of choice sold us a monopoly value system: materialism. Yet myriad examples now exist of the growing demand to reskill, actively create, repair, share and remake things for ourselves, rather than passively consume.

Mutual interest. If we make the world a more equal place, solving problems that are global in scale becomes much easier, and regardless, our inescapable interdependence means that we sink or swim together. Our own well-being depends on that of others. *The momentum*. With the eyes to see it, a great transition has already begun. It may be far from guaranteed, but the opportunities are everywhere for virtuous spirals of change.

That is *why* I think it is within humanity's power and ability to head in a new, more positive direction. But *how* will it happen? That answer is partly contained within the *why*, because change is necessary, desirable and possible for all those reasons described. Humanity is restless, and doesn't tolerate even bad things indefinitely. It will happen also because a critical mass of people will come to want it to do so. Until the banking crisis, the triumph of finance felt like an end of history (as bubbles always do before a crash), its architects lauded and untouchable. How things change, and quickly sometimes completely flip. The resolution to that problem is still being worked through, but a consensus emerged that the financial sector had been out for itself, to the detriment of everyone else – business and industry, unions and environmental groups, governments, families and communities. Disgust at taking risks with other people's money, and the enormous damage done, obscenely high pay for work of no economic, environmental or social value, brazen lack of concern or empathy for the consequences of their actions – all of these things united diverse interests to change the climate of opinion, dethrone the previously unquestionable status of the lords of finance, give new life to more ethical finance, change attitudes on tax and inequality, begin re-regulating finance and chart a new economic path that we are now still making.

New movements and alliances emerge all the time to argue, persuade and seduce us towards new directions. History guarantees change, society determines it. As surely as slavery and child labour, once thought normal, were made illegal, and women's exclusion from democracy was generally reversed, so one day burning fossil fuels and giving financial interests in companies legal priority over social and environmental concerns will seem outlandish. Tomorrow will be different from today, just as today is different from yesterday. It is, of course, all to be fought for. Our task is to ensure that good choices get made. In that sense, this book is something of an open manifesto embracing questions of environment, the economy and lifestyle. Open because no one has a monopoly on solutions, but a manifesto in that I believe the necessary direction of travel is clear.

For reasons explained throughout the book, we can, for example, apply simple tests to all proposals – whether from politician, entrepreneurs or campaigners. Will it increase or decrease pressure on the biosphere, will it lead to a more equal distribution of benefits from economic activity, will it enhance or detract from human well-being? A little hard-nosed rigour in filtering the bewilderment of our options could quickly set us on the right path. The charge of being unrealistic, so glibly levelled against those who argue for radical and urgent change, can straightforwardly now be turned back on those who believe that business as usual can continue.

Between the hopeless doom-mongers and those technological utopians with blind faith in quick fixes, or who reject the existence of a problem, I think there is an important middle ground. It is the place where we look our threats in the face and refuse either denial or despair. There is much to be done, and we can decide to enjoy the doing.

First, though, how did we so overreach ourselves as to end up in this predicament? The mundane hubris of that relatively recent would-be science, economics, has much to answer for. Even worse is the modern notion that the normal laws of nature that govern the material world simply don't apply to economic life, or can magically be removed with assumptions and algorithms. At heart the big issue is something utterly normal, something we don't question and usually experience as delightful, reassuring and good. The next chapter asks, what went wrong with growth?

2

The Model

Growth and the curious invisibility of limits

When paradigms change [it is] as if the professional community had been suddenly transported to another planet where familiar objects are seen in a different light and are joined by unfamiliar ones as well.

Thomas Kuhn, *The Structure of Scientific Revolutions*

Lately in a wreck of a Californian ship, one of the passengers fastened a belt about him with two hundred pounds of gold in it, with which he was found afterwards at the bottom. Now, as he was sinking – had he the gold? Or had the gold him?

John Ruskin, 'Ad Valorem'

We have for over a century been dragged by the prosperous West behind its chariot, choked by the dust, deafened by the noise, humbled by our own helplessness and overwhelmed by the speed. We agreed to acknowledge that this chariot-drive was progress, and the progress was civilisation. If we ever ventured to ask, 'progress towards what, and progress for whom', it was considered to be peculiarly and ridiculously oriental to entertain such ideas about the absoluteness of progress. Of late, a voice has come to us to take count not only of the scientific perfection of the chariot but of the depth of the ditches lying in its path.

Rabindranath Tagore, Nobel laureate

Pencil dashes rise up the kitchen wall, like a tiny, rickety ladder. You've lovingly recorded your child's growth, her slowly changing height carefully marked and dated in the heart of your home. Growth is life. It's a fundamental measure of fundamental progress: the passage from birth to maturity. Look out of the kitchen window into the garden and there's another kind, that of plants. All life depends on plants. Our default understanding of growth is simple: it is a good thing. As children, we learn to be proud if we are above average height. As parents we're proud if our child is taller than their peers. Shorter people are often made to feel like lesser people, in every respect. The absence of growth implies that something must be wrong.

But how much growth is enough? When applied to the economy, the homely wisdom that growth is good lacks something. Absent is any concept of maturity. Yet this idea is central to our very nature. It is, in fact, essential for survival.

Take this extreme, bizarre, yet oddly telling illustration. From birth to puberty a hamster doubles its weight each week. If, then, instead of levelling off in maturity as animals do, the hamster continued to double its weight each week, on its first birthday we would be facing a nine-billion-tonne hamster. If it kept eating at the same ratio of food to body weight, by then its daily intake would be greater than the total, annual amount of maize produced worldwide.[1] As curious as this image may be, when, with friends, I turned it into a short educational animation, it proved oddly popular on the internet and inspired a full-length BBC Radio play that faithfully explored the economic and environmental challenges of growth. There is, after all, a good reason why in nature things do not grow indefinitely.

Yet every major global economy is founded on the premise of continual growth, the possibility of rising consumption stretching infinitely into the future. The resources, ecosystems and raw materials upon which that assumption is based are, however, finite. Over forty years since the limits of economic growth were first vigorously debated, the issue is only now returning to the fringes of economic debate. But questioning economic growth remains, largely, a heresy.

It is taken for granted to such a degree that few even ask the simple question: Why do economies grow? And why do people worry that it will be a disaster if they stop? For most countries in much of human history, having more 'stuff' has given human beings more comfortable lives. Also, as populations have grown, so have the economies that housed, fed, clothed and kept them.

Yet there has long been an understanding in the quiet corners of economics, as well as louder protests in other disciplines, that growth cannot and need not continue indefinitely. John Stuart Mill stated in 1848, that 'the increase of wealth is not boundless: that at the end of what they term the progressive state lies the stationary state'.

The reasons for growth not being 'boundless' too have been long known. Even making allowances for the time in which Mill wrote, his meaning remains clear: 'It is only in the [economically] backward countries of the world that increased production is still an important object: in those most advanced, what is economically needed is a better distribution.' So why is it, that over 160 years after Mill wrote those words, rich nations are more obsessed than ever with economic growth? Countries like the UK are decades past the point where increases in national income lead to similar increases in human well-being and life expectancy for the population overall. We'll come to how and why things get measured in certain ways a bit later, as well as looking at how things vary within a population.

Yet, in spite of decades of data revealing a clear break in already wealthy countries between the growth of an economy and the life satisfaction of its citizens, no mainstream politician argues against the need for economic growth. Neither do they contradict at a fundamental level the economics discipline which, like King Canute's courtiers, seems to believe that the power of assertion alone can hold back encroaching waves of environmental exhaustion.

The American economist Herman Daly argues that growth's first, literal, dictionary definition is 'To spring up and develop to maturity. Thus the very notion of growth includes some concept of maturity or sufficiency, beyond which point physical accumulation gives way to physical maintenance.'[2] In other words, some kind of development continues but growth itself gives way to a different state, one akin to dynamic equilibrium. In this condition, a balance is achieved in the overall system between resources entering and leaving.[3] For example, if water flowed in from the tap at the same rate as it escaped through the overflow pipe, a bath would be in dynamic equilibrium – changing, but with a constant mass and volume.

The laws of thermodynamics, neatly summarised by the physicist

C. P. Snow, tell us two inescapable conditions which have profound implications for economics. First, in the material world, you cannot win, in the sense that you cannot get something for nothing. In a bounded biosphere like ours, you have to work with what you've got, and you cannot end up with more than you started with. Second, and crucially for the economy, you cannot break even. Making things, creating order out of scattered matter, uses energy that then dissipates, meaning you end up with less readily available than you started with. Disorder, entropy, increases. Imagine first making, then shattering and trying to remake a vase. To create it, you put effort into gathering the necessary ingredients: clay, water, a potter's wheel, a kiln and the fuel to fire it to the necessary high temperature. The order you create is the vase. Dissipated is the heat energy from the kiln, along with the fuel's waste carbon and gases from burning. Order and disorder are in a dance in which disorder always marginally triumphs. You've made something beautiful but in a small way changed the world around you. Once the vase emerges new from the kiln, the endless struggle begins against wear and tear, chipping and cracking, the relentless tendency towards disorder. To picture entropy's upper hand, imagine if you then drop the vase and try to glue it back together: it will never be quite the same again. You can't win, and you can't break even.

Thermodynamics means that the energy efficiency of any process can never be 100 per cent. In the real world the practical limits of efficiency are much less than that. In other words, accepting that infinite growth in material consumption is a physical impossibility, we also have to accept that increased efficiency is no 'get out of jail free' card to save growth, because it too is limited.

As we struggle to make things, use great amounts of energy to create systems, structures, factories, transport networks, in doing so, depletion happens, something is always lost at the margins. There are of course short-term benefits, but fundamental longer-term problems.

Economies cannot grow and industry cannot continue without energy, and neither can occur without environmental impact. This is the basis of Herman Daly's 'steady-state economy', which, building on the work of the economist Nicholas Georgescu-Roegen, challenges the failure of the mainstream economics discipline to notice the 'entropic nature' of the economic process.[4]

Just as physical laws constrain the maximum efficiency of a heat engine, economic growth is constrained by the finite nature of our planet's natural resources, the variable but ultimately bounded bio-capacity of its oceans, fields, geology and atmosphere. From the point of view of material science, this too has long been understood. Pre-dating the landmark *Limits to Growth* report (see below), the economist E. J. Mishan published *The Costs of Economic Growth* in 1967. He was assailed by critics who asked: 'What about the costs of not growing? What about the poor people who need economic growth?' And then, the apparently killer challenge, then as now, when people asked: 'What about the fact that raw materials haven't actually run out yet?' To these voices Mishan replied: 'A man who falls from a hundred-storey building will survive the first ninety-nine storeys unscathed. Were he as sanguine as our technocrats, his confidence would grow with the number of storeys he passed on his downward flight and would be at a maximum just before his free-fall abruptly halted.'

Daly once quipped that he would accept the possibility of infinite growth in the economy on the day that one of his economist colleagues could demonstrate that Earth itself could grow at a commensurate rate.[5]

At the moment, that doesn't appear to be happening. Human use of biocapacity – farmland, forests and fisheries – measured by the size of our global ecological footprint is growing. Decade by decade it further overshoots what the biosphere can provide to our economies and the waste it can absorb from them. Now, like two trains speeding in opposite directions, as we collectively consume more, we also appear to be shrinking the available biocapacity on which we depend. Worryingly, it's not simply because we're taking more from nature.

This requires a little explanation. Global warming, driven largely by human burning of fossil fuels, appears to be weakening the ability of key parts of the biosphere to absorb, safely, our carbon emissions. It is a process that scientists describe as 'positive feed-back'. Except that it is not in any human sense positive at all. It is a problem exacerbated, accelerated, by the very nature of its impact. Forests and oceans are referred to as 'carbon sinks' – that is, they absorb much of the carbon we emit from coal, oil and gas. But warming seems to be reducing the ability of oceans to absorb carbon, leaving more in the atmosphere, quickening warming and in turn further reducing the oceans' ability to act as a 'sink'.[6] For some time, it was a popular theory that rising levels of carbon dioxide in the atmosphere would encourage tree growth, and that this would have a cancelling effect as the trees absorbed the carbon. But there is evidence that warming is also compromising forests' ability to soak up carbon.[7] If major sinks become instead sources of carbon, absorbing less and releasing more, for example when forest are cleared or die back, we have a very big problem. Even if oceans greatly increased their absorption of carbon dioxide – and some have suggested 'seeding' the seas in such a way as to encourage this – it would seriously damage the delicate chemical balance for marine life, encouraging acidification and deoxygenation.

Now, according to the measure of our ecological footprint (explained in the next chapter) we are consuming nature's services – using resources and creating carbon emissions – at the global level 52 per cent faster than nature can regenerate and reabsorb what we consume and the waste we produce. In other words, it takes the Earth about eighteen months to produce the ecological services that humanity uses in one year, just two thirds of that time. The numbers already don't add up, and these could be underestimates for reason explored below. The UK's footprint is such that if the whole world wished to consume at the same rate, we would need around three planets like Earth.[8]

Growth is making us hit the biosphere's buffers. It happens as a natural resource is exploited to the point of exhaustion, or because more waste is dumped into an ecosystem than can be safely absorbed, leading, sooner or later, to dysfunction or collapse. Science is telling us that both are happening, and sooner, rather than later.

Yet for decades it has been a heresy punishable by career suicide for economists (or politicians) to question orthodox economic growth. As the British MP Colin Challen quipped in 2006: 'We are imprisoned by our political Hippocratic oath: we will deliver unto the electorate more goodies than anyone else.'[9]

But what is growth? The question is deceptive, because the word has many uses. They range from the description of biological processes, plant and animal growth, to more abstract notions of personal development, I want to 'grow' as a person, learn, develop, become better at doing things. This brushes the concept of growth with an enormously positive gloss. As mentioned above, flowers grow, children grow, how could that be bad? Growth becomes synonymous with all that is good.

But when used to describe the economy, growth has a very specific meaning, causing much confusion. In economics 'growth', or the lack of it, describes the trajectory of Gross Domestic Product (GDP) and Gross National Product (GNP), two slightly different measures of national income (they differ, basically, only in that one includes earnings from overseas assets). The value of imports is deducted and the value of exports added. Hence, an economy is said to be growing if the financial value of all the exchanges of goods and services within it goes up. And, as described above, the laws of physics mean it is not possible to create the order of such exchanges without a little something being lost.

Growth of GDP and GNP differs fundamentally from the meaning of growth usually (though not exclusively) applied in nature, because it means expansion with no sense of development. It is growth in scale. The absence of such growth gets described, pejoratively, as recession. Prolonged recessions are called depressions.

It gets more confusing. An economy may grow, for example, because money is being spent on clearing up after disasters or pollution, to control rising crime associated with inequality, or to counter a pandemic. The riots and looting in Britain's inner cities in 2011, for example, will have contributed to growth. All those shop fronts to mend, the cost of the street clear-up, the insurance claims prior to restocking, etc.

A landmark report (widely ignored by policymakers) on human development from the United Nations Development Programme in 1996 identified five types of negative economic growth.[10] Unusually for a UN body that is typically cautious due to the need to keep happy the many nations it represents, it used quite undiplomatic language. It spoke of the tendency in both capitalist and socialist economies to 'sacrifice' people on the 'altar of increased accumulation'. And of how readily in its regular periods of crisis, capitalism was prepared to cast people aside onto the 'scrap heap of unemployment'. The report identified 'jobless growth' in which an economy gets bigger with more buying and selling of goods and services, but without creating more jobs. Countries ranging from India to Egypt and Ghana have all had times when employment lagged far behind their growing economies.

Voiceless growth is another phenomenon in which an apparently successful economy rides on the back of the suppression of civil rights, union membership and democracy. Parts of East Asia, although demonstrating a form of growth with more equal distribution than, say, Latin America, have had voiceless growth. The long-imprisoned Burmese opposition leader Aung San Suu Kyi contrasted her experience with the Buddhist outlook on the responsibility of leaders: 'The Ten Duties of Kings are: liberality, morality, self-sacrifice, integrity, kindness, austerity, non-anger, non-violence, forbearance and non-opposition to the will of the people.'

Ruthless growth accompanies high or rising inequality. This will also get a closer look later in the book. It has been the experience of the Anglo-Saxon economies, the UK and the US, and other parts of the world like China, India and South Africa, significant in terms of population and global politics. High inequality has also strongly affected Brazil and much of Central America for decades. Effects vary across generations too, with young people facing a disproportionately high and worsening risk of poverty and unemployment.[11] More recent research from the universities of Manchester, Delhi, Cape Coast and Arkansas showed that in India impressive economic growth and a focus on raising the productivity of farmers, fishermen, labourers and factory workers failed to improve poor levels of nutrition among both adults and children.

Rootless growth describes the culturally destructive effects of economic globalisation. It is the homogenising effect of McDonald's, Starbucks and Coca-Cola. It is the triumph of the Hollywood film and concentrated media ownership that is able to push a narrow Western notion of beauty, material success and cultural pride.

Finally, and the subject of much of this book, comes 'futureless growth'. That means growth that steals our collective future by depending on the unsustainable consumption of finite natural resources.

With environmentally destructive growth, a kind of false monetary value is created by liquidating irreplaceable natural assets on which livelihoods depend. The island of Nauru in the South Pacific, which is visited later in more detail, is just such an example. It was discovered in colonial times to contain massive phosphate deposits, hugely valuable to farmers, built up from bird droppings over thousands of years. In just a few generations, though, the island's ore was mined for exports almost to the point of destruction. Money was made, but the island's centre was left a hollow shell. Its people became dependent on expensive imports. They suffered major health problems, and when the phosphate ran out they had no livelihood. Many of these issues might appear comfortably remote to a person living in the UK or United States. But are they really?

The collapse of finance-driven globalisation since 2008 washed onto the shores of our daily lives the detritus of a broken economic model. We are increasingly jobless. Governments on both sides of the Atlantic struggle, pushing policies justified on the basis of restoring economic growth, yet accompanied by large-scale unemployment. In reaction, there are forceful attempts to restrain the voice of protest. Aggressive and increasingly restrictive policing, for example against the Occupy movement, seeks to familiarise public critical voices with the smell of pepper spray, and curtail challenges to the financial system. According to Bernard Porter's review of Christopher Andrew's *The Defence of the Realm: The Authorised History of MI5*, the domestic secret security services consider one of their roles to be protection of 'the Anglo-Saxon model of capitalism' against subversion.[12] If that is indeed the case, their time might be more constructively spent monitoring banks like RBS, Barclays and Goldman Sachs than street protesters. As a child I saw the Western world define its superiority in terms of how Soviet bloc countries suppressed protest. It is suffocatingly ironic to see the victor in that struggle now worship the tactics of control that it fought a Cold War supposedly to defeat.

Growth in the Anglo-Saxon economies also has been 'ruthlessly' unequal. And rootless, too, in terms of the rise of dominant consumer brands, chain stores, clone towns and the destruction of local diversity. Open your eyes on most any high street in Britain and expect to see the same chains of coffee shops, phone stores, supermarket outlets, fast-food places and bank branches (supposing with banks that you have one at all). How do we encounter 'futureless' growth on our doorstep? Even here, far from threatened rainforests, as energy security becomes an issue, communities in both the UK and America witness the return of everything from dirty open-cast mining to 'fracking' for gas – the process of injecting liquid under pressure deep underground to release gas trapped in strata there. But all this is to skim the surface of challenges the book will look into later in more detail.

Altogether, the fact that an economy is growing tells you nothing necessarily about the quality of economic activity happening within it. Conversely, history shows that in times of recession, life expectancy can rise, even as livelihoods are apparently harmed. This happens in rich countries probably due to force of circumstances, as people become healthier by consuming less and exercising more, using cheaper, more active forms of transport such as walking and cycling. But see again how language loads the dice. Growth, regardless of what drives it, equals children flourishing, gardens blooming. Its absence, by definition, is either recession or, left uncorrected, full-blown depression. Downers both, although you might ask: 'What's the difference?' The former US president Harry S Truman, who first worked as a senator in the long shadow of the 1929 Wall Street crash, said: 'It's a recession when your neighbour loses his job; it's a depression when you lose yours.'

There is, in fact, no fully agreed definition of either. Customarily they involve respectively shorter and longer periods of low-to-negative economic growth, and coincide with bad things, such as raised unemployment. Nothing, though, is straightforward. An odd assortment of sectors supposedly does well during recessions. The pub trade, gambling, artistic endeavour, religion and, more predictably, pawn shops and the debt trade all thrive on hard times. This is ironic, given the role of predatory lending to home buyers in the 2008 financial crisis. The marketing of expensive loans to people on low incomes then seems to thrive in recession One company, Wonga, was heavily criticised by the National Union of Students for pushing loans to young people in college that racked up a staggering annual interest rate of 4214 per cent. A proper student loan, by contrast, carried just 1.5 per cent interest.[13]

Good and bad things can happen whether an economy is growing or not. The questions we'll come to are whether the good things associated with growth, such as employment, material security and ensuring public services, can be guaranteed in other ways without it; and whether the bad things linked to an economy not growing in the conventional sense can be avoided.

But, in summary, it is possible to have both 'economic' and 'uneconomic' growth. We cannot assume that growth per se is a good thing, to be held on to at all costs, let alone possible or sustainable at an aggregate, global, level. Even in nature, growth, if it is cancerous, can be malignant. In this case, it is the kind of growth that recognises no boundaries other than the exhaustion of the limits of its host, rather like the limitless growth of GDP.

A little historical context.

There is a kind of inverse political correctness that prevents growth being debated properly. The left associates growth with poverty reduction, the right sees it as the route to progress and individual wealth accumulation. Point out its limitations and you pull off the impressive trick of branding yourself an enemy both of private profit and of public enhancement. One apparently progressive grouping of left-leaning economists whose meetings I attend has resisted every suggestion to discuss the issue.

This has not always been true. Historically, there have been vigorous debates on the optimal scale for the economy. In fact, the logic that an economy must mature and stabilise in size was recognised at the dawn of modern economic thinking by Adam Smith. He foresaw this being the result of several dynamics including resource use, population and limits to the efficiency with which the tasks of labour could be divided. David Ricardo, too, wrote about the idea of arriving at a 'stationary state' in his 1821 work *On the Principles of Political Economy and Taxation*.

The philosopher and political economist John Stuart Mill was shaped by the human and environmental havoc of the voracious Industrial Revolution. In reaction to it, he argued that, once certain conditions had been met, the economy should aspire to exist in a 'stationary state'. It was a hugely radical notion for the time. Mill thought that an intelligent application of technology, family planning, equal rights and a dynamic combination of a progressive workers' movement with the growth of consumer cooperatives could tame the worst excesses of capitalism and liberate society from the motivation of conspicuous consumption.

He thought that all economic expansion must tend towards a point at which any further growth was unnecessary. In 1848 he wrote:

> In contemplating any progressive movement, not in its nature
> unlimited, the mind is not satisfied with merely tracing the laws

of the movement; it cannot but ask the further question, to what goal? Towards what ultimate point is society tending by its industrial progress? When the progress ceases, in what condition are we to expect that it will leave mankind?[14]

Even then, Mill thought that since the increase in wealth could not be 'boundless', then it must 'always have been seen, more or less distinctly, by political economists . . . that all progress in wealth is but a postponement of this [transition from a progressive to a stationary state], and that each step in advance is an approach to it.' He was quite confident that this was no bad thing, and clear that just as much should be obvious to everyone else:

> It is scarcely necessary to remark that a stationary condition of capital and population implies no stationary state of human improvement. There would be as much scope as ever for all kinds of mental culture, and moral and social progress; as much room for improving the Art of Living and much more likelihood of its being improved, when minds cease to be engrossed by the art of getting on.[15]

Perfecting the 'art of living', as humanity's greatest aspiration once its material needs were met, was a theme the great economist John Maynard Keynes would return to about a century later.

Time and again, it is those who have strayed into economics from outside the discipline who have seen the flaw in assuming infinite growth to be either possible or desirable. One interloper was the Victorian art critic John Ruskin. In a comprehensive assault on the conventional economic thought of his time, he famously asserted in *Unto This Last* that: '*There is no wealth but life*. Life, including all its powers of love, of joy, and of admiration. That country is the richest which nourishes the greatest numbers of noble and happy human beings; that man is richest, who, having perfected the functions of his own life to the utmost, has also the widest helpful influence, both personal, and by means of his possessions, over the lives of others.'[16]

At a stroke, Ruskin inspired and laid the foundations for a new economics of well-being, as opposed to one of simple accumulation. On the path of his thoughts walked everyone from Mahatma Gandhi

to a pioneering chemist called Frederick Soddy, whose work Herman
Daly has done much to draw attention to.

The year after Soddy was awarded a Nobel Prize for his work on
radiochemistry and the characteristics of isotopes, he published a tract
he called *Cartesian Economics*. Coming from a scientific background,
he had not internalised the dominant assumptions and abstractions of
economics. This led him to pour scorn on several things accepted
unquestioningly by the discipline's mainstream, such as the growth
of money through the magic of compound interest and what that
implied for unending economic growth per se.

In return, the economics profession ignored Soddy entirely. 'You
cannot permanently pit an absurd human convention, such as the
spontaneous increment of debt [i.e., compound interest],' he wrote,
'against the natural law of the spontaneous decrement of wealth [i.e.,
entropy].'[17] Being an assiduous radiochemist did nothing to constrain
his ability to communicate in popular, accessible language, as this
passage from his *Inversion of Science* (1924) reveals:

> If Christ, whose views on the folly of laying up treasures on
> earth are well known, had put by a pound at this rate, it should
> now be worth an Octillion, and Tariff Reform would be of little
> help to provide that, even if you colonized the entire stellar
> universe . . . It is this absurdity which inverts society, turns good
> into evil and makes orthodox economics the laughing stock of
> science. If the consequences were not the familiar atmosphere
> of our daily lives they would be deemed beyond the legitimate
> bounds of the most extravagant comic opera.[18]

Beyond concerns of the impracticality of endless growth, Soddy
invokes Ruskin on its likely pointlessness: 'Capital which produces
nothing but capital is only root producing root; bulb issuing in bulb,
never in tulip; seed issuing in seed never in bread. The Political
Economy of Europe has hitherto devoted itself to the multiplica-
tion . . . of bulbs. It never saw or conceived such a thing as a tulip.'[19]
Echoing Ruskin's 'there is no wealth but life' almost Copernican
assault on economics, Soddy mocks those who would confuse the
properties of land, which, by combining water, sunlight and minerals genuinely produces the wealth of life, with money, which,

although it can buy land, is not inherently wealth-creating. Money, rather, merely shifts tenure, ownership and management style, and often for the worse: 'the age seems to have conceived the preposterous notion that money, which can buy land, must therefore itself have the same revenue-producing power.'

Soddy, like the other trained scientist turned (ignored) economist Nicholas Georgescu-Roegen, was resurrected by Herman Daly. Soddy's understanding of the material limits described by natural laws led him to argue that, rather than growth, 'economic sufficiency is the essential foundation of all national greatness and progress'. Daly emphasises that 'sufficiency' means 'enough' and growth beyond 'enough' is just 'seed issuing in seed never in bread'.[20]

Mill, Ruskin, Soddy, all brilliant, but in terms of their deeper appreciations of the *purpose* of the economy, even they were walking in much earlier footsteps. Exactly how much earlier makes the current impoverished nature of economic debate even more embarrassing. Take this from the first-century AD letters of Lucius Annaeus Seneca:

> What difference does it make how much is laid away in a man's safe or in his barns, how many head of stock he grazes or how much capital he puts out at interest, if he is always after what is another's and only counts what he has yet to get, never what he has already? You ask what is the proper limit to a person's wealth? First, having what is essential, and second, having what is enough.

More familiarly, the 1960s and early 1970s saw a vigorous debate on the environmental implications of growth that accompanied the birth and rise of the modern green movement. Sometimes, though, it was hampered by insufficient data. Scientists at the Massachusetts Institute of Technology (MIT) were commissioned by the Club of Rome to research and publish what became the controversial report *Limits to Growth*. In the decade before it came out in 1972, Rachel Carson's seminal environmental wake-up call, *Silent Spring*, was published on the impact of industrial agriculture, Garrett Hardin coined the term 'the tragedy of the commons' in an essay for the journal *Science*, the campaign group Friends of the Earth was set up, and protests against nuclear testing led to the formation of Greenpeace. The following year E. F. Schumacher's *Small is Beautiful*, a collection of his essays and lectures, would come out. Something was in the air, and if you listened to the green groups, in the water and soil as well.

Since its first publication, *Limits to Growth* has been successively revised and republished. Matthew Simmons, founder of the world's largest energy investment banking firm, commented on the 2004 update that its message was more relevant than ever and that we 'wasted 30 valuable years of action by misreading the message of the first book'.[21] The Earth system models and computer power available to the MIT researchers were, by contemporary standards, rudimentary. Many dismissed the original report for 'crying wolf' and being, basically, mistaken. Ever since, this early perceived failure successfully to model humanity's interaction with its underpinning natural resources has been used to dismiss almost any kind of environmental warning.

But it appears that the report has, in fact, stood the test of time. A study in 2008 by the physicist Graham Turner from CSIRO (Commonwealth Scientific and Industrial Research Organisation), Australia's leading scientific research institute, compared its original projections with thirty years of subsequent observed trends and data.[22] His research showed that MIT's best estimates on resource depletion due to human economic activity 'compared favourably' with what then actually happened. Hence, rates of pollution and industrial output and consumption have closely followed the model's projections.

It was the scoffers who were wrong, not the scientists. The computer model on which *Limits to Growth* was based, known as World3, is, although simple, in many ways yet to be improved on according to *New Scientist* magazine, providing a balance between 'over-simplification and unmanageable complexity'.[23] Worryingly, when the model was run without deliberately constraining either economic or population growth, whatever the techno-fix applied, the system ended in fairly sudden collapse. Only with some cases in which growth was limited, did the model stabilise without collapse. Without that, sooner or later growth 'swamped the remedies'. 'The general behaviour of overshoot and collapse persists, even when large changes to numerous parameters are made,' Turner told *New Scientist*. It concluded that today: 'no realistic assumptions' produce a stabilised outcome.

The idea remains alien in the political mainstream, however, that there should be any limit to the amount that we consume within our ability to pay. And even that constraint largely dissolved in recent decades in economies built and wrecked upon the financial rocks of debt-fuelled overconsumption. Attempting to recover from just such a crisis, Alistair Darling, the UK chancellor of the Exchequer, said when presenting his budget for 2009: 'I am also confident that, as the global economy recovers to double in size over the next twenty years, Britain can, and will be, a world leader.'[24]

To reprise, the global economy is already exceeding its available biocapacity by at least 52 per cent, and heading in the wrong direction. Someone who was at the time the second-most important politician in a major global economy airily, confidently, reassures his countrypeople that they will float out of troubled economic waters as the global economy doubles in size in just two decades.

The lack of even remote awareness that there might be an issue to address will, I suspect, appear as breathtaking in retrospect as US Secretary to the Treasury Andrew W. Mellon's promise in early 1929 that: 'There is no cause for worry. The high tide of prosperity will continue.'

It seems to be in disciplines other than economics, where people are less in thrall to the unquestioned imperium of growth, that the nakedness of certain assumptions is more likely to be called out.

Roderick Smith, Royal Academy of Engineering Research Professor at Imperial College, London, gave a lecture in 2007 that looked at the notion of economic 'doubling'. Echoing Georgescu-Roegen, he said that, from a physical point of view, the economy 'is governed by the laws of thermodynamics and continuity', and so 'the question of how much natural resource we have to fuel the economy, and how much energy we have to extract, process and manufacture is central to our existence'.[25]

Instead of abstract mathematical equations that rest upon often bizarre simplifying assumptions about human behaviour and markets, engineers must deal with reality. It is not enough to believe that something will or should behave in a certain way: a bridge must carry weight without collapsing, walls must be able to support a roof. Economists are oddly immune to the failure of their theories, even when they wreck lives and livelihoods, whilst a similarly culpable failed engineer who built a bridge that collapsed would most likely end up in court.

Perhaps this concern for the necessary viability of systems and structures – how tall or broad you can build, and with what materials, before it all tumbles down – led Smith to focus on an economy's 'doubling period'. Just as it sounds, this is the time it takes to double, as measured by the indicators for growth, GNP and GDP. With a background in engineering, it occurs to Smith to ask the obvious question – so obvious that in the mainstream it almost never gets asked. Namely, can it double? Given the stresses and strains, the compression and extension of materials, the energy sources and efficiencies, the ecosystems, biosphere and their tolerances, how tall or broad can we build the economy before the biosphere's roof caves in? Because, if we are to play games of trial and error, like the medieval cathedral builders, and we make fundamental mistakes with the biosphere, we won't simply be able to start again and rebuild. The consequences of ecosystem failure inhabit a different order.

Smith points out that even at relatively low growth rates of around 3 per cent, this leads to 'surprisingly short doubling times'. At that rate, typical of a developed economy at least outside of a recession, you get a doubling time of just over twenty-three years. Then, he adds: 'The 10 per cent rates of rapidly developing economies double the size of the economy in just under seven years.'

Now here's the crunch. According to Smith, what people overlook is that 'each successive doubling period consumes as much resource as all the previous doubling periods combined', just as 8 exceeds the sum of 1, 2 and 4. 'This little appreciated fact,' he says, 'lies at the heart of why our current economic model is unsustainable.'

People who tend towards optimism will argue that this view overlooks the way in which economies become more materially efficient as they develop. And in some cases this is true. But in order to escape the growth trap, those efficiency gains have to match, and in the case of the carbon emissions driving climate change exceed, the additional resource burden that growth brings.

It is at this point that trusting to increased efficiency as a technological fix for the exhaustion of resources runs into problems. As mentioned, efficiency has both theoretical and practical limits – 'You can't win and you can't break even.' There can also be unexpected outcomes to pursuing efficiency which, perversely, lead to more not less consumption.

'It is a confusion of ideas to suppose that the economical use of fuel is equivalent to diminished consumption. The very contrary is the truth,' wrote William Stanley Jevons in his book *The Coal Question* (1865). In doing so he coined the 'rebound effect', sometimes also respectfully referred to as the 'Jevons effect'. He observed, quite simply, that because efficiency saves materials and energy use in one place, it drives down prices, saving money which can then be spent on buying more of the same thing (although more efficiently produced), or other things entirely.

The rebound effect has been observed in areas ranging from fuel use to heating homes, making cars, lighting and more. Estimates for how much of any efficiency savings get eaten up by additional consumption vary from a fraction to their entirety.[26] Hence, as appliances become relatively cheaper people buy more of them, increasing both the embodied energy in manufactured goods, and overall energy demand. And, as cars become more efficient, people drive them further and/or buy bigger cars.

More than anything, climate change has forced environmental questions into the debate about economics. Nicholas Stern, former chief economist at the World Bank, was commissioned by the UK government to assess the economics of global warming. I happened to be at the launch of his final report[27] and was able to ask him, as he stood flanked by the prime minister, chancellor of the Exchequer, secretary of state for the environment *and* head of the Royal Society (a full house for the establishment), if they had analysed what level of economic growth, under what circumstances, was compatible with preventing dangerous climate change. They hadn't. It didn't seem as if the idea even to ask the question had ever occurred to them. They hadn't asked whether in theory or practice the unspoken assumption of endless growth was compatible with preventing runaway global warming.

Fortunately, a couple of years later Professor Kevin Anderson and Alice Bows, of the Tyndall Centre for Climate Change Research at Manchester University, did exactly that.[28] There is some necessary background. Many, including the European Union, have come to the conclusion that a 2-degree global average surface temperature rise is the maximum acceptable in order to prevent 'dangerous' warming. Even this, however, is the subject of much debate. Small Island States, a group of particularly threatened countries that often negotiate collectively at international climate talks, fought hard in 2010 to establish a lower maximum temperature rise of just 1.5 degrees as the target to aim for.[29] With bad things happening already in a warming world, before we have reached even a 1-degree rise, understandably, small islands, many of which have their highest point no more than a few metres above sea level, think that a 2-degree rise spells disaster. They were opposed in their lobbying, principally, by the oil producer Saudi Arabia. It was one of those occasions when diplomacy struggles to disguise naked national self-interest.

Anderson and Bows based their work on models that include all sorts of variables, including more or less optimistic political and technological responses to tackling climate change. They also looked at different levels of risk for whether any particular temperature threshold was likely to be crossed, and included the fact that, because poor countries face different economic challenges to rich ones, rich countries are expected, and have agreed, to do more, and earlier, to lower their emissions. They then ran the numbers and looked at what came out. The conclusions were stark.

Presenting the findings in a fringe meeting at the time of the Labour Party conference in Manchester, Anderson summarised that: 'Economic growth in the OECD cannot be reconciled with a 2, 3 or even 4°C characterisation of dangerous climate change.'

Now, a few necessary numbers. For a reasonable chance of keeping to 2 degrees, the rule of thumb used was that greenhouse gases (so-called 'carbon dioxide equivalent' or CO_2e) need to be no greater than 450 parts per million by volume (ppmv) in the atmosphere. Any higher than that, and you are definitely playing climate roulette. As mentioned, some, including James Hansen and the Small Island States, think that even this is too risky, and any more than that, unthinkable.

Anderson points out that, according to the Stern review on the economics of climate change, annual reductions in greenhouse gas emissions of greater than 1 per cent per year have only 'been associated with economic recession or upheaval'. In other cirumstances, for short periods of a decade or so, and excluding the carbon footprints of imported goods, some countries have achieved higher reductions by switching to different energy sources. Denmark, for example, cut its carbon emissions by 2.2 per cent on average between 1994 and 2005. Belgium managed 3.7 per cent between 1978 and 1988, and Sweden

4.5 per cent between 1976 and 1986. This is where things get sticky, as he finds that: 'Unless economic growth can be reconciled with unprecedented rates of decarbonisation (in excess of 6 per cent per year), it is difficult to envisage anything other than a planned economic recession being compatible with stabilisation at or below 650 ppmv CO_2e.'[30] So much for the physical possibility of continual growth without wrecking the climatic conditions for civilisation. What of its simple desirability?

Adair Turner was once head of the Confederation of British Industry, the organisation that lobbies on behalf of big business. It has a reputation for seeing the environment as a distinctly secondary concern next to making money. But Turner went on to head the government-sponsored Climate Change Committee before being made the head of the City regulator, the Financial Services Authority (FSA). One reason for such a far-ranging CV is that Turner is known for creative and independent thought. Writing in a book I edited, *Do Good Lives Have to Cost the Earth?* (2008), he speculated about the value of 'natural beauty', 'happiness' and the threat of environmental crises, at the same time as the 'confused economic concept of "competitiveness"', and the need to 'dethrone growth' as the principal objective of the economy.

Then, in an interview I did with him for BBC Radio 4, he went further:

If you spend your time thinking that the most important objective of public policy is to get growth up from 1.9 per cent to 2 per cent and even better 2.1 per cent we're pursuing a sort of false god there. We're pursuing it first of all because if we accept that, we will do things to the climate that will be harmful, but also because all the evidence shows that beyond the sort of standard of living which Britain has now achieved, extra growth does not automatically translate into human welfare and happiness.

Which once again raises the question: Why do economies need to keep growing? We've seen what growth is, but not why it is continually necessary to grow, beyond the point that we achieve a sufficient level of material comfort. Why do people worry that it will be a disaster if an economy stops growing? One answer can be put quite simply. For most countries in much of human history, having more stuff has given human beings more comfortable lives. Also, as populations have grown, so have the economies that housed, fed, clothed and kept them.

At this point, there's an important caveat to make. Beyond the club of already rich countries, this situation still prevails in many parts of the world. It is almost certainly the case that in societies where millions are subsisting, where many have too little to eat, homes without basic amenities and services, health and education systems that are sparse or non-existent, correcting those problems will almost certainly have economic growth as a side-effect. But even this does not mean necessarily that growth should be pursued as an end in itself. The very different historical experiences of Asia and Latin America, for example, reveal that different types of growth can have very different results, both positive and negative, for people living in poverty. But more of this later.

So why is it that, over 160 years after Mill wrote that for wealthier nations 'what is economically needed is a better distribution',[31] those same nations are more obsessed than ever with economic growth? As we've seen, countries like the UK are decades past the point where increases in national income, measured by GNP and GDP, lead to similar increases in human well-being and life expectancy. Exactly why this is the case will be looked at further on.

No mainstream politician, however, argues against the need for economic growth. The reasons are partly to do with rhetorical and policy habits, partly political posturing, and partly because we have set our economic system up in such a way that it needs growth in the way that an alcoholic needs a drink or a drug addict his next fix: without it there is insecurity and the frightening prospect of cold turkey – much better to keep drinking, inhaling or injecting. It should also be noted that the already wealthy capture a disproportionate share of the financial benefits from growth.

Growth-based national accounting became popular in the 1930s as a guide to quantify the value of government interventions to rescue economies from the Depression, and also later as a tool to aid increased production as part of the war-planning effort.

But the new measurement came with a very big health warning attached. One of the indicator's key architects, the economist Simon Kuznets, was explicit about its limitations. Growth did not measure quality of life, he made clear, and it excluded vast and important parts of the economy where exchanges were not monetary. By this he meant family, care and community work – the so-called 'core economy' that makes society function and civilisation possible. So, for example, if the money economy grows at the expense of, and by cannibalising the services of, the core economy – such as in the way that big supermarkets grow at the expense of independent local stores and the greater number of jobs, local money flows, human contact and relationships that bind communities that they provide – it is a kind of false growth. Similarly if the money economy grows simply by liquidating natural assets that are treated as 'free income', this too is a kind of 'uneconomic growth'.

Robert Kennedy pointed out this weakness in 1968 when he made a speech in which he said that growth measures everything apart from 'that which makes life worthwhile'.[32] Spending on prisons, pollution and disasters pushed up GDP just as surely as spending on schools, hospitals and parks. But growth nevertheless became the indicator of an economy's virility and success which eclipsed all others.

Economics has a reason why. Free-market economics rests upon a number of theories which themselves make interesting assumptions. It monitors and assesses their practical consequences oddly too. Both the Treasury and the Bank of England, for example, use models of the economy that do not include banks, because their impact on the economy is considered to be neutral. However hard to sustain in the light of real-world events, when assumptions get locked into models they tend to go unquestioned and endure. Banks' extreme lack of neutrality is discussed in chapter 6. John Maynard Keynes famously observed that: 'Practical men, who believe themselves to be quite exempt from any intellectual influence, are usually the slaves of some defunct economist.' Step forward Léon Walras, the French mathematical economist whose work in the 1870s laid the foundations for General Equilibrium Theory. Profoundly influential in free-market thinking, it was, of course, not a picture of the real world – nothing so messy – but a hypothetical one. A quick caveat: few economists, even in the mainstream, would say that the simplifying assumptions of neo-classical and neoliberal economics represent reality. Many spend academic careers analysing their flaws. Nevertheless, the power of the models built upon these assumptions is such that a level of folk wisdom about economics, derived from them, continues to operate with extraordinary and uncorrected influence within politics. The basic model has evolved and been adapted in many ways since first devised, but to simplify considerably, here is a flavour of the assumptions behind the models.

One is that everybody has 'perfect information', i.e., everyone involved in the market knows everything there is to know about what is being bought and sold, literally everything (it doesn't matter what it is, it could be a market in bananas or ball bearings). Another is that there is 'perfect competition' between firms. That means, in the theory, that there must be an *infinite* number of small firms each unable to infringe another's ability to trade (think Tesco versus your corner shop, not). Next is the notion that we are all so-called 'utility maximisers'. This was, and remains, a profoundly influential idea in mainstream economics. It has enormous consequences that lock growth into our system, perhaps unintentionally.

The philosopher Jeremy Bentham said that utility was the principle on which things are judged according to their ability 'to augment or diminish the happiness of the party whose interest is in question'. In the long shadow of this theory, mainstream economics says that we are primarily motivated to maximise our utility. But there's a catch, and that is how to measure it. Economists think this can only be done by looking at our 'expressed preferences', or in other words, what we buy. Only when we have made a purchase can the system measure that we are 'expressing preferences to maximise our utility'. It doesn't take much thinking to realise that bizarre anomalies can arise as a result.

Imagine one morning I have two choices. First, I could spend hours travelling by irregular public transport to a grim industrial estate, to visit a big, crowded DIY shop and stand in a slowly shifting queue to buy weedkiller, a gas-burning patio heater or a barbecue that might, optimistically, get used on a handful of occasions. Or perhaps, instead, I could take a stroll in the dappled sunlight among trees in my local park.

In the first of the two scenarios I make a purchase. The system registers that I have expressed a preference and acted to maximise my utility. I must be better off. The system cheers: success. A whole bunch of policies ranging from tax to town planning then take note and encourage me to do more of the same.

In the second scenario, my joy, my connection with the world and inner peace remain invisible. No financial transaction has occurred. The system registers nothing. Therefore there is no feedback to value and encourage more of the same behaviour, even though the walk has probably left me healthier, more productive, and less likely to cost the system money due to long-term problems with health and depression.

Growth is the measure only of money being spent on goods and services. When I spend money, no matter on what, I am expressing a preference, and hence doing something to maximise my utility. It must all be good. In mainstream economics, almost by definition, you're only happy when you're spending. Growth became the proxy indicator for human well-being. More spending means more happiness, means more growth. Therefore growth can only be good. Nonsensical, of course, but this represents the foundation of the consensus that stands for economic thought in mainstream politics.

In brutally simple terms, it implies that there is no such thing as bad consumption. Even those addicted to substance abuse are welcome if their purchasing is captured in the national accounts. For example, imagine a violent alcoholic. He spends money on costly hard spirits, sometimes he gets into fights, breaks things – windows, furniture, china – and hurts other people and himself. As a result, money has to be spent on buying replacement glass and chairs, policing, health care, perhaps prisons, and people living near the pub where he gets drunk and violent feel insecure and so buy extra locks and security. You may, as a result of lax regulation on the price and sale of alcohol, be living in a society that is less friendly, more violent, nervous and unhealthy, but money is being made, and that is good for business and good for growth. This is a real, not fanciful version of events. Big supermarkets aggressively resist controls on the sale of alcohol to defend profits, passing costs directly onto the public sphere, and in the process 'cannibalising' the social, core economy.

At a time when crime in general in the UK has been declining, perception of drink-fuelled antisocial behaviour, which greatly undermines well-being, remains high. Expensive alcohol-related hospital admissions have risen steadily too. Numerous proposals have been made to control more aggressively the advertising of alcoholic drinks and to impose higher minimum unit prices for alcohol. Adverts for the mixed spirits drink WKD (a contraction of Wicked – strapline: 'Have you got a WKD side?'), which appear to be targeted largely at young men, associate consuming the drink with the drinkers carrying out 'pranks' that, seen from another point of view, might be considered as antisocial behaviour. As a counterbalance, the tiny size of the 'drink responsibly' advice to be seen buried at the bottom of drink adverts gives an indication of real priorities. Weak regulation of alcohol in terms of price or advertising is ultimately justified as a 'pro-growth' policy. It is not an arbitrary cultural artefact, but the result of industry lobbying and politicians believing in a particular economic argument.

The tensions become especially clear when private providers begin delivering things like prison services. In the United States, the prison population tripled between 1987 and 2007 to 1.6 million according to the American Civil Liberties Union (ACLU). Laws that reduce the courts' powers of discrimination over sentencing, such as the 'three strikes and you're out' law, led to huge increases in those incarcerated. In that time private companies grew to provide for one in every eleven prisoners. In 2010 the Corrections Corporation of America, the largest private provider, took $1.7 billion in revenue. 'Prisons for profit have a different mission than public prisons: they must earn revenue. This means they have an inherent interest in ensuring prisons stay filled,' comments the ACLU.[33] A study in Ohio showed that states with higher proportions of private prisons had higher rates of reoffending and that private prisons in Ohio itself offered fewer rehabilitation and training courses than publicly owned equivalents.

It gets stranger still, though. The contracting out of prisoner labour to private companies has also spread. Among the companies taking advantage of prisoner labour according to the Canada-based Global Research, a centre for research on globalisation, are: IBM, Boeing, Motorola, Microsoft, AT&T, Wireless, Texas Instrument, Dell, Compaq, Honeywell, Hewlett-Packard, Nortel, Lucent Technologies, 3Com, Intel, Northern Telecom, TWA, Revlon, Macy's, Pierre Cardin, Target Stores and many others.[34] In publicly run prisons, the pay for prisoners might be at the level of the minimum wage or as low as $1.25 per hour. In private prisons it might be as low as 17 cents per hour, or 50 cents if lucky. Inmates find themselves making an interesting variety of goods, from ammunition belts to bulletproof vests and medical supplies – potentially a cradle-to-grave service.

The words of John Maynard Keynes come compellingly to mind, but probably not in the exact context in which he intended them: 'Capitalism is the astounding belief that the most wickedest of men will do the most wickedest of things for the greatest good of everyone.' Whether or not the walls of the prison create a meaningful gap between the 'most wickedest' and others I will leave open.

Now, after noting a small exception, back to *why* we grow economies, as opposed to merely *how*.

As described below, the idea of well-being has risen rapidly up the political agenda. The British prime minister David Cameron called for a measure of 'general well-being' to sit alongside growth, and official statisticians are developing a set of national accounts of well-being. This is progress and welcome news, and partly the result of relentless lobbying by organisations like the new economics foundation, for which I have worked for many years.

In an essay that I commissioned from the future prime minister, which appeared in a book in 2008, David Cameron wrote:

For the past few decades we have witnessed unparalleled prosperity. But it is hard to escape there is something not quite right. In some cases, it is difficult to put your finger on exactly what it is: a feeling of emptiness, and a lack of defined relationships and solid social structures. In other respects, it is clearly identifiable: rates of drug abuse and depression are rocketing. It goes to show what most of us instinctively feel: that the pursuit of wealth is no longer – if it ever was – enough to meet people's hope and aspirations; that over-consumption of the world's resources cannot satisfy our most inborn desires; and yes, that quality of life means more than quantity of money.

But we cannot mistake the development of new illustrative measures, or the expression of particular sentiments, for meaningful change in economic policy. It is the difference between soft and hard issues and how they relate to decision-making. Considerations of economic growth still, at virtually every turn, trump all other concerns at the government top table. Growth remains the beating economic heart. This slightly different point of view from a speech by David Cameron as prime minister three years later, in January 2011, illustrates the point: 'It is a new year and this coalition government has one over-riding resolution, and that is to help drive growth.'[35]

The effects of the pressures of high office can be remarkable, transformative even, and not in a good way. These are some more reasons why.

First, governments plan their expenditure assuming that the economy will keep growing. If it then didn't grow, there would be shortfalls in government income with repercussions for public spending. The same is true for all of us; for example, when we plan for old age by putting our savings into pensions.

Ironically, as a result of the recession that ensued from the banking crisis of 2007–8, many economies like the UK are facing this problem in any case. Weak regulation of financial services was considered progrowth. It was meant to unleash creative free-market forces and allow the invisible hand to steer successful expanding enterprises. Instead it got distracted, and crashed the car of the economy, destroying wealth and pushing growth into reverse.

Second, the legal and inescapable investment-related obligations on publicly listed companies under shareholder capitalism make growth necessary and inevitable. In theory at least, they make the maximisation of returns to shareholders the highest priority for management. In reality, again as the financial crash demonstrated, management also found plenty of time to maximise its own returns and continues to do so at the expense of virtually everyone else, shareholders included. In research commissioned by the company IBM, vastly overpaid fund managers were estimated to actually destroy $1.3 trillion in value each year.[36] Nevertheless, both drivers maintain growth as an overarching goal.

As major investors are generally footloose, they are free to take their money wherever the highest rates of return and growth are to be found. The absence of capital controls is seen as a major cause of economic instability, not to mention a challenge to democratic government.

Third, in the modern world, money is lent into existence by banks at interest. Because for every pound, dollar, yen or euro borrowed, more must be paid back, economies that function largely on interest-bearing money have a built-in growth dynamic. And yet, on the edge of the mainstream, the idea that the levels of growth witness over the last century may be a historical aberration is beginning to take hold. For most of the millennium up to 1900 Britain experienced negligible growth in per capita income, typically far below 1 per cent. Then, for a century the world reaped the benefits of transformational, but frequently one-off, breakthroughs in energy, transport, communication and other technologies. They included things like electric light, domestic plumbing, the car and the computer, and were boosted by cheap, easy-to-access fossil fuels. Growth went up accordingly. But now, in the absence of similar luck and innovation, industrialised countries in particular are returning to a long-term state of low-to-no growth. To illustrate how great technological leaps are likely to be replaced by small shuffling steps, Professor Robert J. Gordon of Northwestern University poses this thought experiment:

> You are required to make a choice between option A and option B. With option A you are allowed to keep 2002 electronic technology, including your Windows 98 laptop accessing Amazon, and you can keep running water and indoor toilets; but you can't use anything invented since 2002. Option B is that you get everything invented in the past decade right up to Facebook, Twitter, and the iPad, but you have to give up running water and indoor toilets. You have to haul the water into your dwelling and carry out the waste. Even at 3 a.m. on a rainy night, your only toilet option is a wet and perhaps muddy walk to the outhouse. Which option do you choose?

How to deal with some of the former problems I'll return to, but first of all, how else can we measure progress other than with GDP? What compass can we use to steer us away from the apocalypse?

One reason for gentle confidence is that a dim awareness of the current unsustainability of how the economy operates is creeping into unlikely corners. The Bank for International Settlements (BIS) is a trade body for central banks which technically is global, but is dominated by the major Northern economic powers. Its job is to set a range of standards for how cautious or reckless banking should be. Its reputation suffered first for failing to see the approaching banking crisis, and then afterwards for not noticing systemic market rigging by banks in the way they lent money to each other. But, to its credit, in its 2011 annual report BIS seemed to conclude that spending money we don't have on things we don't really need isn't such a good idea after all: 'The sooner advanced economies abandon the leverage-led growth that precipitated the Great Recession, the sooner they will shed the destabilising debt accumulated during the last decade.'[37]

If the economy, therefore, is to fit the shoe size of the planet, it cannot grow for ever. So far, so simple. Yet this can be challenging in an everyday way. I'm often asked whether this means that individual firms can no longer grow either. The answer is that while growth is constrained by biophysical limits at the aggregate level, within those aggregate boundaries (and obviously some local ones too, which become obvious if you live on a small island, for example), there can be a lot of variability.

A fossil fuel company will need to shrink, whereas a company specialising in providing renewable energy, repairing and recycling, or the arts, might expand. There are myriad choices and options to be explored about the nature, balance and shape of an economy that functions within the planet's ecological thresholds. More than that, it is a positive invitation to innovate and be enterprising. Life is, after all, an open experiment conducted within the limits of the laws of nature. Accepting such parameters is not defeatist, it is to live in the real world instead of an ideological fantasy land.

There are, in fact, so many alternative ways of doing things that without better ways of measuring the quality of economic activity, confusion might reign and we could become paralysed by the range of choice. Fortunately a profusion of better measures now exist. Here are some leading contenders.

3

The Measures

Planetary Plimsoll lines – finding the biosphere's safe waterline

The prodigy Jedediah Buxton, in his first trip to the theatre to see a performance of Shakespeare's *Richard III*, [was] asked later whether he'd enjoyed it, all he could say was that there were 5202 steps during the dances and 12,445 words spoken by the actors.

David Boyle, *The Tyranny of Numbers*

The nineteenth century carried to extravagant lengths the criterion of what one can call for short 'the financial results', as a test of the advisability of any course of action sponsored by private or by collective action. The whole conduct of life was made into a sort of parody of an accountant's nightmare . . . The same rule of self-destructive financial calculation governs every walk of life. We destroy the beauty of the countryside because the unappropriated splendours of nature have no economic value. We are capable of shutting off the sun and the stars because they do not pay a dividend.

John Maynard Keynes, 'National Self-Sufficiency'

In reasoning upon some subjects, it is a mistake to aim at an unattainable precision. It is better to be vaguely right than exactly wrong.

Carveth Read, *Logic: Deductive and Inductive*

What is the weather like on Mars? Where is the water that might contain microscopic, extremophile life forms? Has the atmosphere on Mars seen past climate change that we could learn from? NASA launched the Mars Climate Orbiter to find out. It was pure science and yet the most romantic of missions – to explore the red planet, source of dreams, myth and nightmares of alien invasion. Here was a perfect adventure for the eve of a new millennium. It also wasn't cheap: the whole programme cost well over $300 million. But, on this occasion answers to those tantalising questions would not be found. Nine months after being launched from the Cape Canaveral air force base in Florida, the Orbiter began descending to find its position in planetary orbit.

Then, on 23 September 1999, at 9.04 a.m., it lost contact with Ground Control. A break in signal had been expected as the Orbiter passed behind the planet, but it disappeared too early, and never came back. Something had gone very wrong. It later transpired that Orbiter's entry angle for its 'orbital insertion' was incorrect. As a result, it burned and broke apart. The best brains in astronautics and space engineering had spent years and hundreds of millions of dollars in preparation, so what defeated them?

For something so complex, the answer came quite quickly, in a terse press release issued just one week later. One team on the project had used metric measurements, another imperial, centimetres and inches, and of course they hadn't matched up. It was that simple and the official explanation was no more complicated. It read:

> The peer review preliminary findings indicate that one team used English units [e.g. inches, feet and pounds] while the other used metric units for a key spacecraft operation. This information was critical to the maneuvers required to place the spacecraft in the proper Mars orbit. 'Our inability to recognize and correct this simple error has had major implications,' said Dr Edward Stone, director of the Jet Propulsion Laboratory.[1]

The error was a false measure. The 'major implication' was complete mission failure. Simplicity, clarity and understatement, something refreshingly rare in official statements, but that can't have eased the sense of loss.

Everything about the space programmes seems to capture the best of human endeavour: striving, curiosity and problem-solving. There is a pure, almost innocent wonder and aspiration to it. For a global economy in need of rapid, low-carbon transition, the programmes teach us something about what can be achieved with boldness and ambition. In the first few months of John F. Kennedy's term of presidential office, he set the tone of America's short-lived new dawn by announcing his intention to put a man on the moon. As fantastic and literally otherworldly as that must have seemed, only eight years later in July 1969 it was achieved. The moon missions cost an estimated \$20 billion by their end in 1973.[2] To see what that would represent today you need to look at it as a relative share of GDP, which gives a sum of around \$200 billion. It's big, but considering the iconic nature and speed of the achievement, from a virtually standing start, it looks rather affordable compared, for example, with the cost and misery of the banking crisis. The Apollo programme was money spent for a handful of men to become the only people in history to set foot on another celestial body. As parsimonious official support to renewable energy is cut still further under austerity measures, what price is it worth paying to preserve for the whole of humanity the conditions under which civilisation emerged? In America they are invoking the Apollo programme as a precedent for the overdue climate response.

A good illustration of what focused purpose can achieve, then, yet there is also something giddily imbalanced and perverse about the hypnotic spell of space programmes. Whether or not rock samples from otherwise barren planets contain evidence of long-gone life can hold the world in pregnant anticipation and dominate the news. But curiosity about even the prospect of former microscopic life on other worlds sits oddly beside the blithe decimation of the rich profusion and diversity of life, much yet undiscovered, on our own planet.

A kind reading of our disregard might be that our attention spans are short and easily redirected. But it might also be a failure, or lack of measurement. If there's no dial to indicate when the pressure in a system is too great, don't be surprised if the boiler blows. BP's *Deepwater Horizon* oil rig above the Macondo Prospect in the Gulf of Mexico, which failed spectacularly in a lethal explosion that killed eleven workers, had an alarm system that could have prevented disaster. It was switched off so as not to be annoying. If you get no statement from the bank, you're likely to just keep spending, but shouldn't be surprised if poverty or bankruptcy await.

Anyone who lives in or visits London is surrounded by the symbol of the London Underground, a circle with a line crossed through it. This symbol has another meaning, one that saved countless thousands of lives when it was adopted, and continues to do so every day, yet however sensible it seems in retrospect, its introduction was bitterly resisted. The symbol, the problem it addressed of safe carrying capacity, and the manner of the struggle for its passage into law are all peculiarly relevant for us today. They illustrate the unending tension between wealth accumulation and safety, between profit and the risk of destruction.

On 11 January 1866, two weeks after setting sail from the East India Docks on the river Thames, a ship, the *London*, was sinking in the Bay of Biscay.[3] The weather was rough, but nothing that would normally trouble something of the *London*'s size and recent build. But the ship, owned by the strikingly titled Messrs Money Wigram and Sons, was overloaded with cargo. As it foundered, some passengers, expecting to die, hurriedly scribbled letters to the people they loved. One, a widower whose daughter Edith was far away on shore, wrote:

> Farewell, father, brother, sisters and my Edith. Ship *London*, Bay of Biscay, Thursday 12 O'C. noon. Reason – Ship over-weighted with cargo . . . Water broken in – God bless my little orphan . . . Storm, but not too violent for a well-ordered ship.[4]

In addition to its 289 passengers and crew, the *London* was thought to be carrying 1200 tons of iron and 500 tons of coal. Even in calm conditions, the distance between the waterline and its deck – the so-called 'freeboard' – had been just three feet six inches. It was horribly overloaded and too low in the water. When it sank, one small boat escaped, but 270 people drowned.

The *Sydney Morning Herald* wondered if the *London*'s owner, the 'millionaire, warm from his wine . . . [found his] feast disturbed by the thought that the stroke that destroyed the husband beggared the widow and the child?'

Contradictory sayings riddle folk wisdom. 'The sky's the limit', meaning there is no earthly limit. 'Look to the stars', meaning that not even the sky is the limit. But there's also 'Don't push your luck' and 'the happy medium'.

Optimism and pessimism struggle with the notions of limitlessness and boundaries. Denial of the latter has become synonymous with empowerment, freedom and aspiration. Meanwhile, the recognition of limits has been hooked to their opposites. Celebrity culture's triumphant paradox is that it hypnotises the mass of the public with ambitions of limitless success linked to material excess which, by definition, only a tiny minority can ever attain. Even then, for the winners, there is nearly always a downside.

The best PR always seems to be on the side of the life untethered by concern for the world around it, taking for granted the circumstances that make its own existence possible. Reminders to the contrary are nearly always unwelcome. Even so, recognising and learning to flourish within the thresholds and tolerance levels of our material world is what keeps us afloat.

The climate scientist James Hansen refers to coal-fired power stations as 'death factories'.[5] In the time that the *London* set sail, the shipping industry was called a 'widow and orphan manufacturing system'. How it was changed delivers both insights and a metaphor for our time.

The merchant navy was a very dangerous profession in the nineteenth century. According to the Board of Trade, during the 1860s, of the average one thousand wrecks per year, around five hundred of them were due to overloading and unseaworthiness. Sailors called these 'coffin ships'. Some were merely decrepit vessels, the 'spongy slums' of the sea that made drowning a common occupational hazard. Others were good ships, but recklessly overloaded by profit-hungry owners. Still others stemmed from shipowners' vicious insurance scams. Unseaworthy vessels were filled with junk, over-insured and sent to sea for the inevitable to happen.

Cases were hard to prove. As one writer put it: 'To start an investigation would involve heavy expense in obtaining witnesses from overseas, and as often as not their evidence would be merely hearsay, the real witnesses being drowned.'[6] Nobody heard any more of the sailors. Either they died or, if they survived, they were too poor and voiceless to get a hearing. Here was a silent apocalypse affecting families all around the country, wherever men were recruited to go to sea.

The real witnesses being drowned are words that echo down to an age of global warming, in which millions too poor and powerless to be heard struggle to survive on the front line of climate change.

In the year 1871, well after the lesson of the *London*'s loss, still 856 British merchant ships sank within ten miles of our coast, in weather that was no more threatening than a strong breeze.

Worst of all, if a sailor, having signed on, found to his horror that he was about to board a coffin ship, there was little he could do. A law made it a criminal offence, punishable by imprisonment, to refuse to board. The police forcibly kept reluctant sailors on ships, and even on occasion shadowed them out of port in police boats until the ship was too far from shore for the sailors to swim back.

It may be well disguised, but there is something darkly similar in the legal compulsion on companies that demands as their first consideration that they maximise returns to shareholders, and the way in which we find ourselves politically and economically bound to a treadmill of endless economic growth and rising consumption, regardless of the environmental consequences.

When complaints were made about the state of the fleet and regulation suggested, there were howls against official 'interference'. Shipowners damned meddling that would 'favour foreign rivals', and get in the way of free trade – the same song sung by bankers, fossil-fuel companies and others resisting regulation today.

In 1872, Samuel Plimsoll published a pamphlet called *Our Seamen*, and led a campaign to introduce a load line – a mark on the side of boats that, when level with the water, showed that you had reached the ship's maximum safe-loading capacity. Plimsoll was instantly reviled by big business and its friendly media outlets and politicians. He was a danger to vested interests, an Arthur Scargill, Chico Mendes or Hugo Chavez of his time – outspoken, a populist with a sense of mission. He was called 'the most dangerous man in Britain'.

Mills and factories were starting to be regulated, but shipowners had largely escaped. The more ruthless the operator, the more money they made. This was unbridled laissez-faire. Plimsoll was born in Bristol, which had been the most lucrative port for the slave trade in Britain, and slavery had been abolished only a few decades before.

Plimsoll would have been familiar with the arguments made in defence of immoral profit.

John Cary, a prominent Bristol sugar merchant, wrote a work on English trade in 1695 that strongly influenced British economic thought for over half a century. Slavery, he wrote, is 'indeed the best Traffick the Kingdom hath, as it doth occasionally give so vast an Imployment to our People both by Sea and Land'.[7] The promise of jobs, even then, was the universal excuse for more broadly destructive and morally indefensible economic activity. As we'll see later, it is heard to this day in relation to military spending and new airport runways.

The excesses of history are easily exposed in retrospect, attractively so when hindsight seems to flatter our moral superiority. But compare Cary's attitude with another view, written three hundred years later: 'I think the economic logic behind dumping a load of toxic waste in the lowest wage country is impeccable and we should face up to that.'[8] These were the words of Lawrence Summers, then chief economist of the World Bank, writing in a memo to other bank staff about six months before the United Nations Earth Summit in Rio de Janeiro in 1991. When his economic reasoning was repeated more recently, it led to thirty thousand people in the Ivory Coast seeking compensation from the oil services company Trafigura over the effects of toxic waste dumping.[9] You see it too with climate change, when rich countries seek to avoid reducing their own emissions by paying into carbon-offset schemes in poor countries of questionable benefit.

Summers, like Cary before him, merely took the logic of an economic system that is proud of being 'value-free' to its inexorable conclusion. Jose Lutzenburger, Brazil's environment secretary, wrote to Summers after the memo became public saying: 'Your reasoning is perfectly logical but totally insane.' Summers went on to be US treasury secretary under Bill Clinton, president of Harvard University, and an economic adviser in the Obama White House. Lutzenburger was sacked shortly after writing his letter to Summers. But the same logic now tells us that the global economy must grow by liquidating its natural assets in order that we may prosper and be free.

Shipowners said the introduction and inspection of Plimsoll's load line would bring 'absolute and immediate ruin' to the industry. The general attitude of the industry could be parodied as:

Thou shalt not kill, but needst not strive
Officiously to keep alive.

It is hard to underestimate the scale of the challenge Plimsoll set
himself. Britain was the dominant global power of the day and its
navy, very much including its merchant fleet, was the mechanism
through which it exerted that power. Any challenge or obstacle placed
in the way of the fleet's day-to-day operations was a challenge not just
to shipowners, but to the British economy and empire.

A newspaper letter said Plimsoll was damning all shipowners (read
bankers and oil men) for 'unmitigated scoundrelism', and accused
him of being sensationalist. In a speech he gave the same evening
that the letter was published, he replied:

So I am . . . Is it not a sensational thing for men to choke in the
water and to die, and is it not fit that I should speak of that as a
sensational matter and in a sensational manner? . . . I have been
made an agitator by the simple fact that when, for years past, the
storms of winter were blowing, I knew that men were being
wrecked and dying, and I could not lie in my bed.

The storms of winter. The real witnesses being drowned. In old age Plimsoll
worried that he had been ineffective, but he'd created the urgency for
reform. His biography says: 'It was not facts alone that were needed,
but indignation and anger.'[10] Somewhat presciently he went on in later
life to campaign against the economic 'Americanisation' of the world,
frightened by the centralisation of power that came with the growth of
corporate conglomerates.

After a decade of furious campaigning combining passion, fact
and crafted argument, Plimsoll succeeded. In 1876 the Marine
Shipping Act introduced what became known as the Plimsoll line,
its symbol a circle crossed by a horizontal line. It is still with us
today, a simple mark used everywhere on shipping. It has saved
untold lives on the seas of the world, and it did so without destroying the industry that once so fervently rejected it. The industry
merely adapted.

A ship overloaded is not dissimilar to an ecosystem or planetary
function overburdened. Push its carrying capacity too far and it will

THE COFFIN-SHIPS

POLLY : "Oh, dear Jack! I can't help crying, but I'm so happy to think you're not going in one of those *dreadful ships* !"
JACK : "What, Davy Jones's decoy ducks! No, no, lass—never more! Thanks to our friend Master Plimsoll, God bless him!"

The relief brought by the introduction of the Plimsoll line.

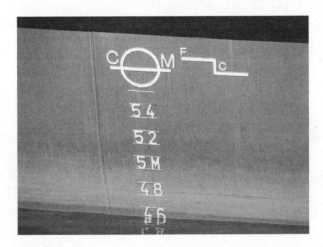

The Plimsoll line, painted on the side of a ship. A simple measure to reveal when castastrophe threatens, if you overburden the life-support system you depend on.

become unstable, more vulnerable to external shocks. A warming climate or exhausted soil equate to a heavy sea. Ignore the warning signals of destabilisation, and sinking or collapse become likely. How, then, can we introduce a Plimsoll line for the ship of the biosphere? The answer is that more than one measure is probably needed.

For the sake of illustration and parallel, imagine our less and less stable climate as a ship being sunk by the weight of carbon we are piling onto it. How low should we let it sink and where should the carbon line be?

In 2009 an important study led by the academic Malte Meinshausen from the Potsdam Institute was published in the journal *Science*, which sought, for the first time, to quantify how much of our remaining fossil fuels it would be safe to burn to retain a good chance of keeping below the 2°C threshold.[11] Around one quarter was the conclusion.[12] The rest of the coal, oil and gas needed to be left in the ground. It is what is coming to be known as 'unburnable carbon'.

Their study was 'probablistic' due to inherent uncertainties in the biosphere's carbon cycle, and the unpredictable, non-linear way that it responds to change. For a sense of what they found, a few numbers are needed. To keep a relatively low chance – 25 per cent – of going above 2°C, in the fifty-year period between 2000 and 2050 we can afford to emit around 1000 Gt (gigatonnes) of CO_2. But in just the six years from 2000 to 2006 around 234 Gt of CO_2 were already emitted, leaving little room for manoeuvre. If humanity felt like gambling a little more, and put three bullets into a six-bullet chamber for a game of climate roulette, emitting 1440 Gt of CO_2 would give a 50 per cent chance of going above 2°C. Emissions since that study mean that, in order to retain the better chance of staying below the temperature target, we can now afford to burn only around one fifth of proven fossil fuel reserves.

There are several attractions to introducing a carbon 'Plimsoll line' for the global economy that would render many fossil fuels unburnable. The industry is very concentrated in terms of major producers of coal, oil and gas, making such a line theoretically easy to implement from a practical, physical point of view (although the politics are quite different). Also, the commercial companies that trade in fossil fuels tend to be concentrated in a small handful of stock exchanges, and the City of London is a major one. Again, theoretically, this makes for an easily isolatable regulatory target (although, once more, the politics of such an action are quite different).

Already, for the benefit of investors wishing to assess value, fossil-fuel companies are required to describe their reserves as 'proven', 'probable', 'possible' or 'speculative'. There is no fundamental reason why a new category of 'unburnable' could not be introduced, using a formula that allocated an appropriate share to each producer of those reserves that could never safely be burned. It would send a clear signal to investors of the risk associated with sending the ship of the economy out to sea with too much carbon loaded on board.

The implications of Meinshausen's work have been spotted in some corners. Nick Robins, head of the bank HSBC's Climate Change Centre in the City of London, noted: 'We're still pricing [companies in the extractives sector] as if they are all going to be exploited. This is a particular concern for the UK as our stock market is overweight with fossil fuels.'[13] From an investor's point of view, this creates potentially 'stranded assets' that might become, in effect, no assets at all if they cannot be used. At the moment though, there is no line on the ship, meaning that economies can set sail dangerously overloaded.

In 2010, the world's self-proclaimed largest producer of coal, Coal India, listed on stock exchanges with a value over $3 billion. An investment analyst with Carbontracker, Mark Campanale, points out that in its 510-page offer document – the information provided to potential investors – there was not a single mention of climate change, meaning that there was no assessment of financial risk, should regulations to tackle global warming affect what the company could do. For him, this beggared belief: 'It is more remarkable that the company counts among its advisers Deutsche Bank, Morgan Stanley, Citigroup and Bank of America Merrill Lynch – all of whom trumpet their climate change research and corporate responsibility.'[14]

Flawed assessment of risk and the mispricing of investments led to the sub-prime mortgage crisis. A failure to assess carbon risk – because there is no carbon Plimsoll line – creates the conditions for the same mistake to happen again, on potentially an even bigger scale. With no proper measure, risk builds invisibly. It's something that touches nearly everyone. BP alone, for example, accounts for about £1 in every £8 of British pension payments.

Carbon is important, vitally so, but it is just one aspect of the economy. How else can the distortions of GDP be corrected, and what might make a better compass?

First, to recap from the previous chapter. The architects of the measure GDP did not devise it to be an indicator of general welfare, but that, in practice, is what it became. Growth or decline in GDP became the politicians' obsession and overarching gauge of the economy's success or failure. Its key problem is that it measures scale, but not quality, of economic activity. So in order to correct that, since the 1970s many have tried to produce more rounded measures of overall economic performance. All of the increasingly elaborate attempts to do so work, basically, by subtracting bad things and adding good things.

In the same year, 1972, that *The Limits to Growth* was published, two Yale economists, James Tobin (more famous for his advocacy of a tax on financial transactions now dubbed a 'Robin Hood tax')[15] and William Nordhaus, developed a 'measure of economic welfare' (MEW).[16] It took GDP, the sum financial value of transactions in the economy, as a starting point, added to that the value of leisure time and unpaid work to take account of positive things ignored by GDP, and then subtracted the cost of environmental damage, also usually ignored. It also made adjustments based on the relative equality of the society, the gap between rich and poor measured by something called the 'Gini coefficient'. Their work was taken a stage further by Herman Daly and John Cobb, who developed what they called an Index of Sustainable Economic Welfare.

What they did was to add yet more things into the equation. For example, they subtracted more 'bads', like public spending on so-called 'non-productive' items such as the military (this will emerge again in chapter 7, on lessons from history), personal spending on health (on the basis that this too is 'defensive' spending and not something to celebrate), time lost commuting and the costs of road accidents (which otherwise show up as the economy doing better), similarly the costs of various forms of pollution, and the using-up or depreciation of natural assets.

Although not perfect, and subject to a variety of value judgements (like almost every other indicator), these efforts produced more nuanced pictures of the economy. Many other subtle variants have been developed, including one, the Measure of Domestic Progress (MDP), by colleagues of mine. The MDP was a collaboration between Professor Tim Jackson of Surrey University and the Centre for Well Being at nef. Compared with the earlier indicators it tweaked the costs of environmental damage, such as from climate change, and included even more 'bads', in particular the costs of social ills ranging from crime to family breakdown (lawyers are expensive). In 2004 it was reported on publication in the *Financial Times* under the headline 'Index Pins Down "The Good Old Days" To 1976'. The journalist, Ed Crooks, picked up on the difference between the graph lines for the MDP and GDP in Britain over the last few decades.

Data going back to 1950 was used. Against this, GDP rose steadily over the subsequent half-century with just the occasional wobble. But the MDP, with all the adjustments made, peaked in 1976, never to reach such heights again.

After the *Financial Times* article appeared, there was an outbreak of bewildered hilarity. Folk memories of the 1970s in general dismissed the decade as naff. Glam rock, flared trousers, economic unrest and a bailout by the International Monetary Fund question whether things were going well either culturally or economically. Newspaper spreads used the MDP as a hook to ask what was so great about 1976. In the UK there'd been a heatwave, leading to water rationing and public standpipes where people queued with bottles. Forest fires broke out in Southern England. The cod war between British and Icelandic shipping fleets rumbled, direct rule from London was imposed over Northern Island as conflict deepened, and Harold Wilson surprised the nation by resigning as prime minister.

But the MDP reflected something else. Then Britain was a more equal and less polluting country. More equal countries have lower bills for a range of social problems, like crime, and this came out in the data. With fewer cars per head of population – we were yet to embrace Margaret Thatcher's 'great car economy' – and using less fossil-fuel energy to heat our homes, our greenhouse gas emissions were also much lower. The scale of public-sector investment back then also boosted the MDP. Factors like these explained the favourable judgement. With great irony, since then, fashion and design from the 1970s has enjoyed a resurgence on the style pages of the very newspapers who scoffed.

The MDP is what gets called a 'composite indicator', many measures rolled into one. Other, different, versions are used by big international development agencies. The United Nations Development Programme (UNDP) created the Human Development Index (HDI). It combines measures of life expectancy, educational attainment and income into a composite index which is a frame of reference for both social and economic development. Using it, countries can be compared in terms of their overall progress, or regression, against individual component elements, such as primary education, or the 'HDI' measure given for everything combined. Across all 187 countries measured, in UNDP's 2011 report Norway came at the top of the index and Congo bottom.

The report also noted that income growth was linked to worsening carbon dioxide emissions, soil and water quality, and loss of forests. In much of the world inequality at the country level was getting worse too. Strikingly it estimated that if resources were available to answer all the current unmet need for family planning up to 2050, it would lower the world's carbon emissions by 17 per cent below current levels. In the data, carbon emissions show a strong link to both income and overall ranking in the index, but key human development concerns such as health and education do not, suggesting that important development objectives can be achieved regardless of the resource use hard-wired to a growing economy.

UNDP says that: 'The HDI was created to emphasize that people and their capabilities should be the ultimate criteria for assessing the development of a country, not economic growth alone.' It sees the index as a way of questioning policy choices at the national level, 'asking how two countries with the same level of GNI per capita can end up with such different human development outcomes'.

Compare Costa Rica and the Russian Federation, for example. Their overall rank on the human development index is almost identical. Yet in strict income terms, Costa Rica is far poorer. That means Costa Rica is doing something positive, choosing policies that deliver far more for the development of its people in comparison with its income. Similarly, the small island state of Vanuatu achieves the same level of human development as South Africa, but with substantially less than half the comparable per capita income. Both these well-performing countries, Costa Rica and Vanuatu, come up again below in a different index, with clues about why they do so well.

Also noted was that the poorest groups in the population stood to be worst effected by environmental degradation. Here is a good reason to argue the counterproductive nature and pointlessness of saying that environmental protection cannot be afforded if we are to eradicate poverty. Some results are unsurprising. Germany and Sweden, for example, are lauded for their performance on the environment, equity and human development. But Costa Rica and the Philippines do well too, measured against absolute targets for greenhouse gas emissions, forest conservation, water use, air pollution and equity, and in comparison with their regional neighbours.

However, all these alternate measures are, in effect, still built on, or contain a substantial element of GDP. The HDI is slightly different, but the others merely illustrate better the downsides of economic activity. The economist and author Susan George, a critic of the GDP measure, was once asked what the alternative to growth was. She replied that this was the wrong question. It was like asking: 'What's the alternative to cancer?', she said: it is not to have it and to be well.

The key issue takes us back to the Plimsoll line. The more goods you pile onto a ship, the more likely it is to sink. You can price the relative risk of different levels of load, and insure it accordingly, and you can put a price on the economic cost of lost goods should the ship turn turtle. But if your life depends on keeping the boat afloat, pricing ultimately becomes irrelevant. The point is to stay on the surface. This is the paradox facing all environmental economists. Without putting a price on nature, the value of ecosystem services goes unregarded. They are, literally, devalued, and therefore there is nothing to regulate their exploitation. But some things it is impossible to value objectively. What is the price of a species gone extinct? How do you value the lost culture and nationhood of a small island nation lost under the waves? The attempt to price carbon is a clear case, and a major problem in the transition to a climate-friendly energy system.

One day renewable energy looks like a sunrise industry, the next, tumbleweed blows before the sun setting on the solar-power sector. What changes in between? The price of carbon.

Since 2005 Europe's Emissions Trading Scheme (ETS) created a market in which highly polluting industries, representing under half of Europe's overall emissions, have to buy permits to emit the greenhouse gas carbon dioxide. The number of permits is limited. Supply and demand set a price that is meant to drive incentives to shift to low-carbon energy. But it's not working.

A steady, rising price would send the necessary signal to invest in clean energy. But the price of a tonne of carbon dioxide in the ETS behaves like a child on a rollercoaster – happily soaring one minute, plummeting sickly the next. In 2008 the price hit €30, but since it has hovered below €10, less than a third of its previous value.

This is the result of there being already too many permits in circulation – a weakness of its original design – and of the economic downturn. As car makers and others mothball factories, energy use drops and demand for permits goes down. At the same time businesses try to raise cash by selling unused permits, flooding the market and further depressing prices. Even the energy giant EDF complained that carbon markets were failing like the market for sub-prime mortgages which partly triggered the global recession. *The Economist* estimated that in 2020 there will be 845 million surplus permits, in effect permanently depressing the prices in the carbon market.[17] Disastrously, a low and unpredictable price for CO_2 removes the economic incentive to decarbonise economies.

But how do you decide a meaningful price for carbon? The reality is more complicated than the ETS might suggest. Getting it right or wrong could determine, as James Hansen said, whether or not we are able to retain an atmosphere convivial to civilisation.

Apart from the classic demand and supply of the ETS, there are many other ways to put a value on carbon. To choose the most economic way to cut emissions, you can work out the 'marginal abatement cost' – what it costs per tonne to reduce emissions. But this is complicated by doubts over the scientific rigour of carbon offsetting, and the lack of reliable (or sometimes any) data with which to compare the full carbon life cycles of different energy technologies (see the section later on energy choices).

Another measure previously used by the UK Treasury, in a still fairly isolated example (others such as the Dutch government and World Bank experimented with it too), is the so-called 'social cost of carbon'. This estimates the full cost of emitting a tonne of carbon based on its whole lifetime in the atmosphere, and is used to assess different policy and planning choices. But with so many variables to account for, that measure generated a cost range of £35 to £140 per tonne of carbon.[18] It was then dropped in favour of a new 'shadow price of carbon', an approach supported by the French government and with backers in the European Commission.[19]

The shadow price is similar to the social cost but, using the government's own words, includes 'other factors that may affect UK willingness to pay for reductions in carbon emissions'. It is claimed to be 'a more versatile concept', allowing decision-makers to second-guess what other governments may do, and so enabling the UK not to make 'greater reductions in carbon emissions than would be efficient'. This is a methodology that, although well-intended, is also vulnerable to abuse.

Each of these methods has its advantages and disadvantages, but there is one problem that none can answer. I'll call it *the paradox of environmental economics*. As mentioned, for many years a small wing of the economics profession has tried to put a price on nature to redress the oversight that treats natural resources as free economic income, thus leading to overuse and degradation. It's a useful but fraught exercise. One study by the European Commission and the German government estimated that forest loss had an annual price tag of some $2–5 trillion.[20]

But here's the paradox. You have a market, like the Emissions Trading Scheme, that is limited in scope, less than global and with a limit to its carbon emissions that is not set by the science of avoiding dangerous warming. That means the players in the market will be allowed to burn enough carbon to take us past a climate tipping point. How do you put a price on that extra tonne of carbon which, once burned, tips the balance and triggers catastrophic, irreversible climate change? What would it even mean if, with some sophisticated algorithm, you did identify a price?

It's like asking: How much is civilisation worth, in perpetuity? Or, if you needed a camel to carry you alive across an expanse of desert, what is the cost of the straw that breaks its back?

The question reveals the limit to market-led solutions for environmental problems. Unless the parameters for carbon markets are set tightly in line with the science of preventing runaway warming, they cannot work. That palpably did not happen with the ETS, which issued more permits to pollute than there were emissions, and now, in the recession, is trading some emissions that don't exist – so-called 'hot air'.

Carbon markets cannot work without a global cap at least compatible with preventing a temperature rise of more than 2 degrees above pre-industrial levels. The idea that we can overshoot and reduce later is belied by the unpredictability and uncontrollability of environmental feedbacks, such as forest death and ice-sheet loss.

Now, in part because of the low price of carbon, all kinds of green energy schemes are grinding to a halt according to the Renewable Energy Association. Governments are there to compensate for market failure but seem to have a blind spot when there are flaws in carbon markets. They could counteract the impact of low carbon prices by spending on renewable energy as part of anti-recession economic stimulus packages, but ideological commitments to austerity measures prevent that at any meaningful scale. When the UK allocated up to 20 per cent of GDP to back the financial sector in 2008, new and additional spending as part of its green stimulus amounted to just 0.0083 per cent of GDP.

'Versatile' carbon accounting such as 'shadow pricing' allows government decisions that lock in fossil-fuel-intensive infrastructure, such as building airports and roads. A high, stable, carbon price would help. Adair Turner, as chairman of the UK Committee on Climate Change, called for a 'floor' price, suggesting £40 per tonne of CO_2. That would be somewhere between an economic nudge and a shove, but not enough. A cap on carbon is more important than its price, and this is also true of the unsustainable use of other vital parts of the biosphere. The point is to stay afloat, not just to make sinking expensive. Creative solutions are needed to tackle the paradox of environmental economics.

Price mechanisms, even manipulated by taxation, are too vague, imperfect and often unjust in outcome. In the Second World War, as we'll see in chapter 7, to prevent overconsumption of key resources, especially fuel, the British government rejected taxation in favour of rationing, because taxation unfairly hit the poor and was too slow to change behaviour. Rationing was the quicker, more equitable option. Carbon rations, or 'entitlements', in line with a truly safe cap on emissions, would provide a surer way of hitting emissions targets.

Even if you could price that killing tonne of carbon, it is a transaction that should never be allowed. Economics, and much else besides, becomes redundant if it can rationalise an exchange that sells the future of humankind. The way out of this paradox of environmental economics is to have quantitative targets for how much of the biosphere humanity should be able to use. Measures for this now exist (imperfect, of course, like all the others) – ecological Plimsoll lines – and can be used to guide key decisions. The concept of 'unburnable carbon' is relatively new and is yet to become a tool of policymakers. But there are others, longer-established.

For one we have to thank William Rees, who has taught at the University of British Columbia in Vancouver since 1969 and is now a professor there. Trained as a population ecologist, Rees raised an eyebrow at how the Western philosophical tradition of enlightenment somehow allowed people to imagine themselves as separate from nature. Nowhere was this more obvious than in the shift to living in cities where, with the occasional exception of a few ordered green spaces, entire technospheres grew in which the only contact with the natural world might be from an office or apartment door to a car, bus or metro station. Seasons in this world become a vague backdrop of varying temperature and dampness, stripped of their deep significance for our livelihood. How could this be turned on its head?

The thing about cities is that they are utterly dependent on the space beyond their immediate geographical limits in order to survive. Modern cities, no less than medieval ones, have a supporting hinterland to keep them going, to provide them with food and fuel. You can have urban allotments – and as we'll see later, these are making an important comeback in response to necessity in many parts of the world – but the sheer concentration of human population demands ecological resources from elsewhere. Rees wondered just how much: how could it be calculated? Working with one of his PhD students, Mathis Wackernagel, he developed the concept of the ecological footprint – how big is the mark we leave on ecosystems in order to stand up and live? Applying this analysis to cities produces startling results. When you add up the land surface area needed for food, building materials, freshwater catchment area and so on, you quickly realise that cities have outsize feet.

Take Tokyo, for example. Its broader metropolitan area has a population of around 33 million people. Rees calculated that to provide its inhabitants with all their needs required an area 344 times larger than the Tokyo metropolitan region itself, or fully 4.3 times the land surface area of Japan itself. It represented a level of consumption that was more than double what the biocapacity of the whole country could provide. This would be impossible were Japan not able to import food, fuel and other materials from beyond its own borders – as of course it can do: this is a rich city in a rich country, it has the kind of lifestyle held up for much poorer people and countries to emulate. But what if every country on Earth did the same? What if all the countries where, currently, the domestic population lives within its national environmental budget, where their ecological footprint is smaller than what their forests, fields and fisheries can provide, ended up like Tokyo and Japan? From where would we import the extra stuff we needed? This is the ultimate logical problem to which global economic development tends.

In a debate at the Darwin Centre of the Natural History Museum in London, I put this question to a fellow speaker from one of the neoliberal economic think tanks. He thought there were no limits to the scale of the economy. Where, I asked, when push comes to shove, will the material content of economic growth come from? He thought for a brief moment, missing only half a beat before confidently replying: 'Asteroids.'

Rees on the other hand saw precisely the logical conclusion, and the danger. If we all start consuming beyond the ability of our biosphere to replenish itself in terms of soil fertility, forest growth, fish stocks, safe carbon absorption and more, then we risk crashing our own life-support systems – just as projected by the original, and updated, global systems model developed by the MIT scientists who produced the original *Limits to Growth* report.

So Rees and colleagues set out to develop a new indicator, the ecological footprint, which would measure levels of human consumption and waste generation against the best estimate for the biosphere's ability to regenerate and safely absorb waste. It is a project still under way today, being endlessly revised as the data available improves, and our understanding of our feedbacks occur within and across complex, interrelated ecosystems. It is another kind of Plimsoll line. It attempts a snapshot, in one composite indicator, of the totality of how sustainable, or not, our lifestyles are. Data showing available crop and grazing land is combined with that for forests, ocean capacity for fishing, and carbon emissions (a big part of the footprint) and land taken up by urban development and then standardised into a measure called a 'global hectare'.

Footprint accounts are maintained and updated by a group of

international statisticians and scientists coordinated by the Global Footprint Network based in North America and led by William Rees's former student Mathis Wackernagel. Worldwide, humanity's ecological footprint has grown steadily. It turns out that since 1980, collectively we have been consuming more natural resources and producing more waste than the biosphere can replace and absorb, leading to a net depletion of the biocapacity we rely on.

The point beyond which overstressed ecosystems continue to function productively is poorly understood, but the more over-stretched they are, the more prone to failure and collapse. Biocapacity is not a fixed amount. Depending on how we treat the natural world it can increase or decrease. Desertification, acidification and oxygen loss (anoxia) in oceans and freshwater systems linked to climate can all reduce productive ecosystems. On the other hand, sensitive agro-ecological farming may increase them. The 2010 set of ecological accounts showed that the human footprint was one and a half times the size of available biocapacity.[21] Put another way, as noted above, it takes ecosystems eighteen months to provide the resources and absorb the waste that we produce in a year. Over-milk a cow, and the animal may tolerate and survive exploitation for a while, but not for ever.

Different groups of countries perform very differently, however. The ecological footprint of low- and middle-income countries is smaller than their available biocapacity. They live within their environmental means. High-income countries as a group, however, have a footprint twice the size of the resources available within their own territories. It is even more extreme where individual countries are concerned. The UK has a footprint per person nearly four times its available biocapacity, Belgium and the Netherlands nearly six times.

More meaningful still, however, as ecosystems respect no national boundaries, and because our world is interdependent, is to compare national levels of consumption per person with what the world as a whole has available to support everybody. In this way it is possible to say how much resource would be needed to sustain everyone at a given level of consumption. Hence, for everyone to live at North American average levels of consumption would require the resources of around five planets like Earth. At the European level it would take three. Wackernagel likens this to living off a credit card when you are spending more than you can afford to pay off. The objective is to get the global economy on-track for so-called 'one-planet living'.

Another way of visualising this that I suggested and was taken up by Wackernagel and colleagues is to imagine how far through the year we could get if we lived within our environmental means, before going into ecological deficit. Performing this calculation gives an ecological debt or 'overshoot' day when we go into the red. Allowing for revisions to the methodology of the footprint, this date has been creeping forward, further into overshoot at the rate of about three days per year since 2001, and now falls in August.

Another approach, published in the journal *Nature* in 2009, attempts to define a range of Plimsoll lines for key ecological life-support systems, distinct yet interrelated. It uses the notion of 'planetary boundaries'.[22] A team of twenty-nine interdisciplinary scientists worked to define thresholds that it would be dangerous to cross concerning nine processes in the biosphere. These were: climate change, the rate of biodiversity loss (both terrestrial and marine), interference with the nitrogen and phosphorus cycle upon which productive agriculture depends, stratospheric ozone depletion (the issue no longer grabs headlines in the way it once did, but is still of concern), ocean acidification, global freshwater use, change in land use (such as deforestation for farming and urban sprawl), chemical pollution and 'atmospheric aerosol loading' (this is the particulate matter from burning coal, crop waste and burning forests that ends up as soot, sulphates and other matter in the atmosphere, affecting both animal health and the climate).

Nine boundaries, like nine lives. How many had we already been careless with? The researchers found that three have already been crossed: climate change, disruption of the nitrogen cycle (with phosphorus close and linked) and biodiversity loss. But setting boundaries is not straightforward. Earth systems react to changes internally and to external shifts in often non-linear ways. There can be domino effects. Overburdening one ecological ship can make waves for another, or lower it in the water, make it less able to carry such a heavy load as it once did. As the researchers pointed out in *Nature*: 'If one boundary is transgressed, then other boundaries are also under serious risk. For instance, significant land-use changes in the Amazon [i.e., deforestation] could influence water resources as far away as Tibet.'

We are at or near the boundaries of four other systems: ocean acidification, ozone depletion, land-use change and freshwater use. On two others – chemical pollution and aerosol loading – they were not, as yet, sufficiently confident of defining the boundary to say which side of it we might be on.

The work on planetary boundaries complements, although at first it made no explicit reference to, the ecological footprint method. The latter, due to a lack of previous research on safe rates of harvest and waste dumping, merely produces a best assessment of full available biocapacity and compares it with human rates of consumption and waste generation. This, conservatively, or rather generously, creates the impression that all biocapacity might be available for human use. But the notion of slack, or lying fallow, is central to the healthy functioning of ecosystems. Nothing can operate at 100 per cent efficiency and productivity, the laws of physics will not allow it. How much slack does a system need? That is a difficult question.

Andrew Price, professorial fellow in the biology department at Warwick University, says it is a grave mistake to think that notions of 'efficiency of industry and development' matter more than 'robustness of ecosystems', and that the latter is fundamentally incompatible with the mainstream understanding of the former. Costs in industry are lowered by getting more from less, but ecological robustness or resilience can require the opposite, getting less from more. In other words, it requires more extensive forms of harvesting. Applying the 'efficiency of industry and development' to nature (and we shall also see, some would argue to people as well) is a road to ruin. Commercial fishing gives a clear example. In his book *Slow-Tech*, Price describes how, compared with pre-industrial levels, 90 per cent of large predatory fish have been lost from the world's oceans. But nature recovers, doesn't it? Sometimes, but not always in timeframes meaningful to human societies. A study looked at twenty-five commercially targeted fish stocks pushed into decline then left to recover. After fifteen years only 12 per cent made a 'full recovery'; 40 per cent of the stocks failed to recover at all. 'The worst enemy of life, freedom and the common decencies is total anarchy,' wrote Aldous Huxley, author of *Brave New World*, 'their second worst enemy is total efficiency.'

In response governments agree on what they consider to be a 'sustainable yield' for different types of fish depending on their rarity, habitat and breeding habits. In practice, however, these prove almost impossible to police. Then there's the problem that the fish don't understand that they're supposed to swim only with their own kind to make catching the right amount of the right kind of fish easy. Because the nets themselves make no distinctions they create the problem of by-catch, in which vast amounts of fish that are not the target species, or that it is illegal for fishermen to land because it would go beyond their quota, are caught anyway and thrown back dead into the water. One 2009 study reported in *New Scientist* concluded that 38 million tonnes of fish are wasted in this way, around 40 per cent of the tonnage originally landed.[23]

In place of this grotesquely wasteful and poorly monitored system a call has grown to establish marine reserves – downtime for fish stocks – to rebuild 'robustness'. A global goal of 20 per cent of the world's oceans by the year 2020 is a popular conservationist target, a long way from the 0.6 per cent already with some degree of protection. Somewhere between a fifth and a third, says Price in conversation, is the fallow space that ecosystems need to function well. If that is indeed the case more generally, it means revising downward in the ecological footprint calculations the amount of biocapacity that we should consider available for human exploitation. In turn this means that we are much lower in the water than even the dire current insights of the ecological footprint data already indicate.

Ecosystems are so complicated that it is tremendously difficult to identify where a tipping point might be that, if passed, would push things over the edge. Some say they are impossible to predict. But the American ecologist Stephen Carpenter, of the University of Wisconsin, and colleagues have attracted attention for noticing tell-tale patterns in nature that foretell a system about to flip. What they saw, first by studying insect populations, is a slowing down of natural variability before a shift to a new state, such as a crash in numbers. The challenge, it seems, is to develop ways of identifying such patterns before the change gets locked in. As an economist working with Carpenter, Buz Brock, told *New Scientist* magazine: 'If you wait for clear evidence of negative environmental impacts, you may well be too late to do anything about it.'[24]

Professor Tim Jackson, author of *Prosperity Without Growth*, talks in terms of a 'productivity trap'. In capitalist economies investors demand more from less. To get their returns, if a factory employing ten people produces 100 widgets in one year, depending on the investor, the following year they might expect the income from production of 108 widgets, or 115 or 120. But, if ecological limits kick in, and it's not possible to produce more than 100 widgets a year, and nothing else changes, in order to still get the expected return on investment, instead they would expect the 100 widgets to cost less to produce, and so be the work of only nine people, and then eight, and so on. An endlessly expanding economy can mask this problem simply by having more people producing ever more goods and services.

So, normal expectations of productivity growth create a huge problem if you seek to establish a steady, or equilibrium, economy. If the scale of the economy stabilises, or reduces, but investors still expect rising productivity from a workforce – more from less – the pressure is in one direction: to produce the same output with fewer workers. All else being equal, unemployment rises along with productivity. But unemployment is bad for people's well-being, socially divisive, and leads to economic instability. More people with less spending power creates a house-of-cards effect, a kind of rapid de-leveraging – conventionally less earning means less spending, less activity and therefore fewer jobs in a downward spiral.

How can the productivity trap be tackled? We live with something like this problem already. It's known as 'Baumol's cost disease' and, delightfully, the health service is a good illustration of it. Named after the American economist William Baumol, who coined the idea in the 1960s, it signals a common debate among economists but one that is rarely explained beyond, leading to much erroneous bluster about the expense of services like health and education in the public sector.

Briefly put, in sectors like manufacturing, fairly open to mechanisation, the costs of labour can be lowered easily by replacing people with machines. But where human contact is central to the job being done, as in the case of a nursery school teacher, speech therapist or nurse, it is much harder. Of course technology can assist, but you can't leave a class of thirty-two seven-year-olds alone in front of a computer monitor and just let them get on with it, much less forty, fifty or seventy young children if the school management were to further 'increase the productivity' of their teachers. We would call that bad-quality education, not highly productive schooling. Perhaps a health care worker has a patient who cannot communicate easily; if they are having difficulties swallowing food at mealtimes, the carer may need to sit and watch them for half an hour to understand the nature of the problem. Haste would be counterproductive and lead potentially to a wrong diagnosis. Similarly there are tasks that are fairly indivisible. Baumol gave the illustration that while many things may have changed in the last two hundred years, such as concert ticket prices and the sartorial fashions of the audience, a Mozart string quartet still requires the same number of players and the same amount of time that it did when first performed in the eighteenth century. Speeding the music up or performing it as a duet might be an amusing experiment, but not necessarily a more valuable musical experience.

What this means is that relative to other sectors of the economy where costs are more easily lowered by rising labour productivity, in areas like health and education it is intrinsically more difficult, and their costs rise in comparison, often to an ideologically motivated chorus alleging public sector inefficiency, requiring the 'discipline of the market' to correct it. Apart from such a view tending in general to be either mistaken or disingenuous, this problem is not limited to the public sector, but affects the whole of what get called 'personal services', which might be anything from hairdressing to plumbing, or someone bringing food to your table in a restaurant.

A whole range of services are inescapably more labour-intensive. From one perspective this creates a problem for those defending labour-intensive public services, from another perspective it is an opportunity to turn ideas of productivity upside down. It's possible to re-imagine the economy in such a way that a fall in classic productivity can mean a rise in quality of service and efficiency of outcome. In *The Skeptical Economist*, Jonathan Aldred puts it like this: 'In so far as service quality is defined in terms of low labour productivity, productivity improvements are impossible without quality reductions.' This verdict goes equally for the overstretching of ecological assets through applying the 'efficiency (and productivity) of industry' to nature.

This is an important insight and advantage for the green economy. Its early mantra of 'repair, reduce, reuse, recycle' is a charter for a more labour-rich service economy, requiring far more enterprises built on human interaction and relationships. This book provides examples from banking to recycling, the rise of refurbishing, urban farming, community-based renewable energy and shared transport, where the intelligent return of a human element to the economy, together with new ideas about how better to share the amount of work available, point towards a positive escape from the productivity trap.

According to Tim Jackson and his colleague Professor Peter Victor: 'Either we can reduce the average hours worked per employee or else we can shift the structural composition of the economy to sectors which have lower labour productivity and lower (possibly even negative) labour productivity growth.'[25] More people in work, but working fewer hours, for example, would capture for a larger share of the population the social and economic benefits of employment. It would have the added advantage of lowering overall consumption in rich countries. People who work less tend to consume less for a number of reasons, such as being more time- than cash-rich, with more time to do things for themselves, and being driven less hard by the culture of long hours towards superfluous consumption. A shorter work week – explored more in the final chapter – would free time to engage in a range of activities that can add to personal and community well-being – being active, social, learning – and doing more for ourselves, rather than having to pay for services.

In one sector alone, moving from old-fashioned fossil fuels and centralised power generation to an energy system based on a variety of small- to large-scale renewable energy technologies, a study by Deutsche Bank, *Investing in Climate Change – Necessity and Opportunity in Turbulent Times*, suggested that for every pound, dollar or euro invested, between two and four times the number of jobs could be created.

Variables that make it more or less easy to prosper in the absence of growth include whether the economy is built around activities that create many or few jobs, and whether those activities are themselves building a greener, less wasteful economy. Another, which will also be explored in more detail later, is how equally the benefits of the economy are shared. More equal societies, for example, almost always have lower bills for everything from health to crime and education. This applies as much to the distribution of employment as to the distribution of income. A report I co-authored called *The Great Transition* looked at the impacts on GDP in the UK of a real national reduction in carbon emissions to meet a target of a fair, safe, global share. Growth would reduce, lowering the national income. But we found that by shifting to be a more equal society, on a par with levels found in a country like Denmark, the commensurate drop in social costs more than made up for the drop in national income from a smaller GDP. We'll also see in more detail how different values can make transitions of this kind harder or easier. Whether we value money, status and image, for example, above caring for others, the environment and the public domain.

The issue now becomes the quality of economic activity. And the question arises, can there be a more meaningful measure of economic efficiency, one that shows not just how we are doing at living within our environmental means, but how well we are living within them? With my colleagues at the think tank nef, we worked with the ecological footprint, I devised the 'ecological debt day' concept, and there was a whole group working on the emerging agenda on human happiness and life satisfaction. Could they all be brought together? It was a challenge I set Nic Marks, trained as a statistician, who founded nef's Centre for Well Being. His answer was to propose a unique new composite indicator that combined three things. First, the ecological footprint. Then two other measures combined into one. Life expectancy, which is a good general indicator of how well countries perform on the Human Development Index, mentioned above. To that was added the measure of subjective life satisfaction.

This last area I'll come back to in subsequent chapters, but it is worthwhile to point out that research into life satisfaction is now decades old, with data allowing many different countries to be compared. While the term used is 'subjective' life satisfaction, that doesn't mean it is merely to do with fleeting and random observations. Surveys are conducted in such a way as to capture people's general reflections on their experiences of their own lives, not just the ephemeral emotions of a given moment. Over time it's been shown that this 'soft' data correlates very highly with other hard data, for example in relation to depressive illnesses and suicide rates. Following up on a pre-election promise by the UK prime minister David Cameron, the government's data division, the Office for National Statistics (ONS), published its first investigation of subjective well-being data in December 2011. As we saw in the previous chapter, in opposition Cameron championed what he termed 'general well-being'. The ONS explained that: 'To measure national well-being it is important not just to rely on traditional indicators of economic progress, but also to collect information from people themselves about how they assess their own well-being,' concluding that: 'Individual or subjective well-being estimates are an important addition to existing official statistics.'[26]

With the new index you end up with an equation. On one side is the ecological footprint, the resources we put into the economy. On the other side is a measure of relatively how long and happy our lives are, in other words the meaningful outcomes of how we organise our livelihoods. It is, in effect, a measure of the ecological efficiency with which we enable long and happy lives. When we first produced this new metric, which was called the *Happy Planet Index*, we did not know what to expect. There were some remarkable and some unexpected findings. The results of the calculations were turned into a score scaled from 0 to 100. No single country scored well on all three counts. There were telling differences between countries and striking individual national scores. In some regard, performance was unrelated to a country's starting point, rich or poor. The United States, China and India, for example, all had higher scores thirty years ago than they do today – they have become less efficient in their resource use at producing relatively long, satisfied lives.

In a similar study conducted for Europe in which the ecological impact was restricted to looking at the region's carbon footprint, Europe was revealed to be less carbon-efficient today than forty years ago in supporting happy, long lives.

Among wealthier countries there is a huge range in the scale of natural resources used to garner similar outcomes. Germany and the United States have similar scores on life satisfaction and their average life expectancy is also roughly the same. But Germany's ecological footprint, the resources consumed per capita, is about half that of the US. Lives in America are locked into much higher levels of consumption, the result of planning decisions, dietary habits, cultural norms on car and house size, and personal aspirations.

Alternately, you can have nations with similar scales of consumption that yield wildly different outcomes. Compare Russia and Japan. They share similar-sized ecological footprints, but the closeness ends there. At the time of the study, you could expect to live on average seventeen years longer in Japan, and your level of life satisfaction was likely to be 50 per cent higher. Russia has lived through extreme political and economic upheaval, and been left with a variant of capitalism sometimes called 'gangster'. It has a less developed civil society and struggling democratic machinery. All of these contribute to the insecurities that undermine well-being. Weak social protection, unemployment, alcoholism and other factors affect life expectancy. A similar comparison can be made comparing the developing countries Jamaica and Equatorial Guinea, in which Jamaica comes off the better. In some cases two countries might have similar footprints and life expectancy, but one much lower life satisfaction. This is the case for Honduras and Moldova – the latter is the sadder.

Larger overall patterns were also clear. Rich countries were pulled down by having large ecological footprints. Very poor countries, such as in sub-Saharan Africa, suffered low life expectancy. Central America is the global region that performs best overall. Once synonymous with being the victim to Cold War, superpower-fuelled conflicts, the region has enjoyed greater harmony in recent years. It also has a history of community engagement – high social capital, as academics like to say – and vibrant cultural life. Now its people achieve relatively long and satisfied lives with moderate levels of consumption.

Being a high consumer is also no guarantee of well-being. Estonia is, but its life satisfaction score is low, whereas the Dominican Republic is the opposite, low-consuming but far more satisfied. Higher levels of satisfaction were found in countries where it was more common to join groups for sport, religion or community activities, and which had open and democratic government and whose value systems tended to favour 'adventure, creativity and loyalty, over material wealth and possessions'.

Earlier we saw how Costa Rica compared favourably with the Russian Federation on the UN's Human Development Index, although technically poorer. On the Happy Planet Index Costa Rica came top in two consecutive editions.[27] Compared with the United States, it achieves higher life expectancy, higher life-satisfaction levels, and a much, much smaller ecological footprint. This begs the question, which, really, is the more efficient economy?

Perhaps the most striking finding of all was that within every global region the countries that tended to do best were smaller island nations. Although roughly equal in terms of income, island nations in general had higher life expectancy and satisfaction, and smaller ecological footprints. These results were pictures of data. Complex forms of social, economic and cultural organisation sat behind them. Interpreting the results is quite another matter. But there is scope for informed speculation. Something about how islands develop creates lives that are healthier, happier, and have lower impact.

Islands, especially those that are smaller, more remote and therefore vulnerable, often evolve adaptive and supportive forms of economic and social organisation. I've seen this for myself in South Pacific islands in studying how communities prepare for and recover from natural disasters. Traditional Pacific agriculture proves remarkably resilient. Instead of starving, Samoa recovered from two 'hundred-year' cyclones and main crops lost to disease in the 1990s, thanks to a wide diversity of hardy crops grown together in a robust mixed pattern. Sharing and gift-giving on the islands that make up Tuvalu are common, and give rise to cooperative, mutually supportive communities. Here, 'tallies of material benefit are meaningless', according to anthropological assessment, and 'as a result, sharing equalises access to resources across a community and serves as a socio-economic levelling mechanism'.[28] The opposite can also be true, however. When things go wrong on small islands, they can go badly wrong, as is the case in another Pacific island, Nauru, which we'll come to later, and famously in Easter Island. Geographical isolation can either insulate from or exaggerate the consequences of political turbulence and conflict. Many studies show a strong relationship between well-being and contact with nature, and on small islands it is nearly impossible to be removed from contact with the natural world (conversely, people are least satisfied at work in urban settings). Close contact with nature and proximity to visible limits – on Funafuti in Tuvalu there are places where you can walk from one side of the island to the other in a matter of seconds – could and should lead to societies developing more culturally ingrained notions of environmental stewardship. It's also expensive importing goods to remote islands, hence likely to reduce personal consumption.

Regardless, no one was more pleased than the people of little-known Vanuatu itself, when it came top of the league of nations in

the first Happy Planet Index. It has an ecological footprint almost at
one-planet living, high life satisfaction and life expectancy superior
to the Russian Federation, large parts of Central and Eastern Europe,
Indonesia and Bolivia. Vanuatu is democratic, peaceful, culturally
diverse and rich in natural resources. There is a strong notion of collective endeavour, its national anthem choruses We, We, We (*Yumi,
Yumi, Yumi*). Local small-scale farming provides around two thirds of
its food needs. It has few exports and little to do with international
markets. Over one hundred languages (the point at which a dialect
becomes a full-blown separate language is open to debate) are spoken
among the population of a quarter of a million who live across sixty-
five islands.

I find this irresistibly fascinating, because, with an altered scale,
what is planet Earth but a very remote, isolated small, blue and green
island in space? All that energy to find evidence of life on Mars might
be the equivalent of swimming ten miles out to sea from the shores
of Vanuatu to see if there is a single algal floret on an otherwise
barren ocean-bound rock. Interesting, but . . . The further study of
successful small islands should reap rich rewards for the broader
survival of humanity. Cuba, for example, is an interesting tale, visited in chapter 7. Although caught up in a history weighed down with
ideological baggage and adverse circumstances, it demonstrates relative success in areas like energy conservation, disaster reduction,
health and organic urban farming. But for some uncertainty over
data, Cuba, surprisingly for some, might once have topped the
Happy Planet Index.

Different ways of measuring provide us with a different compass
with which to plot societies' paths forward. A compass for which due
north is simple growth in the scale of the overall economy will take us
in one direction – ultimately, according to the analysis here, into very
stormy waters. Magnetised towards living within our environmental
means, or maximising the length and happiness of our stay on the
planet, and hopefully a combination of the two, the compass points in
a different direction. On the latter course, nature itself would seem to
have much to teach us. From farming to finance and architecture,
increasingly the professional world is looking to the functioning of
ecosystems to understand and better explain how to organise complex
economic, social and physical structures.

The 'unappropriated splendours of nature', as Keynes said, over-looked by cold financial accounting, in fact have enormous value. Even very small splendours, like beetles. I'd never heard of the Namibian fog-basking beetle until introduced to it by the architect and leading advocate of biomimicry Michael Pawlyn. You might assume that an architect's strongest instinct is to keep insect infesta-tions at bay, rather than bowing to learn at their feet. But there is reason to bow where the fog-basking beetle is concerned. Through evolution it has worked out how to survive in the desert by collecting its own supply of fresh water. It does this, Michael explains:

> by climbing at night to the top of a sand dune, and because it is matt black, radiating heat to the night sky and becomes slightly cooler than its surroundings. When the moist breeze blows in off the sea, droplets of water form on the beetle's back. Then, just before sunrise, it tips its shell up, the water runs down to its mouth, it has a good drink and goes off and hides for the rest of the day.

This is an astonishingly clever adaptation to resource scarcity. 'Look deep into nature,' advised Einstein, 'and then you will understand everything better.' Close observation of nature in this case, copying the beetle at larger scale, led to the development of seawater green-houses allowing crops to be grown in arid regions, and a Sahara forest project. Michael is fond of beetles, which is fortunate, because they are fabulously diverse and successful. More than five thousand species of mammals have been identified,[29] but around 350,000 species of beetle, many of which have hung around since the time of the dino-saurs. As well as helping to build innovative structures for a water-stressed world, Michael has come across others that are set to help with avoiding buildings burning down. The bombardier beetle defends itself with a high-temperature explosion from its abdomen, and is currently helping to develop better fire extinguishers. The bark beetle, which has a unique breeding cycle linked to forest fires, can detect an inferno ten kilometres away with one thousand times greater sensitivity than human fire detectors. Such extreme and particular examples merely demonstrate how much there is to learn from nature.

Not only do we need better measures to align the human economy with its supporting ecology, but we need to get the measure of the world in the sense of understanding it better, to function in harmony rather than conflict with the biosphere. As E. F. Schumacher put it: 'Man talks of a battle with Nature, forgetting that if he won the battle, he would find himself on the losing side.' From countless other examples and the work on biomimicry by Janine Benyus, Michael presents a typology of how nature operates differently, and more effectively, than human systems.[30]

Biological systems	Human-made systems
Complex	Simple
Closed-loop flows of resources	Linear flows of resources
Densely interconnected and symbiotic	Disconnected and monofunctional
Adapted to constant change	Resistant to change
Zero waste	Wasteful
No long-term toxins used	Long-term toxins frequently used
Distributed and diverse	Often centralised and monocultural
Run on current solar 'income'	Fossil-fuel dependent
Optimised as a whole system	Engineered to maximise one goal
Regenerative	Extractive
Use local resources	Use global resources

Cooking, building, making clothes, there's little in life that doesn't rely at some point on measurement and a system. A faulty or mistaken measure or system will be inefficient at best, and fatal at worst. Metrics are not just about numbers, they are the way you understand the world. Failure to measure something important leads to it being overlooked. Measuring can make it matter. Then, of course, there are things that defy or elude measurement or escape price, like the value of culture or stable climate. At the very least we need measures attuned both to current challenges and to assessing human progress more meaningfully. No single figure will do it, but we can stop using misleading measures, and start using a richer range of better ones.

The edifice of the modern consumer economy rests on a denial of limits. However well grounded scientifically, to point out any kind of shaping parameter is seen as a failure of imagination, a lack of vision, profoundly anti-modern and in opposition to progress. Yet these attitudes are not innate, they don't just emerge from the soil like grass on the plains after rainfall. They are culturally planted and nurtured by a host of interests. They play out in almost every theatre of our lives in which aspirations shape our choices. As no book can assess the whole of life, the next chapter looks into one particularly symbolic human activity. It names, and virtually created, a dominant modern lifestyle of conspicuous consumption. It is both an age-old fantasy to defy the physical laws that bind us to the Earth and one of the main veins and arteries of a fossil-fuel-addicted global economy.

If one popular theory among palaeontologists is to be believed, the evolutionary development that saw dinosaurs take to the air is one way in which they guaranteed their own continuation. Many believe that modern birds descend from the dinosaurs.

Paradoxically, humanity's obsessive desire to fly may be the best illustration of behaviour that leads to the opposite for us of the dinosaur's apparently successful evolutionary foray. It has an immediate, direct environmental impact, but also symbolises a lifestyle with certain values that have much broader implications, and it shapes certain human aspirations. Like Icarus, our desire for flight, and what it represents, is taking us into dangerous territory, crossing thresholds of environmental tolerance with potentially disastrous consequences. But how bad is it, and to what degree can we either learn to live without it or find another way to connect in an increasingly complex, interdependent world? The next chapter begins the journey.

4

The Myth (and reality)

The Icarus Complex – living the high life, the jet age and consumer culture

A splash quite unnoticed

> William Carlos Williams, 'Landscape with the Fall of Icarus'

Icarus flew too near the sun
Into the blue his red wax did run

> Hawklords, 'The Only Ones'

Progressive or 'prog' rock music has a lot to answer for. Mincing classical mythology is one of its minor sins. Hawklords – the band also known variously as Hawkwind, Psychedelic Warriors and the Sonic Assassins – sank their psychedelic teeth into the Icarus myth about the dangers of hubris for the song 'The Only Ones'. Why, later in the song, they had to insert a sealed scroll and 'daredevil angels' into a tale already so dark and rich is probably best explained by watching the music mockumentary *Spinal Tap*.

The original story (oral traditions allow variations) included the rage of one king (Minos), the accidental suicide of another (Aegeus), the stolen bride of a god (Ariadne, from Dionysus), bestiality, a labyrinth, human sacrifice, a Minotaur, and a ball of string. The Greeks knew how to party. Icarus enters the story as the son of Daedalus, an Athenian master craftsman commissioned by King

Minos of Crete to build the labyrinth to contain the Minotaur, half man, half beast.

Icarus and Daedalus, father and son, ended up in Minos' prison on Crete. They incurred the wrath of the king because Daedalus took pity on the plight of Ariadne, Minos' daughter, and Theseus, the future king of Athens. Ariadne fell in love with Theseus, son of Aegeus, her father's enemy. The Greeks did soap so much earlier, and better, than modern television.

Theseus was sent into the labyrinth as part of the sacrifices demanded by Minos in payment for the sins of Athens against Crete. Daedalus, the clever craftsman with a simple solution to hand, gives a ball of string to Ariadne, who will pass it to Theseus. He, in turn, will then be able to find his way out of the fiendish puzzle that holds the monster at its centre. First, though, he has to kill the Minotaur. The plan works, but it lands Daedalus and Icarus in prison. There's also a sting in the tail. When Theseus escapes by boat he forgets to send the right signal, hoisting a white sail, to indicate his survival to his father. Aegeus, not seeing the signal and fearing the worst, commits suicide in pointless despair. Meanwhile, the imprisoned father and son use their professional skills to fashion wings for escape.

Considering its complexity, it is extraordinary that the tale of the craftsman and his son took on just one dominant meaning: that over-reaching leads to downfall, reckless ambition will be severely punished. As a motif it litters popular culture, imagination and music, reaching far beyond the comically laboured lyrics of Hawklords. It is carefully poised too. Both fly in seeking escape, but one lives and one dies, suggesting that a single impulse differently interpreted can have opposite results. 'Myths about flight and ascent have appeared in all cultures,' writes Karen Armstrong in *A Short History of Myth*, 'expressing a universal desire for transcendence and liberation from the constraints of the human condition.'[1]

Myths are many things: entertainment, educational cautionary tales, ways to come to terms with the extreme and often inexplicable nature of existence. As ornate representations of the various rites of passage we experience on life's journey to maturity and, hopefully, wisdom, myths help us prepare for and assimilate such experiences. Mythology provides 'the discourse we need in extremity'.[2] When

European conquistadors risked unknown terrors crossing vast oceans to bring their own particular brand of terror to South America in the fifteenth century, they were drawn by a myth of cornucopia, a belief in the fabulous natural wealth of the continent yet to be explored. The same myth drew Viking settlers across the perilous Northern Sea to settle environmentally hostile Greenland (the name itself was advertising 'spin'), and later European settlers to spread across North America in disregard of the existing occupants of the land.

Cycles of death and rebirth form the narrative arcs of numerous myths and accompanying rituals. From pagan stories that personified the seasons, to their co-option and continuing use by contemporary Christianity, depictions of seasonal rebirth help to express the human imagination's ability to conceive of immortality, or godhead, whilst being trapped in a mortal frame. This enables us to 'live more fearlessly and therefore more fully here on earth'.[3] Thinkers interested in understanding the creation of meaning in contemporary culture find the study of folk tales a rich resource. The twentieth-century Russian intellectual Vladimir Propp (considered by some the founder of structuralist thinking) identified common storytelling elements in a vast diversity of Russian folk tales. Issues of 'prohibition' and 'lack' hence frequently correspond to common themes of 'transgression' and 'quest'. Icarus, for example, transgresses in his quest from freedom. 'Both the naturalist and the folklorist deal with species and varieties which are essentially the same,' writes Propp in his classic work of 1928, *Morphology of the Folktale*. Awareness of such deep structures at work in good storytelling could help in the grand cultural project of understanding ecological transgression, and the quest for transition.

Go ahead then, take flight, says the Icarus story, but find a way to do so that doesn't melt your wax. The popular retelling tends to overlook the extraordinary achievement of Daedalus in flying safely.

Life was certainly unfair on the Athenian father and son. They had done the bidding of their masters and mistresses, only to be harshly penalised – collateral damage in the machinations of gods, kings and princesses. Yet Icarus' tale is also one of innocent attempted escape, infected with natural exuberance. Sheer joy at the exhilaration of flight led a young man to ignore the wisdom of his father, a craftsman who understood the tolerance levels of the materials he worked with, and to transgress a natural boundary, flying too close to the sun, melt-ing the wax that held the life-preserving feathers in place. Unlike Hawklords, I'll try not to labour the point, but you can see where this is going.

In one of Belgium's main art galleries in Brussels hangs a famous and haunting painting of the Icarus myth by one of the many Brueghels. The poet William Carlos Williams was sufficiently struck to write about it.

Brueghel's 'Landscape with the Fall of Icarus'.

Far from the immediate drama of Icarus' plight, Williams is dis-tracted by the vibrancy of nature in spring, painted in lush detail. The self-absorbed farmer lost in his ploughing, the 'whole pageantry of the year was awake,' he writes, 'tingling near the edge of the sea'. Icarus' symbolic demise is pushed into the background, his tragic fall and drowning become 'a splash quite unnoticed'. Against the immense backcloth of the biosphere, humanity's predicament becomes local news, perhaps rather important to us, but does the rest of existence care, or even notice very much?

Is that how it will be for all of us if, as a civilisation, we are carried by our own exuberance, against the best advice, beyond thresholds that should not be crossed? We embody both the wise and skilled craftsman Daedalus, who is close to and understands how to work successfully with the material world, but also the more impetuous son, who thinks his will and desire need acknowledge no boundary. There are insights aplenty to excavate from civilisation's founding myths and legends and bring to bear on societies in necessary transition.

Long before scientific explanation, creation myths gave us a sense of place in the evolution of life on Earth. Sometimes, in advance of science, they did so with creditably accurate metaphorical guesswork. In the Babylonian epic poem *Enuma Elish*, a kind of evolutionary process has the gods emerging from an indeterminate primordial soup. Apsu, Tiamat and Mummu are the first gods out. Sweet river, salty sea and misty cloud, their names meaning roughly 'abyss, void and bottomless pit'.[4] The gods evolve in couples and the tale then becomes an allegory of man emerging and making the transition to an ordered society and functioning agriculture within nature, without losing a sense of the divine.

Wisdom and youth, ancient and modern, human society in tension wondering, sometimes quite literally, how close to the sun we can fly. If in escape, then from what? If in joy, does our ride have to flirt with destruction? Where better to reflect than in our failures to learn the lessons of Icarus himself?

Ten years after the Wright brothers were credited in 1903 with the first practical flight in a powered machine that was 'heavier than air' (i.e., not a hot-air balloon), a slim book by Sydney F. Walker was published called *Aviation: Its principles, Its Present and Future*.

Then, as now, safety was a concern. But then, you were statistically far more likely to die trying to fly. The Wrights' first flight was appropriately in North Carolina, at a place called Kill Devil Hills. That event turned out fine, but the Wrights are credited with the distinction of the first killing of an aircraft passenger, when a plane they were demonstrating for sale to the US army crashed in 1908. Sydney Walker understood the dangers of aviation, and he had a no-nonsense answer. The issue was clearly so important at the time that he finished his book with this proposal:

In conclusion, the Author would point out that the consequences of accidents may be minimised if first-aid appliances are carried. What are called 'Tabloid' First Aid outfits are now on the market, the cases containing all that is required in the way of bandages, dressings, etc.

His optimism was laudable, if misdirected, and his other insights go to show how hard it is to predict the long-term evolution and unintended consequences of a technology. On the one hand, having pointed out that some aeroplanes had reached the astonishing speeds of 80 and 90 miles per hour, he correctly predicts that:

A regular aeroplane service will be established between all the great cities of Europe, and between the great cities of America, and eventually between Europe and America, Europe and Asia, Asia and America. Lives have been lost and more will be, but the work will go on.

But, given the great sweep of that vision, and allowing for the fact that he was writing before the industrial slaughter of the First World War, Walker had considerable difficulty imagining that the new flying machines might be put to darker, more destructive uses:

It is supposed also that aeroplanes will be able to drop bombs over fortifications, towns and on the decks of men-of-war. The present writer has considerable doubt as to this being accomplished. Bombs might be dropped over towns, such as London, Manchester, or Glasgow for instance, but that would probably not be allowed. It would rarely get within the necessary distance to drop bombs over forts or ships, if a proper look-out was kept, even in the night, without being subject to attack itself. As its engine and controls are very sensitive indeed, one bullet might put it out of action.

Already by 1913 here are three of the great themes of aviation: a technology that was – contrary to Walker's bland assurance – to be dramatically advanced by conflict and military applications, a whole new ever-spreading, world-shrinking transport system, and the contradictory fear and attraction of flying.

The last of these is fertile psychological territory.

Epic horrors from aviation make whole nations shiver. The first commercial crash happened in 1920 when a transport plane crashed on take-off from Cricklewood aerodrome on a flight from London to Paris. Two crew and two passengers died, four survived. Then there was the apparently graceful, mighty and secure Zeppelin airship the *Hindenburg*, which caught fire in 1937 when seemingly secure at its mooring station, and collapsed as passengers jumped and fell like leaves from a burning tree. There were the two Space Shuttles that failed, one on take-off, the other on re-entry. Watched by millions in hopeless disbelief, it wasn't just the crew that died, but the glamour of space exploration, and a dream of the omnipotence of an economic and technological hyperpower. When a Concorde supersonic jet operated by Air France caught fire on take-off and crashed soon after, the knowledge that the passengers probably realised their fate before the plane hit the ground invites an intimate, exquisite, claustrophobic pain of empathy.

Greater than all of these in terms of cultural and worldly impact, not to mention lives lost at the time and consequently, was one of those rare acts that truly deserve the term 'evil genius'. Whatever the image, the reality of air travel between cities in North America had become routine by the turn of the millennium. Few foresaw that in the minds of zealous terrorists a passenger aircraft could be re-imagined into a giant weapon. But it was, and several were, and on 11 September 2001 history turned.

Like others, I found that the sight of a plane in the sky meant something utterly different after the murder and destruction of the Twin Towers. Contrails behind disappearing jet engines meant something different also after a conversation I had with the author Philip Pullman, but I'll come to that later. The antithesis of these fearful lurking tragedies that dominate the imagination was the dreamlike, almost unbelievable survival of US Airways Flight 1549. It became known as 'the miracle on the Hudson'. The plane had just taken off in New York when it collided with a flock of birds and lost power to its engines. Against all odds, the captain, Chesley B. Sullenberger, a former fighter pilot with thirty years' experience, a safety expert who also flew gliders, was able to float the plane down to land safely on the surface of the Hudson river. Not a single life was lost. 'Sometimes,' as the poem has it, 'things don't go, after all, from bad to worse ... Sometimes a man aims high, and all goes well.' On this occasion the pilot's aim was low, but it too went well.

Events like these form the grand theatre of history. But a more generalised ambiguity towards flying seeps out in popular culture. *Airport*, the 1970 movie about a bomb on a plane, passengers with issues and an airport disabled by snow, virtually created the disaster movie genre. Put another way, it's a film of our cultural ambivalence towards the benefits of flying. It was wildly successful, made a huge amount of money and spawned a movie franchise. It also unintentionally redefined and rejuvenated the spoof genre with a comedy send-up, *Airplane!*, which came out ten years later. Much of *Airplane!*'s script entered the language and is still often quoted. 'There's no reason to become alarmed, and we hope you'll enjoy the rest of your flight,' says the stewardess in the voice of reassuring officialdom. 'By the way, is there anyone on board who knows how to fly a plane?'

From episodes of *The Twilight Zone* to kitsch classics like *Snakes on a Plane*, thrillers such as *Flightplan* and *Red Eye*, television documentary fare like *Air Crash Investigation* and shaggy dog stories like the TV series *Lost*, everywhere are cultural reflections of our unease about something that the world's relatively wealthy now depend upon.

Without routine air travel, our culture tells us, we cannot be citizens of the world, we cannot aspire and, however reduced, we cannot bask in the long, romantic shadow of the jet set. They were a small, elite, ridiculously rich group of people in the early days of flying who indelibly attached the idea of glamour to aviation. So effective was the association from the first few decades of powered flight, that in spite of the queues, the delays, the security, the insecurity, the anti-social hours and deep-vein thrombosis, flying remains, for many, unshakeably aspirational. It's an example of enduring and influential 'stereotype activation', as described in chapter 9.

Sydney Walker's premonition about aviation's future global domination is impressive because, back in 1913, luxury and flying were alien to each other. It would be years before airlines could offer an experience to society's elite that would allow them to take to the air with the same style and comfort they expected and took for granted on the ground.

The dictionary says a high-flyer is an ambitious person, someone who is 'extravagant of opinion or action'. It has an economic meaning too. A 'high-flyer' is a share in a company that rises in price, often out of proportion to the actual earnings and profitability of the company itself. They tend to be volatile, fanned by rumours of potential, and have a nasty habit of crashing.

But the rather obvious root is from the early days of aviation, when only the super-rich could afford to fly as a means of getting from A to B. Adventurers, innovators and test pilots were a slightly different matter.

The first 'jet set' – call them a 'propeller pack' – shaped notions of air travel so definitively that the glamorous associations are still with us. The rich world still operates a kind of international apartheid in which the dividing line is whether you turn left when entering a plane, to sit in first class, or right with the general public, aka civilians.

After planes were used extensively in the First World War, the UK established a Department for Civil Aviation in 1919. In August the same year the world's first scheduled airline route started between Hounslow Heath in London and Paris. Imperial Airways began operating, with the support of a government that saw in aviation a means to 'make the British Empire stable', according to Professor Gordon Pirie of the University of the Western Cape, South Africa. Flying also became a 'statement about modernity', Britain must do it to 'hold her head high'.[5]

A civilian aviation industry (albeit in the service of Empire) may have been a badge of national pride, but it was also an essential attribute of the interwar age of glamour, Art Deco and the flourishing of modernism. In art, architecture and the design of everything from tea services to radio sets and automobiles, to be of your age you had to look sleek, fast and aerodynamic, even if you weren't going anywhere. But how much better when you were, in an aeroplane. The phenomenon of an international superclass in permanent transit may seem very recent, with today's legions of airborne corporate executives, consultants and country-hopping, arm-twisting government advisers. An estimated half-million now float aloft at any one point in time, like a largish town hovering above the Earth. But the restlessness of flying lifted off with little encouragement in the 1920s.

The first in-flight movie was screened in 1925 – a union of two industries that were both to define the century. Decent personal hygiene, however, came a little later. A proper washroom (toilet) wasn't available until 1930 on the Handley Page 42. By this time the once loud, basic and draughty interiors had been replaced with the kind of first-class comfort and style that the passengers were familiar with from ocean liners and the best carriages on trains.

Croydon today has a downbeat, far from glamorous reputation, but when it became London's airport it was not just the epicentre of chic, but 'a little theatre of Imperial endeavour' according to Pirie. It helped that the earliest regular routes linked London, a global power centre, with Paris, a global centre for art, fashion and partying.

In 1933, Britain's comfortable middle classes were allowed a glimpse of the high life. Afternoon 'Tea flights' took off to fly over London, served by waiters dressed in immaculate white. Something about the self-obsession of flight glosses over the fact that this genteel scene of aspiration hovered above a Britain in the grip of depression. The previous year more than one in five were unemployed, and in some towns unemployment hit 70 per cent. But for a new industry that was the almost exclusive plaything of the rich, aviation seemed immune. And in fact it was exclusive only up to the point that Imperial Airways was heavily subsidised by the government to deliver its diplomats and mail around the Empire.

From London to Africa and India, little Englands emerged to cushion passengers in transit from having to experience the real lives of Britain's subjects. Archive footage in the documentary film *High Flyers* pictures an elite every bit as happy, pampered and disconnected as the aristocratic London party scene they were taking a rest from. Flights all the way to Australia were introduced in 1935, and a service across the wide Atlantic to the United States began in 1939 just before the outbreak of the Second World War.

Several things happened after a conflict-driven hiatus to propel aviation towards the mainstream. Huge productive capacity and dramatic advances in technology from the war combined with rising prosperity, America's resurgent global economic status, and the birth of the consumer age. The sheer size of the North American land mass and the time it took to cross it also made flying extremely attractive. Suddenly other classes found they could follow the jet set. Relatively speaking, and in reality only where a still small handful of the global population were concerned, the skies began to be democratised.

International air traffic grew at double-digit rates during the period from the end of the war until the first OPEC oil crisis in 1973. First, turbo-propeller aircraft, then transatlantic jets in the late 1950s, followed by wide-bodied aircraft in 1970, made flying increasingly cheap and created a growing mass market.

Air freight too expanded rapidly in the second half of the last century. It is often measured by the amount of weight carried over a certain distance, or 'tonne/kilometres'. Hence 1 t/km is one tonne carried one kilometre. The numbers now are so large that the acronym used is 'BTKM', or billion tonne/kilometres. Starting in 1950 with an amount of airfreight so negligible that it doesn't register on this scale, by 1998 the world was notching up 100 BTKM. If that's hard to visualise, imagine just one tonne, travelling 100 billion km. For reference, NASA's *Voyager One* spacecraft took thirty years to travel just 17 billion km. It's a big, heavy number.

Sydney Walker's vision of aviation's ultimate ubiquity proved correct. According to the global airline industry programme at MIT, two thousand airlines now operate around the world, serving 3700 airports. At the last count there were twenty-eight million scheduled flights per year, carrying two billion passengers. Over the last three decades air travel grew worldwide on average by 5 per cent per year, and at double the rate of economic growth. At such rates, it could double over again over the next ten to fifteen years.

The industry is enormously concentrated, however, in the world's richest countries. Of those twenty-eight million flights, eleven million were attributed to US airlines, which account for one third of global air traffic, making thirty-one thousand flights every day.[6]

Extreme circumstances can generate extreme behaviour. Almost unnoticed, the growth of aviation created a new global currency specially minted for the international travelling elite. At the height of the growth in air travel in the 1980s a reward scheme for frequent fliers was introduced called 'air miles'. It quickly spread, with different airlines competing to offer better free travel offers. The more you flew, the more you could fly. Air miles took on a life of their own, operating like a currency in its own right. Soon the accumulated free miles could be traded for more than just additional flights. You can buy meals, theatre tickets, car hire, a 'chocolate rub, wrap and massage', or sign on to a course on owl-handling, and much, much more besides. The offers associated with air miles are broad, but fit almost entirely into a category of luxury-oriented, conspicuous consumption, perfectly in tune with aviation's own history.

For some, simply collecting air miles became a lifestyle, often an obsessive one, even developing into a career of its own. Randy Petersen set up FlyerTalk.com, described by the broadcaster CNN as 'an elite group of people obsessed with plane loyalty schemes'.[7] Randy, formerly a marketing manager for a fashion chain, has become an air-mile millionaire eight times over. His group collect air miles and in doing so, says Randy, 'We collect our dreams.'

One such elite flier, Gene Gibbs, travels a little short of half a million miles per year by plane. He racks up so many air miles that he's not averse to going 'on a run', flying for the sake of it, such as the weekend when he flew from San Francisco via Chicago to Tokyo. As well as free miles, you get recognition as a frequent flier. 'If it wasn't for the miles and status,' Gibbs told CNN, 'we probably never would have started flying, and we probably wouldn't continue to do so.' Altogether, it can become a little irrational, as Petersen says of his ultimate motivation: 'He who dies with the most miles wins.'

Even in an age of relative, mass air travel, the idea of luxury and aspiration is still assiduously cultivated. Most only experience being sat in 'economy', knees scraping the back of the seat in front, feet battling for floor space with hand luggage. But open the pages of the in-flight shopping magazine and you're back in the age of self-absorbed glamour.

The front page of the German airline Lufthansa's *WorldShop* brochure sets the tone. 'Vanitas' is a perfume that you can buy either for €60, or in exchange for 17,000 air miles. Everything in the brochure can be bought with air miles. 'Hypnotic Poison', another perfume, can be yours for just 14,000 miles; 'Get Me Gorgeous', an eye shadow, for 10,000.

Here is a treasure chest of irony and accidental association. A €295 silver bracelet named Pandora promises 'unforgettable moments', perhaps not to be opened on board, just in case. A similarly priced watch invokes the memory of Zeppelin airships, impressive maybe, but indelibly associated with crashing in flames. The memory of the radical, anti-war song writer John Lennon is co-opted to endorse a pen costing €425. It carries a 'platinum-plated plaque engraved with Lennon's self-portrait'. Yes, but why? What can someone likely to spend that much on a ballpoint pen have in common with a bohemian peace protester? At least Lennon himself can be excused as having no posthumous control over the licensing of his name and image.

The same can't be said for the self-styled anti-poverty campaigner Bob Geldof, who 'follows his convictions' to endorse a watch selling at €750 (212,000 air miles). 'I don't want to live like everyone else,' he is quoted as saying in the advert. 'I don't want to talk like everyone else. I am myself.' What to think? On the one hand, at these prices he's not likely to be living like 'everyone else'. On the other, here's a classic paradox of adverts promising products that allow you to express your individuality, yet do so with things designed to ostentatiously declare your membership of a 'lifestyle club'. So, oddly, Geldof's wealthy individualism, touted as 'I am myself', also communicates: 'You should be like me.'

After adverts for brandy and whisky, come those for cigars and cigarettes. An accident of layout positions the text 'Passenger Exclusive' above the words 'Smoking Kills'. On the opposite page, 'With Lucky Strike You Always Get More' sits above the list of ingredients: tar, nicotine, carbon monoxide.

Trinkets. Pages and pages of trinkets. If you are already flying, chances are that all your basic material needs have been met. You are a member of the global elite. All that is left necessary to adorn your life is perfume and trinkets. But the way that the hedonistic treadmill turns, and that status competition operates, is that you must be able to move up. Where do you go after becoming an air-miles millionaire, and enjoying seats that turn into beds? The controversial entrepreneur Richard Branson's answer was into suborbital scheduled space travel. Virgin Galactic, the service his business empire is developing, already boasts 430 customers who have paid deposits towards the ticket price of $200,000, available from 'accredited space agents around the world'.

Icarus would be proud. Is that a trifle killjoy? Perhaps, but no more than the glorification of limitless flying is reckless. The difference to the Icarus myth is that this time it's not just the person flying who is endangered. I interviewed the author Philip Pullman for a book about human well-being and the environment. I'd read the trilogy *His Dark Materials* and in one book, *The Subtle Knife*, the implement of the title is used by various characters to cut through the fabric of

space separating different universes. Only, when they do, unknowingly they do terrible damage, and release terrifying spirits. When I
looked at the sky on a clear day, to see it bisected by the contrails of
planes passing overhead, and knowing about the disproportionate
climate damage resulting from the chemistry of airplane emissions, I
thought that there must be a connection and asked him if there was
an allusion to global warming hidden in his book. Pullman answered
that *The Subtle Knife* 'wasn't a completely unconscious echo', adding
that: 'At the end of the first book, there's an explosion that rends the
sky wide open . . . I've been aware of the terms "global warming"
and "climate change" for as long as they've been around.
Unfortunately, unlike the characters in my story, we've only got one
universe to play with, we can't skip through a hole into another one.'[8]

Greenhouse gas emissions from international aviation are largely
beyond the control of the agreement to tackle global warming, the
United Nations Framework Convention on Climate Change and the
Kyoto Protocol. Worse still, the nature of aviation emissions can make
them between two and five times more potent in terms of warming
than emissions at ground level. Already large, between 1995 and 2050
emissions from air travel could increase by a factor of between three
and six, depending on variables like the price of oil and the state of
the global economy.[9]

In spite of the accumulated science, and the crazily high stakes of
threatening a climate conducive to human civilisation, the world in
general is still moving in the wrong direction. The concentration of
greenhouse gases in the atmosphere is rising inexorably, and emissions from aviation are rising faster than the average background rate.
In the last decade of the last millennium global carbon dioxide (CO_2)
emissions grew by 13 per cent, while aviation emissions grew by
nearly double, 25 per cent. In the same period in the UK aviation
emissions grew by a much larger 80 per cent. They account for over 6
per cent of the UK's CO_2 emissions before you allow for aviation's
worse impact, and over 12 per cent once the nature of their emissions
is conservatively factored in.[10]

The UK has committed to reducing its greenhouse gas emissions
by 80 per cent below 1990 levels by the year 2050, and adopted an
aviation target limiting emissions to no more than 2005 levels by 2050.
The latest science, however, suggests that to achieve their necessary

share of worldwide cuts, wealthy industrialised countries like the UK will have to reduce their emissions by 70 per cent by 2030, and 90 per cent by 2050.[11]

This is where things get tricky for the human ambition to fly (and to fly more and more and more). It's the point at which Icarus has to pause for thought. Should he go that little bit higher? What is the balance between risk, desire and experience?

The UK's Department for Transport makes certain assumptions about aviation growth. Depending on where you draw the line, and the degree to which you wish to reduce emissions, looking ahead to the year 2050 extraordinary things happen in terms of the share of the nation's allowable emissions taken by aviation. It ranges from fully one quarter to around 150 per cent, i.e., far more than we can get away with.[12] Taken literally, that would mean that no other economic activity would be allowed to emit a single gram of CO_2. Everything else, in this case, that is currently reliant on fossil fuels – kettle boiling, driving, growing most of our food – would have to stop just to allow flying to continue.

In one scenario that would leave us with a reasonable chance of preventing global temperatures not straying beyond the danger threshold of a 2°C rise, aviation takes up the UK's entire fair share of emissions by 2040.[13]

Somewhat atypically, one of the academics who did this work, Professor Kevin Anderson of the Tyndall Centre for Climate Change Research at Manchester University, draws conclusions for his own life from the research he does. When invited in 2011 to address a conference in China he agreed, reluctantly, but only on the basis that he wouldn't fly, so he took the train instead. Anderson is quietly infuriated by fellow climate scientists who think nothing of globe-hopping by plane to present their work on global warming. He withdrew from a high-profile environmental conference, *Planet Under Pressure*, due to the organisers' insistence that delegates offset their emissions for attending. That may seem counter-intuitive, but he argued in a memo made public that 'offsetting is without scientific legitimacy, is dangerously misleading and almost certainly contributes to a net increase in the absolute rate of global emissions growth'. This happens because of the way that the promise of offsetting makes action to actually reduce emissions less likely – why change your behaviour if you can carry on as normal and pay for absolution? – and makes the continuing development and lock-in of high-carbon infrastructure more likely.[14]

He makes the point that cancelling the apocalypse is going to require behaviour change as well as different ways of making and using things. This fact can be used either as a counsel of despair (People will never change! Oh, but they always are!) or as an accusation that you are intent on denying the poor their place at the overflowing dinner table of life. The latter argument is, to say the least, often self-serving and disingenuous. It is the rich, overwhelmingly, who fly: it is an option substantially limited to the populations of wealthy countries, and to wealthy elites in poor countries. Even within rich countries, it is the wealthy who fly disproportionately. Generally, where climate change is concerned, 80 per cent of worldwide emissions stem from 20 per cent of the population. Staggeringly, according to Anderson, fully 50 per cent are the result of the lifestyles of just 1 per cent.

In the UK, around three out of every four people taking a leisure flight come from the wealthier groups of society, and the proportion of the flying public (a wonderfully visual notion) who are relatively well off is increasing. As the Aviation Environment Federation put it, comparing the mid-1980s with two decades later: '[Artificially] low air fares have not "democratised" air travel. They mainly – and increasingly – benefit well-off people.'[15] The number of business passengers flying internationally grew by 61 per cent in the decade from 1996 to 2007.[16] In the same period the annual number of business passengers using UK airports for scheduled, long-haul flights increased by 3 million, from 8 to 11 million. The comparable growth of business short-haul flights was even more dramatic, from 19 to 29 million annually. When all categories of business traveller are added together, numbers rose from 43 to 63 million, or nearly half as much again. Although the recession of 2008 had an impact on business travel,[17] expectations remain that it will keep growing. Business travel in dedicated aircraft (free of messy leisure travellers), for example, is rising. There were on average 393 such flights a day in the UK in 2011. And businesses expect to travel more and more by plane.[18]

If it is not disingenuous arguments about the freedom of the poor to travel that are invoked to defend the expansion of fossil-fuel-intensive transport infrastructure, it is instead the more general line of defence that we need the economic benefits of aviation. But these too can be wildly overstated.

Heathrow in West London is one of the world's major airports, what is known as a 'hub', an airport linking many international flights with countless passengers not necessarily flying in to visit the UK, but in transit to somewhere else. It is like a town in its own right. Heathrow even has its own 'writer in residence', a role once filled by the popular philosopher Alain de Botton. He was a clever choice, having written a book about the problematic nature of travel. Out of many insights offered, the simple paradox I remember most is his observation that inner turmoil or restlessness often motivates us to travel to change our surroundings, but that wherever we go, we find that we still have our troubled selves for company. For a philosopher, this is an obviously reassuring insight, affirming perhaps the greater importance of the inner philosophical journey.

The advice to calm our ennui before imposing it on foreign countries has done little, however, to reduce the enthusiasm to fly from Heathrow. It served 176 locations in 90 countries with 450,000 arrivals and departures carrying 66 million people in 2010 (as if the entire population of the UK either came or went). It has five terminals and two runways, and is eager to grow. A debate has raged for years about whether or not Heathrow should be allowed another runway.

After years of debate, in 2009 the Secretary of State for Transport in the Labour government approved the building of a third runway. His decision was justified in part by research from the Department for Transport (DfT) that concluded an extra runway would bring an economic benefit of £5.5 billion. But their research used models that are highly sensitive and relied on including certain key assumptions, and omitting other concerns. When the same model was rerun by nef with revised assumptions, and after discussing the impact of increased flight numbers with the local community, the picture changed dramatically.[19]

The new analysis used a more comprehensive approach to evaluation called Social Return on Investment (SROI). It differs from limited conventional approaches by including the views of all the groups likely to be affected by a development. For example, it revealed that the DfT's study failed to give local people the opportunity to register their own objections, such as concerns to do with impact on local heritage and community blight. The DfT had merely asked a series of 'closed, prescribed questions' to help enable the proposed runway to meet its legal obligations for noise and air quality.

The alternative approach to measuring impact took the view that: 'We should value the things that matter, rather than just those things that are easy to monetise.' This means being healthily sceptical about attempts to give definitive financial values to things that are inherently difficult to cost and where no agreed, accurate metric exists, as well as incorporating social and environmental considerations in a more balanced way.

The analysis set different initial parameters, using figures for economic growth, exchange rates, the price of carbon and other factors that they judged to be more realistic. Then they recalculated the costs to the local community of living with a new runway, looking again at noise and air pollution. They also included for the first time something that the DfT had left out: the added costs of surface congestion and community blight. There was criticism too of the way in which it seemed an economic case had been deliberately constructed to support airport expansion. It was, so to speak, policy-based evidence rather than evidence-based policy.

It is not unusual for the ground rules of impact studies to be geared towards delivering a desired result. The case for another piece of major UK transport infrastructure, a high-speed rail link between London and Birmingham (known as HS2), relied on at least one very curious assumption. A key part of its economic justification was the small amount of travel time saved by passengers, added up over the year. But for this to become a saving that could tip the scales in favour of the project in terms of costs and benefits, the researchers assumed that time spent on the train was unproductive, in other words that business travellers would be idle, not working during their journey. Anyone who has seen a forest of laptops flip open as a train pulls out of London will know how ridiculous that is. Another report also commissioned by the government from an engineering firm called Atkins, but ignored, concluded that money spent on HS2 would bring more value if invested instead in upgrading pre-existing trains and infrastructure. Yet another, also from nef, found that HS2 could increase problems to do with the North–South economic divide, part of HS2's rationale being to do the opposite, because instead of encouraging businesses to head north, it would merely make it easier for enterprise to drain south.

The result of the more comprehensive Heathrow assessment, with revised estimates of likely economic growth and a higher, more realistic price of carbon, was to turn something that had been made to look like an economic asset into a liability. Under the new study, the net cost to society outweighed the benefits by at least £5 billion, and at worst £7.5 billion.[20]

Surprisingly for some, many senior voices in the business community agreed more with the latter analysis than with the former. Ian Cheshire, boss of the big conglomerate Kingfisher plc, commented that the more critical view established 'what many in business and civil society have suspected all along – that the case for a third runway at Heathrow is at best incomplete and at worst completely flawed'. After apparently being ruled out by a new Liberal Democrat/ Conservative coalition government, at the time of writing in 2012 Heathrow expansion appeared to be back on the political agenda.

This book will regularly return to the curious economic assumptions that got society into its current predicament. In transport planning there has been a consistent bias over the last half-century in favour of maximising travel by road and air. The mantra has been 'predict and provide': estimate unrestricted demand and then try to ensure that there are enough roads and airports to meet it. Little consideration has gone to designing out unnecessary travel, or the impact of transport on quality of life. The subtle but important difference is how we optimise rather than maximise our mobility as a society.

This oversight, in turn, has meant a bias against the poor, who drive and fly less, against mass public transit, and in favour of burning fossil fuels. For all its superficial sophistication, transport planning has also been oddly self-defeating. The average speed of vehicle traffic in London, for example, is about the same as it was in Victorian times when real horse power was used.

More interesting still, in *The Limits to Travel* Professor David Metz reveals the curious lack of evidence underpinning the 'centrepiece of transport economic analysis' relied on for half a century: 'travel time saving'. The notion is that time spent travelling is dead time, useless time, hours that we would rather spend doing something else. Therefore, getting quicker, but not necessarily in more comfort, between two places is a human and economic benefit. This assumption was key to justifying the London-to-Birmingham high-speed rail link. According to Metz: 'travel time saving' now has the 'quality of myth – a traditional story accepted as fact . . . what economists term a "stylised fact"'. In other words, it is not a fact at all.

You would think that with 'travel time saving' as the organising principle in the development of our roads and airports, we might in fact have saved some travel time. Detailed data is collected in Britain from the National Travel Survey, run since 1972. In that time over one thousand miles of motorway have opened and airports expanded dramatically, offering flights between UK cities. Yet the average amount of time travelled by people over that period has barely changed. We haven't actually saved or liberated any time at all. We've just used the infrastructure to travel further. The average amount of time spent travelling by someone in the UK is around 380 hours per year. The number of trips we take has also remained fairly constant. 'There can be few, if any, measures of human behaviour that show such relative stability in a context involving so much change.'

Another dry-sounding planners' nostrum captures the banality of economic approaches that, left unchallenged, almost guarantee an apocalypse, sooner or later. Predict-and-provide covered swathes of countryside and divided towns with roads. Anticipating levels of car ownership and use and building roads for them was various governments' approach, broadly the same as the one taken to airport expansion. It is a version of Icarus' tale in which Daedalus doesn't even bother to warn his son about the dangers of flying too near the sun. In simple, more general terms, it is also the basis upon which the entire modern economy operates. The only thing constraining demand and consumption – apart from brazen illegality (and not always even that) – is the ability to pay.

And yet, if we adapt to new opportunities without changing some aspects of our underlying behaviour (such as not wanting to spend much more than an hour a day travelling), it suggests that, actually, in reverse, we might quite easily fit into a world in which some things previously taken for granted suddenly are no longer there. Hence an hour formerly spent flying or driving might become an hour walking, cycling or going by train.

You can glimpse what that future might look like by going to the

Mojave desert, or Tucson, Arizona. Both are home to technological boneyards. They are the vast, abandoned *Marie Celeste*s of the modern world.

Photographs of the Mojave Air and Spaceport are mesmeric. Row after row of neatly parked, disused civilian airliners make patterns in the desert. They look like they are waiting for the call to evacuate human civilisation in the event of some previously unimagined horror.

At the Davis-Monthan Air Force Base outside Tucson, it looks as if the world has finally declared peace with itself, because here is the military equivalent of Mojave, a place where planes go to die. The dry conditions preserve the metal and the planes can be cannibalised for spare parts. It's such a strange site that many make pilgrimages to see it.

It is not yet true in reality, but this is a taste of what it would look like if we chose a more convivial way to be in the world, and stopped flapping in Icarus' self-absorbed slipstream. It reminds me of the way in which, more sadly, the railways were retired in the 1960s in Britain, to make way for the expanding road network and private car, and the urban tram systems in American cities likewise. It's a useful reminder that things have, previously, been very different. In 1920 nearly every American town of any size had its own electric streetcar, or tram. They were clean, efficient and convivial. Mass public transport dominated. But, because of the infrastructure involved, trams and cars did not easily coexist on the roads. At the same time the motor industry, with General Motors at its head, was worried that the market for cars was saturated. They saw urban electric rail systems as direct competition and, although not acting alone, established a special unit within the company charged with breaking them.

It was tremendously effective, using a range of heavy-handed techniques, some of which landed GM in court, where they were found guilty. The assistant US attorney general described GM's plan as 'An organized campaign to deprive the American public of their splendid electric railway systems'. In a story known as the 'great streetcar conspiracy', and told in the film *Taken for a Ride*, by the 1950s, of over one thousand electric railways targeted by GM, more than nine hundred had been replaced with motorised transport. At least in the US it took a commercial conspiracy to undermine a more socially and environmentally friendly form of transport, and the losing side fought back. The president of the Electric Railroader's Association, a man called

E. J. Quinby, convinced the government to take legal action against the might of GM.

In Britain, however, it was the chairman of the British Railways Board itself, Richard Beeching, who successfully achieved through two reports published in 1963 and 1965 the closure of a huge portion of the railway network, making way for the rise of the 'great car economy'. Ironically, the UK's 'car economy' had little more than a couple of decades left in it.

Yet sad as these were, the turning points nevertheless are reminders that change is something that human society is quite good at. Possibly even change for the better. But here is a paradox. Apart from the safe escapism of science fiction, it is actually difficult at any one point in time to imagine life being fundamentally different from how it already is around you. Habit, tradition and familiarity weave into social norms that veil from ourselves our ability to live differently. Why is this paradoxical? For the simple reason that, as history demonstrates, change over time is absolutely inevitable. Sometimes, though, there are glimpses of radical and rapid changes that might lie just around the corner. And which, when seen, do allow our imaginations to grasp the possibility of a very different world.

The city of Freiburg, for example, has been called Germany's environmental capital because of its transformative rethinking of transport. It's not complicated. There is a strong inverse relationship between the share of urban trips taken by public transport, bicycle and on foot and the carbon emissions from road use. More of the former means less of the latter. Car makers are a powerful lobby in Germany, but Freiburg was able to coordinate transport and land use to increase journeys by bike threefold, double public transport use, and cut the share of trips by car to less than one third (32 per cent), meaning that over two thirds of journeys are now made by public transport, walking and bike. The number of cars and light trucks owned per head of population has fallen in Freiburg over the last two decades, even as it has risen steadily for Germany as a whole, and rocketed in the US. Freiburg had 419 per 1000 people in 2006, compared with 776 in the US.[21]

Yet Freiburg began with above-average car use until things started to change around 1970. Bike networks, expanded light rail, pedestrianisation and locating new developments for both homes and businesses by public transport all played their part. By 1980 the car officially took second priority to pedal, foot and mass transit. By 2008 the city had several cycle-only streets, and nine out of ten residents lived in areas where traffic could not go faster than 30 km p/h (19 mph). In many areas the speed limit drops to 7 km p/h (5 mph). The city has set a template now widely being copied.

In the US, Portland in Oregon is the nearest parallel. Although using a lighter touch in designing out car use, in two decades from 1990 the town managed to cut the share of people commuting by car, truck or van by around 10 per cent, with journeys by bike or public transport rising to just under one in five. Daily commutes by bike went up by nearly six times, and public transport by over 50 per cent. In Los Angeles, where the car dominates, a new movement has taken to digging up single or double car parking spaces. They are then planted and landscaped to create 'Parklets', micro urban green spaces that invite people to relax and rethink their environment. Ghent in Belgium took the decision to demote cars to being only 'guests' on its roads, and implemented a huge shift towards cycle use. In the late 1990s, beset with congestion, it created a car-free city centre with a progressive 'Mobility Plan'. Ghent not only built new infrastructure for cycling, including three hundred kilometres of cycle routes and 7500 rental bikes, but promoted the culture of cycling with art and exhibitions to increase its appeal. Journeys by bike are now quicker than by car. In a decade the share of commutes by bike rose to one in five, more than double the national average, up from just 12 per cent. Ghent plans to be carbon-neutral by 2050 and won an international prize, the Eurostar Ashden Award for Sustainable Travel, in 2012.[22] If every city followed suit, great progress would follow. But other events in recent years hint at our ability to adapt quickly to far more radical changes.

5

Meaning and imagination

The fall of materialism and the rise of well-being

We are sleeping on a volcano . . . Do you not see that the earth trembles anew? A wind of revolution blows, the storm is on the horizon.

Alexis de Tocqueville

Nowadays you can go anywhere in the world in a few hours, and nothing is fabulous any more.

Roald Dahl

An absolutely new concept is a great happiness, and I can still get this any afternoon. Two or three hours walking will carry me to as strange a country as I expect to ever see. A single farmhouse which I had not seen before is sometimes as good as the dominions of the King of Dahomey.

Henry David Thoreau

We have to show the world that there is a new world of pleasure and fun out there for the taking.

Barbara Ehrenreich

I looked at the sky. There was nothing in it. Watery spacious blue, a few gauze-white strips of cloud, and an absence. Birds flew, curving in graceful arcs, the odd fly sped by but, conspicuously, something was not in its usual place.

I was staring up, standing by the Australasia glasshouse in Kew Gardens, south London. Kew is notable for two things. One, obviously, is its stunning, internationally famous botanical collection. The other, that it lies on the approach to Heathrow, one of the world's busiest airports. Normally, visitors have their appreciation of nature interrupted by low-flying aircraft every few seconds. Birdsong and conversation give way to aircraft engines howling their arrival.

But if, like me, you had visited Kew over a few days in the spring of 2010 you would have seen something quite different. Crowds of people stared in quiet wonder at something that was missing from the air above their heads. None of the normal 1231 daily flights were there.

In the early hours of Wednesday, 14 April, a dormant volcano, covered in ice, with a name that was almost impossible to pronounce – Eyjafjallajökull – erupted. Nobody heard it across northern Europe because the volcano was far away in Iceland. But the skies fell silent.

Within hours, airports all over Europe were closing, as if a giant master switch for the aviation industry had been flicked to off. A continent's transport system was sent back in time by half a century. In a moment, Europe was also isolated from North America. An extraordinary ability that most had come to take for granted was taken away. No longer could we pass thousands of miles, in a metal lozenge, at twelve thousand metres high, through temperatures of –50°C in just a few hours.

Why? By normal volcanic standards this was not a huge explosion. But, a combination of factors made Eyjafjallajökull the enemy of airlines.

The key eruption happened under a two-hundred-metre layer of ice. Meltwater flowed back into the volcano, hugely magnifying its eruptive force. Rapid cooling created an ash plume that was full of fine silica (glass) particles, and because of the volcano's siting, much of the ash went straight into the jet stream directly above. Dust that was lethal to modern jet engines then got spread over a vast area in the shape of a gigantic, mechanically toxic, billowing cloud. Planes that flew through similar clouds in the past had suffered terrifying, nearly disastrous losses of power. As a result, Europe was grounded for days. Quite unexpectedly, one of the main arteries of the modern world – cheap, ubiquitous air travel – was abruptly cut.

The 'sky is as clean as a wiped slate,' wrote the poet Carol Ann Duffy in 'Silver Lining'. What happened next was revelatory. It was a glimpse of a possible future in which both climate change and limited oil supplies clip the aviation industry's wings, compelling us to rethink our expectations, and how we relate to the world.

Philosophers, poets and stranded travellers filled the airwaves with reflections. Yes, it was inconvenient, they said, of course it was. No one was prepared for it. But suddenly the skies were peaceful. People found other ways to get from one place to another. They took trains, buses, taxis and shared cars. They talked to each other and, travelling at a slower pace, found themselves marvelling at scenery, much more aware of the world they were passing through. Most strikingly, as flying was something we thought we couldn't live without, the world did not come to a standstill.

The sky didn't fall, it just looked more peaceful. We heard more clearly and, as Duffy wrote, we heard 'the birds sing in this spring'. Almost everything simply carried on, but not entirely as usual. The airlines suffered economically, but their hiatus revealed how few of the things we depend on for day-to-day life relied entirely, or at all, on the airlines. Life might be different without them (or far fewer of them), people realised, but life would go on, as it had done previously in their absence for thousands of years. Surprisingly, however, several realised that life might even be better.

Shocks to a system and sudden, unexpected challenges, such as natural and unnatural disasters, can be revealing of human potential. Powers to innovate and collaborate surface that were either unknown, suppressed or forgotten. Rebecca Solnit wrote a whole book about the phenomenon – *A Paradise Built in Hell*. In these moments, we can end up feeling so much better about ourselves, each other, and life in general that you wonder why day-to-day life isn't consciously organised to bring out the latent best in all of us, most of the time. Rather, that is, than worshipping an economic system deliberately designed to promote selfish individualism (because that, explicitly, is both the theoretical basis of mainstream economics and the cultural language of its practical reality, consumerism, as spoken in advertising, its means of communication).

It is, in fact, an extraordinary triumph of human nature, that in spite of all the economic inducements to behave selfishly, the rarely acknowledged secret of what makes society work, and tolerable, is that most people, most of the time, are generally kind, considerate and trusting. They bear little similarity to the self-seeking cipher of mainstream economic theory, or the tabloid newspaper parade of daily degradation and evil.

Look what happened when the skies fell silent and business as usual was interrupted across Europe.

Thousands of stranded people turned to each other for help, setting up new social networks. Members of the Swedish carpool movement spread their horizons, setting up a new Facebook group called Carpool Europe, so that people could find others who were also grounded and wanted to hire cars instead.[1] Facebook threw up another, more colourfully named group, When Volcanoes Erupt: A Survival Guide for Stranded Travellers.

On the micro-blogging site Twitter, hashtags (words used to group issues under discussion) included #putmeup and #getmehome. Stranded @hubmum asked if anyone would like to help organise a return trip over land and/or sea from Morocco to the UK. One asked for a lift from Berlin 'towards' England while others offered Nice to Barcelona, and the picturesque-sounding Pisa–Genoa–Milan–Paris return tour.

They were all finding ways to *connect* and, in many cases with the offers of help, to *give*. An informal transport economy emerged overnight. The flurry of rearrangements, the human reshuffle onto boats, trains, buses and cars, shook people from the normal airport torpor, making them more *active*.

To see people in Kew and, come to that, on street corners all over London looking towards the sky, for once not scarred with contrails, it was clear that the sheer difference was making people look again at the world around them. Alain de Botton, mentioned earlier, was commissioned by the BBC to speculate on a future in which air travel ended entirely. He concluded that:

Everything would, of course, go very slowly. It would take two days to reach Rome, a month before one finally sailed exultantly into Sydney harbour. And yet there would be benefits tied up in this languor. Those who had known the age of planes would recall the confusion they had felt upon arriving in Mumbai or Rio, Auckland or Montego Bay, only hours after leaving home, their slight sickness and bewilderment lending credence to the old Arabic saying that the soul invariably travels at the speed of a camel.[2]

One of the problems, said de Botton, was that for all the apparent convenience of air travel, it had become too 'unnoticeable', draining travel of its meaning, connection to place and potential for transformative experience.

In that light, the flight interruption also briefly restored travel as something from which people could learn. A young couple returning from Australia for their humanist wedding ceremony in the UK got as far as Dubai before planes were grounded. Staff at the airport hotel in Dubai baked Sean and Natalie Murtagh a cake, decorated the hotel lobby, and the ceremony took place via a laptop computer and Skype link to London.[3] Norway's prime minister, Jens Stoltenberg, stranded in New York, expanded his range of computer skills by 'running the Norwegian government from the United States via his new iPad', said one of his aides.

But we learned much more than about Mr Stoltenberg's connectivity. Considering that aviation was such an 'unnoticed', taken-for-granted feature of modern life, it turned out that a sleeping, or perhaps dozing, architecture was ready to substitute for many of its purposes.

Other forms of transport proved surprisingly adaptive. The Eurostar train service carried fifty thousand additional passengers over four days. More ferries sailed, with many arriving at ports amazed to find them almost empty. More coaches and trains ran in the UK, particularly over distances, such as London to Scotland, where it had become 'normal' to fly. Parcel-delivery services within Europe like FedEx and UPS shifted from planes to trucks where possible.[4]

Instead of executives spending days travelling to and fro by plane to sit in identical office meeting rooms in other countries, there was an 'unprecedented spike' upwards in the use of video-conferencing facilities. Bookings went up 38 per cent in the UK, 12 per cent across Europe and 9 per cent in the US.[5] 'As one business contracts, another expands,' as BT's advert said of its video conferencing.

Some things, of course, can't yet be sent digitally, like exotic and out-of-season food and flowers. Yet even here it is surprising how quickly people can adapt. Judith Martin from Winchester wrote to the *Guardian* newspaper on 22 April 2010:

> In our local farmers' market I bought pak choi leaves – delicious, and grown within 15 miles of where I live. The first local spinach is starting to appear, as are spring onions. Even supermarket carrots have a fair chance of being from the UK. Leeks and mushrooms ditto. Finely shredded they all go into a stir-fry. I confess I don't know the provenance of my tamari sauce or my sesame seeds but I bet they don't need to be air-freighted.

The cooperative retailer John Lewis reported that a big effort from 'local hero' producers prevented any major interruption of supplies.

Some business were exposed as highly vulnerable to the loss of air freight, such as those dependent on producing luxury horticulture – everything from mange tout to roses – for export. A company called Blue Skies, operating in Kenya, announced plans to shift operations to Thailand and Vietnam (places where labour costs might also be cheaper). But, rather than highlighting the vital importance of air freight, which sixty years ago was virtually non-existent, this rather revealed the weakness of relying on a fragile export-led economic model, vulnerable to many shocks ranging from the whims of consumers to the power of retailers, energy and commodity prices, water availability and the inherent perishability of certain goods.

Thomas Homer-Dixon, author of *The Upside of Down*, argues that: 'First, we need to encourage distributed and decentralised production of vital goods like energy and food. Second, we need to remember that slack isn't always waste . . . This is the fundamental challenge humankind faces. We need to allow for the healthy breakdown in natural function in our societies in a way that doesn't produce catastrophic collapse, but instead leads to healthy renewal.'[6]

To be clear, I'm not suggesting that if the relatively privileged global few who do fly suddenly stopped, then all would be well, our problems solved. That would be nonsense. But I am suggesting that interruptions, in this case of natural origin, to normal service reveal how quickly we can alter aspects of our lifestyles that we take as fixed and for granted. And, also, that as well as being particular challenges, such changes can be surprising and throw up unexpected benefits.

More importantly still, I think that a certain DNA for society and our own well-being is carried in how we identify and organise the delivery of our needs and wants through economic goods and services, finance and technology. This, in turn, strongly influences the prospects for whether or not we will cancel the apocalypse.

'A dance around the circumplex'

Where flying is concerned, I'm a semi-exile. If travelling in Europe for work or pleasure I'll take the train. If the journey is likely to take too long, either I won't go or I'll find out if there's another way to do it. But a few years ago I flew to a conference in the United States that my work had organised. It led, ultimately, to the creation of the New Economics Institute, a North American version of nef.

To get there, first I had to pass through the temple of conspicuous, status-obsessed, luxury consumption that is the airport duty-free shopping zone. I had to ignore the obvious social stratification on the plane – the self-consciously drawn curtains and different goody-bags that separate the various classes of traveller – and the pages of perfume, watches and jewellery in the in-flight shopping magazine. The discomfort of passing through hostile territory, in order to change it, was going to get worse.

How far should the sins of the fathers be passed to the children? Follow the river Hudson north of New York and you come to a place called Pocantico. A family once lived there who were so rich that they could commission Picasso, at the height of his power and fame, to make them giant tapestries to decorate their giant homes (they had several). Even today the estate keeps a spectacular art collection, viewable by appointment, and houses a museum devoted to the family's other collection: cars, lots of them, and again, big ones. This is the former residence of one of the richest families in history, whose wealth stemmed from the exploitation and liquidation of a natural asset that is now warming the global climate. It was the home of the Rockefeller family, which has now become a conference venue. Today, key descendants like the economist Neva Goodwin use their remaining family shareholdings in Exxon to exert pressure on the US oil industry to accept climate change.

The reason it is worth mentioning (apart from expiating my residual guilt for flying there) is that the whole place was a monument to materialism and its obsession with status, money and image. It was here that I first met the world's leading researcher on why the values of materialism are bad for the individual, corrosive of community and environmentally destructive. Our conference concerned the relationship between quality of life, well-being, and whether and how those relate to materialism and rising consumption. We posed the question: Do good lives have to cost the earth?

What do we really need, and what is happy?

'What is a good life?' The question has been debated throughout human history. Why can't you just buy one? Why don't we feel like the smiling people in the adverts when we buy the goods they are selling? Why do we endlessly go back to buy more when experience tells us it didn't make us happy last time?

But in recent decades researchers have moved beyond rhetoric to a more empirical understanding of what helps to create or undermine human well-being. The results are often counter-intuitive to received wisdom and social norms. They suggest also that our dominant value system leaves us vulnerable to many challenges ahead and is a major obstacle to our ability to adapt and change to meet them.

In 1946 the World Health Organization coined a remarkably holistic definition of human health. They described it as 'A state of complete physical, mental and social well-being, and not merely an absence of disease or infirmity'. Aristotle wrote of the desirability of 'eudaimonia', literally 'good spirit', or the life well lived. The psychologist Carl Jung wrote of the aspiration towards individuation, or 'becoming all that one can be'. Famously Abraham Maslow, who coined the term 'positive psychology', developed a hierarchy of needs, the highest of which he called a state of 'self-actualisation' in which the individual explores and experiences creativity, morality, spontaneity and the ability to solve problems, therefore enjoying a high degree of personal agency in the world.

In recent decades, neoliberal economics has been hugely successful at increasing the amount of stuff consumed by a small, wealthy
and very influential fraction of the world's population. In doing so, by
its own logic (which is explored more in the next chapter) it should
have enormously increased those same people's satisfaction with life.
But it didn't. At best, rising consumption was met with levels of life
satisfaction that flat-lined.

Awareness of this apparent contradiction led to a huge rise in the
study of what is variously referred to as life satisfaction, well-being, or
more straightforwardly just plain happiness. Journals, university
departments and piles of popular books stand testimony to its attraction. Nic Marks, who established a centre for the study and promotion
of well-being, defines well-being as 'the quality of people's experience of their lives'.

But some deride the notion that you can even measure happiness
or agree what it is, let alone do anything meaningful to promote it. On
one level, the emotional uplift associated with happiness seems such
a rare and fleeting bird, how could it possibly be caught and domesti-
cated with policy? Certainly the idea carries more than one meaning,
as Daniel Gilbert, one of many authors writing about well-being,
points out. It can refer to a state of mere 'bovine contentment', or to
something more like Aristotle's eudaimonia, knowledge of a life lived
with purpose, engagement and meaning. In another sense it can mean
to pass a sort of judgement. We might say: 'I am happy with the
result,' having seen a sports match or trial in a court of law, and objectively judge the outcome to have been right and just, even if was not
what we wanted.

For these reasons, many prefer to talk about levels of life satisfaction and well-being. These prove to be the less fleeting, if not
unchangeable, scenery of our lives. It is scenery that tends to alter
depending on how far our fundamental needs are being met. But how
do we know what these are?

A large and growing body of empirical psychological research
shows that human beings in general have certain fundamental needs
to meet in order to live, flourish and function optimally. In a summary
of the research, which cuts across ages, cultures and demographic
groups, these needs have been grouped into four areas.[7]

The first is for 'safety, security and sustenance'. This means, for example, not living in fear of attack, hunger, homelessness or abandonment. These are primal, survival needs. The second is for 'competence, efficacy and self esteem'. This is the need to feel that you can accomplish things, do what you set out to do and have worth in the world. The opposite, having low self-regard and -esteem, can be the result of an absence in childhood of having the first set of needs met – of being made to feel secure and confident that what you say and do has value, and all this in a nurturing environment in which you are appreciated, encouraged and recognised.

The third set is to do with our needs for human relationships and being 'connected' to others. We are gregarious social animals who feel better for joining clubs, choirs, campaign groups, churches and classes, who go to parties, watch films in large groups and join huge throngs of fans to follow sports teams. The final set of needs is for 'autonomy and authenticity' – this means having the opportunity and situation in which we can express ourselves, to fashion and shape our lives and environment, and to develop as individuals in society by doing what excites and interests us, so that we do not feel like the puppets of circumstance or somebody else's clone.

When these needs are met we experience higher levels of well-being, a higher-quality enjoyment of our own lives. It does not mean bovine contentment, and neither does it imply a project designed to eliminate difficult emotions like sadness and grief, which can be normal and healthy responses to difficult events in life.

The way that these needs have or have not been met in our early lives, together with our current circumstances, our outlook on life, and the things that we do, collectively set our background levels of well-being. The two strongest influences on our well-being are first, how we were brought up by our parents – that accounts for about half – and only slightly less powerful is the effect of our outlook and the types of activities we engage in (ranging from substance abuse to gardening, or helping in a youth club). This is important because while we can't change our upbringing, we can change our outlook and how we spend the time we have available. Strikingly, beyond the point that our basic material needs are met, our circumstances – such as income and the kind of dwelling we have – exert only a very weak influence on our well-being. Yet when most people think about improving their lives, consumer culture excessively focuses on these.

Yet it is in what we do and how we value things, not what we buy, the image we have or status we acquire, that our needs reside and can be met.

These needs are importantly, and not positively, related to the prevailing values of consumerism and materialism. That is to say that materialism grows in the stony ground of unmet needs, operating as a kind of unfulfilling compensatory mechanism. Worse still, materialism further stunts and blocks our ability to meet those needs.

Tim Kasser is the friendly, unassuming academic who codified the framework of fundamental needs above. Kasser is one of many recent researchers and academics whose interdisciplinary work is challenging mainstream economic doctrines. We'll come across others later, like Dan Ariely, a behavioural economist who turns upside down notions that consumers make 'free choices', and Daniel Pink, who does likewise to assumptions about the relationship between high pay and performance in the workplace.

As a young student, Kasser had a hunch, a moment of inspiration driven not by ideological leaning but by pure research curiosity. Like all the best questions, the one that occurred to him was as simple as its implications were huge. Its unambiguous answer was that our dominant economic doctrine is not fit for purpose, and that the value system underpinning it is misery-making.

Simply, Kasser decided to find out whether people who cared more about money and materialism were happier or not. He devised a survey, ran the results and stumbled on a researcher's jackpot, a clear result. Over time and with greater complexity the strength and implications of the results grew. They would turn the academic into a campaigner as well (something similar happened to the economist Richard Layard when he absorbed others' work on the economics of well-being).

Over time, Kasser then drew together a vast amount of empirical research, from dozens of cross-cultural studies carried out in rich and poor countries alike, East and West, North and South. He's a synthesiser, a pattern-finder, someone who can turn the world upside down in a sentence, but do so with the matter-of-factness of pointing out rain on a window pane.

On one level Kasser's findings were simple, a justification of types of folk wisdom, yet their implications for how we live, the values we uphold and what this means for how we organise the economy are profound. They are as revolutionary and direct as the work of the social epidemiologists Richard Wilkinson and Kate Pickett, whose book *The Spirit Level* summarised a life's work and a mountain of data to show that more equal societies 'almost always do better'. They, too, perhaps to their own surprise, were transformed into high-profile campaigners as a result of their research conclusions, and I'll return to the relevance of their work to cancelling the apocalypse in later chapters.

What Kasser found is that different but related sets of values tend to flock together like birds of the same species, and that the behaviour they encourage tends to create a self-reinforcing dynamic. The more you value one thing, the more likely you are to behave in a certain way, which in turn reinforces the original value. If you get on a good spiral, things get better; slip onto a bad one and things get worse. What constitutes good and bad can, of course, be debated, but Kasser revealed that the value that is the engine at the heart of the modern consumer economy – materialism – has far more potentially disastrous side-effects than just the ones you might expect.

'Values' here means the guiding principles that help us make decisions. In his studies of them, Kasser presents his findings not as ideas or theories, as such, but as 'pictures of data'. In essence, the more someone cares about money, status and image, the less likely they are to have a 'good life', and the more likely they are to suffer distress and have lower levels of personal well-being.

Materialism keeps particularly bad company. It's associated with lower levels of vitality, 'that feeling of aliveness that makes us ready to jump out of bed in the morning', as Kasser puts it, but his findings go much further. The stronger people's materialistic outlook, the lower is their level of satisfaction with life. They experience fewer 'pleasant emotions', more distress, anxiety and depression, are more prone to narcissism and substance abuse, and are more likely to experience negative emotions such as being 'angry, scared and sad'. These negative associations with materialistic tendencies have been found in children as young as ten years old. They occur right across the age range, across cultures and demographic divides, and regardless of the range of established research methods used to gather and study the data. Kasser reports such findings in countries ranging from the United States to Russia, India, Denmark, the UK, China, Hong Kong,

Australia, Germany, Hungary, Singapore and South Korea. For example, a study of business students in Singapore revealed that those with strong materialistic values had lower levels of well-being – happiness, vitality and self-actualisation – and higher levels of anxiety.[8]

Another analysis of a huge international data-collecting exercise called the World Values Survey looked closely at people's attitudes to work and whether they were more materialistically concerned with their pay, or with their quality of employment, determined by their chances for autonomy and creativity at work. From groups of a total of forty-eight countries in Europe, to Africa, Asia and the Americas, the negative link between materialistic values and life satisfaction is clear.

Most of the research on human well-being shows that there is a strong link between income and life satisfaction up to a moderate level of material security. Coherent with that, this study showed that the signal influence of materialistic values on life satisfaction becomes relatively stronger in more affluent countries, but it was still there in poorer countries. There are also fascinating national variations. Of the countries included, Rwanda and Mali were found to value most highly creativity in the workplace. In Latin America income is valued much less than in other global regions, and this, it is suggested, is one reason that Latin America consistently scores well in terms of life satisfaction. In Asia, speculates the study, the opposite appears to be true.[9]

Fair enough, you might think, people are free to choose how they behave and accept the consequences. At least that should be true of adults. There are, though, strong reasons why our choices are far less free than we like to think they are. It is something that challenges not just the assumptions underlying mainstream economics, but the very idea of the modern self, heroic individualism and free will.

Social norms, the general behaviour patterns of those around us, and those reflected in advertising, television, advertising and films, have a huge, largely unacknowledged effect on the choices we make. From the notorious Milgram experiments of the 1960s, which showed how easily people can be persuaded to act against their better judgement when deferring to perceived authority, to research in behavioural psychology on the influence of stereotypes, it may be an affront to our sense of self, but there are invisible strings attached to our free will.

Imagine the effect of exposure to anything from an estimated five hundred to three thousand daily advertising messages, pictures, music and words that persuade us to consume and reinforce materialistic values. Behavioural economics contradicts the mainstream economic notion that individuals make free, rational choices. In practice we are hugely influenced by others. Observing and copying shapes what we do, as does a sense that others will approve of our behaviour. Advertising is influential in these ways because it shows and validates behaviour for us to copy, and similarly provides a cultural mirror of approval when we emulate the behaviour it shows. This could be anything from driving a powerful car fast down a road, to smoking (hence the advertising controls on tobacco) and drinking alcohol (whose advertising is less regulated) to release your 'wicked' side. Overall, incrementally and insidiously (much advertising is designed to be influential without being consciously noticed, such as product placement in films and television programmes, which is a growth industry), advertising reinforces behaving as if the acquisition of material goods, beyond the point of sufficiency, is the path to happiness.

Regardless of the personal damage wrought by materialistic values, they also lead to behaviour that can negatively affect other people's well-being.

It was dubbed 'shopping with violence'. To some, the London riots of August 2011 were not only unexpected, they were peculiar in character. The city has a grand tradition of public disorder, ranging from full-blown political revolution to the sporting violence that periodically accompanies Saturday football matches. In the early 1980s there was an inner-city reaction to poverty, together with a hardline Conservative government and policing tactics. Later, there was that old favourite of history, a riot against taxes, the euphemistically named 'community charge' that led to rioters charging through communities. The Poll Tax riots were explicitly political.

The surprise in 2011, widely noted, was that people seemed just to want 'free stuff'. It was looting, 'pure criminality', as the prime minister David Cameron said. Initially, politicians were wrong-footed. Most were on holiday, Cameron in Tuscany and the chancellor of the Exchequer in America. The riots also coincided with an unprecedented market crash. Our leaders were absent, phoning in decisions to a bewildered nation. Afterwards, though, there was a rush to appear tough.

Looters were identified, courts sat through the night. 'I think for too long we have taken too soft an attitude to people who loot and pillage their own community,' said Cameron. 'If you do that you should lose your right to housing at a subsidised rate.' Had the looting indeed come from nowhere, and been an exceptional instance of reckless greed with no explanatory circumstances, then perhaps that would be, if not uncontroversial, politically understandable. But the irony of Cameron's words was as raw as a knee scraped on concrete. Because there was a host of circumstances that conditioned, if not excused, the looting.

In the build-up to the riots there were brash displays from various social elites of exorbitant and unearned entitlement, greed, disrespect for the law, and outright criminality. The political establishment was convulsed by revelations of grotesque abuse of the system of parliamentary expenses. Not only were members of Parliament enjoying outlandish shopping trips at the taxpayer's expense, buying large and costly consumer goods, but some were supplementing their income through illegally manipulating payments for second homes. Then there were the banks, whose reckless failed gambling in financial markets created a lasting economic crisis and cost the economy trillions. Even after they were bailed out by unprecedented sums of public money, huge bonuses were still paid to executives who presided over the collapse.

Murky in a different way was the scandal that enveloped the police, media and, again, politicians, involving the hacking – listening in to voice messages and calls – of the phones of celebrities and people caught up in often tragic news stories. It led to numerous legal actions, resignations in the police and press, and the closure of a long-established Sunday newspaper, the *News of the World*.

Altogether, a picture emerged of highly privileged groups in society behaving very badly. In a newspaper comment article written jointly with Neal Lawson, the author and chair of the campaign group Compass, we dubbed them a 'Feral Elite'. The term stuck.

Here were high-profile individuals and institutions, whose lives were broadcast to the rest of society. Voluntarily or not, they were role models who, by example, legitimised certain values and types of behaviour. These were highly materialistic lives, marked by an aggressive sense of entitlement, the pursuit of status, wealth and a lack of empathy for others.

The worst of the riots happened in some of Britain's poorest inner-city neighbourhoods in boroughs like Tottenham and Hackney in North London, where cuts in services such as youth clubs were already happening. And in the shattered glass windows of the looted shops could be seen a dark reflection of what the Feral Elite had achieved more smoothly and with far more impunity by playing the system, sometimes legally, sometimes not.

Speaking in Parliament, the Labour MP Gerald Kaufman condemned as abject 'these criminals who looted, stole', and asked the Prime Minister what could be done 'to reclaim them for society'. In painting the rioters as criminal outsiders, it was as though there could be nothing even implicitly political in their actions. As if the redistribution of wealth by whatever means – upward via tax avoidance and creative expenses accounting, or downward via the looting of flatscreen TVs – was devoid of political implications. The exchange acquired a certain poignancy when it emerged subsequently that in 2006 Kaufman submitted an expenses claim for an £8865 Bang & Olufsen Beovision forty-inch LCD television. As there was a £750 limit for such items, the claim was rejected as falling within the 'not allowable category of luxurious furnishings'.

Bearing in mind the usual caveat that to understand and explain does not necessarily excuse, how surprised should we be at the actions of the Feral Elite and the poorer looters? Not very, once the prevalence of materialistic values is taken into account.

According to Kasser's own experiments and to the 'data pictures' emerging from an assessment of a large research literature, people with materialistic values are more likely to demonstrate a wide range of antisocial behaviours. These included: aggression, stealing, cheating and behaving unethically in business. But it goes much further than that, to the point of suggesting that to cancel the apocalypse requires a shift in the values of materialism and the cultural reinforcing mechanisms, like advertising, that glamorise them. Because materialism also correlates with lower empathy, being more manipulative and Machiavellian in personal and work relationships, and being more prone to prejudice and authoritarianism. Nor does it stop there.

The more materialistic in outlook you are, the less likely you are to care about the planet and take positive environmental action.

Materialists tend to recycle less, conserve energy less, and have life-styles exemplified by choices that are worse for the environment. This means that in everything from the type of transport used to choice of diet, materialistic values require and demand a larger eco-logical footprint.

The political consensus around the inevitability of consumer-driven growth, and the lack of imagination to visualise any fundamentally different system, mean that our hardly challenged social norms predispose us towards a set of values that, as Kasser writes, are 'associated with lower happiness, diminished social cohesion, and greater ecological degradation'.

On that basis, a society unable to imagine an alternative to con-sumer capitalism appears to be digging its own emotional, social and ecological grave. But the good news is that, around the circumplex of values, it is possible also to see positive self-reinforcing cycles.

The goals described above are called 'extrinsic'. That's because they are indirect ways in which we go about meeting our other needs. We buy new clothes, electronic upgrades, go for the more important job – not because these actions in themselves are satisfying, but because we see them, however wrongly (the triumph of hope and conditioning over experience), as tickets to a better life. We believe they will make us feel good, deliver recognition, acceptance, belong-ing, love even, and at the very least remove the discomfort of being in another person's shadow.

On the other side of the circumplex there is a cluster of 'intrinsic' goals, so-called because they are satisfying in themselves, and which, when pursued or held as desirable, directly improve our sense of well-being. These are self-acceptance – to do with a sense of relative autonomy and liking one's self; affiliation – developing good relation-ships at home and with friends; and community feeling – a sense of extended responsibility for the world at large.

It goes without saying that we are not exclusively one thing or the other. People's goals and values are typically a mix, but intrinsic and extrinsic motivations do not happily coexist. One or the other tends to get the upper hand and each type tends to reinforce itself along with the associated behaviours.

Where people more strongly pursue intrinsic goals they display behaviour that is the positive opposite of people hung up on wealth, status and image. But this is not just an argument about wealth and luxury goods. It is possible to embrace materialistic values or their opposite whether rich or poor in terms of material living standards. And the values consequently upheld will have a similar effect on life satisfaction. Later in the book I'll look at issues to do with equality and well-being and how these play out on the global stage, between rich and poor countries and within them. Income level loses its strong influence over various constituent elements of our well-being at different so-called 'inflexion points'. These, in turn, vary in different countries depending on the spread of relative income. I will come back to this.

People with more intrinsic goals hence have greater vitality, empathy and satisfaction with life, and are less likely to be angry, depressed, narcissistic and criminal substance abusers. Similarly, they are more generous, cooperative and have greater empathy for others. They are more likely to take positive action on environmental issues and have smaller ecological footprints.

'Intrinsic goals are positively associated with personal, social, and ecological well-being,' writes Kasser, adding that 'enhancing how much people care about intrinsic values should decrease their concern for materialistic values'.

In this light, advertising, when aimed at children, becomes highly controversial. Everyone feels its effect. It is commonly claimed by the industry that it mainly works at the level of encouraging people to switch their consumption between different brands. It is, say its defenders, about aiding informed, conscious choice. Yet, as we'll see later in chapter 9, advertising is shown to increase how much 'stuff' we buy, and is often deliberately designed to work at an unconscious level, overriding rational, informed choice.

Young children are, though, particularly susceptible. They are more credulous, and less able to critically assess the claims and promises made by adverts, or understand that the advertiser has an ulterior motive in telling them things. This is seen by some, unfortunately, as an opportunity rather than a problem. Kasser quotes a number of people being brutally honest about advertising hooking young consumers into a materialistic lifestyle, but none more so than Nancy Shalek of the Shalek Agency in the United States who said: 'Advertising at its best is making people feel that without their product, you're a loser. Kids are very sensitive to that . . . you open up emotional vulnerabilities, and it's very easy to do with kids because they are the most emotionally vulnerable.'

That sounds very much like a description of consumer capitalism as child-abuse, and has led to calls for childhood to become an advertising-free zone. Countries like Sweden and Norway already strongly regulate advertising aimed at children, so does Greece. In the UK the children's television channels that are free of adverts on the BBC are disproportionately popular with parents, who experience first hand the creation of wants, less sociable behaviour and dissatisfaction when children are exposed to advertising, that academics also find in their research.

If the balance of cultural propaganda transmitted through omni-present and ever more invasive advertising is massively weighted in favour of extrinsic values, is there any hope for action to rebalance values and behaviours towards something better for individuals, society and the environment?

One of the more successful attempts at public education was Britain's '5-a-day' health campaign to get people, especially young children, to eat less processed food, high in sugar, salt, refined carbohydrates and fat, and more fruit and vegetables. Simplicity was key. Campaigns run through schools, hospitals and in the press over long periods reinforced the basic message. Food producers and retailers adopted the messaging in promoting products that could help deliver portions of the 5-a-day.

Could the same be done to communicate well-being that worked with diet? Across the already large and burgeoning literature, five themes did emerge as core to raising overall well-being.[10] The 'data pictures' delivered insights that could be summarised and converted into simple recommendations which, if followed would improve well-being. They also bring several directly related social and environmental benefits.

They had little if anything to do with spending money, consuming goods or joining the jet set. They were oriented towards enhancing community and, as part of that community, the individual's connection to and enjoyment of the world around them. When practised, the 'five ways to well-being' demonstratively add to people's life satisfaction. They are, however, the very things that the old economic system tends to limit through the norms of modern working life, town planning, the ubiquitous conditioning of advertising, and subsidies of various types to less beneficial ways of being in everything from transport to food production and retailing.

If supported, alongside other changes, encouraging the well-being 'five a day' is one way in which we can strengthen the invisible heart of the core economy – home, neighbourhood, community and civil society – upon which well-being and the resilience and conviviality of society largely depend. The five are that we should:

Find ways to *connect* with the people around us, with family, friends, colleagues and neighbours, at home, work, school and in our local communities. *Be active*, day-to-day, by going for a walk or run or just stepping outside. Cycle, play a game, garden, have a dance, absolutely whatever works. The trick is to find a physical activity that you enjoy and fits well with your own ability. Next is developing the habit to *take notice* of the world. Like the concept of mindfulness, it involves being curious, or remarking on the unusual or beautiful, such as noticing the changing seasons, or just the everyday – what *are* those pictures hanging on the wall where you're eating lunch? But it is also about becoming aware and appreciative of what matters to you, through consciously noticing what you are feeling, and reflecting on the things you do and what happens to you.

To *keep learning* is another foundation of well-being. This means trying something new without worrying too much whether or not you'll be the world's best at it. You might rediscover an old interest, sign up for a course, or be responsible for something different at work. It's the act of learning itself that makes the difference, from fixing a bike to crushing fresh spices to cook a curry for the first time, or learning to play the recorder. Lastly, if you *give*, you not only enhance your own well-being, you help create the conditions for the reciprocity that helps make more convivial, resilient and adaptive communities. It's not complicated. Do something for a friend, or a stranger. Thank someone. Smile. Volunteer your time. Join a community group. Look out, as well as in. It helps to complete the well-being cycle by connecting to others. Imagine you notice broken guttering on your elderly neighbour's house and offer to fix it. After some quick homework, a job done, tea, biscuits and a conversation full of neighbourhood stories later, both you and your neighbour will feel better. You'll have learned something too, and got to know someone.

There they are: connect, be active, take notice, keep learning, give. It sounds almost too simple. They are now being applied in a range of projects for health and local authorities due to the intrinsic value they bring, and because people with higher overall well-being cost society less in health and welfare services, as well as giving more back. Better still, as we'll see in later chapters, these all overlap and underpin the kinds of activities and attitudes at the heart of the transition to a low-carbon, high-well-being economy. Transition Town initiatives, for example, with their combination of communal organisation, reskilling and multiple activities, tick all the boxes in one way or another. The four 'Rs' of the green economy – repair, reduce, reuse, recycle – similarly fit the bill.

Why wouldn't you engage in the five ways to well-being if they work? Possibly for the same reason you might forget to drink a glass of water on a hot day and end up with a dehydration headache, or forget to check for traffic when crossing the road. In the modern world it's easy to get distracted from things that might be good for us. A cynic might say that the whole system is *designed* to distract us from behaving in a way that might make us feel better, more whole, content (though of course not self-satisfied).

For if we felt better about ourselves we might feel less inclined to stay on the consumer treadmill, working long hours to earn money to spend on compensations and cultivated material aspirations that leave us feeling as bad, if not worse, than before we chased them. The kind of conspicuous consumption promoted in those in-flight magazines is just a glaring example of a system that exploits our desire for novelty, and insecurity about status (often towards people we will never meet and whose opinions we will likely never know). So to make a few people very wealthy, and to keep the rest of us busy and distracted, we encourage a form of materialism that carries high human, economic and environmental costs.

Its futility was long ago mocked by intellectual giants of both left and right. Adam Smith, the much-misrepresented grandfather of market economics, derided the 'multitude of baubles' people wasted their money on. Karl Marx, on the other hand, understood the insatiability of material desire, and how a perfectly good dwelling can shrink in perception miserably to the 'size of a hut' if a larger one is built next door.

'It's a story about us, people, being persuaded to spend money we don't have on things we don't need to create impressions that won't last on people we don't care about,' says Professor Tim Jackson. 'We've created systems, which systematically privilege, encourage, one narrow quadrant of the human soul and leave the others unregarded.'[11]

There are other signs of people seeking practical ways to shift values and behaviour away from spellbinding materialism and towards a better quality of life that is also less demanding of the planet.

The government's Office for National Statistics is developing an official set of well-being indicators to sit alongside more conventional economic data so that shifts in the nation's life satisfaction can be compared with other changes in the economy and lifestyles. It creates the potential to understand the real-world impact on life satisfaction of different economic policies and events.

The advertising industry itself increasingly is in the uncomfortable and unfamiliar position of having to justify itself as much as promote the products of its clients, in the face of renewed criticism and calls for better regulation and 'advertising-free zones'. The economist Richard Layard, once converted to the cause of happiness, helped set up a campaign in its name, Action for Happiness, to both challenge conventional economics and promote the foundations for greater well-being.

Spontaneous protests like the Occupy movement that spread internationally in 2011 often went beyond a simple cry of rage at the excesses of finance and rampant inequality to question the broader value system behind the problems that emphasised the primacy of status, wealth and image. The occupations themselves, such as the one on the steps of St Paul's Cathedral in the City of London, sought as far as possible to operate on a different basis. They organised their microcommunity around consensus decision-making, sharing resources and each according to their needs. They eschewed charismatic leaders, recycled and even tried to provide for the significant numbers of homeless people with mental health problems that their camp attracted. As a protest they were reasonable and cooperative with the Church, police and City of London authorities with whom they found themselves in conflict.

I was invited by the Occupy the London Stock Exchange camp to speak at a teach-in marking the twenty-fifth anniversary of the so-called 'Big Bang' deregulation of financial services in the City of London. We met on the steps of the former Royal Exchange building opposite the Bank of England. Today, inside, instead of the bustle of old-fashioned trading there is a temple to conspicuous consumption. Expensively branded luxury goods from jewellery to watches, scarves and suits vie for the surplus bonuses of City types coming and going during their lunch breaks. In fact, it is rather like a more expensive, more self-satisfied version of an airport duty-free shopping complex, just without the planes or passport control.

The protesters arrived walking in a column led by a bagpipe player who had been kicked out of Trafalgar Square and asked if he could join. We formed an alfresco classroom beneath the pillars of the Exchange and discussed through a megaphone the reform of banking. Around us stood bewildered and blank-faced policemen from the City of London's private force. The huge security men for the Exchange itself were a different matter: intrigued, smiling, itching to join in and speak, but prevented by their uniforms and fear of losing their jobs from doing so. The clash between the poor pay of security work and the brash materialism of the world around and inside the Exchange made them ready listeners.

The act of reclaiming public spaces for collaborative social purposes was itself the demonstration of a different set of values, and one that chimed broadly with a much wider public sentiment. It is perhaps unsurprising that, in one specific piece of research, Tim Kasser was able to demonstrate though studying different groups of people, some who campaigned and some who didn't, that the very act of engaging in constructive protest and campaigning itself has a positive impact on well-being. Good news: campaigning to cancel the apocalypse can make you happy.

Here are reasons to celebrate, fish swimming against the flow of the river. But why does the river flow in that direction in the first place? One reason is that before a nuanced understanding emerged of the foundations of real human well-being, a much more narrow and cautious view took root in mainstream economics based only on people voting with their wallets as consumers.

The shiny flowing surface of the river of consumerism is significantly the result of an economic system hooked on growth. It's a system that convinced itself that the most reliable measure of how an economy meets human needs is simply the amount of money people spend on goods and services. If that increases, everything is supposed to be fine. If it falls, disaster. We've looked at what the big deal with growth is, now it is the turn for scrutiny of money's role in either hastening or cancelling the apocalypse.

6

The Money

The perennial gale

A pandemic spreads. A terrorist detonates a nuclear bomb in a major city and claims to have more ready to explode. Ice caps melt, coastlines are submerged, and crops wither from drought. Clean fresh water becomes increasingly difficult to obtain. Or maybe it is oil that becomes scarce. Or a global financial panic erupts that regulators cannot contain. Any one of those scenarios could occur in our lifetimes. The one thing they all have in common is that their occurrence will touch off panic and, in some cases, hysteria. As a result, these events will also contain the seeds of profit for investors who stay calm and think rather than panic and run.

The Wall Street Journal Guide to Investing in the Apocalypse

The sense of responsibility in the financial community for the community as a whole is not small. It is nearly nil.

J. K. Galbraith, *The Great Crash: 1929*

I wish I had written those words. I wish someone had joyously commissioned me to lampoon the excesses of speculative capital. I wish that, grinning and laughing at my own audacious caricature, I'd so effectively distilled the detached, self-absorbed nature of finance and its lack even of residual empathy for human suffering. Had I tried, however, I'm not sure that I could have bettered reality. Because I did not make up these words, neither the passage nor the title of the *Wall Street Journal* guide. These remarks are real, serious, not remotely ironic, and published in a book by a mainstream publisher. They were written by one man who was a reporter and editor on the *Wall Street Journal* for twenty-six years, and another contributor described as an 'entrepreneur, investor . . . and media personality'. With a grasp of euphemism to match any government functionary, word for obfuscating word, they set out to show how to 'execute an event-based investment strategy'. Albeit the events are all apocalyptic in nature.

Financial markets have an idea of themselves as being a life force. Nothing ever happens in this version of events but for the verve, personal risk-taking and adventurism of the investor. Similarly, the breathless suspense with which media and government await the verdict of the markets to any decision suggests that they can be denied no less than gravity. Testosterone (now much studied for its negative role in financial crashes) fuels creative vision and finds opportunity to make the world a better place. Without the City's 'masters of the universe', we are led to believe, we would still be in caves, or crouched around a homely hearth, at best with the news and weather forecast to listen to on the radio. If the process of reshaping the world driven by the imperatives of finance caused commotion and dislocation, well, it had its one explanatory and legitimating narrative to fall back on. In 1942 the Austrian-American economist Joseph Schumpeter described 'the essential fact about capitalism' as being a 'process of Creative Destruction'.[1] The way in which capitalist markets rip up and replace what exists, denying any form of continuity or cohesive force other than their own overarching search for profit and accumulation, he termed a 'perennial gale'. And, to be clear, he considered this a thoroughly good thing.

It is pure modernism translated into economics. Whether or not Schumpeter had read Goethe's great work *Faust*, he was certainly channelling the final incarnation of the anti-hero who made a pact with the devil.

First Faust plays the dreamer, before assuming the role of lover. Then, finally, in his 'romantic quest for self-development', writes the academic Marshall Berman, 'he will be the consummate wrecker and creator, the dark and deeply ambiguous figure that our age has come to call, "the developer"'.[2]

Berman's Faust has the self-belief – typical of the modern financier – that whatever the short-term inconvenience of his actions, ultimately the majority will benefit. He dramatises the central contradiction of the global economy. Faust is 'convinced that it is the common people, the mass of workers and sufferers, who will benefit most from his work . . . [but] he is . . . not ready to accept responsibility for the human suffering and death that clear the way'. Hence, the 'deepest horrors of Faustian development' stem from powerful actors convincing themselves that they are acting for the common good, when they have, in fact, made a pact with darker forces to advance their own interests.

These are two explanations which, slightly oddly, absolve finance as the beating heart of capitalism at least of malign intent. Either it represents a type of carrion economics, omnivorously feeding off any victim of disaster, natural, economic or otherwise, or else it represents a clumsy, damaging delusion, in which deep self-interest is disguised as beneficent good works, in which ends justify means. The approaches are, on the one hand: bad things happen, who are we to judge, why not make money? And on the other: we flooded the valley to build a dam, made a few thousand homeless, caused the river to silt and lost an ecosystem or two, but now we have electricity to export and power factories.

But there is a third explanation that accuses finance and pro-market ideology of explicitly malignant intent. For all the more left-leaning economists hunkered down in academia (of course they are: government departments and financial institutions generally only employ those with obediently neoliberal inclinations), it took a non-economist to rebrand 'event-based investing', 'the logic of the market', or simply 'development'. The Canadian author Naomi Klein called it 'the shock doctrine'. Massive shocks can hit society through premeditated acts like war or terrorist attacks, a system failure like a financial crisis, or a natural disaster like a flood, hurricane, earthquake or tsunami. In the worst cases it could be a combination of several events. In her book of the same title, *The Shock Doctrine*, Klein argues that political conservatives deliberately exploit the 'public's disorientation following massive collective shocks' to advance corporate and financial interests.

Moments of upheaval are consciously targeted by vested economic interests, writes Klein, because that is when it is easiest, when there is least organised resistance, to push policies that pass control of natural assets, public services and economic sectors into private, profit-seeking hands. This kind of economic shock therapy has been employed for decades, ranging from Pinochet's coup in Chile in 1973 to the collapse of the Soviet Union in 1991, the Asian Financial crisis in 1997 and Hurricane Mitch in 1998. Impressively, it also seems to have been used in response to the massive financial market failure of 2007–8 in Europe and the United States. I say this is impressive, because it takes a certain steely chutzpah for the financial markets to profit from a crisis that was of their own making, the detail of which I'll come to later. While it is perfectly obvious, according to the *Wall Street Journal*, that any fool can profit from any other disaster.

Hence we are advised that putting money into the pharmaceutical giant GlaxoSmithKline is wise because the corporation is 'a solid long-term bet to profit from pandemics'. Then, whilst remaining agnostic about whether global warming is real or not, and noting the doubts sown by deniers, the authors enthuse that 'it is precisely this confusion and obsession about the environment and about climate change that creates opportunity for the investor. Money,' they underline, 'is going to be spent.'

Later I'll look at how the opposite can also be true, at how upheaval and disruption can open up possibilities to create better, more convivial ways of organising our lives, communities and livelihoods. *A Paradise Built in Hell* is an entire book devoted to the subject by Rebecca Solnit.

Of course, the financial community cannot be accused of having no powers of self-reflection. On the contrary, key figures made quite remarkable admissions. Alan Greenspan was chairman of the Fed, the US Federal Reserve, from 1987, during the presidency of Ronald Reagan, all the way through to 2006, after having been appointed for a fifth term by George W. Bush. For two decades he reigned supreme as possibly the most influential man in the global economy.

His period of office spanned several financial disasters, starting with the Black Monday stock market crash of October 1987 that followed a speculative boom, and of which *Liar's Poker* by Michael Lewis is a palm-sweating eyewitness account. Black Monday happened just months after Greenspan took over at the Fed. It didn't get less interesting after that. There was the Asian financial crisis of 1997–8, the

Russian financial crisis and the overlapping crisis of the hedge fund Long Term Capital Management (LTCM) in 1998.

LTCM, once the darling of the financial markets, was a previous operation during which very clever people (two Nobel Prize-winning economists sat on its board) thought they had found the secret to making vast amounts of money at low or zero risk. In a few months it then lost nearly $5 billion, once thought a lot of money, and Greenspan had to coordinate a rescue sufficient to prevent a domino banking collapse.

Yet, as if he needed a real test and these financial disasters were only for wimps, Greenspan was about to help unleash a deregulatory financial equivalent of the dogs of war.

One significant piece of legislation stood between the modern United States and the devastation of the Wall Street Crash of 1929. Back in the Twenties, different types of banking had got mixed up. Risky speculative investment banking contaminated its duller but important retail twin. Bankers were gambling with people's homes and life savings without anyone fully understanding the risk, and yet convinced, just like Treasury Secretary Mellon in 1929, that all was well and 'The high tide of prosperity will continue.' It didn't, of course. It ended catastrophically and took decades to recover from.

One of the preconditions for recovery was separating the two types of banking, investment and high street retail, and in 1933 a new piece of legislation, the Glass–Steagall Act, was introduced to do that. Even though Greenspan undermined the Act by loosening controls, it lasted until 1999. Then with liberalisation in favour, and under fierce pressure from financial lobbyists who argued that segregation was inefficient (they basically wanted a free-for-all), and with the support of Alan Greenspan's Federal Reserve, the Act was repealed.

History could have been our friend at this point. The collapse of the South Sea Company in 1720, fuelled by massive speculation, led to the superbly named Anti-Bubble Act, by which Parliament banned any joint-stock company without a royal charter. The act was withdrawn in 1771 in the middle of another credit bubble, which quickly precipitated another crash and bank failures the following year, 1772.

Back to the future, and from 1999 it took less than a decade for the financial system to destroy itself by doing precisely the sort of things that the Glass–Steagall Act had been introduced to prevent. The US house-price bubble began seriously to inflate in the year 2000, immediately after the Act was repealed.

Oblivious to the warnings of history from Andrew W. Mellon's overconfidence, in December 2004 the New York Federal Reserve responded bullishly to concerns that a dangerous asset-price bubble was inflating in the housing market. This was happening for a reason. By cleverly, or so they thought, mixing up housing loans that were both low- and high-risk to create new opportunities for investors, the financial markets thought they had spread risk in such a way as to make it effectively negligible. Mortgage debt became more profitable than investing in boring concerns like factories that made things, and money poured in. The Nobel Prize-winning economist Joseph Stiglitz calls much of what happened 'predatory lending'.

People on low incomes who had built up comfortable levels of equity in their homes were encouraged to 'unlock' their wealth and spend it by remortgaging, but typically on terms they couldn't afford. People with no savings, assets or sufficient income were given big home loans because, once their debts were blended with those who did have such things, the risk of overall default seemed small. In reality the opposite happened: bad debts contaminated the good and, to cut a long story short, it all fell down. What was happening in the US was also happening in the UK. Paul Ellis runs a small, UK-based environmentally friendly financial institution called the Ecology Building Society. At the peak of the housing boom he recalls larger lenders boasting of being able to offer a five-second mortgage. 'Before making a loan,' he says, 'all they were doing, literally, was checking to see that the property existed.' It's been said often that the cause of the crisis was too much cheap money. A closer look reveals it to have been a crisis of money easily lent, but on costly terms.

In America, by 2004, house prices when adjusted for inflation had risen well above the price variability of the previous century. This was entirely new territory for the economy.

Nevertheless, the system under Greenspan saw nothing to worry about. In December 2004 the Federal Reserve Bank of New York published a report titled *Are Home Prices the Next 'Bubble'?*[23] It concluded that 'market fundamentals are strong enough to explain the recent path of home prices and that no bubble exists'.

Even in 2006 the authorities did not see a major threat from the house-price bubble, which continued to inflate, and from the complex financial instruments underpinning it. That year Greenspan was succeeded by Ben Bernanke. He merely echoed the belief that market cleverness had somehow immunised the mortgage system against the fact that many people had been lent money on terms they could not afford to repay. 'The management of market risk and credit risk has become increasingly sophisticated,' said Bernanke. 'Banking organisations of all sizes have made substantial strides over the past two decades in their ability to measure and manage risks.'

Confidence brimmed on both sides of the Atlantic. It did so to a degree that is well worth recalling every time we are told to place our faith in a deregulated market. In his Mansion House speech, also in 2006, the UK chancellor of the Exchequer, Gordon Brown, swaggered to an incautious extent for such a seasoned politician:

I will be honest with you, many who advised me including not a few newspapers, favoured a regulatory crackdown. I believe that we were right not to go down that road which in the United States led to Sarbanes-Oxley, and we were right to build upon our light touch system.

The following spring in 2007 he promised: 'we will never return to the old boom and bust,' and that financial services and the city would help us 'to secure our place in the high value-added, investment-driven growth sectors of the future'.[4]

Then in September 2007 Northern Rock, the bank that aggressively engaged in sub-prime lending via a deal with Lehmann Brothers, had to be saved from collapse by the Bank of England. Customers wanting to take their money out were turned away. It was the first really visible sign of the financial markets seizing, of banks refusing to lend to each other, panicked at the sudden realisation that they were all sinking in a sea of bad debt, not knowing which, if any, would be able to struggle to the surface and say afloat.

Early in his career Alan Greenspan was an acolyte of Ayn Rand, the ideologue of individualism and unregulated capitalism, and author of the resurgently popular novel *Atlas Shrugged*. More than anyone, the arc of his life personifies the rise and nadir of finance-driven globalisation,

underpinned by an almost religious or perhaps childishly simple faith
in the efficiency of markets.

That is why, when questioned by a congressional committee, his
response carried a sense of history similar in weight to the end of the
Cold War and fall of the Berlin Wall the previous decade. It is pivotal,
candid, and worth allowing time to soak in. Greenspan was being
questioned in October 2008 by Henry Waxman, the Californian
Democrat representative. Waxman had just asked Greenspan, very
simply: 'Were you wrong?', to which Greenspan replied: 'Partially.'
Then Waxman elaborated: 'The question I have for you is, you had
an ideology, you had a belief that free, competitive – and this is your
statement – "I do have an ideology. My judgment is that free, competitive markets are by far the unrivalled way to organize economies.
We've tried regulation. None meaningfully worked." That was your
quote.'

Greenspan's next response was the economic equivalent of the
Pope admitting his own fallibility whilst simultaneously questioning
the existence of God: 'Well, remember that what an ideology is, is a
conceptual framework with the way people deal with reality.
Everyone has one. You have to – to exist, you need an ideology. The
question is whether it is accurate or not. And what I'm saying to you
is, yes, I found a flaw . . . ' He continues after a prompt: '[a] Flaw in
the model that I perceived is the critical functioning structure that
defines how the world works, so to speak.'

Oddly, the slightly sheepish phrase 'so to speak', which seems to
want to box and contain the enormity of what has been said, only ends
up magnifying it. It's a bit like attending a doctor's appointment and
being told: 'I said you were cured, but actually you're going to die, so
to speak.'

Advocates of a winner-take-all market system have a certain swag-
ger, a machismo dismissive of fey bleeding-heart liberals who worry
about things like society and the environment. When Greenpeace
staged a protest on a trading floor in the City of London, it was with
visible relish that the traders physically assaulted the unresisting
protesters. And, indeed, neuroscience has established links between
testosterone overdrive and the speculative bubbles that lead to financial crises. Behind the confidence is the notion that they have
understood human nature, and its motivations. Having done so they

live in the only real world; others who think differently are naïve, romantic, impractical dreamers.

Greenspan was the swaggerer-in-chief of this brigade. What stunned many, including his followers, was not only the rare clarity of his admission, but the air of bewilderment accompanying it. It was Greenspan whose beliefs suddenly seemed almost childishly naïve. 'I made a mistake in presuming that the self-interest of organizations, specifically banks,' he told the congressional committee, 'is such that they were best capable of protecting shareholders and equity in the firms.'

So this human keystone of the global financial system didn't believe that greed, multiplied by opportunity, when gambling at no personal risk with other people's money, could go wrong. It did. The world's largest economies came within hours of a complete financial meltdown. Cash machines nearly stopped issuing money. It was, as Joseph Stiglitz put it, 'a total crisis of markets'. The United States and the United Kingdom, and possibly other nations, came close to the kind of collapse that hit Argentina in 2001. Then all bank accounts were frozen. Barter quickly replaced cash and communities survived by inventing local currencies and improvising forms of exchange to allow local life to continue (see chapters 6 and 9). Trillions in public bailouts and guarantees prevented system collapse, yet even four years later, in 2012, the aftershocks were so great that whole nations, like Greece, teetered on the edge of chaos and ungovernability. Worse, major banks such as JPMorgan Chase still engaged in reckless speculation on a huge scale. When it emerged in 2012 that its chief investment office had lost multiple billions in high-risk trading, ironically the bank was also planning what to do if a 'catastrophic, idiosyncratic event' took place. In the world of casino banking that could mean, of course, simply turning up for work.

A lingering irony touches Greenspan. In 1977 he was controversially awarded a doctorate by New York University. When he was made chairman of the Fed in 1987, Greenspan had the only public copy of the dissertation he submitted removed from the university's library. When a copy emerged, dusted from an ageing professor's shelf and sent to an offshoot of the *Wall Street Journal*, it contained surprising observations. Those were the days before complex financial instruments like the now infamous collateralised debt obligations (CDOs) – a way of blending debts that carry different levels of risk that was supposed to reduce if not eliminate risk altogether, but ended up doing the opposite, spreading risk to all they touched – allowed speculation in mortgage debt. The sub-prime crisis was barely imaginable. Yet Greenspan wrote: 'There is no perpetual motion machine which generates an ever-rising path for the prices of homes.'[5]

Deregulating finance had greater consequences than mere instability and recession. It supercharged an economic model of debt-fuelled overconsumption. Generally speaking, the rich already have a lot of stuff, so when they are given the opportunity to leverage assets, like their homes, they buy more assets, more homes. The poor, who have less stuff, given the same chance but from a more modest basis, use their equity to buy household goods and other consumables that depreciate in value. This creates a particular, divisive dynamic. A rising asset market pushes up prices, giving the already rich more to borrow against, and hence more confected wealth to buy even more assets. The rich get richer, generally speaking, while the poor get further into debt. Inequality widens at high cost to society. The few triumphal decades presided over by Greenspan's all-American lords of finance saw inequality widen dramatically.

As Andrew Haldane, Executive Director for Financial Stability at the Bank of England, pointed out, the ratio of chief executive pay in the seven largest US banks rose when compared to median national pay from 100:1 in 1989 to 500:1 in 2007.[6] More generally, chief executive pay as related to average pay rose from a multiple of between 30 and 40 in 1960 to 344 in 2007. In the same year the fifty highest-earning hedge and private equity fund managers took home an almost unimaginable average of $588 million each. That's a sum that the average-earning US employee would need to toil 19,000 years to accumulate over 400 working lifetimes.[7] John Paulson, the top-earning private investment fund manager, personally took home $3.7 billion. To put that into perspective, it is equal to the total flow of foreign direct investment into East Africa in the year 2010.[8]

Much has been made of the fact that, in terms of the distribution of benefits, the rise of an economy driven by liberalised finance has led to the emergence of a cohort of 1 per cent riding high at the top, and the other 99 per cent significantly beneath them. The facts appear strongly to support this view. Comparing 1979 with the peak year before the crash, 2007, the top 1 per cent of households has seen a huge rise in average income, from around \$0.5 million to nearly \$2 million, in constant 2007 dollars.

The top 20 per cent, lifted by the 1 per cent, saw a much more limited rise. But, below that, the rest of household's saw their incomes stagnate. The result is that the bottom 80 per cent of households saw their share of income shrink over the period. Specifically, between 1990 and 2005, while chief executive pay rose 298 per cent, and corporate profits went up by 107 per cent, when adjusted for inflation the pay of production workers fell by 4.3 per cent and the minimum wage by 9.3 per cent.

The share of US national income going to the top 1 per cent showed sharp peaks at two points over the course of the last hundred years. They came in 1928, before the Wall Street Crash, and in 2007. Its low point was 1976, just as the era of serious financial deregulation was beginning again. Some of the practical consequences of such high levels of inequality are now obvious, but later in the book we'll see how odd, exactly, it is, given the deeper attitudes to equality that are held, even by the rich.

Strange too that the period of modern American history most likely to produce sighs of nostalgia for lost innocence, quality of life and community, the 1950s and 1960s, were the times when America was most equal. And that was the result of Franklin D. Roosevelt's New Deal package, which had heavily regulated the banks after 1929 and made huge investments in the public sphere.

Taking back the banking system

Of all the many ways of organising banking, the worst is the one we have today.

Mervyn King, Governor of the Bank of England[9]

When the revelation came in a church in Dulwich, South London, it was nothing to do with religion. David Boyle was listening to an unoriginal sermon based on the Bible story of feeding the five thousand.

In it, Jesus, hearing of the death of John the Baptist, retires to a quiet spot beyond the nearby town boundaries to reflect, but is followed by crowds of people. When evening comes his disciples suggest that Jesus send them back to town because there isn't enough food to go around. This is the point when he is said to have performed magic, feeding the multitude with five loaves and two fishes.

David sat there thinking about scarcity. In particular he wondered why, with a few notable exceptions, there never seemed to be enough money to go around. Loaves and fishes are products of nature, limited by the seas and lakes in which we fish, and the land where crops are grown. But money is made by people. Why, then, is there always too short a supply to adequately pay for schools and hospitals, homes, or simply to be able to afford to work less?

Years earlier a similar thought occurred to J. M. Keynes. In his classic essay on national self-sufficiency, Keynes elaborately bewailed the impoverishment that resulted from an artificial shortage of money to pay for things:

> We have to remain poor because it does not 'pay' to be rich. We have to live in hovels, not because we cannot build palaces but because we cannot 'afford' them . . . London is one of the richest cities in the history of civilization, but it cannot 'afford' the highest standards of achievement of which its own living citizens are capable, because they do not 'pay.' If I had the power to-day, I should most deliberately set out to endow our capital cities with all the appurtenances of art and civilization on the highest standards of which the citizens of each were individually capable, convinced that what I could create, I could afford – and believing that money thus spent not only would be better than any dole but would make unnecessary any dole. For with what we have spent on the dole in England since the war we could have made our cities the greatest works of man in the world.[10]

It was a simple, yet profound question that would lead to David becoming a world expert on the money that is created and exchanged outside the mainstream – so-called 'complementary currencies'. Already a published author, David got a grant to tour America visiting communities that were printing their own money.

Can people really do that? The answer is yes, with both ease and great difficulty, occasionally leading to prison. Money is the strangest thing, worshipped, ubiquitous and yet widely misunderstood. Confusion reigns not only over how money functions, what it is, but also where it comes from.

This deep, popular incomprehension is one of the reasons that banking escapes greater scrutiny. It infects financial regulators, as much as politicians, business journalists and the broader public.

'The study of money, above all other fields in economics,' wrote J. K. Galbraith, 'is one in which complexity is used to disguise truth or to evade truth, not to reveal it. The process by which banks create money is so simple the mind is repelled. With something so important, a deeper mystery seems only decent.'[11]

That process is basically a franchise operation in which the government allows private banks to lend money into existence. When you or I, for example, go to the bank to ask for a loan, say a mortgage to buy a house, and the bank agrees, something simple but magical happens: a credit is added to your named account. You now have money to buy things with, and the bank adds the same, negative, figure against your name on their computer, and that is what you now owe them. The latter figure will, of course, increase with interest that is the wonder of so-called fractional reserve banking, a wonder at least from the bank's point of view. Banks are legally allowed to create money, for nothing, which then earns them interest from you when you take their loan.

Quite staggeringly, around 97 per cent of the money supply, broadly speaking, is created in this way (I say 'broadly speaking' only because the measure of the money supply is slightly more varied and complicated than need detain us). Much criticism of government argues that while it has franchised out money creation to private banks, it has not exercised the responsibility, quality control and rigour that might be expected of a franchiser over its franchisees, especially where something so vital to the daily functioning of society is concerned.

The notion that banks largely act as intermediaries, mainly taking in savings and recycling them as loans to borrowers, is a charming, remarkably enduring and yet fairy-tale version of banking. Because banks do not have to wait for one customer to make a deposit before they lend money to another. As counter-intuitive as it seems, even to those who daily oversee the system, the opposite is the case. In making a loan the bank creates money, and a new deposit in someone's account.

There is meant to be a limit on the degree to which a bank can do this, measured against the actual reserves they hold. This is called, rather cumbersomely, the 'capital adequacy requirement', or 'ratio'. It is set, in any case, rather low. It's another measure that isn't straightforward. But under a bank agreement called Basle III, the minimum reserves a bank should have against the loans it makes rose from just 2 per cent at the time of the crisis to a modestly larger 7 per cent (in practice the number varies somewhat according to risk, financial conditions and the quality of the reserves). When the crisis hit, banks held only £1.25 worth of reserves for every £100 they issued as credit. What this meant, in effect, was that £98.75 of every £100 on a bank's balance sheet was bluff – there if you believed it. Once upon a time bank money was connected to something real, a cold commodity that you could, if insistent, actually touch. Up until 1971, the US dollar was, technically at least, redeemable against gold at $35 an ounce. President Nixon ended that arrangement over the weekend of 13 August 1971, symbolically marking the end of one financial era and the beginning of an age of increasingly liberalised flows of capital.

David Boyle recounts a conversation after the 2008 crisis with a baffled financial journalist working for one of the red-top UK newspapers who was utterly convinced still that behind the cashier windows and ATMs of modern banks sat great piles of gold securing our notes and coins. Wry, maybe, but nothing like as concerning as misunderstandings at the heart of attempts to re-regulate the banks.

The Independent Commission on Banking (also known as the Vickers Commission after its chair, John Vickers) was set up by the UK government as an arm's-length inquiry into the financial crisis, tasked with making recommendations for a safer banking system. I think it reasonable that such a body might, as a starting point, understand the role of banks in creating money.

Altogether, colleagues and I met them more than once. At one meeting, Tony Greenham, a former banker who once worked under the same roof as the controversial chief executive of Barclays, Bob

Diamond, pushed them to acknowledge banks' role in making money in order that it should become more appropriately regulated. Having the right to do so is worth tens of billions to the banks every year. Simultaneously, the guarantee of state bailouts in the event of failure, which lowers their risks and therefore the costs of their borrowing, is worth anything from £40 billion up to £100 billion, the lower figure according to nef, and the higher figure according to the Bank of England's Andrew Haldane.

The official was utterly resistant to the characterisation of banks as the main creators of money. Tony pushed his case by asking the official which of two strategies would be more successful if he wanted to walk into a car showroom to buy a brand-new Audi car: a) a promissory I.O.U. note from Tony for £20,000 or b) a bank loan from the bank for the same amount. The word (or rather computer) of the bank is enough to bring money into existence, Tony's word, although remarkably well informed, is not. We did challenge the Commission in writing, but never received a response that addressed the question.

A greater irony lingers here too. The reason that banks, rather than governments, create most money rests on the belief that if governments created money they would make a mess of it. It would be poorly allocated, runs the argument, inflationary and lead to a crash. Leaving it to commercial banks, of course, led only to massive asset-price inflation, the allocation of vast sums to gambling with exotic financial products (socially and economically useless activity, according to Adair Turner, head of the UK's Financial Services Authority), and caused the biggest crash in living memory. That governments can create large amounts of money when they want to was revealed by Ben Bernanke in a famous speech as governor of the Federal Reserve Board in 2002. To considerable shock and some derision, Bernanke revealed a truth that proved magnetically repellent to the economic orthodoxy.

'The US government has a technology, called a printing press (or, today, its electronic equivalent), that allows it to produce as many US dollars as it wishes at essentially no cost,' he pointed out. '. . . Under a paper-money system, a determined government can always generate higher spending and hence positive inflation.'[12] When explaining the post-crash US stimulus package of 2008, he again reminded a sceptical, uncomprehending commentariat that the hundreds of billions of spending had not required new debt, but that the government had simply done what commercial banks do, entered a minus figure in one column on a computer, and a plus in another. It was that simple.

A textbook definition of money is that it is a means of exchange (you can swap it for goods and services), a store of value (you can keep it under the mattress or in the bank, and spend it now or later) and a measure of value, or unit of account (a huge range of things from ice cream to computer repairs and a wild-flower meadow can be compared, controversially some would say, by their price in a common currency). In brief, that might tell you everything but leave you cold. Much better was the joke that began circulating widely on the internet as the financial crisis worsened in 2011, and which fell into David Boyle's in-box. It goes like this:

It is a cold day in the small Saskatchewan town of Pumphandle and the streets are deserted. Times are tough, everybody is in debt, and everybody is living on credit.

A traveller comes to town and lays a $100 bill on the hotel desk saying he wants to inspect the rooms upstairs to pick one for the night. As soon as he walks upstairs, the hotel owner grabs the bill and runs next door to pay his debt to the butcher.

The butcher takes the $100 and runs down the street to retire his debt to the pig farmer. The pig farmer takes the $100 and heads off to pay his bill to his supplier, the Co-op. The guy at the Co-op takes the $100 and runs to pay his debt to the local prostitute, who has also been facing hard times and has had to offer her services on credit. She rushes to the hotel and pays off her room bill with the hotel owner.

The hotel proprietor then places the $100 back on the counter so that the traveller will not suspect anything. At that moment the traveller comes down the stairs, states that the rooms are not satisfactory, picks up the $100 bill and leaves.

No one produced anything . . . No one earned anything . . . However, the whole town is now out of debt and now looks to the future with a lot more optimism . . . and that, folks, is how a 'stimulus package' works.

On its own it's a good story, a modern moral tale about the unnecessary consequences of enforced austerity. But David noticed something: he spotted at once that the story wasn't new at all. It was an updated version of a tale originally told by a man called Charles Zylstra in the 1930s and recorded by Professor of Economics Irving Fisher in his 1933 book *Stamp Scrip*. During the Great Depression money was in short supply – the hotel owner didn't always have access even to that $100 in the safe – with the result that even though people had goods to sell and people wanted to buy things, the lack of money in circulation caused economies to seize up. Both Zylstra and Fisher advocated the creation of 'stamp scrip', an alternative currency that could be issued by a local authority. It was not entirely new. Big companies in remote locations such as mining and logging areas used types of scrip to pay workers when normal currency was hard to come by.

The clever thing about stamp scrip was its simple system, which encouraged people to actually use it. If hoarded it became worthless. Each week the holder paid 2 cents for the note to be stamped. At the end of the year the issuer made back $1.04 for every $1. If unused the notes were cancelled and were withdrawn after twelve months. In the meantime, though, they put cash in the hands of the hotel owner, butcher and all their business associates, freeing up the economy.

There was a revealing sting in the tale as told by Zylstra. In the morning, on seeing that his hundred-dollar bill is still secure in the safe, the traveller expresses relief, explaining that he didn't want the note to fall into anyone else's hands because it was a fake. Yet, it hadn't mattered, because money isn't in essence a note or a coin; it is not an object at all, but a social contract, the note or coin merely a crutch, a reassurance upon which it rests.

Different types of currencies, different contracts, work in very different ways and have different purposes. One solution to finance failing large parts of the economy – small businesses who cannot get loans, for example, and the poor and unemployed who cannot get bank accounts – is therefore to have greater variety.

When he travelled to the US, Boyle found that complementary currencies were anything but consigned to history. Although infinitely varied, there were two main kinds: those enabling social exchanges that might not otherwise happen, often taking the form of so-called Time Banks, and those offering a more straightforward alternative to conventional money in the form of local currencies.

To illustrate the former approach, in Washington he found an extraordinarily imaginative yet simple solution to the problems of an overwhelmed youth justice system. Criminalisation of the urban poor in America had taken root during the Reagan administration, and rates were rising so fast that, had they continued on the same trend, by the year 2053, bizarrely, half the population would be looking out from a prison cell. This was when the radical lawyer and former speech writer to Bobby Kennedy, Edgar Cahn, stepped in. He often found himself on America's social front line, having opened the first legal practice in Washington to employ a black female lawyer.

Cahn proposed involving the peers of the very young people who were finding themselves in youth court, focusing on non-violent first-time offenders. Hundreds of young people were trained to operate 'teen courts' under licence from the District of Columbia, with jurors paid in 'time dollars' in return for the hours they spent running the courts. The time dollars were then redeemable by the young people against refurbished computers from another local project. It was astonishingly successful. Not only was the initiative itself educational for those involved and able to reduce reoffending rates (teen courts in the US have been shown to reduce reoffending to as little as 5 per cent), it saved the local authority a big slice of its budget. A resource – the time, knowledge and peer sensibility of the young people – was released by turning time into a currency, with benefits that went far beyond the walls of the teen court.

'I was short of money and it occurred to me to print some' were the words that introduced the other main type of complementary currency. It was Paul Glover speaking from Ithaca in upstate New York. He identified exactly the same problem that the joke above addressed. A lack of conventional dollars was an obstacle to several things happening. So he produced a new currency for the local area. Confusingly, it was called Ithaca Hours, but it was not a time bank, it was a parallel currency designed only for local circulation.

This latter feature was included in order to address a key economic problem facing some areas: as Edgar Cahn put it, money has a bad habit of 'defecting' or leaving an area. If conventional money is spent in a given community in a business that is national or international, also has remote shareholders to appease and procures many of its own goods and services remotely, the money local people spend in that business is likely to leave the area. If this happened evenly, every-where, that would not, of course, be a problem. But in reality it doesn't, it tends to lead to islands of accumulated wealth both geo-graphically and demographically (for example among fund managers working in the City of London and living in somewhere like Surrey).

Conversely, when money is spent in a local store less wired to the outside, where the centripetal forces of the markets concentrate wealth into fewer hands and places, the money is more likely to recir-culate locally in a beneficial pattern – again, as in the joke. The more it does that the bigger is what economists call its 'local multiplier effect'. Creating your own local currency not only increases the chance of more things happening in a more vibrant economy, it also helps prevent money defecting, ultimately into the black hole of a fund manager's back pocket somewhere.

All Glover had to do in Ithaca was persuade businesses to accept the new money as tender. He did that by advertising its benefits, which he said were: it helped create new business by linking skills and products with those who need them and therefore made new jobs; it was a form of interest-free credit insulated from inflation; and it insulated Ithaca from external economic shocks. With that, many were hooked. A local farming cooperative ended up paying some staff entirely in the new currency. More and more local enterprises got involved and, remembering that this is not a big town, in the first five years of operation the new currency conducted the equivalent of $1.5 million worth of business. Quite early on it was even praised by *Forbes* magazine.

A similar scheme was launched in 2006 in the Berkshire region of Massachusetts. In its first nine months over one million Berkshares, the currency unit, were circulated. Four hundred businesses agreed to accept the currency. In recognition of its multiple local benefits there is a special incentive to use Berkshares: put simply you get more for your money. Berkshares are bought with conventional dollars. In local businesses that take the local currency you can pay in either dol-lars or Berkshares. But one Berkshare only costs 95 cents to buy, meaning that you get an automatic 5 per cent discount when buying with local money.

Five different regional banks support the new currency through a network of thirteen branch offices. Centred on the town of Great

Barrington, when I visited to see the scheme in operation a few years ago, not only did the coffee I bought with my Berkshares taste the same as one bought with dollars, I knew the currency wouldn't leave the area.

The scope of local currencies is limited only by the range of services and enterprises that choose to accept them. Once they exist an individual then has complete discretion about whether to pay for something in the local or national currency at any outlet which accepts both.

In the UK, much more recently, similar local currencies have emerged in places as diverse as inner-city Brixton, which launched its own in 2011, rural Totnes in the south-west of England, whose scheme began in 2007, and city-wide in Bristol in 2012.

Neither time banks nor local currencies seek to replace, wholesale, the circulation of dollars, pounds, euros or yen (Japan also has a vibrant scene of local currency innovation). As the name suggests they 'complement' mainstream money, and act to compensate for some of its failings. In doing so they help to lubricate parts of the social economy (people with useful skills to offer but no medium or encouragement through which to interact with others) and the system of local economic exchanges where the cost or lack of formal currency is an obstacle.

Time banks work well in the social economy addressing problems like an overworked youth court, or perhaps a doctor's surgery overburdened by an appointments book filled with the psychological results of a lonely, alienated urban community. Giving patients a role through a time bank-type scheme, some kind of reciprocity relationship, which could be as simple as elderly Mrs Brown agreeing to phone elderly Mrs Smith on a Tuesday afternoon to see how she is (we're not talking about her standing in for a doctor or nurse), can have transformative results.

In Camden, London, the Holy Cross Centre Trust (HCCT) uses a time bank to help deliver mental health day services on behalf of the local council. It builds on the skills and capabilities of members to support each other, extending their social networks, and confidence to work and get involved in the local community. Staff put 10 per cent of their time into the time bank, whose purpose is to encourage and reward both them and the members. This approach, based on reciprocity, or give and take, is referred to in policy circles as 'co-production'.

Fair Shares is a network of time banks working with criminal offenders and their families in three prisons: Gloucester, Leyhill and Eastwood Park. Prisoners earn credits by, for example, fixing bicycles or training with the Samaritans to become 'listeners' who offer support to other prisoners. They can then use their credits to gain different types of support for themselves, or give them to friends and family for use in other connected time banks. Fair Shares developed a 'toe-by-toe' approach in which the new skills they learn, including literacy and numeracy, are passed on prisoner to prisoner. There are now over 250 time banks in the UK.

In the United States an initiative called Nurse Family Partnerships uses the approach of encouraging peer support to strengthen young, especially first-time mothers in high-risk social groups. Apart from its direct social value, it has a remarkable preventive and cost-saving effect. Where applied in the US, child arrests fell 59 per cent and child abuse and neglect by 48 per cent. Behavioural difficulties up to age six went down by two thirds. For every $1 invested in the programme, savings of between $2.50 and $5.70 were recorded across every field from crime to education, welfare and health. After costs, the benefits of the scheme per child are around $17,000, and a 20 per cent cut in months on welfare for the parent.[13]

Time banks can be very localised, whereas local currencies need to circulate more broadly to be effective. Credits earned and used up in the former can be unlimited, and don't need to balance. Local currencies, on the other hand, have to 'add up'.

There are, of course, many other ways to create new types of money for specific purposes. Trade or barter exchanges are a huge but almost entirely unreported part of the global economy, with deals each year worth the equivalent of trillions of dollars. These are commercial operations with a trading platform organised by an exchange that does the book-keeping for the system. But their trade, or barter, is denoted using an internal, non-conventional electronic currency called barter or trade dollars, usable by members of the exchange, within the system. An international currency called universal is used to barter remotely if local exchanges can't provide what someone is looking for.

New local currencies emerge in times of crisis, from Depression-era America to turn-of-the-millennium Argentina, and modern Greece, as we'll see in chapters 8 and 9. Boyle points to still others like the NU-Spaarpas scheme in Rotterdam, where people earn credits on a smartcard for behaving in a sustainable way, and the long-established Swiss complementary currency the WIR, from the word 'Wirtschaftsring', or 'economic circle' (it is also the German word for 'we').

Although sometimes opaque and typically operating beneath the radar, it would be wrong to think of complementary currencies as purely back-yard, corner-shop or village-green affairs. The WIR is a parallel currency created in Switzerland in response to the financial crisis and ensuing shortage of capital caused by the Wall Street Crash.

It as designed as an independent currency for small and medium-sized businesses, so that those who knew and trusted each other could extend credit against collateral for purchases among their number. Swiss first mortgages are typically only for around 60 per cent of a property's value, so buildings are often used as collateral. And their number grew to be large and diverse, reaching around 60,000 by the end of the century, in which was included '167 lawyers, 16 undertakers, 1853 architects and 18 chimney sweeps'. Trades to the value of $1.6 billion were reported during the WIR bank's seventy-fifth anniversary in 2009 (the currency is denoted in, but not exchangeable with, the Swiss franc).

This is very different to the cliché of local exchange-trading schemes, which are sometimes dismissed as offering a lot of aroma-therapy, but not much else. The WIR bank is now licensed by the state, a big change from when the state conspired against such initiatives with the main banks who feared being marginalised. The late radical economist and author of *The Ecology of Money*, Richard Douthwaite saw great benefit because it 'avoids the two main defects of national currencies: it should never be in short supply, and because no interest is charged for its use it does not create the growth compulsion'.[14] The JAK members bank in Sweden is yet another that grew in response to the Great Depression of the 1930s, but was only officially licensed in 1997. It has nearly forty thousand members who use their collective savings, denoted in 'savings points' and amounting to around €100 million equivalent, to make interest-free loans to each other through a local branch network run largely by volunteers.

This kind of innovation is by no means limited to the world's wealthier countries. Latin America has a well developed network called the Social Trade Organization (STRO) that operates widely in

Brazil, Uruguay and Central America. Their small and medium-sized businesses face many of the same difficulties as those in Europe and America: problems getting credit, and money leaving communities due to the 'leaky bucket' phenomenon in which money spent in other big, non-local businesses quickly gets sucked away to head offices and pays shareholders and remote suppliers. They set out to devise 'new ways to make money work even in conditions of a semi-permanent economic depression'. STRO used state-of-the-art software to develop a system they call the Commercial Credit Circuit or C3. Like some of the schemes already discussed, it creates additional credit for companies and promotes more local purchasing to keep money circulating in the area. They have a strong ethos of supporting in particular environmentally progressive businesses that meet local needs and build varied, resilient local economies. Hence, when they support a biofuel business, they make sure its products are for local use, not export. 'A community that offers only one commodity to the world market tends to lose its social and cultural structure,' says STRO, closely echoing the new development model explored later in chapter 10. 'Social trade emphasizes the development of diversified local economies. Production of fuels for local use is a logical first step.'

'It's all a matter of what counts,' says David Boyle. 'We have to escape from the old idea that money is one, indivisible, totemic, semi-divine, golden truth – issued from on high by an infallible Federal Reserve and handed down to a grateful populace. Complementary currencies can reveal to us that, even in the poorest places, there are vast living assets – ideas, skills, time, love even – that can turn our ideas of scarcity on their heads.'

What we find when the many, subtly varying approaches to making our own money system are put together on a map is a hidden architecture of a different way to run an economy. As the cracks in the walls of mainstream banking grow ever wider, the obvious question is whether this hidden architecture can accommodate and bear the weight of our livelihoods, in the event that the structurally unsound house of finance continues to subside and crumble.

Some of the examples described may seem small and local, and some recent examples might be dismissed as atypical artefacts of particularly progressive communities. But they can be found in big cities and rural areas, in prisons, courts, doctors' surgeries and schools. They work for businesses and the unemployed alike.

Complementary currencies are not automatically easy to get the hang of – either how they work or why you might need them. It is perfectly understandable that many would only discover their value if their personal circumstances left them few other options, or if mainstream currencies ceased to function. Under such conditions, the do-it-yourself culture of complementary currencies can prove lifesaving, as it did after the Wall Street Crash, Argentina's economic collapse and Greece in the aftermath of the 2008 crisis.

These alone instil some confidence that human ingenuity is capable of escaping the tight corners that we create by subjecting ourselves to monolithic (yet internally complex) unstable institutions like the world of finance.

But there is an even bigger sleeping architecture of alternatives out there which, were it to take up a larger share of the financial system, could revolutionise its resilience and usefulness, creating stronger economic foundations to face other threats. Simply encouraging greater diversity could, by itself, produce a less vulnerable system.

The academic Professor Margrit Kennedy spent years looking at monetary innovation and reform. Trained as an architect, she turned to working on the money system after finding that mainstream finance was an obstacle to the application of ecological principles in building and, come to that, everywhere else as well. Speaking at a meeting on complementary conferences at the Institute of Chartered Accountants in the City of London in February 2012, Kennedy said: 'We are living in an interim time, a transition between a system that we know doesn't work any more, but are not yet sure what will replace it.'

This is a view increasingly being entertained not just in the colourful world of communities who gather together to make their own money, but now also at the highest levels of the scientific and monetary establishment.

Andrew Haldane, Executive Director for Financial Stability at the Bank of England, joined forces with the former government chief scientific adviser Robert May to see if natural systems could teach them anything about the functioning (or rather dysfunction) of financial markets. They looked at the dynamics of ecological food webs and the networks within which infectious diseases spread.

What they found was the now familiar tale told above: before crisis, 'an increasingly elaborate set of financial instruments emerged, intended to optimise returns to individual institutions with seemingly minimal risk'. But the result of this was to echo Galbraith's observation of Wall Street in 1929, when individually financial actors showed little or no concern for the effect of their behaviour on the structural integrity of the overall sector and economy. 'Essentially no attention was given to their possible effects on the stability of the system as a whole,' wrote Haldane and May in the science journal *Nature*.[15]

They looked at the explosion in the notional value of outstanding derivatives contracts over the course of a decade from 1998, during which they rose from under $100 trillion to over $600 trillion – for comparison, the latter figure is over 240 times the size of the UK economy in 2011. They also looked at the dramatic concentration of assets following the final repeal of the Glass–Steagall Act. The largest three US banks doubled their share of the sector's assets to around 40 per cent of the total in less than a decade. Looking at the rapid growth, concentration and complexity of the banking sector, they saw direct analogies with the dynamics of increased instability in ecological food webs.

The financial markets had, in effect, created a 'shock-propagation' system. Some of Haldane and May's recommendations for corrective action were the same as those made by others, but with a rather different rationale. Setting higher liquidity ratios, for example, is explained as a way of protecting individual banks and their clients. Haldane and May write that it can also be seen as 'a means of strengthening the financial system as a whole by limiting the potential for network spillovers'. With a broader view like this, regulation follows 'in the footsteps of ecology, which has increasingly drawn on a system-wide perspective when promoting and managing ecosystem resilience'.

One implication of this approach is to treat differently banks that represent different levels of risk to the system as a whole – in epidemiological terms, these are equivalent to the 'super-spreaders' of disease. That would mean, for example, setting the capital requirements of a bank (how much real money it should hold to underpin everything else it does) in such a way as 'to equalise the marginal cost to the system as a whole of their failure'. So banks that are bigger and have more 'connectivity' (if they fail the shocks propagate faster and further) need a shorter, tighter leash. 'The failure of Lehman Brothers in October 2008 is testimony to the force of such super-spreader dynamics,' observe Haldane and May. 'Protecting the financial system from future such events would require the key super-spreader nodes to run with higher – potentially much higher – buffers of capital and liquid assets.' Also to improve resilience, they advocate what any sensible community does to manage a food supply, namely store reserves in the good times to eat in the bad. This is 'counter-cyclical' regulation, 'with buffers rising in booms and falling in recessions'. Next they call for simplification of the massive complex array and trading of exotic financial products and derivatives; instead of a mesh of trades between many players – the tangled-hair model – they suggest a 'hub and spoke' approach with deals being checked and cleared centrally.

In a run-down East End student house I found myself in a room full of people waving jazz hands. They weren't rehearsing for an amateur musical, but deciding how best to reform the financial system. It was autumn 2011 and perhaps the beginnings of a much broader social movement to create a more balanced banking system.

As government austerity plans tightened, and the public were told that 'we are all in this together', it seemed to some that the opposite was true. A conversation in a London pub led to the formation of a new campaign group that called itself UK Uncut. Its focus was to be the large-scale tax avoidance of major companies in the UK.

The reason that hands were being waved, jazz-style, was because several of the young campaigners had learned their skills in a new, much more democratic style of activism. Many had been to annual 'climate camps', where short-lived, fully functioning micro-communities were set up to highlight the issue of global warming, and where decisions were mostly taken by consensus. To aid consensus, when somebody speaks in a meeting, if others are in general agreement, one hand will be waved, strong agreement gets two waving hands. Hence, by the time it comes to make a decision, there is already a sense in the room of where people are at, making choices easier. It may look strange to a newcomer, but once tried, it does seem to lessen conflict.

Over several months UK Uncut carried out a series of creative, quite theatrical and non-confrontational direct actions against companies it considered to be avoiding significant tax payments to HM

Protesters in the City of London creatively join the dots overlooked by government. Multiple billions were found to bail out a broken, reckless banking system, but no such resources have been mobilised to prevent irreversible destabilisation of the climate system.

Revenue & Customs (HMRC). It frequently involved appearing in stores, in costume, enacting roles to make their point. The clothing retailer Philip Green was one target, communications company Vodafone and chemist Boots were others.

Vodafone's case involved a long-running dispute over a £6 billion potential tax liability. The company faced a similar issue in India over a potential tax liability of £1.6 billion. It described its approach to its own tax affairs quite openly on its website: 'The maximisation of shareholder value . . . will generally involve the minimisation of taxation.' After seemingly winning all the legal arguments, HMRC appeared to let the company off, even though the sum of money was close to the amount of the first wave of UK public spending cuts.

The campaign seemed to come from nowhere but quickly stole headlines, making tax avoidance by big companies at a time of public spending cuts a political issue. Over time, a picture emerged of an overly cosy – some might call it indulgent – relationship between HMRC and the companies owing them tax.

The focus on the Vodafone deal, and another in which the vast investment bank Goldman Sachs was let off paying millions of pounds of interest on a disputed bill, drew attention to the top civil servant at HMRC, David Hartnett. According to a table published by the Bureau of Investigative Journalists he headed a league of senior civil servants who were most frequently 'wined and dined' by companies.[16] Among the most frequent corporate hosts were the big four accountancy firms KPMG, PricewaterhouseCoopers, Ernst & Young and Deloitte – a large part of whose work is advising businesses on how to avoid paying tax.

Goldman Sachs was likened by the investigative journalist Matt Taibbi to 'a great vampire squid wrapped around the face of humanity, relentlessly jamming its blood funnel into anything that smells like money'. After it emerged that a £10 million bill for interest on tax HMRC said they owed to the UK Exchequer was 'waived on a handshake'[17] with Hartnett, the civil servant initially refused to accept that a mistake had been made and refused to apologise.

More than that, the HMRC solicitor, Osita Mba, who brought the case to light because he feared it was illegal, was put under internal investigation and threatened with disciplinary proceedings by his employers under Hartnett, even though Mba acted under legislation introduced specifically to protect whistleblowers. As Mba's version of events was seen to be correct, action against him was suspended. Hartnett apologised to Parliament and later announced his early retirement.[18]

Why was this such an ultimate success for the band of poorly resourced, yet hugely enterprising campaigners? First, it raised the idea that the government had a real option in responding to the financial crash. Instead of their default position of cutting public spending, they could instead pursue some of what gets lost to a mixture of tax evasion (illegal), tax avoidance (legal but probably immoral) and simple non-payment. The leading UK tax expert Richard Murphy estimates that, in all, that sum is in excess of £100 billion annually, and the business minister Vince Cable conceded that it amounts to at least £40 billion.

The second reason is perhaps obvious, but worth spelling out. How the government manages the collection of taxes ultimately determines how the benefits of economic activity are distributed around the country and throughout the population. Taxing and spending is one half of a government's macroeconomic policy. Crudely put, how it is executed determines whether the world fills more with superyachts and luxury cars, or with affordable homes, schools and hospitals.

Allowing large sums to wash up in tax havens results in the negative redistribution of wealth, a less, not more equal society that itself carries further knock-on costs to society, and higher social bills. UK Uncut found a nerve, pressed it cleverly, and changed the shape of the debate about economic policy. It certainly needed revising. The most recognisable banker in the country, Mervyn King, governor of the Bank of England, made perhaps the most astonishing statement possible for a man in his position. Giving a speech in New York in October 2010, King said, bluntly: 'Of all the many ways of organising banking, the worst is the one we have today.'[19] A bad system had failed and been bailed out by the public purse. The irony of what happened at first went under-reported and was later thoroughly twisted. The financial sector championed the supremacy of markets. For decades, any new public policy was routinely tested against the question: 'How will the markets react, will they approve?' But when their model of private self-interest failed, they took without question and little gratitude (or obvious admission of fault) the public support and guarantees that, all along, had underpinned them.

The controversial, very highly paid, chief executive of Barclays at the time was Bob Diamond. It's the sort of name that Charles Dickens, were he alive today, might choose for a wealthy banker, but if you consider it comically unlikely, check out Diamond's similarly well-paid colleague at the bank, Rich Ricci (pronounced Richie).

Barclays, like all other major UK banks, enjoy public guarantees in the case of their failing. These save them huge amounts of money. Because they are in effect, and almost uniquely in terms of the modern economy, underwritten by the state, it means they can themselves borrow money much more cheaply. This so-called 'too big to fail' subsidy was estimated to save the biggest five UK banks £46 billion in 2010, and Barclays in particular £10 billion through lowering the cost of borrowing. The UK version of this subsidy to banks was 62 per cent larger than the equivalent in Germany, revealing a greater, and not innately necessary, indulgence of the financial sector.

Under questioning from the UK Treasury Select Committee in January 2011, Diamond was asked by the Conservative MP David Ruffley if he was 'grateful to the British taxpayer for subsidising you in this way'. Diamond refused to give an unambiguously positive answer. Then, intentionally or not, he created for himself the persona of a Victorian stage villain, exactly the sort that Dickens would have lampooned and campaigned against. Diamond said that he thought the time for 'remorse and apology for banks . . . needs to be over'.[20] Subsequently he was forced to resign, not because of that, but because it emerged that Barclays had engaged in large-scale market rigging, having manipulated for their own advantage the rate at which banks lend money to each other, known as LIBOR – the London Interbank Offered Rate. Extraordinarily, the banks' own trade association and lobby group, the British Bankers Association, was allowed to play a formal role in regulating this money market. It was a bit like allowing the National Rifle Association to run gun control.

At this point, and still as I write, no meaningful structural banking reforms had been implemented. It was still a time when, as Mervyn King concluded, the 'massive support extended to the banking sector around the world . . . has created possibly the biggest moral hazard in history'.[21] If the banks had been bailed out once on such a scale and got away with it, ditched remorse, and now wanted to move on without reform, what was to stop it happening all over again?

And while the banks wanted to move on, the consequences of their misdeeds meant that the rest of the economy would be changed for ever. According to King's colleague at the Bank of England, Andrew Haldane, the long-term cost to the global economy in lost output was between $60 trillion and $200 trillion. For the UK economy alone it was between £1.8 trillion and £7.4 trillion.

'To call these numbers "astronomical",' said Haldane, invoking the Nobel Prize-winning physicist Richard Feynman, 'would be to do astronomy a disservice: there are only hundreds of billions of stars in the galaxy.'[22]

There are various ways in which economics seems to melt in the face of physics and higher maths. John Lanchester's brief but magisterial account of the banking collapse, *Whoops! Why Everyone Owes Everyone and No One Can Pay*, provides another example from Goldman Sachs. The financial system is the foundation, currently shaky, upon which the economy rests. In turn, the financial system rests upon assessments of risk. Yet, in the calculations of the banks, risk and reality were strangers. The massed ranks of modern financial capitalism bet trillions, as we saw above, on the fact that people with often no income, job or assets were unlikely to default on large, relatively expensive mortgages. After these debts had been chopped up, sold on and insured, the 'masters of the universe' convinced themselves, using impressive mathematics, that the chance of something going badly wrong (having lent lots of money to people with no obvious means of paying it back) would be, in Lanchester's words: 'literally the most unlikely thing to have happened in the history of the universe'.

The risk of what actually happened over several days in one of the worst periods of the banking crisis was, according to the CFO of Goldman Sachs, a so-called '25 sigma' event. What's that? It's a way of expressing how likely something is to happen expressed as a number in a ratio to the number one. And, this is a really big ratio that demonstrates just how wrong very influential and self-confident people who run things can be. Imagine, says Lanchester, a number equal to ten times all the particles in the known universe, and then move the decimal point fifty-two places to the right. Bang. We live with the trillion-dollar consequences of that quite extraordinary collective delusion.

In chapter 2 we heard from the uncommonly enlightened former head of both the Confederation of British Industry and Financial Services Authority, Adair Turner. In a speech to the Mansion House in the City of London in 2009 he also drew a direct link between banking failure and a future in which 'British citizens will be burdened for many years with either higher taxes or cuts in public services'. The irony was not lost on him that in the trading rooms responsible 'many people earned annual bonuses equal to a lifetime's earnings of some of those now suffering the consequences'.[23]

Turner caused mild consternation among some members of the business lobby by describing much of the activities of financial trading rooms as 'socially useless'. Many who identified themselves as pro-enterprise were yet to distinguish between the interests of business and the interests of finance, for too long considered to be one and the same. An attack on one seemed to be an attack on the other.

But Turner understood that it was, in fact, self-interested finance that was proving to be the great enemy of productive enterprise. Later the following year Turner clarified what he meant, in case he had originally been misunderstood: 'People have asked me whether I regret those comments. The answer is no, except in one very small respect. Which is that I think it would have been better to use the phrase "economically useless" or "of no economic value added".'[24]

Even the chancellor of the Exchequer, George Osborne, senior figure in a Conservative Party that derives over half of its funding from the financial sector, came to declare who primarily was at fault. Announcing an 'emergency budget' in June 2010, he conceded that: 'In putting in order the nation's finances, we must remember that this was a crisis that started in the banking sector. The failures of the banks imposed a huge cost on the rest of society.'

Yet while a consensus on fault grew, exactly what to do about it is another matter. One reason is because reforming a system that has failed partly due to its own complexity is – well, complex. In the United States, the Dodd Frank Act was passed in January 2010 to clean up after the banking crisis. It was 848 pages long, and its full implementation relied upon an open-ended timescale.

To avoid potentially terminal torpor I will avoid the detail of how internally to reform the big banks (this can be pursued via the bibliography), but mention some of the broader principles. In any case, without revolutionary reform there is a limit to what a range of technocratic institutional fixes can achieve – after all, we do have the worst of all imaginable systems, as the governor of the Bank of England said. More interesting, I think, is how the hidden architecture of a better banking system can expand to meet our modern challenges and reduce the scale and threat of the old, flawed, system.

With the big banks now even bigger, the best that could be done by the Commission under Sir John Vickers, set up to propose reforms, was to recommend ways to soften the impact when the next crisis hits. Candidly, if subtly, the Commission accepted, given the basic structure of banking, that future trouble was highly probable. There is, it found, 'inherent uncertainty about the nature of the next financial crisis', thereby taking for granted that there will be one.

But the question too infrequently explored, by this Commission and other official inquiries, is: What should be the purpose of the banking system? One good working definition is that it should: 'facilitate the exchange of goods and services, allocate capital to financially sound activities that generate the highest long-term well-being for society, with the least environmental impact, finance a low carbon transition, and redistribute and share risk'.[25]

Several practical steps in the direction of reform gathered broad support. These included that retail or 'high street' banking should be separated from speculation to protect their retail services from volatile international capital markets. Banks that are 'too big to fail' should be broken up and reduced to a size at which their failure would not threaten the wider economy. Exotic financial products should be licensed and incentives that encourage counterproductive risk-taking removed, along with controls on excessive speculative activity. The UK should also introduce a US-style 'community reinvestment act' that obliges banks, wherever they are happy to take deposits, also to lend. Very often banks do the opposite, taking money in from some communities but failing to lend.[26] None of these proposals, though, have been implemented.

A great economic failing is that, in spite of huge public financial backing, and quite apart from imposing huge costs on society from their own ill-advised activities, the big banks were also retreating from serving big sections of society and the economy and, even after being bailed out, continue to do so.

Kept interminably on hold on the phone, hit with huge charges for minor overdrafts amongst countless other things, rejected by automated credit scoring, unable to find a branch open when you need it, customers' dissatisfaction with their treatment by the banks is rife. In the lead-up to the crash, speculation proved so profitable compared with running an everyday, useful bank branch network that the tail of investment banking began to wag the dog of retail. Michael Geoghegan, chief executive of HSBC, said: 'The economics of running a major retail network in the UK no longer stack up.' In other words, humble high street customers simply didn't make enough money for the banks compared with the casino world of complex derivatives.

And so the branches that served us closed. Their number fell by nearly half (43 per cent) in twenty years. At the last count the UK had substantially less than half the number of bank branches per head of population that Germany can muster. And there are 1500 rural and suburban communities with only one or two bank branches left, which may in any case have very restricted opening hours of one or two days a week.[27]

A post-bailout agreement between the banks and the government set lending targets for the banks to support small and medium-sized enterprises, but by early 2012, four years after their public injection of cash, these targets were being missed consistently.

Which brings us back to the jazz hands in the East End of London student house. Banks, it was consensually agreed, were behind many of our problems and would be the target of a wave of actions. In this way, quite unintentionally, I found myself a few weeks later holding an old school bell, dressed in academic professorial robes, standing beside John Christensen, a leading tax expert and reformer, and surrounded by police in an Oxford Street branch of Lloyds Bank. Some UK Uncut activists turned bank branches into children's crèches, others into libraries or mock hospital A&E departments. Ours was a schoolroom. All were making the point that a crisis of private finance had been magically transformed into one of public debt and spending cuts. From all of this, the idea was born among the UK Uncut campaigners of a new initiative. They would repeat in the UK what had proved highly successful in the US – a campaign for people to move their money out of the big, badly performing banks into better financial institutions.

As a global 'Occupy' movement took off, in which people built semi-permanent camps in public places to protest about the damage caused by the banks, and the failure to re-regulate them sufficiently, a 'move-your money' campaign was sparked by an article on the US *Huffington Post* website. Business switching or boycott campaigns can be dismissed as token, with little actually changing, even if high-profile. This one, however, seemed to be different. During a single 'move your money' month in October 2011, 650,000 switched to open new accounts with credit unions, which are radically different to the mainstream US banks.

Over 4 million accounts were estimated to have left the big Wall Street banks in the first year and a half of the campaign. The Bank of America lost 400,000 accounts in the single year 2010, and not only individuals were changing. In Massachusetts a 'Move Money' initiative was announced by the state treasurer, Steve Grossman, to allocate $100 million for community banks to loan on to small local businesses. Previously the state diverted $243 million from Bank of America, Citibank and Wells Fargo. Elsewhere, the city of San José diverted nearly $1 billion from Bank of America, explaining that it was because of the bank's failure to act sympathetically to prevent mortgage foreclosures and home repossessions.

Move Your Money UK launched in January 2012. The day before the launch it was announced that home repossessions had hit a two-year high,[28] and that the share of income of the UK's poorest fifth of the population was now 43 per cent lower than it was in 1978.[29]

The first thing the campaign did was set out to remind people of the hidden architecture of better banking. Already, a host of alternatives existed. From a range of banks with explicitly social and environmental objectives, like the Co-operative Bank and Triodos, to a choice of fifty-three building societies, 580 credit unions and a range of other community development finance institutions and peer-to-peer lenders.

There are still other, more conventional, alternatives that nevertheless do business differently. The Swedish Handelsbanken, for example, has a network of branches in the UK and a policy apparently unthinkable elsewhere in the City – the bank doesn't pay bonuses to top staff.

But these were just alternatives that we already have. There is also the opportunity to grow a more vibrant, diverse local banking infrastructure similar, for example, to that which successfully supports local economies and small businesses in Germany.

The Captain Mainwaring age of local bank branch managers, respected, solid but dull, who drove a Rover saloon and knew the names of their customers, is smugly derided in the modern City of London as an irrelevant, romantic relic of lost times. Yet what the Captain represented – a form of local, relationship-based banking when a human judgement rather than automated credit scoring by computer determined whether you got a loan or not – could well be the future of a more resilient, business-friendly banking system.

Compared with the UK, the shape of banking is very different in Germany, for example. In the UK eight out of ten mortgages, and nine out of ten smaller company accounts are held by just the five biggest banks, but in Germany the small or community banking sector has 70 per cent of the market.

Germany and Switzerland have regional and local banks that are substantially mutually owned. In Germany there is the combination of the regional Landesbanks and the local Sparkassen, or 'savings banks'. There are 430 Sparkassen with over 15,000 branches (the UK has only just over 9000 bank branches left in total). These explain why Germany has so many more branches per head of population. In Switzerland they have what are called cantonal banks.

The differences are striking. Generally theses banks avoided the risky investments that were the downfall of the big commercial banks. They function as much to support business as to 'turn a profit'. Decisions get made at the local level too, where branches develop substantial local knowledge rather than deferring to protocols set by a remote national or global HQ.

Something more needs underlining here. These aren't the relics of a more innocent age, these local banks are the foundations of Europe's dominant economy, Germany. They underpinned a far more resilient endurance of global recession, and a more successful recovery from it. Germany's economic performance in terms of manufacturing, employment and especially jobs for young people, and protection of workers' rights, too, all outstrip the UK.

Compared with their international, commercial big brothers, the German savings banks avoided volatility, producing stable returns on capital. And they kept lending to business throughout the crisis when big bank lending fell off a cliff. Reliable, useful and serving the public economic interest, it's a very different face of banking, virtually forgotten in the UK.

Another successful model is the state bank. Since the crisis, people have looked again at examples like the municipal Bank of North Dakota, set up in 1919 as a response to another, earlier financial failure when farmers were facing foreclosure at the hands of Wall Street. Today the bank makes money for the state ($300 million over a decade) whilst lending to underpin local banks so that they, in turn, can make loans to support local businesses, with a portfolio worth about $2.8 billion. As a result North Dakota has fourfold more local banks than the national average, and over a third more even than neighbouring South Dakota, and none went bust after 2008. The states of Oregon, Washington, Massachusetts, Maryland, Illinois, Hawaii and Virginia have all either produced legislation to establish their own state banks or are investigating doing so.

Ironically, in the UK, the Birmingham Municipal Savings Bank was fully established in the same year as the Bank of North Dakota, and along the same lines. Suggested by Neville Chamberlain, then a local politician, it was opposed by both other banks and the Treasury. Later, in the 1970s, it became a separate Trustee Savings Bank before being privatised in the mid-1990s and absorbed into Lloyds TSB.

While its savings bank might be gone, Birmingham's tradition of civic leadership isn't. The city launched its own version of a 'Green New Deal', setting aside millions to invest in the environmental makeover of housing stock and related job creation.

There are several ways in which, relatively quickly and easily, the UK could evolve an effective local banking structure to echo successful international examples including Germany's.

France, Germany and Italy all operate banks born out of their postal services. Not only, by providing universal access, do these keep poorer people out of the hands of predatory and costly payday lenders, they can also help to enhance the economic viability of the postal services themselves.

La Poste, the French postal service, had over eleven million postal banking accounts not long after its banking launch, accounting for nearly a quarter of La Poste's turnover. Within two years of Poste Italiane, the Italian postal service, launching BancoPosta in 2000 it made a net profit for the first time in half a century. Success saw Italy's post office network grow, not shrink as in the UK, and it now has over fourteen thousand post offices. Germany's Postbank, born out of Deutsche Post, is the country's largest retail bank in terms of customers, with over fourteen million. Banking functions account for €4 out of every €10 worth of business at their post office counters.[30]

In 2012, four years after the crash, the major UK banks had missed their government-set lending targets for small to medium-sized business every quarter for a year. More than that, they lacked the local infrastructure and model built on relationships that works well for small businesses. Yet the UK post office network has twelve thousand branches, nearly double the branch office network of the four biggest banks combined. Even without operating a proper banking service, they already contribute significantly to local economies, generating on average £16.20 worth of local economic activity for every £10 earned in income. One analysis of branches in Manchester showed that each post office, through its convenience and range of services, saved local small businesses in the region of £270,000 each year.[31]

A UK Post Bank could build on this, with a remit to support local communities and enterprise, whilst shoring up the Post Office itself in a virtuous cycle. UK Business Secretary Vince Cable MP said of its potential: 'The Post Bank is an attempt to clean up banking. This is a cleaner principle based on sound banking ideas, but driven by public interest rather than narrow short-term profits.'

Its diverse advocates, which range from unions to small business, and from research groups to campaigners, say it would 'offer current accounts, access to credit, direct debit facilities, and expand its savings capacity. It would not be shareholder driven and would, through a Universal Banking Obligation, be locally based through post office branches.' It could also help develop a broader, more stable and productive local banking ecosystem by linking with other local credit unions and community development financial institutions.

Another initiative could help redeem the troubled Royal Bank of Scotland (RBS). Once so proud of its involvement in financing the exploitation of fossil fuels, RBS called itself 'the oil and gas bank'. It was so deeply implicated in the financial crisis that its chief executive at the time, Fred Goodwin, was later stripped of his knighthood (although not his substantial pension). RBS was rescued by the public sector and remains a bank with British taxpayers as the majority shareholders. It still invests substantially in fossil fuels and, still underwritten with public finances, pays millions in bonuses to its senior executives. Two significant proposals that are not mutually exclusive have been made for RBS's future. They go beyond the unimaginative assumption that, sooner or later, it will simply be sold back to the private sector once it is again a sufficiently profitable option.

The first is that the meaning of its initials should change to stand for Royal Bank of Sustainability.[32] It would be a themed industrial bank supporting investment in Britain's low-carbon economic makeover, which some suggested could lead to yet another name change to the Responsible Bank of Scotland. A second proposal is that RBS could be broken up to form a network of regional banks similar to the

German Landesbanks. It would, of course, be possible to do the latter in tandem with giving the new bank a remit to favour in particular businesses and projects that are helping to deliver the low-carbon transition.

Given RBS's lack of reform since its change of ownership, a change of direction is overdue. In the two years after its public bail-out in October 2008, RBS provided nearly £13 billion worth of funding to the oil and gas industries, loaning nearly £3.6 billion and helping to raise equity finance worth a further £9.3 billion. The companies supported include BP, Shell, Conoco Philips, the highly controversial Trafigura, implicated in toxic waste dumping in the Ivory Coast, and Cairn Energy, who are in the vanguard of pushing to exploit the Arctic for oil. The bank also helped raise £448 million for the British-based multinational Tullow Oil, who have been criticised for their activities in Uganda and the Democratic Republic of Congo, the latter since the infamous days of the Scramble for Africa considered to be a nation victim to the 'resource curse'. This is the spell under which countries blessed with extensive natural resources are torn apart by the competition for them and their exploitation.

A fundamental shift presents enormous potential, as the debate around the creation of another new financial institution, the Green Investment Bank, demonstrates. After much lobbying a new investment bank was set up, essentially to finance the infrastructure for a low-carbon Britain. It now exists, although exactly how it will operate is not decided, and the amount of money it has to invest is very small compared with the scale of necessary change and, many argue, the size of economic opportunity.

This speaks to one of the abiding myths that are holding back transition, namely the simple, powerful, and utterly erroneous notion that we cannot afford to do what we need to do.

In order to keep the economy going, since the crisis the Bank of England has increased the supply of money in the UK economy by over £300 billion, through a mechanism called 'quantitative easing'. All this means is that the Bank creates new money by crediting itself out of thin, digital air and then uses this to buy financial assets like gilts and a few commercial bonds from the ordinary retail and investment banks, inflating their balance sheet. This keeps the cost of borrowing low, but is poorly targeted, and if the other banks don't lend sensibly, or enough, its benefit is very limited.

Other suggestions include that the government should simply spend money directly into the economy, for example on a Green New Deal. Or it could perform a similar operation to quantitative easing, but do it via the Green Investment Bank, at the same time giving it special instructions to lend to green enterprises and projects on especially attractive terms. If it did this, the benefits could be extraordinary, according to the Green New Deal group (of which, for the sake of transparency, I am a member). For example:

- £10 billion invested in the energy efficiency sector could create 60,000 jobs, cut carbon dioxide emissions by around four million per year, and save £4.5 billion over five years in reduced benefits and increased tax intake alone.
- £10 billion invested in onshore wind could increase wind's contribution to the UK's total electricity supply from its current 1.9 per cent to 10 per cent, create over 36,000 jobs in installation, direct and indirect manufacturing, plus a further 4800 related jobs, and cut emissions from the power sector by up to 16 million tonnes of carbon dioxide annually.
- Or £10 billion could reskill 1.5 million people for the low-carbon skills of the future, bringing 120,000 people back into the workforce, and increasing the earnings of those with a low income by a total of £15.4 billion.

Beyond creating new money to green and stimulate the economy, a range of measures on tax such as incentives on green savings and investment could go even further. Future ISA tax relief, which currently costs over £2 billion a year, more than the whole £1.4 billion green stimulus package announced in the 2009 Budget, could be made available only for funds invested in green savings. And much more could be done to tackle the £100 billion-plus lost to the public purse in tax that has been avoided, evaded or simply not paid. A general tax-avoidance provision targeting the abuse of tax allowances could raise £10 billion a year if only half successful. Looking globally, a Financial Transaction Tax, now supported quite widely in Europe, applied at a rate of 0.05 per cent could raise more than £400 billion a year, several times the total global aid budget. It could underpin a Green New Deal in the Global South (see chapters 8 and 10), playing a significant role in enabling the majority world to adapt to climate change as well as 'breaking the carbon chains of fossil fuel dependence'.

New savings mechanisms such as green bonds, local authority bonds and carbon-linked bonds would be safe and productive, putting savings to good use and ensuring a world for future generations (just what saving is meant to be for).

When the economy fell apart in Greece a government was pitted against its people and some sections of society against others. Tear gas filled the streets and otherwise ordinary politicians on mainland Europe thought it perfectly normal to suggest the suspension of democracy. This was, for them, the logical price to pay in return for economic support that would ensure Greece's creditors could continue to be paid. The people would pay the price in terms of cuts and austerity for original flaws in the design of the Eurozone, and for the reckless lending decisions of financial institutions over which they had no meaningful control. The banks who failed correctly to assess the risks of lending to Greece would be protected from their own mistakes. The market's supposed method for self-correction – that you lose money when you get things wrong – would not be allowed to work on the very players who created the market.

It's not always obvious, but support from other European countries like Germany was really for the financial system, not the people of Greece. Finance again came first. But before and after the financial crisis in Greece, what really had changed? The sun still shone, ancient olive trees still produced their fruit from the Mediterranean earth, buildings stood and the population was the same. All that changed was the wholly artificial construct of the economy. It was a financial apocalypse made by people that could, similarly, be unmade.

The purpose of this chapter is to make one simple point. Financial systems are not innate or beyond our control. We do not need to suffer our finest aspirations to cower before the ratings agencies, whose role in the financial crisis exposed them as, in any case, frankly useless. Artificial scarcity of the resources needed to do good things should be treated with maximum suspicion, as being the result of some other agenda. Michael Linton is the architect of local exchange trading schemes, or LETS, which are 'local, community-based mutual aid networks in which people exchange all kinds of goods and services with one another, without the need for money'. He points out that: 'Money is really just an immaterial measure, like an inch, or a gallon, a pound, or degree. While there is certainly a limit on real resources – only so many tons of wheat, only so many feet of material, only so many hours in the day – there need never be a shortage of measure.'[33] A lack of money, he argues, is no more an excuse for providing something society needs, than the lack of inches would be an excuse not to build a house.

We can make the banks we need, and we can create the money we need. Lack of money should never be a reason to thwart the progress or salvation of a society.

The next excuse that must be shot down is that we're never going to change things. Belief in an unchanging status quo invites and excuses despair. Change, however, is the one thing that we can rely on. Believing in our own permanence is dangerous for two reasons. First, disgruntled or not, the fact that we are here today is no guarantee that we will be here tomorrow. Second, repeatedly throughout history certain societies facing great threats have managed bold and rapid transformations. Ignore the former, and we risk a false sense of security. Ignore the latter, and we fail to realise the extraordinary things we are capable of. Memory matters.

7

The Memories

If a way to the Better there be, it exacts a full look at the Worst.

Thomas Hardy, 'In Tenebris II'

I marvel at the resilience of the Jewish people. Their best characteristic is their desire to remember.

Elie Wiesel

The age of diminishing returns – warnings from history

Nauru is a small, remote South Pacific island. If its history had been different it would fulfil a rich-world fantasy of exotic escape. In the late 1980s when the Intergovernmental Panel on Climate Change began its work Nauru was named among the world's vulnerable nations, living on the front line of global warming. But the island's problems started long before that. Its earliest encounters with Western habits and values came from European whaling vessels and traders. They named Nauru 'Pleasant Island', and brought with them a colonial cocktail of guns, alcohol and sexually transmitted disease. Even that wasn't the worst of it, however, just the typical trappings of a first brush with modernity. Full progress arrived courtesy of a Pacific prospector called Albert Ellis in 1900. He would make them rich and ultimately ruin them. Ellis worked for a company that traded copra, from which coconut oil is derived, and phosphates, which were in huge demand by the farmers of New Zealand and Australia. Soil phosphorus is essential for plants to store energy and produce healthy crops, and even though the ground is full of it, only small amounts are usable by plants. Continual cropping quickly exhausts topsoil of the sort that plants can easily use. In Ellis's time, scientists had only recently devised ways to treat phosphate rock to make it useful for farming.

In 1899 he noticed a rock being used as a doorstop at the company's Sydney office. He could tell that it was rich in phosphate, the result of guano, bird droppings, building up over a vast period of time and fossilising. The rock came from Nauru. Ellis must have known he was on to something special. It was the days before flight and it was a tiny island, just twenty-one square kilometres in size, with a population of around nine hundred, and it was over 2500 miles away by sea. But he set out at once, and his instincts proved correct. He had stumbled onto one of three exceptional phosphate rock islands in the region (the others were Banaba in Kiribati and Makatea in French Polynesia).

When he arrived Ellis found the phosphate equivalent of a huge diamond set in precious metal. The whole centre of the island was rich in the resource, the gift of geographical isolation and countless generations of nesting seabirds. Within a few months of finding the rock he began to organise the extraction of the island's phosphates, striking a deal with Nauru's German colonial masters.

Steadily, over the course of the next century, the island was mined for the benefit of farmers thousands of miles away, and the population grew to over ten times the size it was when Ellis visited. Today the phosphates are largely exhausted, the centre of the island left looking like a science-fiction film set on a barren rocky planet. The people cling to a rim of land around the island's edge and depend almost entirely on imports to sustain them. The United States Bureau of East Asian and Pacific Affairs comments that due to 'poor diet, alcohol abuse, and a sedentary lifestyle, Nauru has one of the world's highest levels of diabetes, renal failure, and heart disease, exceeding 40 per cent of the population'.[1] Life expectancy is around fifty-five years for men, and fifty-seven for women.

Ellis went on to get a knighthood and be appointed commissioner for New Zealand with the British Phosphate Commission, which managed mining on Nauru after the First World War. Relatively speaking, the local people of Nauru became cash-rich, even though only 2 per cent of the actual proceeds of their natural capital was returned to the island in the form of a trust fund (whose administration they were also charged for). After independence in 1968, in terms of per capita income, for a period it was one of the richest third world nations. But that didn't stop the sad lament of Kinza Clodumar, president of Nauru from 1997 to 1998, who regretted that: 'What was once a tropical paradise was changed to a jagged, uninhabitable desert of coral tombstones. Our sad history serves as a poignant example for the rest of the world of what can happen when humans disregard the good earth that sustains us.'[2]

In an attempt to claw something back from a century of despoliation, Nauru took Australia to the International Court of Justice in 1989. They argued that for decades they had been short-changed over royalties due from the mining and were owed reparations for the immense physical damage done to the fabric of the island. Nothing, however, was going to put the phosphate rock back. In 1993 Australia agreed to pay $73 million spread over twenty years, and the UK and New Zealand made one-off payments of $8.2 million each. If this all seems a little distant, consider that if you have ever eaten food imported from New Zealand or Australia, as you almost certainly will have done, then you have benefited personally from the island's woe.

Were Nauru a small planet like Earth, rather than a small island, its fate would now be sealed. Having outgrown, overconsumed and exhausted its natural resource base, it would have nowhere else to import anything from and would face collapse. But Nauru's sad case became stranger still when it was embroiled in 2001 with Australia's controversial and hard-line attempt to control immigration – called, with extraordinary historical insensitivity, its 'Pacific Solution'. Australia determined to intercept at sea as many inbound refugees as possible, and instead of allowing them to land in Australia, to house and process them in centres on willing regional neighbours.

With its mining industry in severe decline, Nauru was one of those persuaded. Australia paid them to hold around a thousand refugees in conditions that the human rights group Amnesty International described as inhuman. The Australian minister for immigration described Nauru as being like paradise.[3] Those detained there seemingly had a different experience. An Australian promise to remove asylum-seekers from Nauru's detention centres in 2002 was broken, and conditions remained bad enough in 2003 for some to go on hunger strike in protest.

As these disoriented newcomers stared out from behind fences, expatriate workers from the mines were being sent home. To complete the irony, some of the mine workers being sent home were from Tuvalu, another small island Pacific nation even more threatened by global warming and sea-level rise than Nauru. Tuvalu's highest point above sea level is just a few metres, compared with tens in Nauru. Each year at high tides large parts of Tuvalu's main inhabited island, Funafuti, disappear under water. In the face of long-term projections for climate change, Tuvalu previously had approached Australia to investigate the prospects for a gradual relocation of some of its most threatened inhabitants. Tuvalu has a modest population of nine to ten thousand, but was rebuffed by Australia. The policy of the Pacific Solution was ended in 2007, but the future of many of the small island states grows more and more precarious.

Nauru is a very modern parable.[4] Unequal economic relations between rich and poor, natural capital built up over millennia squandered in a few generations, with just some trucks, large houses and offshore bank accounts to show for it. Even the phosphate itself was being used in an ultimately doomed attempt to allow industrial farming to defy ecological gravity (something that will be explored more in chapter 8). Unlike its distant, more famous South Pacific neighbour, Rapa Nui, better known as Easter Island, Nauru's downfall has been minutely observed. All the tonnes of phosphate rock extracted passed through company books, and the island's occasionally dubious bookkeeping has been scrutinised by international observers. Its tragedy also seems more prosaic than Easter Island's. There are not the extraordinary monumental tribal achievements left behind to puzzle anthropologists, just the obviously exhausted mines.

Yet microcosms are useful arenas within which to see much larger dramas played out. The message is the fairly simple one put by Kinza Clodumar about what happens when we fail to respect the limits of the 'good earth' that sustains us. For a time perhaps it seemed worth it to the people of Nauru. Perhaps, frankly, they had little choice, given colonial power play. But from the point of view of history, in a fairly short time frame, the law of diminishing returns began to operate.

Quite apart from Easter Island, human civilisation is littered with examples of societies, whole civilisations, that appear to crumble when they ignore environmental limits. I don't intend to repeat these case studies at length. But it is vital to understand the signs and patterns that warn when we are about to repeat the mistakes of the past. It is, though, at least as important, if not more so, to see whether there are examples of societies adapting successfully, and making positive transitions in the face of great threats. A few more examples of the downside of living beyond environmental means and the failure to adapt are worth examining, as is an analysis which argues a slightly more complex case than that the problem is merely one of crossing ecological boundaries.

Any society must assess both the fragility of its supporting ecosystems, in other words its 'susceptibility to damage' – argues the anthropologist Jared Diamond in *Collapse* – and its resilience, or potential for recovery. This is the first of five factors that he says a society must take into account to avoid collapse. The second is one that tests fragility and resilience, how a climate varies in different ways – year-to-year, on multi-decadal scales, and over much longer time frames counted in centuries and millennia. Even more so than for our modern understanding, which struggles to comprehend the difference between the variability of weather and longer-term changes in the climate, this was a problem for older societies with brief human lifespans and little or no written history. They didn't know what they might have to deal with, or understand the nature of environmental change when it happened.

The third factor is competition for limited environmental resources from potentially hostile neighbours. Ecological decline might weaken a society from within, making it an easy or attractive prospect for conquest, or shortages themselves might provoke conflict for acquisition. This leads to the fourth factor, which is the way in which a neighbour or trading partner who, in good times, is friendly can turn hostile when shortage arrives or other circumstances change. The final factor concerns the questions that we are all facing right now: how, once having perceived a problem, does a society respond? The nature of its politics, institutions, culture and values can determine whether or not a threat is even recognised, let alone acted upon.

The Norse Sagas tell the tale of intrepid North European sailors –

we would think of them as Vikings, strongly linked to Scandinavia – who journeyed past the known world of Iceland to find and settle Greenland. The name of this huge landmass, subject to harsh climatic extremes, was an early example of the art of spin and public relations, knowingly chosen to make the land sufficiently attractive to persuade otherwise happily settled families to risk the long, unpredictable sea crossing. These were the same sailors who got as far as North America centuries before Columbus. What they did not and could not know was that they were building their homes and farms in a relatively benign mild period that wasn't going to last.

The type of subsistence farming they took with them was suited to the less harsh climate that they were familiar with, and their established culture and religion gave them habits and an outlook that inhibited their adaptability to change. The Norse settled in Greenland during the so-called medieval warm period in the North Atlantic (also known as the medieval climate optimum or climatic anomaly). It lasted for two to three hundred years from the middle of the tenth century. Unfortunately it was followed by the 'little ice age', several centuries more of intermittently very cold periods. When the settlers arrived they did what they knew, grazing cattle (their ancestors had been dairy farmers for millennia), sheep and goats, and put great effort into building Christian churches. But when the climate changed and the summers cooled, the arctic soil could not grow enough grass to sustain the livestock. Gradually the settlements dwindled and eventually died out altogether, leaving only archaeology behind.

But the Norse weren't the only people living in Greenland. There was already an indigenous Inuit population, and they did not die out. So what did the Norse do wrong? They failed to learn from the Inuit who developed a better survival strategy, concludes Diamond. While they did take advantage of caribou and arctic hares, they didn't fish, or hunt ringed seals and whales as the Inuit did (a modern sensibility might consider this impressive, though self-defeating restraint). From Greenland to Ladakh in Northern India, it was still common, even in the last century, for European-trained commercial agriculturists to attempt to introduce into harsh environments poorly adapted dairy cattle.

It seems it was the Norse settlers' strong self-image that constrained them from learning from the Inuit. In good times their

European links and Christian identity bound them together, but in bad times it was a cultural obstacle that prevented them learning from the indigenous population, whom they considered pagan and inferior. Their dismissive attitude not only prevented them from developing new ways to thrive, but meant that the Inuit would not behave as friendly neighbours to help when times got hard. The Norse also had a rich elite who directed much of their economic resources into trading to acquire luxury and prestige goods for wealthy households and the Church. Instead of iron and wood, for example, shipping was devoted to fine household items, stained glass, jewellery, bells and vestments. It created a 'conflict between the short-term interests of those in power, and the long-term interests of the society as a whole'.[5]

On a far grander, climate-changing scale, it is arguable that much the same is true today on a worldwide scale. One difference is that the pendulum has swung from the consequences of a periodic cooling event to global warming. Today, the Greenland ice sheet is melting rapidly. In response the Earth's crust beneath it is bouncing back. That means more chances for a range of disasters. The weight of ice acts to dampen fault lines; its release creates the potential for greater earthquake activity. These, in turn, could cause underwater landslides propelling tsunamis towards North Atlantic coastlines. Deep-sea earthquakes created the devastating Indian Ocean tsunami of 2004, and the Japanese tsunami of 2011, the most expensive disaster the world had seen, with a Japanese government cost estimate of $309 billion.

It was once fashionable to scoff at the range of likely impacts being ascribed to global warming, but as more ice melts and sea levels rise, the change in relative weight on different parts of the Earth's surface points to a future of 'escalating geological havoc' according to Professor Bill McGuire of University College London, an expert in geophysical and climate hazards.[6]

Different combinations of the factors outlined above can be found in the collapse, among others, of the Mayan civilisation of Central America, which developed beyond the capacity of its ecosystems to support it, the Indus valley civilisation in Asia, which failed to adapt to a changing climate that became cooler and drier, and Easter Island in the Pacific, as mentioned, which, in short, favoured monumental exhibitionism at the expense of trees.

A slightly different analysis adapts a common term from economics to argue that a society's days are numbered when it enters a period of 'declining marginal returns'.[7] This is, in essence, another expression of the critique of growth-dependent economies made so far in this book. The law of diminishing returns describes how, with everything else being constant, the additional benefit gained from adding more of one thing will sooner or later decline. Imagine a party in a room. With just one person it's not much fun. As more guests arrive it gets better and better until the atmosphere is buzzing. But if more keep coming, suddenly you can't get to the drinks, there's no room to dance and it's too loud even to talk. You've passed optimum and hit the diminishing return on the benefits of new guests arriving.

In a bounded biosphere, an economy growing in scale, but which cannot indefinitely match or better its growth rate with increases in the efficiency with which it uses resources, must sooner or later experience diminishing returns. It can occur under four simple scenarios, when (i) benefits are constant and costs are rising; (ii) benefits are rising but costs are rising faster; (iii) benefits are falling and costs are constant; or (iv) benefits are falling and costs are rising.[8]

In this way the Western Roman Empire grew overextended and over-bureaucratic, and then collapsed under the weight of the diminishing marginal returns of attempting to maintain itself. For a period Rome expanded, the spoils of one conquest funding the next. It then 'plateaued' during the first two centuries of the modern era. But with the scope for further conquests reduced, the empire proved too expensive to support merely from annual agricultural surpluses. Successive administrations nevertheless attempted to do so. They responded by controlling and milking the population within their borders, becoming administratively more complex in the process.

The empire developed a system of government that became inward-looking and weakened by internal dissent. The singular focus and range of new territories available for conquest from the golden days of the Republic was lost. At first a small, trusted coterie of around a thousand administrators ran the whole empire with extraordinary efficiency. In its place a bloated, inefficient and suspicious bureaucracy of thirty-five thousand developed, seeking power and personal advantage. Distracted by their own internal struggles for ascendancy, complacent and self-obsessed, they took their eyes off the Goths at the gates, and paid the price with half an empire. Every subsequent age could and often did project its own experience onto the Romans, and it is tempting to do so now.[9]

We can shake our heads with hindsight, wondering why a creeping pattern of failure was not obvious at the time. Yet both the Greenland Norse and the Roman Empire survived for considerably longer than modern consumer society yet has. The Egyptian Old Kingdom of the Third Millennium BC lasted for nearly one thousand years. To its own people, such a civilisation must have seemed timeless, eternal. When it did collapse it did so amidst 'looting, killing, revolution, [and] social anarchy'.[10] Here a dominant push-factor was probably environmental. Farming was dependent on the fertile flood plains of the Nile, but climatic variability led to successive failures of the Nile floods. However mighty and divinely ordained the Old Kingdom's rulers considered themselves, their order and authority could not survive a hungry population.

It is as if all societies require a cautionary warning, like the ones that appear on television concerning the value of your investments: 'Beware – civilisation can go down as well as up.'

Unless you have lived through a time of great upheaval and reversal, it is hard to shake the notion that, generally speaking, history is the march of progress. Here we are in the world's wealthiest nations, with our basic needs largely met, substantially protected by the rule of law, with leisure time, the opportunity to travel, and to enjoy as never before the culture and goods of countries the world over. We are at a kind of peak. What could possibly go that wrong? If, for example, you didn't live through the Second World War, as my parents' generation did, it is very hard to imagine things being fundamentally different to that.

Mesopotamia was the cradle for much of Western civilisation. It stretched across areas of modern-day Turkey, Iraq, Iran and Syria. Early written languages evolved there, along with complex maths, astronomy, theories of rational analysis underpinning medicine, the first recorded religion, and technologies for working metal. It was, for example, one of the birthplaces of the Bronze Age.

But there was a major collapse of civilisation in the Mesopotamian alluvium between the seventh and tenth centuries AD. The area of land under human occupation shrank to a fraction of what it once had been, just 6 per cent of its level five hundred years before. Actual population fell to its lowest level for five thousand years. It was one of the most complete breakdowns of a society recorded. Tax revenues fell by 90 per cent in a single lifetime. Lands became ungovernable, permanently uninhabitable, and abandoned largely to nomads. Not just a ghost town, but something of a ghost civilisation.

What happened in Mesopotamia was the development of an increasingly large and intensive agricultural system. For a while the climate supported unusually good harvests and the population grew in tandem, with an impressive spate of cities being built. For a time complex irrigation systems and the exploitation of increasingly marginal farmland sustained the growth. However, too much fresh water was used, drawing up increasingly saline groundwater, destroying the soil's fertility and causing diminishing returns. Collapse was more sudden than gradual. The fragile ecological foundations of the society were undermined, causing the output of the farms to vary wildly. More state resources were invested to try to halt the decline, paid for by higher taxes. Yet a sort of reverse ecological leverage made this even more unsupportable, causing collapse.

At more or less the same period in history, around the globe in Central America, the Mayan civilisation was suffering a similar fate. Here, writes Joseph Tainter, the development of competing Mayan cities led to a downward spiral of diminishing returns from their natural capital. There was a 'high-density, stressed population, practising intensive agriculture, living largely in political centres, supporting both an elite class and major public works programmes, and competing for scarce resources'.[11]

With all of these examples, what stands out is the one that began the chapter: Nauru. Because it happened in the modern era, even when its ecology was despoiled and its population grew to the point whereby its local ecosystems could not, alone, support it, there were others who could. The world came to its aid, importing the food and pretty much everything else that the islanders needed, or wanted and could pay for, over thousands of miles of sea. We have what the ancients didn't – global communications technology and the ability to move large amounts of stuff very quickly around the world by land, sea and air. It feels as if we have turned a page. With a modicum of good will we can help each other out of our difficulties.

On the other hand, what if we do at the aggregate, global level what these other societies have each individually done? What if we live beyond our means for sustained periods, enter a period of diminishing returns, and respond by trying, in increasingly complex ways, to prop up a flawed system? Tainter's conclusion in his study of the failure of complex civilisations is haunting: 'Collapse, if and when it comes again, will this time be global. No longer can any individual nation collapse. World civilisation will disintegrate as a whole.'[12]

It would be wise then, to keep an eye open for signs of diminishing returns, and we have already seen some of those. We should be watchful both for evidence of clear signs being ignored, but also for societies responding with increasingly intricate, over-engineered and over-complicated attempts to carry on as usual in the face of diminishing returns. Such as Rome's bureaucratic centralisation, and the Mayan and Mesopotamian exhaustion of the land, those other telltale signs of endangered societies. We should also be mindful of a reluctance to adopt new ways of doing things because we consider them backward, alien or beneath us, even those with a proven track record of success, as when the Norse in Greenland failed to learn from the Inuit. All these tensions can be found in the current debate about the future of global farming examined further in chapter 8.

Stress surges and signs of diminishing returns are there for those willing to see them. We've already noted climate change, soil loss, conflict for limited fresh water and living through a mass-extinction event – the whole concatenation of environmental stresses that result from a dominant species, us, living beyond our means. There are the nine 'planetary boundaries' either crossed or nearly crossed where confidently identified.[13] There's the work by researchers at Kew Gardens and the IUCN indicating that over one fifth of plant species are under threat of extinction. In the UK we are becoming increasingly reliant on imported energy, steadily rising in its share of the energy mix since 2004, when declining North Sea oil production meant we first became unable to meet our own energy needs. Similarly, our dependence is rising on imported food. Our level of national food self-sufficiency recently hit a thirty-nine-year low.

There are the clear signs too, in the richer societies, of humanity continuing to increase its levels of material consumption beyond the point where it adds to our well-being. The way that, in Europe, for example, for every unit of fossil fuel energy consumed today, we derive less human well-being from it than we did decades ago. The efficiency with which we convert that natural resource into relatively happy and long lives has declined. But instead of fundamentally rethinking how to live on planet Earth, and share it for the betterment of all, the default position of almost all governments appears to be to seek new ways to carry on business as usual.

Hence, at least two presidents of the United States – both called Bush – made it clear over the decade that saw climate change rise to prominence as a political issue that the American way of life was not up for negotiation in the face of environmental challenges. A British chancellor of the Exchequer in 2011 spoke of 'endless' environmental goals being a 'burden' on businesses and the economy. None but a handful question the logic of an economy growing endlessly in scale.

At best, it seems, there are promises of marginal additional funding to new energy technologies, as well as the opposite: deeper exploitation of old, fossil fuel energy systems. Yet no matter whether a better or a worse technology, even the basic impulse towards some technological fix, rather than social and economic innovation – changing the shape of our lives rather than just the plug-in technologies – may be a mistake.

We saw in the original and revised working of the model behind the *Limits to Growth* report that whatever technological innovation was used, the system tended towards collapse if neither the scale of output nor the size of population was constrained. That technology can and will solve our problems is an article of faith among many environmental organisations as much as governments and the private sector. What lies behind this notion, writes Jared Diamond, is the idea that from today, technology will solve our existing problems without creating significant new ones, and it will do so fast enough to get us out of trouble. But history teaches that technologies often fail, and even successful ones take time to diffuse. Also that unintended consequences which create new problems are common, not exceptions, and that it is almost always cheaper and more effective to take prior preventive action than to rely on a techno-fix to clean up afterwards.

New technology increases the human capacity to do things, and on a far greater scale than previously imagined. But there is no guarantee attached to those things. Even benignly motivated advances can bite back. The introduction of stable, odourless, non-toxic coolants for refrigerators seemed like a wonderful idea – what could go wrong? Chlorofluorocarbons (CFCs), it turned out, had the unlooked-for side effect of corroding the atmosphere's ozone layer, without which we cannot survive. Even when that problem was largely solved, a massive and unsustainable rise in per capita energy use resulted from the steadily increasing numbers of household electrical goods. Challenges like climate change and soil loss are unintended consequences of existing technological innovation. Cars were praised for making our towns and cities quieter and cleaner when first introduced. Now the car is one of the greatest global threats to health according to the World Health Organization, and a threat to the very climate we depend on. The question is whether purely technological solutions can outpace the problems they create, inadvertently or not.

Yet our mainstream culture is such that to be sceptical of technology in any way is to be dismissed as a Luddite, an irrational, anti-progress machine-hater. This is both unfortunate and ironic. To be sceptical means to 'withhold from prevailing doctrines'. Yet what is a doctrine but a system of belief, not rational analysis, while to be 'doctrinaire' means carrying principles to 'logical but unworkable extremes'. The latter phrase is, for me, quite a good summary of the point arrived at by the mainstream economics discussed earlier. I'll look at how this manifests itself in terms of the energy and food debates in chapter 8. But, to summarise, it could be asked with regard to both: Is the problem faced by the world that we lack sufficient food and energy, and therefore need more and new technologies applied at ever-greater scale to produce them? Or is it that there's plenty to go around, but that the concentration of power, waste, and poor allocation and distribution mean that some people get more than they need, while others much less? If, as I think, it is the latter, the agenda for change, for surviving and thriving in difficult times, looks very different.

This is not to say that technology doesn't matter. It does, of course, but not in isolation, removed from social, cultural and economic context. The trick we need to learn is how to solve several problems at the same time. How do you revive economies, create mass employment, high well-being and maintain the environment simultaneously? The technologies you choose carry with them a different DNA for the economy and society that surround them. And whatever we choose may lock in a particular way of being for decades (even longer in the case of nuclear power, for example, whose full life cycle needs ultra-high security maintained for millennia). We need to find technologies for which low carbon and lots of jobs are part of that DNA.

Accusations of being Luddite are ironic. Even a casual reading of history reveals that the original Luddites were nothing like the cartoonish, progress-hating bogeymen handed down by officialdom, which is a folklore shaped by 'victor's history'. Paradoxically, it seems, the Luddites weren't even Luddites themselves.

Two hundred years ago new weaving machines were being introduced by mill and factory owners in the Midlands and North of England. Accompanied by different working practices, they greatly reduced the number, and changed the type, of workers required in the textile industry. Up to that point, a lot of cloth work had been done by skilled artisans. And in response to the threat of unemployment, the debasement of their craft and the general downward pressure on earnings, there was a spate of planned machine-wrecking. What happened was part of much broader changes during the Industrial Revolution. The enclosures created a class of dispossessed, unskilled potential factory workers in the expanding urban areas. The textile artisan's lifestyle was tough by modern standards, but they lived in mutually supportive communities and had a certain control over their own output, a kind of dignity and modest self-reliance, growing some of their own food to supplement their diets. Life for the mill workers, by contrast, would prove grim, dangerous, dependent and unremitting.

In Nottingham in 1811 the first uprising took place; it spread to Lancashire and Yorkshire the following year. But the Luddites' assault was anything but a mindless rage. It was a calculated use of the only power they had to defend their livelihoods against what they saw as a technology that would serve to make a very few people very rich whilst enslaving in awful conditions many more. They targeted those machines, such as the shearing frame, which they considered 'hurtful to the commonality' – others on the same factory floor might be left untouched. Luddites were not per se opposed to technology, but to how particular machines were used. Some of their targets were not new inventions at all. What they resisted was the use of machines as weapons by factory owners to erode their rights and wages. Their targets were those they considered most guilty of doing so.

The Luddites were organised and worked in secret. In action they would sometimes dress subversively in women's clothing. Factory owners were given warning to remove the offending machines, and only when they refused was action taken. The stakes could not have been higher. Smashing machines became a crime punished by death when the Frame Breaking Act was passed in 1812. The Romantic movement made its own elite critique of industrialisation, whereas the Luddites were a revolution from below, but the latter drew support from the former, with Mary Shelley and Lord Byron counted among their backers.

A group called Luddites 200, formed to mark their two-hundredth anniversary and reappraise their legacy, appropriately enough argue that it was the nearest thing to revolution since the English Civil War. To those who contend that, given enough time, the new machines would bring 'progress and prosperity', they suggest that they 'should ask themselves what they would have done to save their families in the dire situation that the Luddites faced'.

In modern debates about choices of food and energy systems, particular technologies claim support from science and progress, and therefore immunity to challenge. In this way technology becomes an imposition, not a choice. And with it comes the pattern of ownership and control of resources that the technology leans towards. Questioning what else lies embedded in technology, more than its straightforward function, is part of the Luddites' useful legacy to us. Another might be an insight into what happens when a system that we have come to depend on for our livelihood gets interrupted. How prone have we become to social upheaval? How resilient are our societies to external shocks? Chapter 8 looks at how we have fared more recently, and where we sit now.

The Luddites were part of a much older tradition of militant reaction to threats to livelihoods, which give us a taste of what might be expected in a more stressed future. Every ancient Roman consul and emperor knew that if Rome's grain basket ran low they would be stripped of their purple robes. But food riots became something of a European speciality. The second half of the eighteenth century in England has been called 'the golden age of food rioting'.[14] In September 1795, for example, London witnessed nearly a week of rioting in which the targets were bakers, food wholesalers and monopolists. This was not mob rule, but according to the historian E. P. Thompson 'a highly complex form of direct popular action, disciplined and with clear objectives'.[15] Most of these actions were responses either to shortages or to unfair distribution. Eric Hobsbawm called them 'collective bargaining by riot'.[16] The rioters themselves tended not to be the typical culprits of popular imagination. Farm labourers and the poorest of the urban poor were among them, but were often a minority compared with artisans like the Luddites and industrial workers. Protests were frequently begun by women, who were the quickest to spot unfair price rises and engineered shortages, and quickest too to organise demonstrations.

As the Industrial Revolution accelerated, Europe echoed to the sound of riots, often triggered by issues with food. Some rioted when attempts were made to export grain from areas with shortages; some seized food in response to price hikes and sold it on at a 'fair price'; some destroyed their own produce in protest; still others conducted 'market riots' targeted at the dealers, authorities and commercial agents deemed most responsible for price rises.

It was my job in 1999 to attend the infamous meeting of the World Trade Organization in Seattle where protests erupted into rioting met with brutal force from paramilitary police. There was a widespread sense that the trade interests of the wealthiest countries were being placed ahead of both the environment and the needs of poorer countries. To many the diplomatic meltdown, broken windows and tear gas came as a shock. But in many ways the 'Battle in Seattle' was merely the culmination of decades of modern food riots that had been sweeping across the majority, developing world, largely in response to the economic doctrine emerging from the governments and financial institutions of Europe and the United States.

In the Mayan and Mesopotamian cases, economic policies such as higher taxation and agricultural intensification to generate surpluses were responses to the problems of stressed ecosystems that only functioned to make matters worse. The nature of a society's response to threats, and the economic policies it chooses, form a large part of how, as Diamond puts it, societies choose to fail or survive. In the modern world, these choices operate at an unprecedented scale and in a global context. But economic historians note that 'modern food riots ... are generated by processes analogous to economic liberalisation policies that produced classical food riots'. The difference today is internationalisation, and that this is happening 'in response to a new and ever more integrated global system'.[17]

For a time, food riots were a dominant form of civil unrest. But there were other causes too, such as religious disputes, opposition to enclosures, poor working conditions and military conscription. And it was into broader political shifts like the rise of the labour movement that food riots were absorbed, and into protests over that other lifeline, energy from fossil fuels. Without their widespread use the Industrial Revolution would not have happened as it did. Without their long-term effects we would not be faced with potentially catastrophic global warming.

In October 1902 President Theodore Roosevelt faced a major coal strike, and feared that the result would be 'untold misery ... with the certainty of riots which might develop into social war'.[18] In solving the crisis, Roosevelt set a precedent by introducing Federal Government-led arbitration. He also saw the future, writing in his letters: 'I fear there will be fuel riots of as bad a type as any bread riots we have ever seen.'[19] Roosevelt was as nervous then, about government intervention in the private sector, as our government is timid in confronting the energy companies today. But although he feared setting an 'evil precedent', he concluded that he would prefer to 'run the risk of impeachment rather than expose the Nation to chaos'.[20] He made a choice, on balance, between adherence to strict ideology and the public interest.

Today we have the power to apply new technologies at unprecedented scale, whether through social networking via the internet, or nuclear power through energy grids. That means their encoded re-engineering of society will work at a similar scale, as will any negative, unintended consequences, or, indeed, positive benefits. That is what demands our healthy scepticism. It was at the heart of E. F. Schumacher's critique, *Small is Beautiful*. He wrote:

There is wisdom in smallness if only on account of the smallness and patchiness of human knowledge, which relies on
experiment far more than on understanding. The greatest
danger invariably arises from the ruthless application, on a vast
scale, of partial knowledge such as we are currently witnessing
in the application of nuclear energy, of the new chemistry in
agriculture, of transportation technology, and countless other
things.

Such ambivalence towards technology, sceptical but aware and
prepared to garner potential benefits, underpinned another more
recent phase of our history. This period, despite its hardships, might
have even more to teach us, and it is where we will travel next on
the journey to cancel the apocalypse. All through history, civilisations – and the values, culture, order and technological achievements
they represent – repeatedly grow, flourish and often disappear. And,
not always, of course, for the worse. The comedian Omid Djalili
quipped that he'd been out for an Indian meal at a restaurant called
A Taste of the Raj where the waiter had beaten him with a stick and
forced him to build a complex railway system.

The reason to dwell on these cycles in history is to make one point
inescapable, a notion that is hard truly to accept. There is no guarantee, no special right, that we are here to stay – that human foibles, our
Icarus-like yearnings, will be endlessly indulged by a benign biosphere.

Our future is in our hands and will be determined by how we
react to, and pre-empt, the range of 'stress surges' to our system,
civilisation's ark, and how effective we are at mid-voyage re-
engineering. It will be determined by whether or not we are able
to manage a great transition successfully. For the collapsed civilisations just mentioned, at their peak each must have seemed as
permanent as the mountains and rivers – as natural and endless a
part of human order as the movement of the tides and the passage
of the seasons. Their leaders considered themselves divinely
ordained. But each of them ended. We cannot simply trust and
expect to continue as we are. The drivers of collapse were diverse,
but often share common features. Many had the defence of
being unaware of the cogwheels turning to drive their demise.

That is an excuse we lack. Whether we accept the signs or not, they are there.

Nature can drop quite obvious hints when disaster is approaching. The side of the volcano distorts before it blows, the ground may tremble before the big earthquake. Stories of signs missed with terrible consequences fill folklore and popular culture. We have many already noted, and not acted upon. But it doesn't always go wrong, and sometimes the opposite can be true. On 26 December 2004, a ten-year-old English girl called Tilly Smith was on holiday when she noticed that the sea water on the beach had a strange consistency. It was 'all frothy like on the top of a beer. It was bubbling,' she said. Two weeks earlier in her geography class she had been taught to recognise the signs of an impending tsunami. The beach where Tilly stood was in Phuket, Thailand. She and her family were seconds away from joining the quarter of a million estimated victims in one of the world's most lethal natural disasters, the Indian Ocean tsunami. But the sun was shining, and all the people swimming and languishing on the beach were relaxed and having a good time.

Tilly pleaded with her parents. It's easy to picture the scene. People rarely want to believe the worst, and if you've never experienced a disaster on that scale, and few have, it must be hard to imagine one happening. As hard as picturing the collapse of a superficially stable civilisation, where everything seems fine. But not only did her parents eventually believe her, they acted, persuading others to clear the beach too, saving possibly a hundred lives. Timescale is the only thing that separates Tilly's warning from the alarm signals to cut drastically greenhouse gas emissions, and to stop overstretching our other planetary environmental life-support systems. Imagine the beach scene in slow motion, and those few seconds in which life-saving decisions can be made dragged out as the months we are living through now.

Civilisations collapse. We don't like the idea, but they do. Throughout history, looking out from within, each probably seemed timeless, superior to everything that came before and likely to last for ever. Few of them did. Do they now include ourselves? Life-or-death decisions made in circumstances of great uncertainty faced my parents' generation when another potential apocalypse loomed. What can we learn from how they responded?

The art of rapid transition – hope from history

Cutting spending on low carbon technologies now would be like cutting the budget for Spitfires in 1939.

Tim Yeo

The amount of state intervention (in the banking system) in the US and UK at this moment is at a level comparable to that of wartime. We have in effect had to declare war to get us out of the hole created by our economic system.

John Lanchester, *Whoops!*

It is not enough for us merely to do our best – we have to do what is necessary.

Winston Churchill

Major natural catastrophes must feel apocalyptic. Earthquake, tsunami and volcanoes create landscapes from the medieval imagination of hell. War is probably the nearest we come humanly to creating such conditions.

Cigar, bowler hat, fat lower lip and an occasional two-fingered salute are the motifs by which we remember Winston Churchill. Oddly, we should probably remember him in a lab coat, because Churchill was intrigued, even morbidly fascinated, by the potential of science in both peace- and wartime. Even so, his attitude was ambivalent, an echo of very modern sentiments that we'll explore later in the book, and led to one of his most famous observations, that scientists should be 'on tap, but not on top'.

Nevertheless, without marshalling Britain's best scientific brains, we might not have won the war. But the signature of success left to history was not just the triumph of science, it was a remarkable combination of scientific, economic and, importantly, social innovation.

Today we face equally large but different threats, from energy insecurity and a global food chain under threat, to climatic upheaval, overuse of fresh water supplies and a mass extinction of plants and animals. Is there something we can learn from Britain's past that could help us today?

War, famously, accelerates all kinds of technological development, sometimes with ambiguous outcomes. During the Second World War, for example, science planted the nuclear seed of what became known as 'mutually assured destruction' (M.A.D.: an appropriate acronym), but also led to rapid advances in everything from nutrition and transport to information and communication technology.

Scientists working today for the accident-prone oil company BP might long for the day when their predecessors had heroic opportunities to work on projects of national significance like PLUTO, the 'pipeline under the ocean', a supply line to France designed to support the invasion in 1944, and FIDO, 'Fog Investigation Dispersal Operations', to work out how to keep airfield runways clear.

Especially on tap for Churchill when he became prime minister was the physicist Frederick Alexander Lindemann, 1st Viscount Cherwell. Churchill appointed him his chief scientific adviser and he also served as paymaster general. *Scientific American* called him the 'most powerful scientist ever'. Known as 'The Prof', Lindemann's scope and range of involvement in government was as wide as his judgement was sometimes faulty. He dismissed out of hand, for example, evidence of Germany's V rocket development programme. My house in South London was built on the site where one of these fell, so I have a daily reminder of how wrong he was.

But he set up the innovative, meddling and vitally important S-Branch, a statistical unit cutting right across government. It presented Churchill with a vast range of information on the war effort, allowing him to make swift, intuitive decisions on life-and-death issues. For an island nation at war it meant that quick strategic assessments of Britain's food supply could be made.

Lindemann already had a long view of science embroiled in conflict. As a German scientist working during the industrial-scale destruction of the First World War, he knew that Germany's ability to fight had depended on a recent scientific breakthrough. From 1913 a process developed by Fritz Haber and Carl Bosch combined nitrogen and hydrogen gas to produce ammonia in large amounts, which in turn was used to make artificial fertiliser (see chapter 8 for the longer-term consequences and more recent challenges of this development). When war broke out production was switched to its other use, making explosives. Germany was poor in the natural nitrate deposits needed (and which now present something of a global challenge, relating to one of the nine planetary boundaries), and the Haber–Bosch process made it possible to compete with the British Empire, which had plenty. Without it, reflected Churchill, 'The Germans could not have continued the War after their original stack of nitrates was exhausted.'

In 1940, Lindemann backed a department known as 'Churchill's Toyshop'. Its proper name was Ministry of Defence 1 (MD1), and it grew out of Military Intelligence Research, itself set up in 1939 as part of the War Office. The upstart division trod on the toes of more established departments like the Ordnance Board and Ministry of Supply, but got results. Sticky bombs, limpet mines, the puff ball (an anti-tank weapon), pencil detonator and other cunningly destructive weapons all came from the inventors it supported.

Lindemann's supreme self-confidence and failure, sometimes, to see the human dimension of issues justified Churchill's views on the proper place for scientists. Arthur 'Bomber' Harris is often credited with pushing the controversial area bombing of civilian targets during the war, but it was Lindemann, himself a German émigré, who put the scientific case for the destruction of civilian targets in German cities with cold detachment. This was dark science. It wasn't just any housing that should be bombed, he argued, but the closely packed homes of the working-class poor. Why? Because by concentrating on these, rather than less densely built middle-class neighbourhoods, for every pound of explosive dropped, bombing would be more efficient. It would cause more damage, create a larger refugee problem, tie up more enemy resources, and be even more demoralising to the foe, over and above actual mass fatalities.

Although Churchill came to see area bombing as a grim necessity, to him this was the scientific as horrific. After the furious development of weapons during the war culminated in the dropping of atomic bombs on Japan, he said in 1946: 'The Dark Ages may return – the Stone Age may return on the gleaming wings of Science; and what might now shower immeasurable material blessings upon mankind may even bring about its total destruction.'

But there was another, vital side to the role of science in wrestling with the apocalyptic conflict. Wars tend to be won on information and logistics. The tale of scientists gathered in secrecy at Bletchley Park to decrypt Germany's Enigma code is now well known. Among them was the brilliant mathematician and computer scientist Alan Turing, later victimised for his homosexuality. Their work on encryption laid foundations for the coming information age, along with other major breakthroughs.

Conflict took fully to the skies during the Second World War compared with the war two decades earlier, and navies expanded. But how to keep track of all those planes and ships? Today, the answer, which many say won the war, is probably sitting in your kitchen, warming up yesterday's leftover dinner. Microwave ovens use a cavity magnetron.

It's a vacuum tube developed by John Randall and Harry Boot in early 1940 that generates microwaves at high power using electron streams and magnetism, and it made radar practical. It seems odd now, but at the start of the war we still listened out for enemy planes with the equivalent of giant concrete ears, positioned at key points around Britain's coast. The cavity magnetron was such a significant development that it formed the centrepiece of a top-secret mission led by the scientist Henry Tizard, chairman of the Aeronautical Research Committee, to persuade the United States, still not at war, to support Britain's struggle.

A more important invention is hard to imagine. For an island nation at war, knowing where your enemy's ships, submarines and planes are, and ensuring the safe arrival of food and fuel supplies, is the difference between victory and defeat, life and death. Today, radar plays an important role in monitoring weather systems and climate change.

On the home front it was the scientific approach of the Ministry of Food to health and nutrition that witnessed one of the war's most surprising and unexpected outcomes. To win the war, the government knew that huge savings were needed at the household level in the use of food and fuel. The ministry began as part of the Board of Trade just before the war, later disappearing into the Ministry of Agriculture. With the biochemist Jack Drummond as its chief food scientist, a radical rationing system was devised that reduced consumption. This was necessary both because an island nation was vulnerable to isolation during wartime and had to rely on its own, limited, resources, and because the war effort itself had substantial additional needs. After the difficult winter of 1940, and as the ministry's scientifically planned diet, high in fruit and vegetables, took effect, the health and well-being of the nation improved significantly.

By April 1943, 31,000 tonnes of kitchen waste were being saved every week, enough to feed 210,000 pigs. Food consumption fell 11 per cent by 1944 from before the war, even as health, especially of those more vulnerable in society, broadly improved. The Women's Institute set up 5800 food-preservation centres where people learned to make pickles and jams and store food. Alongside these and the Village Produce Associations were more coercive measures. Wasting food was socially demonised and fined. 'Waste the food and help the Hun,' said Fougasse's poster. New eating patterns were helped by a rapid growth in communal eating. By 1944 10 per cent of all food was being eaten in works and school canteens, cafés and restaurants. The so-called British Restaurants that grew out of emergency feeding measures during the Blitz were widespread and their communal eating approach proved popular, with 60 per cent of people wanting them to continue post-war.

As part of the push for greater food self-sufficiency, not only was more land brought into production (10,000 square miles), but the balance of farming was changed. Land was used more efficiently to feed people by promoting a shift away from livestock. It was calculated that one acre used for grazing animals could feed one or two people, but cultivating wheat it would feed twenty, and potatoes, forty. Accordingly, while the output of sheep, pigs and poultry fell enormously (cattle increased marginally to provide milk), production of cereal, potatoes, wheat and vegetables rose enormously. With his talent for public messaging, and against the background of this wholly pragmatic shift, Churchill appealed to the public to, so to speak, save the nation's meat and eat it too. The public was called on to rear pigs, rabbits and poultry to compensate.

By 1943 there were 3000 rabbit clubs and 4000 pig clubs, the latter producing enough bacon for 150 million breakfasts. The number of allotments leapt from 850,000 in 1939 to 1,750,000 in 1943. By then, six million were growing vegetables. They were Britain's willing 'Garden Army', a little like the Carbon Army we need today. Digging for victory drew on older traditions too, such as the radical Victorian gardeners who transformed neglected scraps of public land, planting them with fruit trees and herb gardens, and the culture of the small 'guinea' gardens, so called because their maintenance was cheap. Overall, dependence on food imports halved between 1939 and 1945.

As the changed consumption patterns took hold, history also judged kindly the overall effect on people's health of the new ways of living. Reminiscing in his memoirs in 1981, Dr Magnus Pyke, a former nutritional adviser at the Ministry of Food, recalled how: 'The figures for infant mortality and, indeed, virtually all the other indications of nutritional well-being of the community, showed an improvement on the previous standards.'

Mortality rates fell dramatically among both men and women.[21] As a strong indicator of broader health improvements, between 1937 and 1944 infant mortality (up to age one) fell from 58 per 1000 to 45 per 1000.[22] After being relatively high during the 1930s, suicide rates also fell during the war.

History suggests then, that the shift to a low-energy economy could create more convivial and certainly more healthy lifestyles.

Oddly, food science grew in the modern age to be synonymous in the public imagination with turkey twizzlers, additives and types of adulteration and factory farming that have nothing to do with nutrition. Drummond was a hero in his time for weaning the nation onto healthy eating, but a pall hangs over his memory. He was murdered in mysterious circumstances along with his wife and daughter in France in 1952. In *The Vitamin Murders*, James Ferguson speculates about the involvement of the burgeoning chemical industry. It quickly becomes an investigation into who killed healthy eating in Britain.

A study conducted in 2012 by the nutritionist Amanda Ursell, advised by Marguerite Patten, who worked for the Ministry of Food during the war, found that even allowing for resistance to change, children could in fact rapidly adapt to a rationing-type diet, experiencing a range of benefits. The group of eight-year-old schoolchildren studied were fed on a much lower-calorie diet, similar to what was available during the war. They got 1800 calories per day compared with a modern equivalent closer to 3000 calories. Compared with fellow pupils eating a modern diet high in sugar and fat, those on the rationed diet had above-average height gain (they grew up, not out). Behavioural improvements were reported too, with children in the study complaining less of feeling hungry. Similar results emerged from a campaign in Britain by the activist celebrity chef Jamie Oliver, who fought successfully to improve the quality of school meals.

Ways to actively create health rather than just treat sickness are something that societies seem sporadically to stumble over and then forget. Before and after the war there was an exercise that came to be known as the Peckham Experiment. It was shaped by some of Britain's experiences and social challenges during the First World War and its long shadow, including the Depression of the 1930s. As with some other activities that happened between 1939 and 1945, it displayed a certain boldness, practical and intellectual curiosity and willingness to experiment.

Between 1926 and 1950 the experimental biologists George Scott-Williamson and Innes Hope Pearse, who were husband and wife, developed a pioneering project that set out to make health 'more contagious than disease'. The principles of the Peckham Experiment were self-organisation, local empowerment, organic farming and a holistic focus on human relationships, the social connections within a community being fundamental to health.

Early health checks on the Peckham community in South London where Williamson and Pearse worked revealed widespread, and often untreated, disease and ill health among families, but an early insight of their research was to realise that simple health examinations, information and medical treatment were not the answer. The problem was not just one of money. Peckham at the time was peopled mainly by artisanal working families. Their approach was to do with lifestyle and environment, but it also meant asking a different question. Instead of following normal medical practice and saying: What makes us ill?, in the best tradition of simple revolutionary questioning they asked: What are the conditions that make us well?

The Pioneer Health Centre that Williamson and Pearse went on to found became a research project and a living experiment, established to explore new ways to improve health and well-being through meeting people's needs for 'physical, mental and social activity'. At its height it received ten thousand visitors a year. Here was the seed of a progressive modern public health movement.

The Centre, a modernist architectural gem in its own right, which still stands, run as a subscription club, provided for a range of activities, including a swimming pool, gym, theatre, nursery, school and cafeteria with food from the Centre farm. Whole families were members, paying a small fee and taking part in annual 'health overhauls' and consultations. It operated like a 'social contract' pre-dating the National Health Service and perhaps with greater reciprocity between those providing and receiving a service. Asked about their innovative group, one member commented: 'You use the word "community". The Centre needs a much warmer word than that, we did feel mutually responsible for each other.'

The families were, in effect, actively creating their own wellness, rather than simply seeking cures for illness.

The Centre was linked to Oakley House in Kent and its surrounding farmland, which provided milk, bread, fruit and vegetables to the Centre's cafeteria. During the war the farm was used to evacuate twenty-nine member families. Some stayed on even after the bombing stopped and even greater improvements in their health and well-being were noted. In spite of a severe winter, and living in a cold house with few obvious comforts, the biologists were surprised not only by the health and vitality of those who stayed, but also by the quality of the relationships between parents and children and husbands and wives. They were also impressed with how families from a poor urban area had adapted to the hardships and hard work of farm life. Compared with their lives in London, however, they were growing their own food, which was better-quality than that available in Peckham's shops at the time, and they found new interests and learned new skills. This was in addition to improvements in their quality of life that being involved with the Centre had already produced.

Findings from the Experiment's research were subsequently hugely influential, informing developments like the World Health Organization's Healthy Cities Programme and the Healthy Living Centres in the UK. Yet, now, over half a century later, the design of the UK's economy, food system and health service still lags behind the Peckham Experiment's successful approach to public health.

Radical in its time, the lessons of the Peckham Experiment still resonate. For all our apparent advancement as a society since, we're challenged by inequality and poor health. These are themselves to an extent the products of our very progress, of the bad diets and sedentary days of consumer lifestyles, and a food system more interested in profit than nutrition.

The Experiment showed that healthy, equitable, economically resilient and environmentally thriving communities can be cultivated by neighbours working together in their locality. Now, a small steering group has been established to investigate the potential for a New Peckham Experiment. It is built on the understanding that such communities are possible, and can be cultivated alongside environments that increase well-being, revitalise local economies and increase equality.[23]

It's a myth that achieving a consensus to mobilise for the war effort was easy in the 1930s, and that this alone rules out useful insights or analogies with our current circumstances. Even as Germany militarised heavily under Adolf Hitler in the 1930s, a powerful part of the British establishment favoured positive engagement and appeasement, a story told in Stephen Poliakoff's film *Glorious 39*. Lord Rothermere, one-time owner of the *Daily Mail*, was close to both Hitler and Mussolini. In 1933 an opinion leader column about the Nazi Youth was published in the *Mail* under the heading 'Youth Triumphant'. In November 1936 Winston Churchill took to the floor of the House of Commons to say:

> Owing to past neglect, in the face of the plainest warnings, we have now entered upon a period of danger . . . The era of procrastination, of half-measures, of soothing and baffling expedients, of delays, is coming to its close. In its place we are entering a period of consequences . . . It is this lamentable conjunction of events which seems to present the danger of Europe in its most disquieting form. We cannot avoid this period; we are in it now . . .
>
> Two things, I confess, have staggered me, after a long Parliamentary experience, in these Debates. The first has been the dangers that have so swiftly come upon us in a few years, and have been transforming our position and the whole outlook of the world. Secondly, I have been staggered by the failure of the House of Commons to react effectively against those dangers. That, I am bound to say, I never expected. I never would have believed that we should have been allowed to go on getting into

this plight, month by month and year by year, and that even the Government's own confessions of error would have produced no concentration of Parliamentary opinion and force capable of lifting our efforts to the level of emergency. I say that unless the House resolves to find out the truth for itself it will have committed an act of abdication of duty without parallel in its long history.[24]

The appeasers, along with the atmosphere of complacency, were defeated, however, and at this point the big question was how to find the resources to fight an industrially resurgent Germany. By the outset, even the fiscally conservative magazine *The Economist* argued that government expenditure should be raised to more than three times the contemporary level of revenue. John Maynard Keynes lobbied the Treasury through a series of articles in *The Times* newspaper and through a groundbreaking pamphlet called *How to Pay for the War*. He set out to 'bring home the true nature of the war-time problems' and pointed out that even a 'moderate development of the war effort necessitated a very large cut in general consumption'.[25]

If taxes, rationing and scarcity were inadequate to reduce consumption, Keynes foresaw the danger of an unbridled inflationary spiral of wages and prices. In that case the 'spirit and efficiency' of the nation would be at risk. To avoid it, he proposed a plan of compulsory saving, backed with the promise of a payback at the end of the war. Yet, even with the spectre of Nazism looming, Keynes's medicine was thought too strong. Opinion was not ready. Keynes lamented: 'My discomfort comes from the fact, now made obvious, that the general public are not in favour of any plan.'[26]

He faced problems not dissimilar to those that haunt government officials today, who sooner or later must plan for a re-geared economy to be low-carbon, climate-friendly and resilient in the face of climatic upheaval. Yet Keynes understood that the size of the obstacles was no reason for inaction. His key to unlock official intransigence was agitation. His 'great service', wrote *The Economist* in 1939, 'has been to impel the so-called "leaders of opinion" to reveal the state of their ignorance on the central economic problem of the war'.

As the war progressed, purchase taxes were introduced as a curb on luxury spending. As time passed, the taxes became more sophisticated. Real luxuries like fur coats, silk dresses and jewellery were hit with the top rate. Essentials such as towels, bed-linen and utility clothing were exempt. Famously, there were collections of pots and pans and the railings from outside houses to provide extra metal to help the war effort. Some believe that the more important purpose of the collections was demonstrative – they were to convince the public of the seriousness of the war situation – and that the metal itself was secondary. They were an advert for collective action and said, unmistakably: 'We are all in this together.' The weight of reality in that judgement makes the modern redeployment of the term by politicians selling austerity measures in the wake of banking failures seem disingenuous to the point of insulting history.

There should be no illusion about the hardships that restrictions and rationing led to. Rationing itself was to last from January 1940 until June 1954, and there were celebrations when it ended. But some of the good habits it engendered, such as avoiding waste, were to stay with people for life. It left a generation aghast at modern consumer waste, built-in obsolescence and the disposability of goods.

Agitation from Winston Churchill about the threat of war led in 1936 to the creation of the Shadow Factory plan. The name was given because new factories to increase the production of aircraft engines were to be built 'in the shadow', or 'under the wing', of existing ones. Logically the government turned to the growing vehicle industry to help. Morris Motors, based at Cowley in Oxford, was approached by the government about the possibility of making aero-engines. At first there were to be nine new factories. Rover was commissioned to build two of them. The new factories would operate well within capacity to begin with, but if the international situation worsened, the capacity was there to increase output rapidly.

From the early summer of 1940 until after the war, Rover's only service to cars would be providing spares and maintenance for vehicles considered part of the war effort. Its focus had become making engines for aircraft and tanks, vehicle bodies and aircraft wings. Key manufacturing sectors were not simply charged with aiding the war effort in addition to their usual business – that business was put on hold until the challenge of winning the war was met. In America Franklin D. Roosevelt similarly summoned the nation's vehicle manufacturers to come up with production targets for tanks and armoured personnel carriers. When the manufacturers complained that alongside car-making they lacked capacity, he told them this didn't matter, as for the foreseeable future they wouldn't be making any cars. A modern analogy might be, for example, the manufacture of wind-turbine blades in place of commercial aircraft wings.

To create the climate in which the transition would be possible, the general public were drenched with information about the need for a war effort. Short films in cinemas, public billboard posters, cartoon strips, newspaper advertising, radio programmes – every available means of communication was employed.

Fear, hope, family and responsibility – different messages work for different people. The winners of a modern 'New Home Front' poster competition imagine how to apply the lessons of history.

The complaint might be raised today that we are far too savvy and cynical to accept what would be, in effect, propaganda. We no longer have the deference and acceptance of authority that we imagine was common back then. But what is the modern industrialised world but drenched in propaganda? It is of a different kind, perhaps, in favour of the relentless march of consumerism, but propaganda nevertheless, and it may be even more ubiquitous, both subtly flying beneath the radar of our critical consciousness, and in head-on collision with our senses. Chapter 9 looks into this in more detail.

In an earlier book, *Ecological Debt*, I described how wartime information campaigns were not only conducted officially in a top-down fashion. The messages decorated daily life, cajoling as well as instructing through civic groups, leisure magazines and even in hotel bathrooms. 'Grow fit not fat on your war diet!' said 'Food Facts No 1', from the Ministry of Food in 1940. 'Make full use of the fruit and vegetables in season. Cut out "extras", cut out waste; don't eat more than you need. You'll save yourself money . . . and you'll feel fitter than you ever felt before.'

Good Housekeeping in 1942 suggested that people 'Learn to regard every type of waste as a crime' and 'If you have the will to win, Save your Rubber, Paper, Tin.' In *Feeding Dogs and Cats in Wartime* the RSPCA advised: 'Potatoes are plentiful and if you put in extra tubers when digging for victory you will not have it on your conscience that shipping space is being taken for food for your animals.'

The government dubbed the need for energy conservation 'The Battle for Fuel'. If you stayed in a hotel in late 1942 and went to wash away your anxieties, a sign would remind you: 'As part of your personal share in the Battle for Fuel you are asked NOT to exceed five inches of water in this bath. Make it a point of honour not to fill the bath above this level.' The rail companies reminded us that: 'At this most important time, Needless travel is a "crime".' And the Ministry of Fuel and Power pointed out that: 'Britain's 12,000,000 households are 12,000,000 battle fronts in this great drive to save fuel.' Such concerted campaigns, focused on changing public attitudes, were successful and dramatically cut waste. Scrap metal was being saved at the rate of 110,000 tonnes per week.[27] In just six years from 1938 British homes cut their coal use by 11 million tonnes, a reduction of 25 per cent.[28]

While these initiatives were successful in their own terms, there were also several unexpected outcomes. In the process of prosecuting its war effort, Britain almost stumbled into being a more inclusive and socially cohesive society. Soon after the war began, egalitarianism and the idea of community became something to aspire to. They were a new social ideal. 'The political influence of the ration book seems to me to have been greater than all of the left-wing propaganda of the war years put together,' wrote the historian Paul Addison.[29] 'Fair shares' was not a Labour propaganda slogan dreamed up in 1945, but drawn from the Board of Trade's 1941 campaign to popularise clothes rationing. Hugh Dalton, head of the Board of Trade, famously put it in 1943: 'There can be no equality of sacrifice in this war. Some must lose their lives and limbs, others only the turn-ups on their trousers.' Behind all the schemes to manage demand, the objective was to 'Secure the fairest possible distribution of whatever supplies are available and to ensure . . . that as far as possible the things that everybody needs shall be within the reach of all'.[30] Also worthy of further exploration is the relative success in wartime Britain of efforts explicitly to substitute cultural activity and production – theatre, music, film, art, festivals, sport, and numerous other local entertainments – for material consumption.

Britain's wartime experience highlighted critical choices over which economic mechanisms were most likely to achieve key objectives. Where changing behaviour with regard to consumption was concerned, the government deliberately chose rationing over taxation for reasons that were rational and progressive. Taxation alone, it concluded, apart from disproportionately and unfairly placing a burden on the poor, would be too slow to change behaviour. Rationing was quicker and more equitable. Tradable rations were rejected through fear of encouraging fraud and inflation and 'undermining the moral basis of rationing'.[31] The historian Mark Roodhouse derives specific lessons for policymaking. If transferred to now, government, he writes, would need to 'convince the public that rationing levels are fair; that the system is administered transparently and fairly; and that evaders are few in number, likely to be detected and liable to stiff penalties if found guilty'.[32]

In 1940, Mary Adams, one of TVs earliest producers, moved to Whitehall and was given the task of monitoring domestic morale. Inspired by Tom Harrisson's Mass Observation surveys before the war, from May to September 1940 information was phoned in from the regions daily, and from then on weekly. The reports relayed ordinary conversations – or 'verbatims' – providing vital information that quantitative analysis cannot. They revealed that the population were solid in the main; it was the authorities who were perceived to be wavering: 'we are all anxious to be up and doing'. All people needed was 'to be told precisely what to do'.[33]

Government was not only emboldened by the evidence from these reports, it also included practical proposals:

Not only people in executive positions but also ordinary working classes are demanding that Government should take over and make use of every able-bodied man. It is suggested that Government should order all private gardens to grow at least 50 per cent foodstuffs.[34]

Information in wartime was sensitive, but: 'News broadcasts were condemned for being too repetitive, too flippant and – most seriously – for not telling the truth.'[35]

Neither were people motivated by Britain's interests alone, but: 'for a community of interest for the people of Europe'.[36] The effect of 'national unity' was to open up the political agenda through the experience of collective endeavour. Without it, some of the subsequent achievements to do with universal healthcare and the provision of education and social housing might have proved impossible.

Britain's wartime mobilisation had many dimensions. Political leadership was crucial. There was cultural change based on mass public education, leading to peer pressure and shifts in the social norms for what was considered either decent or antisocial behaviour, to do with waste, among other things. (More recent but less rapid examples of change might include those to do with smoking, drink-driving, racism, football hooliganism and domestic violence.)

In each successful case, explaining why people were being asked to make changes in their lives was critical, and quite different to many modern 'stealth' approaches to action on climate change. Change was not tentative and incremental, it was deliberately bold and visible. Signs were hung from public building and parks and gardens were given over to growing fruit and vegetables. There was rationing, perhaps better understood as the distribution of fair entitlements to available resources and key goods. And there were taxes on luxury goods. Altogether this led to reductions in waste and domestic consumption. Crucially there was an active industrial policy and a major reorientation of priorities for production and consumption. It wasn't left to the whims of the marketplace or to 'nudges' from economic policy. Behind it was a major programme of war savings and bonds in which people's money was invested in securing a better, collective future for all. The big question now is: What would a modern equivalent look like?

One difference today is likely to be the precise role of the state. Whilst the modern state is unlikely to be the sole architect, agent and judge of change, it would have to set the parameters for the delivery of key transition objectives, through a combination of local, community and private actors. A proper, and increasingly shared, grasp of risk and the need for change, planning, local initiative, enterprise, vision, ambition and shared objectives, coupled with a rugged collective endeavour – all need to be part of the dynamics of rapid transition. These create the conditions in which change becomes possible.

The surprising past of a modern consumer superpower

In planning any operation it is vital to remember and constantly repeat to oneself two things: 'In war nothing is impossible provided you use audacity,' and 'Do not take counsel of your fears.'

General George S. Patton, Jr

Britain was not alone in discovering another side of itself in the war that allowed it to survive and thrive in the face of new threats. Post-war America sets the global standard for enjoying apparently consequence-free conspicuous consumption. In the late 1930s, however, and during the war years, the US demonstrated the possibility of a very different 'good society'. Its lifestyles were, by today's standards, almost unrecognisable. According to the American historian Mike Davis, wartime produced 'the most important and broadly participatory green experiment in US history'.[37] After half a century of heavily promoted individualistic consumerism, the nation at war seems strange indeed:

Americans simultaneously battled fascism overseas and waste at home . . . millions left cars at home to ride bikes to work, tore up their front yards to plant cabbage, recycled toothpaste tubes and cooking grease, volunteered at daycare centers and USOs, shared their houses and dinners with strangers, and conscientiously

attempted to reduce unnecessary consumption and waste ...
Lessing Rosenwald, the chief of the Bureau of Industrial
Conservation, called on Americans 'to change from an economy
of waste – and this country has been notorious for waste – to an
economy of conservation'.[38]

Victory gardening had been used during the First World War. In
the heart of New York, parks like the one attached to the National
Public Library became high-profile exercises in encouraging a country
to come together in shared purpose. In the Second World War it was
promoted again by the Department of Agriculture and the First Lady,
Eleanor Roosevelt, who grew beans and carrots on the White House
lawn, and led a national 'Food Fights for Freedom' campaign. At its
peak, twenty million gardeners were producing between 30 and 40
per cent of vegetables consumed. It was more than national self-
interest too, it was an act of solidarity. With that spare capacity the US
farming system was able to provide food for its allies, Britain and
Russia.

Victory gardening became something much more than an exercise
in supplementing the wartime food supply: it evolved into a celebration of self-reliance and the greening of urban spaces. Even though
this predated the massive post-war highways building programme,
the 'dethroning' of the car as the 'icon of the American standard of
living'[39] was remarkable. King-of-the-road individualism was out. One
poster declared: 'When you ride ALONE, you ride with Hitler!'

In 1942, the USA limited gasoline to three gallons per week for
'non-essential' vehicles. Rationing was motivated by a patriotic desire
to ensure that both citizens and soldiers received a fair distribution of
goods. Gasoline entitlement was set by how necessary a person's
vehicle was to them. When, decades later, the USA prepared energy
rationing at the time of the first OPEC oil crisis in the early 1970s, a
similar logic was used. A 'Congressional Declaration of Purpose'
announced that 'positive and effective action' was needed to protect
'general welfare ... conserve scarce energy supplies' and 'insure fair
and efficient distribution'.[40]

The power of Britain's own high-profile, energetically communicated example had an effect in America too. Over one in four people
in Britain were cycling to work, and it inspired a huge resurgence of

the bicycle in the US. A 'Victory bike', made from non-critical resources, was launched. Municipalities 'sponsored bike parades and "bike days" to advertise the patriotic advantages of Schwinn over Chevrolet'.[41] Confident national leadership successfully set an international example. Holidaying by bike became popular as fuel rationing reduced leisure driving. Health and well-being benefits from the combination of victory gardening and victory cycling were noted by public health officials.

After receding for a few years, New Deal values returned in wartime housing, employment and childcare programmes, and the post-war economic conversion of factories from military to civilian production. This latter trend did, though, also lay the foundations of the productive capacity that would deliver the later consumer boom. Notably, the Office of Civilian Defense (OCD) sponsored a 'rational consumption' movement. Its consumer committees promoted 'buying only for need'. In Britain, an equivalent was the work of the National Savings Committee, which reminded citizens that: 'The "Squander-bug" causes that fatal itch to buy for buying's sake – the symptom of shopper's disease.'

Consumer information centres in the US were established that advised on nutrition, food conservation, and how to mend and prolong the life of appliances. Many of these initiatives could sit easily on the wish list of the contemporary Transition Town movement. As such, some mainstream media might dismiss them as 'nice ideas' but hopelessly idealistic and unlikely to happen. Yet, amazing as it may seem to a modern audience, these things did happen, and governments made them happen, with support from families, communities and local organisations. Mass consumption was challenged in the home of mass consumption. The cultures of restless, replaceable fashions and built-in obsolescence were replaced with ideals of the household 'economy soldier' operating along lines of 'frugal efficiency'.

A *New York Times* feature from 1942 contained interviews with young women in a community near a defence factory in Connecticut. The paper expected to find them 'yearning for the post-war future of suburban homes and model kitchens that the 1939 New York World's Fair had prophesied'.[42] But they found women war workers enjoying both their jobs and their simple trailer-style homes that needed little upkeep and housework. Long before the 1960s liberation movement,

here were 'wenches with wrenches', living values as championed by
women like the radical fashion designer Elizabeth Hawes, author of
the 1943 book *Why Women Cry*.

A new sense of fairness prevailed and the rich found themselves on
the defensive in a way not unlike the recent wave of protests in the
UK against big businesses and the wealthy avoiding tax payments.
For example, war workers needed affordable homes, so the War
Production Board ruled that no home should be built costing more
than $500 – much less than the average home at the time. In the
potential 'dead zones' of America's burgeoning suburbs, people were
relearning old skills and picking up new ones, from gardening to
cycling, and fixing and mending everything from radios to clothes.
The *New York Times* observed 'the rediscovery of the home – not as a
dormitory, but as a place where people live'. Less of one thing, consumerism, really did become more of something else, quality of life.

The French writer and aviator Antoine de Saint-Exupéry, who
disappeared for ever on a reconnaissance mission in 1944, once wrote:
'What saves a man is to take a step. Then another step.' The characteristics of wartime decision-making are daunting – urgent choices
made under pressure in complex circumstances with imperfect information and long-term, probably life-or-death consequences. Yet they
apply equally to our modern age. The temptation under such pressure
is strongly towards inaction – perhaps it just feels easier. But ultimately stasis is never an option. History suggests we must take a step,
and then another step. Much more recently there was a country that
had to take a quick, giant leap.

The Cuban laboratory of rapid transition

Whatever your political point of view, it is hard to deny that Cuba has
struggled with adversity. You may think it is the self-imposed result
of Fidel Castro's communist government, or due to being subjected
by the United States to one of the longest-running and most comprehensive international economic embargoes imposed anywhere in the
world. The country's restrictions on free speech and elections vie
with achievements on health and education that made Cuba the envy
of the developing world. Some aspects of Cuban medical research

outstripped the most advanced laboratories of Europe and the US. But at the end of the Cold War the country hit a massive rock.

During the 1970s and 80s, heavily subsidised by the Soviet Union, Cuba became dependent on cheap oil for its transport, farming and wider way of life. So the collapse of the Soviet Union in 1990 devastated the Cuban economy. Some 80 per cent of imports and exports were lost virtually overnight. Oil imports dropped by around half, with the potential to cripple both Cuba's transport and energy systems, and at first there were real shortages that caused hardship.[43]

Before the Soviet collapse, Cuba imported most of the goods required to meet the needs of its people. It exported sugar and tobacco to the Soviet Union at agreed premium prices and took oil in return, some of which was re-exported. This situation created a distorting incentive, leading to large amounts of Cuban land being given over to export crops grown in industrial monocultures, heavily dependent on oil-based inputs. Just before the collapse, in 1989, three times more land was dedicated to sugar than to other food.

Following the collapse, use of chemical pesticides and fertilisers dropped by 80 per cent, putting an end to the country's industrial, high-input approach to farming. The knock-on effect on people's daily lives was dramatic. The availability of basic food staples like wheat and other grains fell by half and, overall, the average Cuban's calorie intake fell by over one third in the course of around five years.

Cuba's response has become a test case. Prior to the shock, it was already investigating forms of ecological farming less dependent on fossil fuels. When the shock came, a system of 'regional research institutes, training centres and extension services' was already in place to support farmers. Immediate crisis was averted by food programmes that targeted the most vulnerable people – the old, young, pregnant women and young mothers – and a rationing programme that guaranteed a minimum amount of food to everyone. The threat of serious food shortages was overcome within five years by a radical transition to self-sufficiency. At the heart of the transition after 1990 was a rapid shift to the use of organic fertilisers and pesticides, crop rotation and intercropping, plus the use of animal labour and manure – in other words, they went over to a substantially organic system. But the shift was not led by the government and the big state farms, it was a triumph of small farms and urban farms and gardens. Their demonstration effect pulled the state behind them.

Shortages and rising food prices made urban farming very profitable. Backyards in Cuban cities became home to food crops and farm animals, grown and reared almost exclusively along organic lines. Half the food consumed in the capital, Havana, is grown in the city's own gardens and, overall, urban gardens provide 60 per cent of the salad vegetables eaten in Cuba.[44] Havana alone ended up with more than twenty-six thousand food gardens.[45] The Cuban experience both echoes and – statistically, at least – surpasses what America achieved in its lauded push for 'Victory Gardening' during the Second World War, led by Eleanor Roosevelt. Since then America's more recent First Lady, Michelle Obama, has led by example, digging up part of the White House garden in an attempt to encourage more American families to reap the health and well-being advantages of growing their own food.

Although Cuba's change in farming was driven by necessity rather than choice, just as in Britain during the war, there were some surprisingly positive consequences. Eating a healthier diet, and exercising more as walking and cycling became more necessary in the absence of petrol, created a healthier country. As calorie intake fell by over one third, the share of physically active adults more than doubled while obesity halved. In just five years between 1997 and 2002, according to the *American Journal of Epidemiology*, deaths due to diabetes fell by half, coronary heart disease by over one third, stroke by one in five, and all causes by just under one fifth.[46] The article's authors comment: 'These results suggest that population-wide measures designed to reduce energy stores, without affecting nutritional sufficiency, may lead to declines in diabetes and cardiovascular disease prevalence and mortality.'

Cuba had stumbled into being a remarkable laboratory test case, to see how a society could respond to the modern challenges of overconsumption, declining oil supplies and climate change. It was eating less, emitting less, finding ways to live without, or with much less, oil, and it was getting healthier as a result.

How to power homes, transport and the economy would prove a trickier problem. At the same time as its urban organic food revolution was taking place, energy consumption across society and the economy needed to be radically reduced. I remember being at school during the time of the OPEC fuel crisis in the 1970s, and how by every light switch there was a sticker encouraging you to 'turn it off'. In Cuban schools in the 1990s teaching energy conservation became common. Renewable energy projects and aggressive energy efficiency programmes were started. Quite apart from the loss of cheap imported oil, Cuba's energy system relied on an antique and wasteful centralised grid and some very dated generating stations. In addition, the decades of economic embargo meant that Cuban households clung to old, inefficient electrical appliances.

The country was well organised for natural disasters – the island sits in the flight path of the annual hurricane season – and suffered far less disruption and virtually no casualties when struck by a hurricane of equal force to Katrina, which wrecked New Orleans in 2005. But hurricanes in 2004 did damage the run-down energy system.

A *Revolución Energética* moved the country to a more efficient, decentralised system with smaller generator stations and shorter distances to transmit energy. It took over 100,000 small new pylons, thousands of kilometres of cable and half a million new electricity meters. But in this way Cuba made estimated savings of close to 1 million tonnes of oil. Fidel Castro's comment at the time was: 'We are not waiting for fuel to fall from the sky, because we have discovered, fortunately, something much more important: energy conservation, which is like finding a great oil deposit.'

The approach to Cuban homes was even more dramatic. Old, inefficient incandescent light bulbs were removed almost entirely, by mandate, in just six months – very different to the kind of gentle encouragement used recently in British homes. From that point, only energy-efficient bulbs would be available. Changing other household appliances was not obligatory, but made attractive. The poorest families could replace their old basic electrical goods for free; other families got them at cost price. Again, the scale of change was impressive. Over a two-year period, something like 2 million fridges were changed, along with 1 million fans and 200,000 air conditioners. In Cuba's kitchens, kerosene, smelly and dangerous, was used for cooking. As part of the *Revolución Energética* around 3.5 million efficient rice and pressure cookers were brought into homes. Dr Kathy Riley is an academic who lived in Cuba and studied the *Revolución Energética* and saw how it was made to work. She reports:

> Compared with virtually all other nations of a comparable level of development, the level of top-down management of the Cuban economy is striking. However, in the policy areas where this central planning is most successful it is strongly linked to an architecture of engaged local administrations that are capable of rapid mobilisation.[47]

A clear reason why it worked is that it was made easy for people and the whole process was kept on track by Cuba's network of around fourteen thousand '*trabajadores sociales*', who are, in effect, volunteer social workers operating under government approval.

Although separated by time, circumstance, politics and much else, there are odd echoes of both crisis and response between Britain and the US in the 1940s and Cuba in the 1990s. In between, Britain and the US faced another challenge that forced them to think and act on energy conservation.

Levittown in Philadelphia was built as a planned post-war suburb in the 1950s by William J. Levitt, credited by some as setting the blueprint for countless more across the US. Its repeating streets and house design made it the definition of the new American consumer dream, a smart, sprawling uniformity of detached homes, gardens and expectations of a better life. It also happened to be utterly dependent on cars and gasoline, which indicates the thread by which that dream has always hung.

Because when the major oil-producing countries organised under OPEC flexed their muscles for the second time in a decade in 1979, restricting supplies and raising oil prices to the rest of the world, Levittown couldn't take the strain. The price of gasoline hit $1 per gallon (in early 2012 the price is nearer $4 per gallon in the US and considered very high, although in the UK it is closer to $10 per gallon). Two nights of rioting broke out in the once iconic suburb founded to showcase the sight of a lifestyle dream cruising around in a large car. When the rioting was quelled, one hundred were injured and nearly double that arrested.[48] During this period of tension there were other riots at US petrol stations. The authorities should, perhaps, have been better prepared, because contingency plans to ration gasoline fairly were available from the first crisis in 1973, whose catalyst had been the Arab–Israeli war. Then, oil prices went up fourfold.

A Congressional declaration of purpose stated that 'positive and effective action' was needed to protect 'general welfare . . . conserve scarce energy supplies' and 'insure fair and efficient distribution'.[49] Britain had similar plans to reintroduce official rationing. It didn't happen, but some petrol stations did limit how much they sold to individual customers.

In 1979 rumblings began from a particular geopolitics that regularly repeats itself, and is doing so again as I write. The revolution in Iran, itself the result of decades of colonial and post-colonial skulduggery to do with access to oil, led to a halt in exports. The price of oil is increasingly volatile, going up and down, but remains at historically high levels as sabres rattle again between Europe, the US and Iran. Reality confounds the habitual over-optimism of the industry. At the end of the last millennium, the International Energy Agency (IEA), US Department of Energy and the US Geological Survey all confidently predicted that oil would remain at around $20 per barrel.[50] For reasons explored below, the long-term direction for prices is one-way: up.

One difference is that in 1979 Saudi Arabia was able to act as a so-called 'swing producer', increasing production to compensate for a loss of supply elsewhere. Today, producers lack the slack production capacity to do that.

Although on the verge of introducing rationing in the US during the 1979 OPEC crisis, instead drivers were exhorted to drive at optimum, fuel-efficient speeds, share cars and avoid unnecessary leisure travel. In the US there was reduced car use, and shifts to car sharing and an increased use of public transport. Actual car ownership levels didn't change, but there was evidence of people buying more fuel-efficient cars.

In one study of vehicle use in the state of Washington, over half of the people questioned, 58 per cent, had changed their travel habits in some way.[51] A quarter altered their mode of transport and there was a short-lived increase in the use of buses, against a long-term downward trend.

That was around the height of the Cold War, when Middle Eastern politics were a theatre of influence for the two great wrangling super-powers, the United States and the Soviet Union. The end of the Cold War had an obvious, dramatic effect on countries like Cuba, which lived on the front line between them, but the subsequent period of transition gives much to reflect on. For one thing, there was meant to be a peace dividend at the end of the Cold War. It never lived up to expectations.

The loss of the bipolar world when the Soviet Union collapsed meant that Britain and the rest of Europe no longer faced a large-scale strategic threat. There was potential for the major reorientation of military spending. Swords into ploughshares had the chance to become reality. And, indeed, some things did change.

Over a ten-year period from 1985 the number of jobs in the UK's military and defence sector fell from around 625,000 to 410,000, work-ers who were generally reabsorbed into the wider economy.[52] Today there are planned reductions to the year 2020 in the numbers of key types of UK military hardware (as much the product of generalised spending cuts brought on by economic problems as chosen strategic changes). These range from battle tanks to heavy artillery, ships (destroyers and frigates) and jet fighters.

And yet, the UK has the fourth-largest military budget in the world, behind only the United States, China and France. It has risen by 28 per cent since the year 2000. Dr Stuart Parkinson of Scientists for Global Responsibility points out that military spending per person in the UK is twice that in Russia, twelve times the level in China, and both per person and in relation to the scale of its economy it is far above the average level in the European Union. The UK is also the fifth-largest arms exporter.

More than that, it recently recommitted itself to one of the more expensive offspring of the Cold War, the Trident nuclear missile system. It was a decision made in full awareness of the radical changes in security threats of the previous two decades that rendered the system strategically of little if any use. Over a thirty-year period the Trident replacement is expected to cost an estimated £97 billion. Two new aircraft super-carriers whose strategic value has also been questioned (and which will have to operate for several years without the aircraft they were designed for) are expected to cost a further £31 billion over fifty years.

When it comes to costs, however, there is always the need to be extremely circumspect even about generous-sounding estimates. Military procurement is notorious for delivering late and over budget. A report leaked from within the Ministry of Defence itself in 2009 made the candid observation: 'How can it be that it takes twenty years to build a ship, or aircraft, or tank? Why does it always seem to cost at least twice what was thought? Even worse, at the end of the wait, why does it never quite seem to do what it was supposed to?'[53]

Late, over budget or even not very strategic, the defence of military expenditure sooner or later resolves into an argument about jobs. However pricey, useless, or indeed murderous, the cry of job protection is heard.

Yet the military sector has long been known as a capital- not an employment-intensive sector. For every pound or dollar of public money spent, if it is simply jobs that are wanted there are many more productive sectors to choose from. The University of Massachusetts studied how many jobs would likely be created in a range of public spending arenas in return for a notional budget of $1 billion. They took the military sector as a baseline against which to compare other significant public spending budgets like education and health, but also those of particular interest for a society that needs to make a rapid transition to a low-carbon economy. Hence, public transport, new house building (new homes are built to much tougher energy-efficiency standards) and retrofitting existing homes for energy efficiency were included. They didn't especially focus on broader notions of social value and general productivity (not for nothing is military spending known among economists as 'unproductive expenditure'). But even where just employment was concerned, for every dollar invested, all these other sectors created more jobs, some many more so. Health care and housing both produced 50 per cent more jobs, education 107 per cent and public transport 131 per cent.

It would seem that, far from a peace dividend, in the period since the end of the Cold War hawkish foreign policy has turned public spending priorities away both from investing in jobs and social development and from making the urgent transition to a low-carbon economy. For example, the cost of a single £90 million Eurofighter aircraft would pay for a 90-megawatt wind farm. That is the size of the

30-turbine Barrow-in-Furness offshore wind farm in the Irish Sea opened in 2006.

In terms of publicly funded UK research and development, Parkinson points out that as of 2009, at just over £2.2 billion, military spending in this area is over thirty-three times greater than the sums being invested in renewable energy.[54] Apart from all the previous arguments, the broad-spectrum threats of climate change and energy insecurity to the UK suggest that investing in renewable energy could even be a much better bet where the security of the nation is concerned (see chapter 8). Joseph Stiglitz and Linda Bilmes estimated in 2008 that the Iraq war cost the US a minimum of $3 trillion, and much more in the long term, which might have been more productively spent.[55]

It is little comfort to know that we were not the only side at the end of the Cold War to make mistakes and miss opportunities. The meaning of the term 'transition' in economics is shifting. Today, increasingly, it refers to the shift towards a low-carbon economy. But for years after 1989 it applied mainly to the weaning of former communist bloc countries onto market economies, and similar shifts elsewhere.

Andrei Shleifer is a Russian-born but American-trained economist based at Harvard University, who was invited on the twentieth anniversary of post-Cold War economic change to reflect on the lessons of that transition.[56] Comparing the fully centralised state control of the economy that came before with the broad spectrum of market-based alternatives, Shleifer concluded that the latter worked. But there was much more to it than that.

Far from the instant benefits that were expected from a shift to a market system, to the architects of change the speed and scale of economic decline actually witnessed in Eastern Europe and the former Soviet Union 'was a big surprise'. Market theory dictated that deregulation and the free movement of prices would automatically improve the allocation of resources in the economies. Instead, things fell apart. Positive change would take longer. In fact, life expectancy in Russia fell noticeably as a kind of terrifying 'gangster capitalism' took hold. Dubious deals were done, selling off national assets through networks of political cronyism. For those who could afford them, there were more and different goods in the shops, but there was great insecurity too. Depending on their contacts, enterprising individuals who wanted to 'get on' could easily end up either rich or dead.

This legacy still shrouds modern Russia, with economically motivated assassinations not unusual and oligarchs of the early transition period either operating as precariously balanced political kingmakers, or in prison.

This goes some way towards explaining what remains to Shleifer the 'surprise and major puzzle' that 'people in all transition countries were unhappy with transition: they were unhappy even in countries with rapidly improving quality of life'. I suspect that by 'quality of life' – more usually a subjective assessment of life satisfaction – Shleifer means 'standard of living' – a description of income and consumption levels. We have seen that these are two different things.

In relation to the large body of evidence surrounding the determinants of human well-being, it is neither surprising nor puzzling for someone to experience a higher material standard of living and yet, due to circumstances of extreme economic, social, cultural and political insecurity, to be very unhappy at the same time. To think otherwise is to have internalised the propaganda of marginal utility theory, described at the start of the book, which takes the one-dimensional view that the only meaningful indication of economic welfare is how much we spend, as by doing so we are 'expressing our preferences and maximising our utility'.

The other 'surprise' was that the oligarchs emerged at all as a 'new economic elite' to dominate politics. Although why, again, this proved a surprise is a good question. These were states where for decades real democratic civic participation had been suppressed. There was an utter asymmetry of benefit between those in power, with connections both inside and outside the old state apparatus, and those without. Overnight deregulation made a grab of state assets by the powerful almost inevitable.

In this light, Shleifer comments with delicious understatement that 'economists and reformers overstated both their ability to sequence reforms, and the importance of particular tactical choices, *e.g.*, in privatization'. The architects of change, he writes, 'had a vastly overstated sense of control'. With lessons for more recent crisis periods, he also observes that debt defaults or restructuring (usually the same thing, but more orderly) are nowhere near as bad an option for wrecked economies as the self-interested financial markets often make out. Very often they clear the way for recovery, as happened in

East Asia and Argentina. 'This experience bears a profound lesson for reformers, who are always intimidated by the international financial community,' he adds.

Times of extreme upheaval offer great lessons. They expose hidden stresses, exaggerate mistakes and reveal the benefits or costs of the decisions a society takes like no other time. They are, as Churchill put it, periods of consequences. A combination of economic chaos, resource depletion, inequality and climate change creates our own 'period of consequences'. In each of these historical examples lie lessons about impermanence and the possibility of collapse, but also about the great human potential for rapid transformation. We should not attempt merely to copy examples from history, but they can give pointers to successful approaches, and also to the scale of what we might expect from ourselves as societies. At the very least, history invites us to raise our sights.

Memory is as important to resilience as yeast is to bread. One reason that Hurricane Katrina in 2005 became so disastrous for New Orleans was that the carefully recorded lessons of Hurricane Betsy, forty years earlier, were ignored by hazard planners in Louisiana.[57] Work with Holocaust survivors also shows the importance of memory for resilience. Remembering the past, sharing stories of how and why people survived, and reconciling great injustice, all support rebuilding of lives and future endurance. The next chapter looks at challenges and responses to do with food and energy. Even where major global challenges are concerned, some answers can be found very close to home, in seemingly prosaic places. With ecosystems in decline and food chains under threat, a study of allotment gardens in Sweden found them to be rich crucibles of memory, key to ecological and community resilience.[58] They help the wider urban environment by aiding pollination, pest control and seed spreading. At the same time the stories, practices, rituals, as well as the human relationships, and gardens and tools themselves, all strengthen ecosystems and the communities that depend on them in times of crisis. As the next chapter shows, such memories will be increasingly in demand.

8

The Mechanisms

Nine meals from anarchy

Man has lost the capacity to foresee and forestall.

Albert Schweitzer

One morning in the first summer of the new millennium, the year 2000, it looked as if Britain was about to be returned to a much earlier age. An unusual gathering at the heart of the British government in Whitehall was full of worried men from several very powerful companies.

Around Britain farmers and truck drivers, angered by the rising cost of keeping their vehicles on the road, were blockading fuel depots. They had found, and were paralysing, the critical infrastructure of a major industrialised country more effectively than any terrorist organisation had ever done. At the height of the protests, hunkered down in nervous meetings, Britain's biggest supermarkets, accounting for around 80 per cent of the nation's food supply, told ministers and civil servants that their shelves could be bare within three days.

The country was, in effect, nine meals from anarchy.

Nothing reveals the thin veneer of civilisation like a threat to its food or fuel supply, or the cracks in society like a major climate-related disaster such as the collapse of public order in New Orleans following Hurricane Katrina. A blend of all three will give cold sweats to the most hardened emergency planner. But, increasingly, that is what we face. Looming, potentially irreversible global warming; the global peak and decline of oil production; and a global food chain in crisis – these are three linked, interacting dynamics. All are complicated by that other shock, the after-effects of the rich world's debt crisis.

Since I was a young teenager, I've been quietly haunted by Doris Lessing's book *The Memoirs of a Survivor*. In it, for some reason left vague, society has broken down. Everywhere people are on the move, displaced, the lucky few leaving the city to stay with relatives in the country. The presiding government is useless but just about able to 'adjust itself to events, while pretending probably even to itself that it initiated them'.

In Britain, the outset of the Second World War became known as the 'phoney war' because there was no fighting and the conflict seemed distant, theoretical and unreal. In spite of all the reporting, there remains something of a 'phoney calm' surrounding current apocalyptic threats that belies their seriousness.

For an official assessment of the issues at stake in the fuel protests of 2000, it was easier to find Canadian sources than British ones. A search for the term 'fuel protests' in general, not even specifically for the year 2000, on the website of the prime minister's office (Number10.go.uk), returned '0' hits. Odd in any circumstance, given that they became a regular feature of political life, and can quickly and efficiently destabilise civil order. A similar search of the Department for Transport's website returned fifteen hits. Almost entirely these dealt simply with the fact that road traffic and congestion statistics for that year had been affected by the protests, and included no other analysis.

Finally, I turned to the Home Office, whose brief covers policing, public disorder, crime and counterterrorism, and found not a single document concerning 'fuel protests'. Odd, very odd. A last throw of the dice. I type 'cobra' into direct.gov.uk, the official website covering 'public services all in one place'. Cobra is the name of the special civil contingencies committee, made up of representatives from multiple government departments, emergency services and the security establishment. It deals with threats to the state. A single item appears. I click on the link. It takes me to an 'error' page.

Of course this doesn't mean that key British government departments did not reflect in detail on the implications of the fuel protests

(I hope and think that they did). But it does mean that, in a democracy, they are oddly reticent about sharing their conclusions. Canadian sources, however, were more forthcoming.[1] Public Safety Canada is the government department charged with keeping 'Canadians safe from a range of risks'. It deals with emergencies and threats to critical infrastructure, and studied carefully what happened in the UK.

In case you weren't there, or can't remember, fuel prices became a political issue over the course of that summer. The opposition Conservative Party, led by William Hague, encouraged protest by organising a day of action in late July. In August there was a call to boycott petrol pumps. Then in early September 2000 a group of British farmers and truck drivers decided to stage large-scale protests. They were angry at the price of fuel and, worse, embarrassed by the fact that French farmers had been quicker and better at demonstrating, and had already won concessions from their government.

While the British protesters were determined to make a point, even they were astonished at the speed and staggering degree to which they brought the country to a standstill. A blockade of fuel terminals and oil refineries spread quickly. As the Canadian government warily observed: 'The impact of the protest was much deeper than anticipated because it struck at a particularly vulnerable point of the UK economy – the oil distribution network, which had been organised along just-in-time delivery principles.'

These 'delivery principles', used by the fuel companies, were the same as those used to organise the food system. Within days the protests created 'a fuel crisis that paralysed Critical Infrastructure sectors and brought the country to a virtual halt'. Anticipated shortages and panic buying then created 'a chain reaction' across sectors ranging from transport to health care, food distribution, and financial and government services. The weakest, as usual, were most vulnerable. The NHS, for example, has to serve nearly one million meals per day and would quickly have faced having to deprive those weak from ill health.[2]

The government finally realised the seriousness of the situation and strong-armed the key parties – farmers, truck drivers, oil companies – into signing a Memorandum of Understanding to prevent anything similar happening again. But the incident revealed just how fragile were the foundations of public order. Here was a heavily interconnected industrialised economy, over-reliant on oil and highly centralised distribution systems, brought to the edge of upheaval by a simple disruption of supply.

A subsequent assessment in a journal article commented that:

> At one level, it [the government] seemed totally unprepared for the fuel protests, with its crisis management strategies, which centred on a combination of public discourse and crisis management committees, appearing to lack strategic planning ... the tanker drivers appeared reluctant to drive through the 'blockades'; the police and oil companies appeared reluctant to clear the protest sites; the public engaged in widespread 'panic buying' of fuel.[3]

More protests were seen in the following decade, though with less effect, but we remain as dependent on oil as ever, and any impression of long-term stability is a dangerous illusion. Because the downside of globalisation and complex economic interdependence is a world in which shocks, stresses and crashes are transmitted ever faster through the media, financial markets and along supply lines which, in the name of economic efficiency, have been stripped of the 'slack' that any system needs to be resilient, the crucial ability to tolerate shocks. This is the 'shock propagation' described earlier by Haldane and May in relation to banking and the lack of resilience in an over-exploited ecosystem. In earthquake zones regulations demand that buildings are constructed with special architectural features to withstand seismic shocks.

The infrastructure and logistics of globalised food and energy supply chains, by contrast, is like a cheap shack built where multiple faultlines intersect but lacking any feature to brace or dampen shocks. It would be hard to do better if someone had deliberately designed a system made expressly to amplify and convey shocks with devastating consequences.

Decades of unsustainable financial markets and rising levels of consumption have left fissures everywhere, from the rocky ground of US sub-prime mortgages to farms that once grew food for people to eat but that now produce biofuels to keep roads clogged with cars. The inherent resilience of the systems we depend on is taken for granted, largely on the broad assumption that the market can and will always provide. Yet the very narrow efficiencies demanded by the market have themselves driven the vulnerabilities of the infrastructure depended on by the market. As J. K. Galbraith observed of banking in the United States, it is a system that needs saving from itself (and then, of course, replacing with something better).

Nature provides a perfect example, and accidentally a broader analogy, for this false assumption. When the full scale of the 2008 financial crash became apparent, it wasn't only businesses, neighbourhoods and bank branches that were falling silent. Stress and substance abuse may have been common in banking, and led to a toxic environment in which parasitic behaviour flourished, but there was another community suffering in a similar but far more blameless way – the community of bees.

Their fate introduced the phrase Colony Collapse Disorder to public debate. Something was killing the bees, but what exactly? Was it pesticides, pathogens or parasites?[4] Possibly a combination of all of these, exacerbated, interestingly, by poor diet. The spread of industrial agriculture and its monocultures, in which vast areas of land are planted with single crops, seems to have left bees sickly, their defences down, just as a diet of only one thing would do to your or my immune system.[5]

It's a crisis, and not just for the bees. About one in every three mouthfuls of food you eat relies, more or less, on honey-bee pollination. Everything ranging from fruit and nuts to salad plants, broccoli, rapeseed, coffee, beans, turnips and pumpkins needs bees to pollinate it. The journal *Scientific American* reported that this placed one hundred crops at risk.[6] Since 2006, in the US beekeepers have been reporting losses of between three and nine out of every ten of their hives. Even if it was physically possible – imagine, momentarily, the fields and orchards of the world crowded with human legions carrying pollen-loaded loaded cotton buds, a floral army of millions to stand in for the public-spirited honey bees – the cost of replacing bee pollination in the US alone has been estimated as up to $92 billion.[7] The British Beekeepers Association warned that honey bees could disappear from Britain by 2018.[8]

It is, perhaps, a reflection of our inverted priorities that while overpaid bank executives are still very much with us, the bees are so threatened. There is the honey bee: productive, useful and communal –

a deliverer of free, life-giving, ecological services worth billions. Then there is the investment banker: destructive, rent-seeking and self-satisfied – a wrecker of homes and livelihoods, who loses billions.

In 2008 the UN reported that the rising price of food, driven by fuel prices, climate impacts and speculation, added over 75 million people to the roll-call of the hungry in the world, those rated 'undernourished' by the World Health Organization, bringing the total to around 1 billion (this figure has subsequently been revised down somewhat due to improved data collection, but remains very large).[9] In April that year, thirty-seven countries were facing a food crisis due to a mix of conflict and economic and climate-related problems.[10] There was rioting in the streets from Haiti to Egypt, India and Burkina Faso.

Stocks of rice, on which half the world depends, hit their lowest level since the 1970s. At the same time, US wheat stocks were forecast to drop to their lowest levels since 1948, when the country was helping to rebuild a shattered and hungry post-war Europe. Down from over nearly eight hundred million bushels in 2001 to fewer than three hundred million,[11] the USDA estimated supplies were enough to last thirty-five days. The American Bakers Association said it left them a supply-cushion of just twenty-four days, compared with a more typical three months. The National Family Farm Coalition and other groups called for a strategic grain reserve to be set up, emulating what is done with oil in the name of national security.[12]

In Britain, until the early 1990s secret food stocks of easily stored basics like biscuits and flour were held officially. Today, the government depends on retailers to keep 'buffer' reserves. But our highly centralised supermarkets, which dominate the grocery market and food chain, operate on the basis of 'just in time' delivery. It is designed to lower their costs. They don't want to keep large stocks lying around just in case of emergency, taking up expensive space.

After another road hauliers' strike in 2008, *The Times* reported that there was government pressure on the retailers to take responsibility for future contingency plans in the event of immediate threats to food supplies.[13] A key role in the discussions was highlighted for Tesco. Reportedly the supermarket pushed to be represented on the Cabinet's high-level and highly secret emergency civil contingency committee, Cobra, should there be a crisis. Were that the case, it would make a private company, a supermarket that otherwise lacks any democratic accountability, a party to the state's highest levels. Cobra has powers under part two of the Civil Contingencies Act, which means it can, if circumstances are considered sufficiently serious: suspend Parliament, close businesses by declaring a bank holiday, shut down businesses, destroy or requisition property, ban the freedom of assembly and movement, mobilise the armed forces and set up 'special courts'.

Against this backdrop, the UK's national food self-sufficiency has been in long-term decline. It fell by over one fifth in the decade from 1995.[14] But official statistics can obscure the real picture. The government claim that we are 60 per cent self-sufficient has been criticised as misleading by the Soil Association, who point out that less than 10 per cent of the fruit we eat is grown here, up to half our vegetables are imported and 70 per cent of animal feed used across the EU is imported.[15]

In the UK, rising dependence on imported food now sees the national level of self-sufficiency at a four-decade low point. Let alone Schweitzer's fear that humanity has lost its ability to 'foresee and forestall', it would help if it could retain just a little short-term memory. Three years after the food–climate–oil–banking quadruple whammy of 2008, food and oil prices globally were rising again. (For the record, the banks were also still in chaos and in spite of the ensuing recession, which normally reduces greenhouse gas emissions, those too were rising.) There were foreign land-grabs in Africa, food nationalism was on the rise and grain export embargoes out of Russia, an important global wheat producer. The geopolitics of food has easily become a match for the geopolitics of oil.

The different crises followed each other's examples. At the height of the banking crisis in 2008, George Soros, compared the behaviour of banks and capital markets to the hoarding of food during a famine. In an interview with the German magazine *Stern*, he said about the financial crisis: 'Speculators create the bubble that lies above everything. Their expectations, their gambling on futures help drive up prices, and their business distorts prices, which is especially true for commodities. It is like hoarding food in the midst of a famine, only to make profits on rising prices. That should not be possible.'[16]

Ironically, in 2011 Soros was reported to be 'making a move to control food and grain production' in the United States.[17] He had, it was said, 'both the economic, and political clout to begin consolidation of purchasing and shipping domestic agriculture around the world'. If successful, he would be left with a stake in America's third-largest grain company, creating a situation that leads to 'the same results that we see in the energy markets as oil is controlled by a small group of corporations, and the price can be dictated by an artificial control over its supply'. A proposed merger between the giant and secretive Swiss commodity trader Glencore, whose annual revenue most recently stood at $186 billion, and the equally giant Swiss-owned mining company Xstrata, with sales of $34 billion, would take this trend to another level. Glencore trades food crops like wheat and sugar, metals, coal (92 million tonnes in 2011) and shares in mining companies. Xstrata digs things out of the ground: 85 million tonnes of coal in 2011 and a range of metals. If successful, the resulting merged company would be so powerful according to the *Financial Times*, becoming the seventh-largest firm in the FTSE 100 list, that it would 'reshape the industry'.[18]

Commodity speculation increased dramatically in the aftermath of the financial crisis, as investors sought more tangible investment opportunities from which to profit than esoteric financial products. The consequence for those at the bottom of the global income distribution was to see food taken out of their reach. The World Development Movement, a UK-based campaign group, estimated that Barclays Capital made up to £340 million per year from speculating on food prices, and in the process drove up the cost of food, 'leaving millions facing hunger and malnutrition'.[19]

Speculation is not the only increased stress on the world's food chain. There is the rise in demand for feed for meat production to supply the rapidly expanding affluent middle classes in China and other developing nations. Rising competition from the use of agricultural commodities, such as maize in the USA, as biofuels has an impact that is likely to worsen as conventional oil supplies are constrained and demand for fuel increases. Poor harvests resulting from increasing climatic extremes – such as Australia's failed wheat harvest in 2007 – put pressure on global prices. And the volatile but in the long run high and rising price of oil raises the cost of farm inputs.

So, having relied on global markets for decades to provide when-ever needed, countries like the UK are increasingly dependent on imports at precisely the time when, for several reasons, the guarantee of the rest of the world's ability to provide for us is weakening. Add to all these vulnerabilities the fact that up to three quarters of agriculture biodiversity is thought to have been lost over the last century. The most significant driver of this trend, large-scale monocultures, has left us in a situation whereby three quarters of the world's food is grown from only twelve plant types and five animal species – cattle, sheep, pigs, goats and chickens. In this worldwide variety show, our ability to feed ourselves wobbles like a waiter carrying trays, stood on a chair, balanced on one leg on top of a ball, while the audience holds its breath and waits for the fall.

'Oil is the trouble, of course,' wrote Gertrude Bell in Baghdad in 1921. 'Detestable stuff!' In her time it had fuelled one world war and already was causing upheaval in the politics of the Middle East. For all that, the problem for Bell, and now the rest of us, is that oil proved just too useful – concentrated energy, easily transported and hugely versatile. In Lord Curzon's famous phrase about the First World War, Britain 'floated to victory on a wave of oil', which then carried before it the modern age and the whole of consumer society.

We all became, and remain, addicted to its convenience. Today's energy supplies provide the equivalent of the work of 22 billion slaves, according to the former oil industry worker Colin Campbell. But now the wave of oil looks set to leave us high and dry. A funda-mental problem looms more and more visibly ahead, in which rising demand departs from flattening supply, leading to a shortage in the supply of the global economy's lifeblood. In economic textbooks demand always equals supply, but because this doesn't happen in any meaningful way in the real world, economists have the quaint notion of 'unmet' demand for when the market fails to provide, which makes everything add up once more.

Unmet demand in energy is set to provide a major external shock to global livelihoods. Until now, two beliefs have provided false reassur-ance that we can carry on as we are. The first is that there is still oil, the second that new oilfields are still being discovered. And, yes, there is still oil and small new amounts are being found. But the situation is like knowing there are ten mouths to feed tomorrow, yet only stores enough for eight. Worse, each day less food is replaced than the amount eaten, while the number of mouths to feed increases. In the late 1980s fifteen big oilfields were capable of supplying 1 million barrels a day. In two decades that fell to only four able to produce at that rate.[20]

New discoveries of oil peaked in the mid-1960s, and based on a range of estimates we are either near to or possibly living through the peak of global oil production.[21] After that, the gap between demand and production inexorably widens. The difficulty of knowing exactly when is heightened by the political and economic sensitivity of gauging the size of a nation's oil reserves. Publicly available figures are open to question. Let's dip into some conventional 'old economics': oil and the rudiments of supply and demand, as surveyed in a publication called the *Medium Term Oil Market Report*. Given that the global economy still wholly depends on a steady flow of oil to function, the report's publisher, the International Energy Agency, an official adviser to most of the major economic powers, words its warnings carefully to avoid panic.

But this is what it said against a background of protests in 2008 about world oil production. There would be 'a narrowing of spare capacity to minimal levels by 2013', and compared with the previous year alone it had made 'significant downward revisions' on 'both non-OPEC supplies and OPEC capacity forecasts'. Until fairly recently, interest in the subject and implications of so-called 'peak oil' was a specialist affair. The IEA may not have said so explicitly, but the words sat on the page: the fuel price rises of that year were almost certainly a foretaste of a far more massive crunch to follow.[22]

The Agency's motto is 'energy security, growth and sustainability', which is odd, given that none of those conditions seem actually to apply. For example, since North Sea production peaked around 1999, hopeful eyes have looked to the major producers like Saudi Arabia to keep the economy's arteries full of oil. Saudi Arabia is the world's leading oil supplier, and just seven producers account for more than half of all production. The others are Russia, the US, Iran, China, Mexico and Canada.

The true level of the Saudi Arabian reserves is widely open to question, however. Official documents released by the website WikiLeaks showed US embassy communications pouring scorn behind the scenes over Saudi claims for the size of its reserves.[23] But however much oil Saudi Arabia has left, it has other ideas about how it will be used than simply helping out Europe and North America. Over the next twelve years it will be spending around $600 billion on a massive domestic infrastructure programme, including power stations, industrial cities, aluminium smelters and chemical plants (about the same staggering figure that the US injected into its economy at the height of the bank crisis to prop up its financial system). And while doubts persist that their reserves are a lot less than publicly stated, all these new developments will be powered with Saudi oil. The rest of the world should not hold its breath waiting to be rescued.[24]

Some people might think that the decline of oil is a good thing from an environmental perspective. After all, if the oil is running out, doesn't that help solve climate change? Unfortunately not. As the price of oil goes up it makes other, dirtier fossil fuels like brown coal and tar sands more attractive. And here is a problem even for people who discount the threat of global warming. In key areas of the economy like transport, especially aviation, and agriculture, oil is hard to replace.

During the 1970s OPEC crises, the worst effects were moderated by swing producers, oil exporters who replaced access lost by the West to key suppliers. Those options are no longer available. Back then, Britain turned to its own fossil fuels. Today it no longer can. The 'energy dependence' factor describes the ratio of net energy imports to demand. When it becomes 'positive' it means that a country is obliged to import energy to meet its demand – in other words, energy independence declines, and meeting domestic needs relies increasingly on the whims and vagaries of global energy geopolitics. Britain lost its 'independence' in 2004, five years after North Sea production peaked, and its energy dependence factor rose fivefold by 2008, increasing by 30 per cent between 2007 and 2008 alone.[25]

In Britain, high hopes rest in the giant pipelines bringing liquefied natural gas from Norway and the Netherlands. The single giant 1200-km Langeled pipeline from Norway is set to provide up to a quarter of our demand for gas. Currently there are just two terminals where the gas comes ashore. Where domestic oil is concerned, a strike at the Grangemouth oil refinery in 2008 halted a large proportion of the UK's

North Sea production. As Jeremy Leggett, the head of Solarcentury, a renewable energy company, and author of *Half Gone: Oil, Gas, Hot Air and the Global Energy Crisis*, puts it: 'We smell in that drama just how fragile the whole energy edifice is.'[26]

Gal Luft, executive director of the US-based Institute for the Analysis of Global Security, told *New Scientist*: 'There is absolutely no slack in the system any more,' leaving the magazine to conclude that: 'This has left the oil market so fragile that a few well-placed explosives, an energy-sapping cold winter or an unusually intense hurricane season could send shock waves across the globe.' Emergency planners face the prospect of what is termed a 'psychological avalanche'.[27]

An international fleet of four thousand tankers delivers over 43 million barrels of oil a day along just six main routes, many of which have narrow 'choke points'. In one official exercise, described by a former head of the CIA as 'relatively mild compared to what is possible', a chain of events that disrupted supply lines led to the price of oil hitting $295, around three times its cost at the time of writing when high prices are already causing hardship.

Fossil fuels, food and climate change are impossible to separate. It was front-page news when the head of the Intergovernmental Panel on Climate Change, Rajendra Pachauri, called on people to reduce their intake of meat to help combat climate change. Amid the predictable culinary stirring of outrage, Pachauri successfully highlighted an easily overlooked fact. Not only is our food system especially vulnerable to global warming, it is also a major contributor to the problem. In the last year for which figures are readily available, 2003, Tesco's lorries alone travelled 68 million miles, the equivalent of about 142 round trips to the moon.[28]

Overall, greenhouse gases from farming are similar to those from industry and greater than those from transport.[29] According to another branch of the UN, the FAO, livestock production accounts for nearly one fifth of all emissions.[30] As a long-term vegetarian I should declare an interest. But leaving aside other concerns, such as animal welfare, there is a startling difference in energy efficiency between predominantly meat- and plant-based diets.

There are almost as many different ways to farm as there are farmers and ecosystems, and any system can be organised with greater or lesser efficiency. But it can take on average 2.2 kilocalories of fossil fuel energy to extract 1 kilocalorie of plant-based food.[31] Meat, on the other hand, has been estimated to have an average input/output ratio of 25:1.[32] Researchers at Cornell University calculated that producing beef cattle requires an energy input to protein output ratio of a staggering 54:1, and that the grain eaten by US livestock at the time of the study in the 1990s could feed eight hundred million people.[33]

The FAO predicts that on current trends the 60 billion count of global livestock will double by the year 2050 to 120 billion.[34] Globally, one third of arable land is set aside for growing animal feed, and over 90 per cent of soya beans and around 60 per cent of maize and barley are destined for cattle, pigs and poultry.[35] Aside from choice between meat-based and plant-based diets, the other great, important distinction is between intensive farming, reliant on large inputs of fossil-fuel-intensive, artificial chemical fertilisers and pesticides, on the one hand, and the range of organic approaches on the other. Intensive farming's biggest energy use stems from its need to defy ecological gravity. Over one third, 37 per cent, is used in the manufacture of nitrogen fertiliser, without which the soil upon which it depends would be rapidly exhausted, and its superficially impressive productivity would be impossible.[36]

According to figures from the UK's Department for Environment, Food and Rural Affairs (Defra), organic farming uses, in general, over a quarter less energy compared with non-organic farming to produce the same amount of food.[37] Today's high and volatile price of oil means, says the Soil Association, that the 'linchpin' of industrial agriculture's efficiency claims is now lost.[38] In the wake of increasingly energy-intensive meat-based diets, the WHO also warns of a dramatic growth in diseases linked to lifestyle and diet. Conditions like heart disease, strokes and cancer are set to rise rapidly alongside the incidence of obesity. It sounds strange the first time you say it out loud, but obesity, too, is a climate-change issue.

Those indulgences that spend a moment on your lips before spending a lifetime on your hips typically come from an oil-addicted farming system, not to mention the petrol-hungry car transport that reinforces sedentary lifestyles. The clue is in the term of measurement – calories – and the fact that we need to consume a lot less of those that stem from fossil fuels. But it's not just about climate change, it's about social justice too. While food prices pushed the number of hungry people to nearly 1 billion, there are also over 1 billion overweight people in the world.[39] Both the hungry and the overweight suffer from a different kind of malnutrition.

For my part, I have a daughter who, as a four-year-old, was not yet ready to read or write. She was given a plain cardboard lunch box at an event, not from any food chain, but it had some writing on it, including one crucial letter. She looked at me enquiringly and said: 'With the "M" – food in a box is a Happy Meal.' No, it wasn't, and she had never been taken through those golden arches for a burger of any description. But why she was susceptible is explained in chapter 9. Academics at the London School of Hygiene and Tropical Medicine say that tackling obesity is an essential part of both halting climate change *and* dealing with the food crisis.[40] They point out: 'Petrol tanks and stomachs were competing well before biofuels wer proposed to tackle climate change.' Ian Roberts, professor of Public Health, commented that: 'Fats and refined sugars, which tend to dominate the diets of obese people, are particularly carbon intensive.'[41] Heavier people require more energy to move around, just as bigger heavier cars use more petrol, and bigger people also burn more calories while at rest. Roberts and fellow researchers made headlines when they calculated that if everyone in the world had the same body mass as the average American (Americans weigh in at an average 80.7 kg compared with a global average of just 62 kg), it would be the equivalent of having an extra 58 million tonnes of humanity, or nearly 1 billion more people to feed. Levels of consumption, therefore, matter as much as absolute numbers in the debate on human environmental impact.[42]

The push factor of massively rising biofuel demand is also having striking effects. The IMF estimated that this caused 70 per cent of the rise in corn prices and 40 per cent of soya bean price rises in 2008.[43] The president of the FAO lamented how in 2006, 11 to 12 billion dollars a year in subsidies and protective tariff policies had 'the effect of diverting 100 million tonnes of cereals from human consumption, mostly to satisfy the thirst for fuel for vehicles'.[44]

He added, for good measure, that in the same year rich countries distorted world food markets with $372 billion in subsidies, that a single country (he means the US) wasted $100 billion worth of food, and that the 'obesity bill' came to $20 billion. Yet all it would take to guarantee the right to food, and thus the right to life, would be an extra $30 billion spent on a mixture of supporting small-scale farming, land reform and better distribution. In some areas the food crisis has been cynically co-opted to promote existing, asymmetrical market liberalisation and commercial agendas.[45] So-called EU cooperation programmes stand to make matters worse where, directly and indirectly, they promote the increasing dependence of small-scale farmers on highly volatile and rising oil prices; and in energy policies that promote agrofuels for transport.[46]

Then, of course, there is the appalling wastefulness of an international trading system that ignores the real cost of transport. Its arteries and veins quietly ossify with carbon as we watch the most peculiar range of goods going backwards and forwards, something we'll discuss at greater length in chapter 10. We worship the supposed 'efficiency' of supermarkets, but forget the fact that, according to the government waste agency WRAP, in the grip of their marketing we end up simply throwing away one bag in every three of the groceries they sell us.

In the face of such waste, worsening projections for climate change present a growing threat to our food supply. Even as we sit in the early days of the disruption, statistics indicate combined annual losses of wheat, maize and barley measuring around 40 million tonnes since 1981 due to temperature rises.[47] But what keeps me awake at night are projections for what could happen to the planet's hydrological cycle. Much of the food of the poor, especially in Africa, comes from rain-fed farming, yet new models of future global drought patterns come to genuinely apocalyptic conclusions for the food chain and human survival.

The UK's Hadley Centre for Climate Prediction and Research looked at the share of the Earth's land surface prone to extreme, severe and moderate drought.[48] It found that the area of the Earth's land surface suffering from extreme drought has trebled from just 1 to 3 per cent in less than a decade. The model projects that this trend will continue until extreme drought conditions affect over 8 per cent of the land surface by 2020 – and no less than 30 per cent of the globe by 2090. In recent history, a total of 20 per cent of the Earth's land surface has been in drought at any one time, be it extreme, severe or moderate. This has now risen to 28 per cent and is predicted to reach 35 per cent by 2020 and then half the Earth's land surface by 2090. Droughts will also be much longer in duration.

Crops become vulnerable to pests if rains come late and yields can drop sharply if the end of the season is too hot and dry. The international farming research group CGIAR (originally the Consultative Group on International Agricultural Research) points out that: 'Even a short reduction in the growing season can mean a complete crop failure.'[49] Reduced growing seasons are expected to hit West Africa and South Asia, where the 'entire breadbasket of the Indian subcontinent is at risk'.

Drought is projected to affect the great grain-growing areas of Europe, North America and Russia, as well as the Middle East and Central Asia, North Africa and Southern Africa, Amazonia in Brazil, and Central America. Although the models forecast a severe overall drying pattern, certain areas will get much wetter. A wetter future is forecast for Central Africa, the Horn and East Africa and parts of coastal West Africa, China and Eastern Asia, and high northern latitudes. In a warmer system, extremes become exaggerated, which means that higher rainfall could trigger destructive, heavy inundations, like the almost biblical floods that hit Pakistan in 2010.

If people cannot grow food to eat they will migrate. If they migrate there will be more competition for resources, and there will be conflict. Energy use, diet, transport and climate change are linked in many ways both as cause and consequence. Analogous to what has happened in finance, fossil fuel use has leveraged many into unsustainable lifestyles (whilst marginalising many others). Its sudden withdrawal due to rising prices and restricted availability could trigger 'de-leveraging', with dramatic consequences.

You might think that a logical, even self-interested response would be to ensure maximum self-sufficiency among the poor in the most populous parts of the world. Instead, the world's estimated four hundred million small-scale farmers, who feed over two billion people, mostly in Asia, face another threat: further marginalisation and insecurity as their national food economies are re-engineered, consolidated and centralised along Western lines by the major supermarkets. Asia, Latin

America and Africa are all targets of the likes of Wal-Mart, Carrefour and Tesco. As supermarkets increasingly capture the market for food in towns and cities, this also cuts off an economic lifeline for small-scale farmers, who once supplied the urban population through smaller stores and open-air markets. If wealthy farmers in Europe and America can't stand up to them, what chance for the smallholders of Asia?

All of these changes combined, along with the lasting inequities of global trade rules and bilateral economic bullying, explain why food riots are back with a chaotic vengeance. In Britain, another type of critical infrastructure is under threat from the inexorable rise of monopolistic retailers, whose model of expansion is the US-style suburban dead zone fed by the out-of-town big box retail park. Vibrant, diverse and independently owned local economies provide the social and economic glue that holds communities together. We've understood this at least since Jane Jacobs wrote *The Death and Life of Great American Cities*. As much as their vulnerable 'just-in-time' logistics, it is the surgical removal of the economic heart of communities by big retail that increases the frailty of society.

If you rip the oil drip from the economy's arm, the choice then is between economic seizure or transition. Driving to the supermarket, the range of food on the shelves, the family holiday in the sun, even how we brush our teeth in the morning – the whole character of modern living in rich countries relies on the assumption of cheap, abundant oil. Yet that can change as fast as the price of a commodity on the stock exchange. What would more secure, people- and environment-friendly food and energy systems look like? Will magic-bullet technologies save us, or are there better bets?

When I read that the author and high-profile environmentalist Mark Lynas wanted 'an environmental movement that is happy with capitalism',[50] I thought of the now infamous comment by Peter Mandelson, chief architect of the UK Labour Party's transformation into 'New Labour'. He quipped, in an accidentally era-defining way, that New Labour was 'intensely relaxed about people getting filthy rich'. To be fair, he went on to add: 'as long as they pay their taxes'. But his party in power presided over a tax system that included rules for the 'filthy rich' that guaranteed they wouldn't pay, such as non-domicile tax status.

At a stroke Mandelson distanced the modern party from its folk roots in the class struggle between rich and poor, between the owners of capital and its servants. Depending upon your point of view, this might be seen in modern terms as 'detoxifying' a brand, a betrayal of foundations and purpose, or simply conceding that there was, after all, only one way to organise the economy, with markets dominated by finance.

After capitalism's monumental failures, and having seen the filthy rich take the rest of us for a very unpleasant ride, Mandelson recanted. (Many politicians did likewise, even as they failed to reform a system that was commonly acknowledged to be broken, or to promote meaningful alternatives.) His rebrand foundered upon a deep contradiction. The means by which general prosperity had been pursued – giving excessive privileges to finance and its controllers – wrecked the objective. Self-interest and lack of concern for its impact on the wider economy introduced extreme instability and ultimately bankrupted the public purse, leading to a downward spiral of cuts, unemployment, recession and depression. Mandelson's newly chastened public persona arrived in time to witness the profit motive implicated in everything from the corruption of politics and the media to the asset stripping and undermining of care homes for the nation's elderly.

How was it then, just as capitalism's once ardent advocates grew aware of its flaws, that a prominent environmentalist should suddenly fall for its charms? Could it be simple contrarianism, driven by frustration at the lack of progress by other means? Lynas's views mattered because the media tend to be drawn, irresistibly, to those who appear to go against the grain, challenging received notions of what it means, in this case, to be an environmentalist.

But what exactly did Lynas mean by capitalism? It wasn't clear which variant of a market system would save us – aggressive Anglo-Saxon free-market capitalism, Scandinavian social democracy or emergent Chinese totalitarian capitalism. Clarity matters because if mainstream capitalism had to take a fresh MOT, it probably wouldn't be allowed on the road. Lynas's book *The God Species* was largely a sanctioned account of the work of the group of scientists behind the planetary boundaries research project described earlier. But Lynas went further, and his case struck sparks.

First, business as usual in economic terms looks bad for precisely the stressed planetary environmental boundaries he writes about. From the carbon cycle of the atmosphere, to biodiversity and the nitrogen cycle at the heart of farming, an expanding global economy has already pushed us beyond natural limits. Yet capitalism respects no such boundaries. It is hard-wired to indefinite accumulation and growth, with all that implies for resource use. It ushered in an age of rising inequality (examined more closely in chapter 10), an issue of social justice that Lynas chastises the environmental movement for also championing.

Turbo-capitalism, or the 'capitalist threat', as George Soros calls it, dramatically worsens inequality within and between countries. It results from a competitive, winner-take-all approach in which power is unequally distributed to begin with, and whereby the already wealthy further strengthen their position. As the income spread widens in weakly regulated capitalist markets, paradoxically the rich have to consume ever more, just to stop the poorest getting poorer. With a shrinking slice of the economic cake, the level of global consumption necessary to lift the poorest in the world onto just $3 per day would then need the natural resources of about fifteen planets like Earth to feed it.

In a physically limited system where growth is ultimately constrained, simple logic dictates that to increase the material standards of living of the poor must require better, more equal, distribution. If you cannot bake a bigger pie, you must get better at sharing what you have, otherwise you either condemn the poor to go without or crash the ecosystems that livelihoods depend on through overburdening them. That can't be good for anyone, including Lynas, who criticises others for conflating environmentalism and social justice. But he then performs an intellectual flip by invoking the needs of the poor to justify controversial technologies like genetic modification in the food system, and nuclear power as a means of energy generation.

In this, he and others find themselves advancing a point of view that, while possibly newer in environmental debates, is part of a much older, larger struggle of ideas. From how to feed and power the world and the climate-change issue, huge complex debates are being reduced to arguments about simply whether you are for or against particular technologies. So if you agree with genetically modified food and nuclear power you are cast as modern, rational, pro-science and in favour of human progress. If you disagree, you are anti-modern, Luddite . . . the whole reactionary ticket. There is the historical irony about accusations of Luddism that I explored in chapter 7, but this polarising proposition itself is open to charges of being unscientific, a self-interested claim to the mantle of modernity and progress. In both cases large-scale, centralised, top-down techno-fixes are offered as economically and politically neutral choices, in tune with scientific human advancement.

Yet both technologies carry with them, as mentioned, a sort of self-replicating DNA for the kind of food and energy systems they create. Which technology you choose – depending on the economic interests that own, control and promote it – determines a particular pattern of benefits that is likely to favour some groups over others. Choices are rarely if ever neutral. Nuclear power stations employ relatively few people directly. The technology requires secrecy for security reasons and, in the UK, has a dedicated, separate and routinely armed police force authorised to spy on public critics of nuclear power. Wind energy is different on all counts. The tension between energy technologies is explored more below.

That is why Professor Andy Stirling of the Science and Policy Research Unit (SPRU) at Sussex University makes the point that, even in the face of extreme environmental challenges, a range of energy systems is possible. Like Lynas, the journalist and environmentalist George Monbiot argues pointedly that other environmentalists must embrace nuclear power, and is scathing of those who reject it. Stirling, however, rebuked Monbiot for being so absolute, writing that 'the crucial issues include contending social values, political interests and future visions. To deny this and seek instead to assert ostensibly definitive technical answers is undermining equally of science and democracy.'[51]

Where genetically modified food is concerned, rather than an evangelical embrace, the technology has in each case to answer two questions: Can the problem be solved using existing research and technology, and will the GM crop replace something else more harmful to people and the environment?[52] Yet there is a sense in which, from finance to food and energy, the response to system-threatening 'apocalyptic' challenges is to reach for more of the same approaches that are deeply implicated in creating the problems. Hence further marketisation of the economy, which strengthens finance, follows a finance-driven economic crisis. The problems of intensive, industrialised agriculture call forth further industrialisation and intensification.

And an insecure, polluting and wasteful energy system chases its own shadow in an attempt to predict and provide for seemingly uncontrollable demand.

At least two factors seem to drive the reluctance to experiment, at scale, with different courses of action. First there is a significant cost, psychological and otherwise, in admitting failure, when whole careers, reputations, large sums of money and vast zones of infrastructure have been invested in one way of doing things. Second, the comfort of the familiar in both industry and politics exerts immense inertia, warding off change and experimentation. There is fear too, when it comes to social and technological innovation. At one extreme it is: 'Better the devil you know than the potential angel that you don't.' In taking on apocalyptic challenges, I don't want to proclaim single alternative solutions, but rather to propose that far bolder and more ambitious experimentation is vital for survival. More of the same, even if incrementally enhanced, genetically modified and nuclear-powered, doesn't appear to be working. What follows explains why and looks at the richness and potential of other paths. Technology, I argue, should be a choice, not an ultimatum.

Why feeding ourselves shouldn't be a problem, but a joy

The transition from a paradigm in crisis to a new one from which a new tradition of normal science can emerge is far from a cumulative process, one achieved by an articulation or extension of the old paradigm. Rather it is a reconstruction of the field from new fundamentals, a reconstruction that changes some of the field's most elementary theoretical generalisations as well as many of its paradigm methods and applications.

Thomas Kuhn, *The Structure of Scientific Revolutions*

We've seen that global food production is challenged both by a world in the grip of warming, and by shifts towards more energy- and resource-intensive diets. Pressure on scarce water resources in particular not only raises the spectre of competition for water – for example between communities and crops grown for export – but is a flashpoint for regional conflicts. Yet on top of all of these stands the question of population growth. There is a consensus voiced among a policy elite that, even following the great leap in production that accompanied the ironically named green revolution in the 1960s and 1970s, a bigger, bolder leap of a similar kind is required again.

And, true enough, global population is set to rise during the course of this century, that much is generally agreed. By how much is another matter. Many things influence how large the human population will grow. Fertility rates may vary according to economic and social conditions and cultural mores; better or worse disease control, such as over HIV AIDS, exerts influence too. The UN's best estimate is that there will be 9.3 billion people in the world by 2050, and 10.1 billion by 2100. However, within their estimates there is a high curve that takes the figure above 15 billion by the end of the century, and a low one that leaves population below the 7 billion it was thought to reach in 2012. A constant fertility rate, which no one expects, would start the twenty-second century with over 25 billion.[53]

When the projections of the original *Limits to Growth* report from 1972 were reviewed against actual data, most of them, to the surprise of many, closely matched reality. The global use of natural resources, pollution and environmental pressures followed the lines of their graphs. Population, however, rose more slowly than they expected. In forty-nine countries, populations are actually expected to fall between 2011 and 2050, and in the following half-century that number is expected to rise to 123 countries. Some are set to see significant falls in population, by up to 20 per cent. These are mostly rich or middle-income countries, ranging from the Russian Federation to Japan and Portugal. But fertility is falling in the great majority of poor countries too. The UN lists six countries that are expected to account for half of the world's population increase: India, Nigeria, the United States, the Democratic Republic of Congo, Tanzania and Uganda.

And today population is rising. Since 2005 the world has added around 77 million people per year. That is a lot of extra mouths to feed. This trend has been used by a succession of government ministers and their chief scientific advisers, such as Professor John

Beddington and Sir David King, along with the National Farmers Union and, crucially, large multinational agrochemical companies such as Syngenta and Monsanto, to emphasise how much more food the world needs to grow.

Two facts in particular are cited repeatedly. First that global food production needs to increase by half by 2030, and that it will need to double by 2050. 'Intensification' is the name of the farming game. The implication when these facts are used is that the world must take the only realistic path open to it: which is to say an approach to farming characterised by large-scale, hi-tech, industrial and market-driven food production and trade (although, ironically, typically backed by large amounts of tax payers' subsidies).

This was, broadly speaking, a conclusion reached by Professor Beddington in a report with global reach written for Defra.[54] The report itself – *The Future of Food and Farming* – was an important statement of official thinking, involving several government departments covering international development and business, as well as environment and food. It was also, if nothing else, an interesting example of the political arts of drafting. For example, its executive summary has five 'high-level conclusions'. Number four states boldly: 'Policy options should not be closed off.' Number five is equally but contrarily bold, asserting that: 'This Report rejects food self-sufficiency.' The rapidly growing international movement for 'food sovereignty' on the other hand, very popular with civil society groups that champion social justice and sustainability, receives a single, fleeting and unexplained mention in the report's forty-page summary. Yet, as we shall see, 'food sovereignty' represents a profoundly different and competing narrative for how we might feed the world, as compared with industrial agriculture and a faith in the ability of global commodity markets.

The report grants a fleeting appearance to the more and more popular term agro-ecology, elsewhere used to describe the application of ecological principles to agricultural production. A term that does appear repeatedly, however, is 'intensification'. Although it is prefixed with the word 'sustainable', in food policy circles it is unambiguous code for a certain type of approach to food and farming. There is a stronger emphasis, for example, on the development and exploitation of new technologies, including genetic modification of crops, than on improving support for the deployment of existing farmers' knowledge about productive, ecologically sound farming techniques. Another theme is that markets should not be interfered with by governments, and pointedly that the striking recent concentration of power and ownership within the global food chain into a handful of ever larger multinational corporations does not require action – 'there does not seem to be an argument for intervention to influence the number of companies in each area or how they operate'.

The clear implication is that while intervention in markets by governments is unwelcome, intervention by corporations in markets is okay. Why so? One reason why companies in any sector grow large and operate globally is so that they can escape market forces and avoid paying tax. Among other techniques, they do so by incorporating most activities they need to operate under one corporate roof, and then trading with themselves. This allows them to set prices internally to conduct business across borders – something known as transfer pricing – which gives them the ability to both control markets and avoid taxes. Stripped of caveats, at the heart of this approach is a faith in new high technology, the efficient functioning of markets and a relaxed attitude to the benign power and influence of big corporations.

The report's account of the purpose of public engagement with controversial subjects makes interesting reading. On the one hand, where GM crops are concerned it seems to view public discussion on the issue, not as intrinsically important to deciding whether they are a good or bad idea, but as an instrument 'to obtain public acceptance and approval'.[55] On the other, in the debate about how to feed the world, prefixed by the need to massively increase production, any reality or strategy other than market-driven intensification, even if discussed, tends summarily to be dismissed.

But has the scale of the challenge been correctly measured? And whether it has been or not, can the most commonly promoted solution of intensified output actually succeed, and are there no realistic alternatives? Simple, useful facts can quickly assume an authority that leaves people incurious about their origins and be used to tend in one direction only. But when, having heard some 'facts' used often to promote the further global industrialisation of farming, a group that promotes organic farming, the Soil Association, bothered to check, several things surprised them. The first thing was how hard it was to track down the original source of the claim that global food production would have to increase by half by 2030, and double by 2050.

The first figure was used in a speech by Ban Ki-moon, Secretary General of the UN, and the second, at the same time and place, by Jacques Diouf, Director-General of the FAO. But then things got murkier. After considerable digging and enlisting the support of a specialist House of Commons committee, the first figure was claimed to have derived from a background paper written for the World Bank's World Development Report 2008.[56] But even the paper's authors would not provide a copy, instead pointing to other papers in which the figure was not to be found.

On checking the second figure, closer examination of the FAO report on which it was based – *World Agriculture: Towards 2030/2050* – revealed that the data it contained implied not a 100 per cent increase in food production by 2050, but a significantly smaller 70 per cent. Although this is still a big number, the UK government conceded that the difference is equal to more than the food production of the entire American continent.

Furthermore, even this sum depends on a number of key assumptions made by the FAO that are, to say the least, problematic. They are worth dwelling upon because they crystallise several important choices to be made about the shape and nature of the global food system, ones that stand to lock in very different possibilities for humanity, depending on which choices are taken.

For example, the projections take for granted that people in developing countries will eat more meat as a proportion of their overall diet. Much of the anticipated need for increased cereal production is to go towards feeding animals in the first place, not people. The Soil Association points out that the projected doubling by 2050 is actually 'of meat consumption in some developing countries – not a doubling of global food production'. As we saw above, this has major implications in terms of both climate change and fossil-fuel dependence. It is a choice, not innate. Other assumptions concern rates of economic and population growth that, equally, may vary, and that developing countries will continue to import larger shares of their food needs, in spite of rising oil costs and the potential for more 'food nationalism'.

Perhaps most importantly, at a fundamental level it is still assumed that for people to have enough to eat is a matter of how much food is grown, rather than how easy it is for them to get access to food. These two things are not the same. Even in circumstances of shortage and drought, as Amartya Sen famously described in *Poverty and Famines*, hunger comes about because people are powerless, or too poor to afford the food that is available, and because governments and markets fail to provide, not because food isn't somewhere available. Hence, under British colonial control of India, millions starved while the country exported food, just as food was exported from Ireland during the great nineteenth-century famine, and food exports actually rose from Ethiopia during its chronic famine in the early 1970s.[57]

The other problems, once named, seriously challenge the assumptions and conclusions being drawn at the level of official government policy. A high meat-based diet carries significant health and social costs. Measuring food security based on levels of production rather than 'access to food, distribution and affordability' is fundamentally flawed as an approach and will not solve food insecurity.

An enduring, influential folk memory of the green revolution in farming (which would be more properly known as the 'chemical revolution', as it heralded intensive farming with artificial chemical inputs) – a change that comprised mechanisation, large farms, new hybrid seeds and synthetic inputs – may be one reason why the further conventional industrialisation of agriculture appears to be the default option for many governments. The belief is that only the revolution in farming allowed an expanding world population to be fed. Yet the picture is more complex.

Modern agricultural science began in the 1930s, but it wasn't until the 1960s and 1970s that it became huge in scale. The food science writer, and a biologist by training, Colin Tudge points out that even in 1930 world population at over two billion had increased two-hundred-fold over our hunter-gatherer days – growth that was achieved with traditional, organic farming. From 1960 to the end of the millennium, population rose from three to six billion. But even here, can the green revolution take all the credit? Probably not. Tudge estimates that the simple increase of the amount of land under cultivation and the spread of traditional, non-industrial farming is what four of the six billion people alive in 1999 owed their existence to. But there is a further quandary that leaves an assessment of the potential of organic and agro-ecological farming at a disadvantage in the modern world. By far the most research funding over the last half-century has gone to the latter, not the former. This leaves us with guesswork: we don't know how much further advanced we might be in soil and biodiversity preservation, water conservation, less nitrogen pollution and lower greenhouse gas emissions, if equal or greater support had gone to organic farming this last fifty years. Even so, what we do know about its potential, on its own terms and in comparison with well-supported industrial techniques, is impressive.

This is not to say that the revolution did not increase farming yields. It did so in the way that when you put more ingredients into a cake tin, you bake a bigger cake. In place of flour, sugar, eggs and baking powder, think phosphate, nitrogen, hybrid vigour, organochlorine pesticides (e.g., DDT), systemic herbicides (e.g., glyphosate) and, of course, lots and lots of fossil fuels. Notwithstanding the total dependence of industrial farming on oil for its machinery and transport, at least one other ingredient of industrial farming is extremely energy-intensive. Nitrate fertilisers use the Haber–Bosch process, which allows nitrogen cheaply to synthesise ammonia upon which they depend. Methane from natural gas is central to the chemical reaction, and the Haber–Bosch production of fertiliser consumes about one twentieth of global natural gas production.

For several decades, and on its own terms, the revolution was a success. But as early as the publication of Rachel Carson's *Silent Spring* in 1962 it was clear that there was a price to pay. Soil erosion, over-extraction of fresh water, chemical pollution, biodiversity loss, rural unemployment and depopulation, and huge greenhouse gas emissions all pervade industrial farming.

It is in this light that alternatives to even adapted forms of industrial farming have to be assessed. And, when assessed, raise the question why they have not been given more serious attention by governments. Especially, as we shall see below, when a group of experts even more comprehensive than those convened by the UK government came to strikingly different conclusions than those in *The Future of Food and Farming*.

First, it's worth noting the actual contribution of small farms using non-industrial techniques, especially in the poorer parts of the world. Worldwide, there are approximately four hundred million small farms, which directly support the livelihoods of around one third of humanity. Around nine out of ten of those are to be found in the most populous parts of the world in Asia. Africa accounts for most of the rest. India alone is estimated to be home to six hundred million farmers. Most all of these small farms will be using low-input, so-called traditional techniques. It's worth pausing to consider what 'intensification' would mean for them, and that, unambiguously, is unemployment as industrial techniques replace labour. The loss of work in developing countries easily sets in motion a chain of events leading to deeper poverty, hunger and early death. Advocates of agricultural industrialisation speak of farmers being 'freed' to work in modern, emerging sectors, but that depends on an equal number of new jobs being made available, and they aren't. And, unlike working your own farm, where at least you have the opportunity to guarantee your immediate, basic needs, many of those who do get work elsewhere find that their jobs deliver only subsistence.

As the International Labour Organization pointed out in 2010:

the majority of young people in South Asia and sub-Saharan Africa and other low-income regions are trying to make a living at whatever job they can find, most often working long hours under poor conditions in the informal economy. There are by far more young people around the world that are stuck in circumstances of working poverty than are without work and looking for work.[58]

The international financial crisis of 2007–8 made things worse. In one year alone, between 2008 and 2009, the number of unemployed youth went up by 4.5 million worldwide. The average annual increase in the pre-crisis decade 1997–2007 was under one hundred thousand young people.

Farming is often described as 'multi-functional'. That means it's not just a business to provide food. It has to preserve ecosystems, cultures, landscape, jobs and livelihoods. There's been a rush to proclaim that the global future for humanity is city-based – 2008 is meant to be the year in which urban dwellers outnumbered the rural population. The logic of feeding and employing a growing world population, and doing it in a less resource-intensive way, could well mean that the opposite is true.

China alone accounts for almost half of the total number of small farms, at 193 million, and China's successes in terms of industrial modernisation and poverty reduction have forced it to scour the world for land and other natural resources to feed its growth. This is a strategy that is not available to less economically powerful developing countries, and in any case, where many key resources are concerned it is ultimately a global zero-sum game. In chapter 10 I discuss this in terms of emerging patterns of interdependence between countries. After China come India, Indonesia, Bangladesh and Vietnam as bases for small farms. Eighty per cent of Africa's farms are small – an estimated 30 million in total. But even Europe is still home to around 16 million small farms, mostly in Central and Eastern Europe. Russia, too, has many.

Compared with Latin America, where inequality and the concentration of land ownership means the average farm covers about 70 acres, in Africa and Asia the average farm size was around 1.6 hectares in the late 1990s, and falling since, as plots get subdivided. Smallholders hugely outnumber larger farmers, yet they regularly have to survive on smaller proportions of the land. Indian family farms represent 80 per cent of the total, but have only around one third of the farmland to work. The 20 per cent of farmers in Brazil who are smallholders have less than 1 per cent of the land. Contrary to the popular myth underpinning the green revolution, however, and with the odds stacked against them – most farm support and research money goes to industrial agriculture – small, often family farms are highly productive. The International Food Policy Research Institute points out that in India small farms dominate dairy and livestock and produce 40 per cent of foodgrains, and in Africa they account for up to 90 per cent of farm production.[59]

Any benefits of commercialisation and industrialisation of farming would need to be weighed against likely impacts on small farmers. The green revolution certainly increased outputs, but it did so at a cost in terms of pollution and the loss of farming's very foundation – the soil. With the application of machinery and synthetic inputs, globally the yield of cereals went up from 1.4 tonnes per hectare in the early 1960s to 2.7 tonnes per hectare at the end of the 1980s. One part of India, the Punjab, saw increased yields of wheat and rice of 120 per cent and 174 per cent.

But by the turn of the millennium a global assessment of ecosystems highlighted the price paid. A combination of mechanical tilling, bad irrigation and soil exhaustion through overproduction and poor management was to blame. Around 40 per cent of the world's agricultural land had become degraded, including three quarters of Central America's cropland, one fifth of Africa's and 11 per cent of Asia's. It seems that topsoil is disappearing sixteen times faster than it can naturally be replaced. To form an inch of soil can take between two hundred and one thousand years.

It became clear that continuing with conventional approaches would be something like an arms race against nature. Innovations from within industrial farming would need to cancel out the rising negative impacts of its way of growing food, whilst finding ways to extract still more from nature.

One study in America followed the fate of farms over decades from 1948. It found a striking loss of soil resulting from industrial farming, with more than a quarter lost – 16 cm worth from an original 60 cm of topsoil. It then noted, appropriately drily: 'at some point the increasing yield reduction from erosion may exceed the diminishing yield increase due to technical progress.'[60] More and more people question whether there might not be a better way. In fact, there are many.

'Sustainable agriculture', 'agro-ecological' farming and 'agro-forestry' are terms denoting a huge range of practices that differ substantially from industrial farming. In place of chemical pesticides and fertilisers, for example, farmers use a mix of techniques that include composting, botanical and natural pest control, growing legumes to aid nitrogen fixing, animal manure and water conservation. These improve the soil, lower erosion and benefit nutrition. The FAO reported such techniques raising farm yields by between 60 and 195 per cent, easily on a par with the short-term gains of the green revolution, and not prone to their diminishing returns over time.[61] Another study for the FAO demonstrated average gains in yield from agro-ecological approaches of 94 per cent, and up to 600 per cent in the best cases.[62] Indeed, surveying a range of case studies that looked at organic food growing in Africa, specialist UN bodies dealing with the environment, trade and development found that in all cases for which data was available, productivity increased, challenging 'the popular myth' that organic farming can't raise output.[63]

One reason that many credit industrial farming with greater efficiency is because, compared on a single crop-for-crop basis, it can produce bigger yields. But on agro-ecological farms the total outputs are higher. A study by the UK Food Group explains why:

> A simple focus of crop yields per hectare is also misleading: agroecological approaches in particular demand a focus on the output of the whole farm, including livestock that are an integral part of the agroecology. Raising fish in rice paddies, growing crops with trees or including goats or poultry are all common practices and all contribute to the total farm output beyond crop yields. Other advantages that accrue to agroecological approaches include lower variance in crop yields and labour needs. On-farm labour is an average of 15 per cent higher and is more evenly distributed through the year, offering realistic full time employment in place of the demand for seasonal workers.[64]

In Zambia, for example, farmers practise something called 'alley cropping'. A shrub that is good at fixing nutrients in the soil is planted between vegetable crops along with ginger, which helps repel pests. It saves money and saves the soil. In Ghana, small-scale farmers grow food and tree crops together to raise soil fertility and produce wood for fuel using a similar system of intercropping. A case in Tigray, Ethiopia, saw yields double due to organic soil-management techniques.

Smart, low-tech approaches applied at small scale can yield big benefits for farmers and produce more resilient farming, especially where life-saving water conservation is concerned. In Burkina Faso and other countries in the Sahel simple planting pits, stone lines and permeable rock dams increase productivity, economic benefits and environmental conservation whilst protecting the water table. Yields of both millet and sorghum rose by 50–60 per cent using such techniques.[65] In Mali, rice yields were raised by up to 100 per cent compared with conventional irrigation, using less water under a system of sustainable rice cultivation.[66]

Using a range of agroecological techniques to raise the amount of organic matter in soils, in Kenya water use was reduced by up to 90 per cent compared with conventional methods,[67] and in Lesotho the use of simple drip irrigation and treadle pumps both saved water and raised output, helping to generate surplus crops.[68]

There are many ways of farming more ecologically that might not pass a test of being strictly organic. And much farming in Africa may be organic by default, simply because farmers cannot afford chemical inputs. However, with the price and availability of oil supplies likely to diverge, one up and the other down, that situation is unlikely to change.

What would happen if through either choice or necessity the world changed over to organic farming on a big scale? The International Food Policy Research Institute (IFPRI), part of a large international network of agricultural research centres, developed a model to assess the likely consequences of different choices in farming. It was applied to non-intensive approaches to see what would happen if the world did indeed go organic at scale. Results were reported to a special session in 2007 of the FAO.

It is a vital question. Several influential voices have publicly doubted that organic food can provide for anything but a relatively wealthy niche market (leave aside the irony that it currently feeds hundreds of millions of the world's poorest people, far more than those shopping in Waitrose and having dinner parties in North London). In April 2010 Sir John Krebs, the former head of the UK's Food Standards Agency, described organic food as 'a complete side-show' to the important tasks both of feeding the world and of ensuring that people had healthy diets.[69] Prior to his appointment, Krebs had no direct involvement with food or farming issues, but he was also on public record as favouring genetically modified crops, and co-founded an organisation called Oxford Risk Research and Analysis Ltd, which provides consultancy advice for, among others, the oil and pharmaceutical industries.[70]

Another establishment figure dismissive not just of organic food but also of small farms is (Lord) Christopher Haskins. Unlike Krebs, before he was made the UK government's 'Rural Recovery Coordinator' during Tony Blair's Labour government, Haskins ran the huge food-processing conglomerate Northern Foods, as well as a large subsidised farm. (A thread joins Haskins to Mark Lynas and John Krebs, which is that they all embrace industrial farming approaches in the name of the poor.) As well as commenting that 'the world simply cannot go organic', Haskins also predicted that half of UK farms, especially small farms, were likely to go out of business. Small farms, he added, should diversify into tourism, and open bed and breakfast guest houses to stand a chance of surviving.[71]

Such views permeated through to the Beddington review on the future of world farming, which expressed the sort of self-conscious pragmatism attractive in the world of policy making, especially when a conclusion must fit neatly into the existing, dominant world view of the powerful. Organic and small-scale approaches become ritually dismissed as 'idealistic' and 'romantic'. However, the UN FAO special conference on organic agriculture and food security came to just the opposite view, with some very practical and positive conclusions. It found that:

> Even at high levels of conversion to organic agriculture (up to 50 per cent) in Europe and North America, there would be relatively little impact on the availability of food and price changes would be limited. For the case of sub-Saharan Africa, a conversion of up to 50 per cent would likely increase food availability and decrease food import dependency.[72]

Leaving no doubt, it stated boldly: 'These findings . . . contrast starkly with critics of organic agriculture and proponents of old paradigms.' The list of reasons in favour was comprehensive: raised yields, energy use lowered up to 56 per cent, 'enhanced economic efficiency' through cost savings on expensive inputs, more employment created, enhanced nutrient cycle, improved food quantity, quality and diversity, organic urban gardens improving access to food, raised incomes and reduced risks to farmers, and better use of locally available resources. There were other benefits, and of course there were challenges too, surrounding support for research and conversion from conventional farming, and the dissemination of best practice. But the advantages were rated as considerable, especially to the farmers themselves and their local environment, including: 'risk reduction, conservation of natural resources, health protection, increased resilience to adverse weather and farmer empowerment through the acquisition of knowledge and higher reliance on local inputs'.

Far from being a romantic dream for some of the world's poorest people, organic approaches often seem custom-made, with raised productivity of between 50 and 100 per cent common. Where crops relied on most by the poor are concerned – rice, beans, maize, cassava, potatoes, barley – output can be raised many times by using 'labour and know how' in place of costly bought inputs.[73] Even elsewhere, when industrial and organic methods produce similar yields in normal years, such as with corn (maize), in drought years organic approaches deliver 30 per cent more of the crop.[74]

It's not surprising then, that when Krebs made his derogatory remarks about the potential of organic farming, the chief executive of his Irish counterpart agency The Food Safety Authority, Dr Patrick Wall, dismissed Krebs's views as 'extreme', and said that organic food was more 'environmentally friendly, more wholesome, and better produced'.

What you grow and how you grow it are two big questions in terms of cancelling the apocalypse in the food chain. But there is another key question, and it is controversial. Who do you grow the crops for? Whether they are grown for export, aiming to earn hard currency with which you then buy the things you need, or whether food is grown first and foremost for local human consumption, can have a big impact on the resilience of a food system and its ability to feed people. In chapter 10 when the issue of global interdependence is addressed, this question will recur.

Perhaps the most striking illustration that the direction of policy is not a rational, evidence-based process is that the UK government's *The Future of Food and Farming* report was published after another, more comprehensive, international assessment that came to very different conclusions.

The International Assessment of Agricultural Knowledge, Science and Technology for Development (IAASTD) was a joint initiative of the UN and the World Bank. It produced a very long report which, in summary, to solve the world's food problems favoured as the way forward: 'An increase and strengthening of agricultural knowledge, science and technology towards agroecological sciences [that] will contribute to addressing environmental issues while maintaining and increasing productivity.'

A litmus test of these reports' approaches was their different attitudes to some of the new, more invasive farm technologies, like genetic modification of food crops. As mentioned above, like nuclear power in the energy debate, which I'll explore later, the issue of whether you are for or against GM food crops has been made to stand for whether you are for or against the modern world, and even whether you are for or against ensuring that the world's poor have enough to eat. It is an expression of laboratory science that has grabbed the mantle of modernity, and sought to close debate on our collective choices about the future.

Hence, generally speaking, those who deride or downplay the potential of organic food claim to see GM crops as synonymous with a rational, scientific approach to solving problems of hunger. Questioning and opposition to genetic modification, similarly, gets dismissed as emotional, unscientific, even unethical or – worst of all in some eyes – political. But there is another irony here, which is that several who wave the banner of scientific rationalism and set great store by specialism, peer review and scientific method, feel free to eschew the rigour they demand of others when it comes to speaking outside their own disciplines on the complex political and economic matters of tackling hunger and poverty.

The influential scientist Sir David King, the UK government's former chief scientific adviser, whilst having no obvious background or expertise in humanitarian issues, complex emergencies or food security as they relate to poverty reduction, felt confident to assert in a speech at London's Guildhall in 2010 that: 'A lot of people have lost their lives because gene splicing has not been acceptable.' He added: 'There is a desperate need for biotechnology if we are to feed the 50 per cent increase in the population.'[75] Quite apart from King's apparent lack of obvious qualification in the relevant field, the second remark is at least very widely contested, while the first appears hugely emotive, quite unscientific, and on even a casual inspection, seemingly lacked evidence.

The claim referred to those who suffered from hunger in 2007 when, as explored above, a combination of high oil prices, commodity speculation and crop failures due to extreme weather events sent prices up and made food unavailable to many. Would modified crops have made a difference in these circumstances, and supposing that they had, would it have been more of a difference than other practices? It would seem to be a quite outlandish claim for a leading scientist to make – suggesting that some deeper, less rational motivation was at work.

Yet King is far from being alone. He reflects a particular elite view. A few years earlier, in 2003, the United States trade representative, Robert B. Zoellick, also an ardent advocate of free markets and later to be president of the World Bank (2007–12), said that to oppose the acceptance and use of GM crops was 'immoral' because it would lead to starvation in poor countries. His comments were in the context of the EU having tighter controls on GM crops and Zambia having rejected US food aid that contained genetically modified crops.

This is perhaps a good point at which to remember the tests mentioned above, when assessing a new crop technique: 'can the problem be solved using existing research and technology and, will the GM crop replace something else more harmful to people and the environment?' Similarly, I argued in the late 1990s, in a report triggered by Monsanto's promotion of so-called 'terminator technology' – the modification of seed to become infertile in its second generation, preventing farmers from collecting and sowing their own seed, in order to force them to purchase seed afresh each year from the company – that, in terms of hunger prevention GM crops need to meet several tests. In addition to environmental health and safety, will the pattern of patents and inputs surrounding GM crops leave poor farmers better or worse off? How will GM crops perform in types of multi-cropping farms most advantageous to the poor? Will their call on research funds distract from other better solutions? What will be the possible long-term effects of novel crops?

A decade after the introduction of a plant variety – Bt-cotton – genetically engineered to be pest-resistant, a briefing sent to cotton-growing states by India's Ministry of Agriculture, based on observations from the Indian Council of Agricultural Sciences and the Central Cotton Research Institute, painted a grim picture.

Introduced with a promise of rising yields and lowering costs, in fact, the briefing reported: 'cost of cotton cultivation has jumped . . . due to rising costs of pesticides. Total Bt-cotton production in the last five years has reduced.' Cotton farmers were 'in a deep crisis since shifting to Bt-cotton. The spate of farmer suicides in 2011–12 has been particularly severe among Bt-cotton farmers.'[76] Earlier research on Bt-cotton in China found that the crop's initial pest-control benefits against its target, the bollworm, were cancelled out by farmers having to use more pesticides to control other pests.[77] Yet another study concluded the opposite, that there were broad benefits to the use of Bt-cotton in China.[78]

Meanwhile, in the US, corn engineered similarly to be pest-resistant shows signs of failing, as pests adapt. Illinois saw crops devastated by pests they were meant to be immune to.[79] Higher seed costs for GM corn have also been criticised in the face of negligible rises in yield.[80] And a coalition of civil society groups from Africa, South East Asia and Latin America found that no food crop had benefited in terms of yield from genetic engineering, but that the technology had led to increased use of chemicals and the spread of 'superweeds'.[81] Far from reducing the application of herbicides overall, GM technology was seen to increase their use from when crops were introduced at scale in 1996 to the year 2011 by around 11 per cent.[82]

Will traits out-cross, creating 'superweeds', what will be the impacts on biodiversity of more thorough pest elimination, and will this, leaving the field clear, merely create the ideal evolutionary conditions for 'superpests'? Ironically, after all the bluster and moral blackmail used to promote invasive and corporate-led genetic manipulation of food crops, that approach looks set, in any case, to be superseded by a less invasive technique, known as 'marker-assisted selection', which allows plant breeders to select desirable genetic traits which are then brought out using conventional breeding. Other non-GM techniques look set to bring dramatic crop improvements. One, for example, stimulates the plant's own self-defence mechanism to dramatically improve pest resistance when applied to barley, the fourth-most important cereal crop in the world, and could potentially be used on other cereals.

This table gives a simplified view of some of the choices and alternatives available:

The Problem	Genetic Engineering Proposals	Agroecological Solutions
Weeds	Crop resistance to a chemical herbicide	Ground cover, mulches, soil fertility management, rotations, mechanical weeding, varietal choice (of vigour, habit), transplants, stale seed beds, canopy cover, 'weed' crops as food/predator attractants
Pests and diseases	Crop resistance to a pesticide or pest/disease	Variety/crop/farm diversity, multi-varietal planting, buffer zones, predator attractants/antagonists, biological controls, rotations, mechanical covers (fleece/mesh), forecasting/monitoring – timing, mixed cropping, varietal selection/breeding, grafting, module planting
Poor nutrition	Crop containing added vitamin or mineral content	Multi-species cropping, biodiversity, varietal selection/breeding for nutrition, soil management, efficient irrigation (higher dry matter), availability of wider range of nutritious foods in local markets

Source: *Securing Future Food: Towards Ecological Food Provision*
UK Food Group

Olivier De Schutter is UN Special Rapporteur on food issues. He is unequivocal about what is needed to create a world food system capable of meeting human needs:

From a right-to-food perspective, host States and investors should . . . establish and promote farming systems that are labour intensive – instead of highly mechanised operations – in order to ensure that investment agreements contribute to reinforcing local livelihood options and provide living wages for the local population, which is a key component of the human right to food. Sustainable agriculture, in particular agro-ecological approaches and low external input farming practices should also be privileged in contract agreements.

Why we can generate sufficient energy, without getting dirty

There is another human defect which the Law of Natural Selection has yet to remedy: When people of today have full bellies, they are exactly like their ancestors of a million years ago: very slow to acknowledge any awful troubles they may be in. Then is when they forget to keep a sharp lookout for sharks and whales. This was a particularly tragic flaw a million years ago, since the people who were best informed about the state of the planet ... and rich and powerful enough to slow down all the waste and destruction going on, were by definition well fed. So everything was always just fine as far as they were concerned.

Kurt Vonnegut, *Galapagos*

One million years in the future humanity has evolved into sleek, furry creatures with flippers and small brains. At least they have in Kurt Vonnegut's novel *Galapagos*. And there aren't many of them left. The only ones to make it, in fact, are the descendants of a handful who managed to climb aboard the shiny and new (at the time), state-of-the-art ship the *Bahia de Darwin*, sailing out of Ecuador on the 'Nature Cruise of the Century' to the Galapagos Islands. As they sail, an economic collapse and their own redundancy triggered by the inventions of their large brains incrementally finishes off the rest of humankind. Just a random selection is left, eventually stranded on the islands to evolve like oversized Darwin's sparrows. In the process most of human culture is entirely lost. A pocket electronic gadget preloaded with twenty thousand quotes from literature is virtually all that remains.

Forewarned is forearmed. Somehow Vonnegut's absurdism, liberally scattered, is more chilling than a shipful of facts rationally delivered. There is always a danger to the reader of science fiction of retrofitting real events in such a way as to make the original work prescient. Yet just over a decade after Vonnegut published his novel there was a real and devastating economic collapse in Latin America, which also hosted a global gathering – the Earth Summit held in Rio de Janeiro in 1992 – that was expressly designed to prevent the extinction of human beings. On that occasion this urgent purpose was shelved for a decade or two by those who were 'by definition well fed'. They probably thought, much like the doomed captain of the *Bahia de Darwin* when most of his crew failed to appear before sailing, that nothing too bad, or demanding really urgent action, was going on. 'Be patient. Smile. Be confident. Everything will turn out for the best somehow.' This attitude was not successful in the novel. I doubt it will be in the real world.

Then I saw photographs of a shiny, state-of-the-art non-fictional ship, the MS *Turanor*, cruising the waters of the Galapagos Islands. On one of the floats of its vast trimaran hull there were sleek, furry creatures with flippers and relatively small brains. They too appeared to have no human culture, probably because they were seals. I stared at these pictures, in equal parts heartened, and yet disturbed by the echoes of Vonnegut's fiction. I was heartened because these were images of an impressive solar-powered ship, full name MS *Turanor Planet Solar*, on a visit to the islands to promote renewable energy sponsored by the environmental group the World Wide Fund for Nature (WWF), the Galapagos National Park and the Galapagos government. As we saw much earlier, small island states tend, in any case, to manage their natural resources for human benefit generally better than other countries. And the Galapagos Islands were already well aware of the importance and potential of renewable energy.

One thing that focused minds was the wreck in January 2001 of the oil tanker *Jessica*, which spilt 800,000 gallons of oil into the appropriately named Wreck Bay in San Cristobal. In the event, the islands made famous by Darwin had a lucky escape, as most of the oil dispersed at sea rather than washing onto their shores, so rich in animal life. Six out of ten iguanas on one island were less fortunate, however, succumbing to the contamination.

Diesel engines and generators are a common source of power on islands, but many did make the connection between their energy dependence and the livelihood-threatening pollution. The Galapagos Renewable Energy Project was formed, and now one third of the electricity used on San Cristobal comes from a new wind farm. Solar power was installed on another island, Isabela, in 2007 to reduce annual consumption of diesel by 146,000 litres per year, a 60 per cent reduction, saving 350 tonnes of carbon dioxide emissions. On Floreana Island solar power provides electricity to one third of households, which local people are eager to improve on. Under this umbrella project, the islands' objective is to replace diesel with renewables 'as much as technically and economically feasible'.

But these are not the only islands with plans for the uptake of renewable energy that are far more ambitious than many of those who are 'best informed . . . and rich and powerful'.

Six kilometres off the mainland in West Bengal, India lies Sagar Island, home to two hundred thousand people living in over forty-three villages. Typically, many lack access to grid electricity. As in the Galapagos, diesel-powered generators were common. In response, starting in 1996, the West Bengal Renewable Energy Development Agency began to develop stand-alone solar photovoltaic power plants that provide grid-quality electricity. An innovative feature of the project is how the Agency works in cooperation with rural energy development cooperatives formed by the beneficiaries of the power supply. There are now eleven small solar PV power plants on Sagar Island and nearby Maushuni Island. Each is attached to its own mini-grid system supplying adjacent villages, which operate for six hours a day in the evenings until midnight. A wind–diesel hybrid power plant was also built.

Apart from bringing electricity to 1600 homes, the mini-grids bring power to businesses, streetlights, schools and hospitals, and integrate power with water supplies to bring drinking water to people's houses. It has boosted the local economy, as additional lighting creates new job opportunities and improves existing working conditions for many others, making work outside daylight hours safer, cleaner and more efficient. One of the reasons for renewable energy's success on Sagar Island is the stake that local people have: the initiative stems from the level of the local village government, 'Gram Panchayet'.

Each January the population grows when more than one million pilgrims visit the Gangasagar Mela festival. Evenings used to be dangerous with little lighting. Now spiritual enlightenment is assisted by better street lighting.

'Sagar Island has its unique ecosystem. It falls under the Sundarbans delta. Diesel-power generation is responsible for environmental degradation not only in Sagar Island but in the entire delta zone. Solar energy is totally eco-friendly,' says Gon Chaudhuri, director of the Agency, who wants the entire island eventually to be powered by renewable energy. 'There are no emissions and no sound pollution from solar PV. Local people are now very conscious about the protection of the environment of "Solar" Island.'[83] Meanwhile, the islands of Tokelau in the South Pacific, comprising the three atolls of Atafu, Nukunonu and Fakaofo that lie between Hawaii and New Zealand, once dependent on diesel generators became in 2012 the first territory able to supply all its electricity needs from solar power.

The Maldives, one of the group of islands in the world most vulnerable to climate change and sea-level rise, is another place plotting an entirely renewable future. The islands don't rise far above the sea, and former President Mohamed Nasheed caught world attention when he held a press conference underwater to highlight their plight. His flair for publicity, however, was married to serious intent. Under his leadership, the Maldives declared the intention to become the world's first carbon-neutral country by 2020. A partnership was formed with Robert Gordon University in Scotland to study the islands' potential for a combination of wave, tidal and ocean thermal energy. 'If the Maldives can demonstrate that low-carbon development is not just practical but also profitable, we hope larger countries will follow suit,' said Mohamed Aslam, the Maldivian environment minister, in 2010. 'As an island nation spread over a thousand kilometres of ocean, I believe marine renewables hold enormous potential to make the Maldives an international energy leader in the zero-carbon economy of the future.'[84]

Nasheed, the Maldives' first democratically elected president in 2008, was deposed in 2012, leaving the country's political future in doubt, along with its world leadership on climate change. Fortunately, an example had already been set. The partnership with Scotland traces a line around the globe to yet another bold experiment in renewable energy.

Take the overnight sleeper train from London to Fort William in the Scottish Highlands, along the coast, over the moors, around the glacial valleys, under the low mountains, and then another hour and a half by road out along the Ardnamurchan peninsula, and stand by that remote coast. From there you can see the outlines of the islands of Eigg, Rhum and, wonderfully, Muck. They are the Inner Hebrides, lying south of Skye. Rhum is a nature reserve. Eigg has the biggest population and unusual distinctions. In 1997 it became the island that bought itself out. Each year in summer there is a party to celebrate when the islanders freed themselves from an unhappy history of being under the control of private owners (including a former Olympic bob-sleigher and heir to a gelatine fortune). They formed the Isle of Eigg Heritage Trust to manage the island for the benefit of both residents and nature. Thirty volunteers and one member of staff run it day-to-day. Now Eigg has achieved something that the rest of the world struggles to do. The local people have largely freed themselves also from their carbon bonds and the volatile price of fossil fuels.

Energy saving and careful use, combined with generating 90 per cent of their electricity from renewable energy sources – hydro, wind and solar – has enabled the islanders to cut their carbon by around half. As on Sagar Island, the success is due to it being a community-led scheme. Homes and businesses have their energy use capped and monitors installed that warn if the limit is being approached. One in five homes has solar thermal water heating and buildings are well insulated, altogether lowering household carbon emissions by 47 per cent.[85] In 2010 the island won a national award for its approach to sustainable energy.

Renewable energy, onshore wind power in particular, can incur resistance from individuals and pressure groups, ostensibly on the grounds that turbines spoil views of landscape. The example of Moel Maelogan in Wales shows again how community involvement and ownership of a project can turn objections into an enthusiastic embrace. One reason why this is so is that sustainable energy, like sustainable agriculture, has more benefits and solves more problems than simply supplying an end product or service.

Hill farmers in Britain have struggled for years. Falling incomes, rising suicide rates, the long-term impact of foot-and-mouth disease and, in Wales, the even longer-term fallout from the Chernobyl nuclear failure whose cloud of radioactive contamination left livestock restrictions in place for decades, all form a pall that hangs heavily.

Faced with such bleak prospects, three Welsh hill-farming families concluded that they had to try something different. Livelihoods based on farming alone were no longer viable for them, either now or in the future. They had to diversify and formed a cooperative to explore alternatives. The answer, they found, was blowing in the wind.

Britain has access to 40 per cent of the total available wind energy in Europe. Theoretically, at least, according to the British Wind Energy Association (BWEA) it is enough to meet the country's electricity needs eight times over. Of all renewable technologies, wind energy seems to be specially divisive. The two most common concerns are aesthetic and ecological: that wind turbines are unsightly and that they are a danger to birdlife. The former worry is real for some, but also in Britain whipped up by interests linked to competing energy interests. Bernard Ingham, for example, the former press secretary to Prime Minister Margaret Thatcher, was also a paid lobbyist for British Nuclear Fuels Ltd. At a public meeting on 19 June 2004 at Saddleworth Moor in Lancashire he memorably claimed that wind power was for 'the brainwashed or the braindead'. When I appeared alongside him on the BBC Radio 4 *Today* programme in 2005, he said that nuclear, on the other hand was cheap, clean and did not want subsidies.[86]

It happens that Alan Moore spent thirty years building and installing nuclear, coal, gas and other power stations before becoming chair of the BWEA and head of renewable energy at National Wind Power. If we are to believe Bernard Ingham, someone managed to hypnotise this seasoned industry man into a plan to invest nearly £1 billion in wind power over the course of a decade. For Moore, too much tendentious bluster was destroying any sense of proportion in the energy debate. 'In the seventeenth century we had ninety thousand windmills in Britain. They were a part of life,' he said. 'What we're looking to do is install perhaps four thousand, making five thousand in total.'[87] Half of these were planned to be onshore and half offshore, and at that point in 2004, Germany already had seven thousand turbines.

A combination of government departments and industry groups working together as the Offshore Valuation Group assessed the contribution that wind turbines located only at sea could make to the UK. They found that if just under one third – 29 per cent – of the practical offshore wind resource was harnessed by 2050, it would generate the equivalent in electricity of 1 billion barrels of oil – equal to the whole North Sea oil and gas production, turning Britain into a net electricity exporter. It would also create 145,000 jobs and cut 1.1 billion tonnes of carbon dioxide emissions between 2010 and 2050.[88]

Back in North Wales, the hill farmers realised that while the soil was no longer making them a good living, there was another, literal, windfall that they could exploit. Together they owned some of potentially the most productive wind-power sites in Europe. They devised a plan to develop, finance and build a wind farm that would not only underpin their own livelihoods with regular, reliable income but bring new economic benefits to the community. Within five years, after hard work and a steep learning curve, having started with little knowledge of the technology or how to manage such a project, the first turbines were erected. On the day in 2002 that the first phase of the wind farm went up they had a surprise. About 200 people were expected; 1500 local people showed up to congratulate the enterprise and celebrate the hope it brought to the local economy. One local said the atmosphere was like 'Glastonbury without the music'.[89]

The project's success and community support led to another phase they called 'Ail Wynt', meaning 'second wind'. To raise some of their funds, bonds were issued giving people in the community a deeper stake, and profit, from hosting the turbines. A total of twelve were eventually built. A curious footnote is that the only real resistance to the project had come from non-native (English), more recent arrivals to the area.

But do a few ambitious islands and rural communities amount to anything more? In some places failed by national energy grids, people find enterprising ways with convenient renewable technologies to overcome their problems. My favourite, and a rather poetic example, encountered as a judge of a renewable energy award scheme, was the engineer in Africa who recycled parts from the wheels and axles of broken-down, petrol-guzzling four-wheel-drive vehicles to build wind turbines. For others, renewable energy is, initially at least, simply another way to generate an income by farming the wind, or the sun, or the fall of a river, instead of planting crops and grazing animals. What can renewable energy offer to everybody else, including the urban masses? Could it ever hope to meet all our needs? The answer, though not without challenges, would seem to be an unequivocal 'yes'.

In 2004 the United Nations held a special conference dedicated to renewable energy. In a paper summarising the state of knowledge for delegates it concluded: 'Renewable energy flows are very large in comparison with humankind's use of energy. Therefore, in principle, all our energy needs, both now and into the future, can be met by energy from renewable sources.'[90]

Obviously not all of it could be recovered, but the potential energy available from wind, wave, tidal, solar, geothermal and biomass greatly exceeds current and expected future human energy needs. The existing technical potential to generate renewable energy could see its capacity increase by over 120 times. The theoretical potential is vastly more, at over 2 million times. While that could never practically be achieved, it does suggest that there is an awful lot of scope. And with up to an estimated 1.6 billion people globally who lack access to electricity, and 2.7 billion who do not have clean-fuel cooking equipment, there is a strong argument from the perspective of human development to pick technologies that, once again, answer multiple needs.

In that light, José Goldemberg, former minister for science and technology in Brazil and secretary for the environment for the state of São Paulo at the time of the special 2004 UN conference on renewable energy in Bonn, was unequivocal about what direction energy policy should take: 'renewable energies will dominate the world's energy system, due to their inherent advantages such as mitigation of climate change, generation of employment and reduction of poverty, as well as increased energy security and supply.'

Wind and biomass in particular, according to Goldemberg, create far more jobs than conventional fossil fuel or nuclear power sources. Nuclear is by far the weakest at employment creation. In terms of like-for-like electricity output, wind created between twelve and thirty-two times the number of jobs, as well as more cheaply reducing carbon emissions, and with both onshore and offshore projected to be substantially cheaper energy sources in 2020.[91] The technical potential already exists to increase the uptake of wind power three thousand times.

As well as tackling energy poverty, climate change and job creation, there is the added double allure of insulating economies from volatile oil prices. And on top of the other advantages offered against both nuclear power and fossil fuels is the security benefit of renewables. No country yet has knowingly been invaded to have its wind farms annexed, and neither do wind farms present the same attractions to terrorists as the nuclear fuel cycle.

How badly, though, do we really need a change of direction? For a particularly hard-nosed assessment, perhaps it is best to listen to those who have the most to lose from a big change in the status quo, the oil industry itself.

Looking into its crystal ball of energy scenarios, Shell breaks down where it thinks we've got to and where we might be going in a report called *Signals & Signposts*. It warns that we face an upcoming 'zone of uncertainty' – a frank admission that it really cannot say with any confidence what is going to happen. It labels a large block of time in the period between now and 2050 as a 'zone of extraordinary opportunity or misery'. These two conditions unfortunately are not necessarily mutually exclusive, as those communities might attest, for example, who live in the Niger delta with the pollution and conflict that thrived in the wake of Shell's pursuit of economic opportunity.

Nevertheless, using optimistic assumptions, the company sees a gap emerging by 2050 between 'business-as-usual-supply' and 'business-as-usual-demand'. It is a gap so large as to be equal in size to the whole of the industry as it stood in the year 2000.

The US mission in Saudi Arabia, a country long relied on to increase production when times are hard, questioned in a cable made available by WikiLeaks 'whether they [Saudi Arabia] any longer have the power to drive [oil] prices down for a prolonged period'. Revelations like this give markets the jitters, intensified by continuing instability and the complex geopolitics of other major producers ranging from Libya to Iran.

And the industry has other mounting problems of its own making. For example, it can no longer safely rely for production slack on the potential of more marginal fields, such as the Macondo Prospect in the Gulf of Mexico, now famous as the scene of BP's *Deepwater Horizon* debacle. Elsewhere, the US oil giant Chevron paid for large press adverts declaring: 'Oil companies should support the communities they're part of.' But Chevron itself was struggling to avoid paying a court order from Ecuador which fined the company £5 billion, half its annual profits, for polluting the communities that they're part of. Initially, at least, instead of having the amount reduced, in February 2011 the Ecuadorean court raised to $9 billion the sum to compensate thirty thousand plaintiffs in the eighteen-year law suit. Meanwhile the unhappy oil company BP sees output falling in key countries like the US, Russia and the UK, and is now caught up with dark machinations in Russia that smack of the old days of the 'great game'.

The whole industry is faced with a paradox. The more successfully they conduct their core business of finding and pumping oil, the sooner they will do themselves out of a job. A comparison of numerous forecasts by Steve Sorrell and colleagues, published in the journal *Energy Policy*, revealed a list of fifty-six oil-producing countries already apparently past their point of peak production.[92] They concluded that any forecast putting the global peak and decline of oil production more than a couple of decades away was based on assumptions that were 'at best optimistic and at worst implausible'. Some thought it had already happened, more still that it would occur in the next five years.

Writing in the journal *Nature*, James Murray of the University of Washington and the UK former chief government adviser David King argue that, in effect, oil production peaked in 2005, hitting a ceiling at around 75 million barrels per day, and would be unable to respond to any further rising demand.[93] They consider that 'the oil market has tipped into a new state, similar to a phase transition in physics: production is now "inelastic", unable to respond to rising demand, and this is leading to wild price swings'. Also, and crucially, 'other fossil-fuel resources don't seem capable of making up the difference'. Looking at the ebb and flow of production in response to changes in price since 1998, supply can no longer, it seems, 'respond elastically' to rising prices driven by demand. This exacerbates instability and has massive consequences for the rest of the economy where prices more generally track the price of oil.

Production did, in fact, rise beyond the level discussed by King. Around 91 million barrels per day (bpd) were produced in 2012 according to the International Energy Agency. Economists sceptical of the importance of peak oil, and the limits insisted on by geologists, saw this as the promised effect of markets responding to a higher price, investing and raising production. Some in the industry even began speaking of a new boom for oil. Research funded by BP and published by Harvard University with the title *Oil – The Next Revolution: the Unprecedented Upsurge of Oil Production Capacity and What It Means for the World* makes the case for the industry having a bright future.

Yves-Louis Darricarrère, president of the giant Total company's oil and gas exploration division, has a different view and publicly stated: 'We think it will be difficult to produce more than 95 to 97 million barrels per day in the foreseeable future.' To meet demand and compensate for declining fields, he said, two new Saudi Arabias would be needed by 2030 to produce an extra 25–45 million bpd.[94] The Harvard paper suggested that with new production capacity by 2020 a figure of 110 million bpd will be reached.

One reason for the latter, much larger figure is that the paper's author, Leonardo Maugeri, made very generous assumptions. He took at face value unproven claims by Saudi Arabia about increasing production, and long-promised but yet to be delivered growth in Iraq. He also assumed that new capacity would be developed at a cost of around $70 per barrel. Actual production costs for the fifty biggest listed oil producers were at $92 per barrel in 2011, and likely to rise to $100 per barrel and beyond.[95]

Importantly, new oil sources being brought into production are not the same as the old. Production of conventional 'easy' oil peaked in 2006, according to the IEA. Further growth must come from unconventional sources like dirtier and more problematic tar sands and oil shale. One such is the shale of the Bakken formation in North Dakota, US. The problem was vividly described by Rob Hopkins, founder of the Transition Network:

> There may be as much oil in Bakken as there is in Saudi Arabia, but getting it out is another challenge altogether. Extracting the oil from the Saudi oil fields was a breeze, like drinking hot chocolate through a straw as compared Bakken, which is more like trying to extract the same amount of chocolate from a chocolate brownie.[96]

Although it has many other important aspects, peak oil can be seen in this light as overwhelmingly an economic problem to do with the price and availability of liquid fuels. An IMF research paper said: 'we suspect that there must be a pain barrier, a level of oil prices above which the effects on GDP becomes nonlinear, convex.'[97] The price of oil helped trigger recession in 2007–8, and the IEA warns consistently of the barrier to recovery represented by the price of oil. Historically, spikes in price correlate one-for-one with recessions.

This means that even if, with considerable investment, it is possible to raise production, the rising cost of doing so, coupled with rising demand, will inflict a major economic impact. Bob Hirsch, the former Exxon adviser to the US Department of Energy, points out that the world currently has anything from $50 to $100 trillion of infrastructure designed to run on liquid fuels which cannot easily and quickly, if at all, be adapted to a different fuel source.[98] The IMF paper's conclusion was far from sanguine: 'small further increases in world oil production come at the expense of a near doubling, permanently, of real oil prices over the coming decade.' Such a sustained increase in prices is described as 'uncharted territory for the world economy', and will be very different to past experiences when prices have spiked and remained at very high levels for a few months.

In circumstances like this, the foundations of the economy could change as fast as a Middle Eastern regime in the summer of 2011. But within the industry there remains the same kind of blithe confidence in its ability to continue as before to prop up our economy and lifestyles, that governments just a few years ago placed in the banking system.

The cost of oil imports as a share of GDP for the US, Europe and Japan is back around the level it was in 2008, at around 2–3 per cent, roughly double the average for the past four decades. That doesn't sound much, but it's misleading. Because, in effect, 100 per cent of the productive activities that comprise GDP depend on energy.

The Shell report spoke of 'volatile transition', and of economic outlooks that range from 'severe-yet-sharp' to 'deeper-and-longer', and the catchy, if dated, 'Depression 2.0'.

With so much insight into the frailty of the future of a fossil-fuel-dependent economy, it is remarkable then that Shell, like BP, reversed at speed out of renewable energy. Shell dropped investment in wind, solar and hydrogen energy in 2009, the same year BP closed the London headquarters of BP Alternative Energy, along with its solar plants in the US and Spain. Ironically, and revealing impressive depths of cynicism, the BP-funded paper by Maugeri concluded that for the oil industry to succeed, 'A revolution in environmental and curb-emissions technologies is required to sustain the development of most unconventional oils.' That, he notes, is the alternative to 'over-regulation'. Without it, he foresees, 'a continuous dispute between the industry and environmental groups' that 'will force government to delay the development of new projects'.

The International Energy Agency (IEA) was formed in 1973 at the time of the first OPEC crisis. As a representative body of twenty-eight different member nations with a coordinating role on energy policy, its outlook tends to reflect the conservatism needed to serve a membership that ranges from the Republic of Korea to the United States, Norway, Japan, the United Kingdom and Turkey. Yet Fatih Birol, chief economist at the IEA, said that we have moved beyond Shell's 'uncertainty' into the 'danger zone' for the global economy. In 2010, oil import costs for the mostly wealthy thirty-four OECD countries had risen by $200 billion to $790 billion.[99] 'Oil import bills are becoming a threat to the economic recovery,' said Birol in January 2011 when oil prices were nearing $100 per barrel again. 'This is a wake-up call to the oil consuming countries and to the oil producers.' A year later prices were over $120. Birol warned that this scenario alone could 'bring us to the same financial crisis times that we saw in 2008'.

A growing consensus suggests that fossil fuel production will only get more difficult, and oil prices higher and more volatile. The cost of maintaining dependence on these fuels will also rise, and it is already very high.

According to the OECD, if you combine the subsidies given to the oil, coal and gas industries – a mixture of tax breaks and subsidies on exploration, production and consumption – in twenty-four of their member countries (presumably the other ten were reluctant to provide data), together with subsidies given in emerging and developing countries, annual totals in the second half of the last decade varied around $500 billion,[100] roughly equivalent to the entire GDP of Denmark and Finland combined. (Alternatively, if you remove Nigeria and South Africa, it is more than the combined annual national incomes of the remaining forty-six countries in sub-Saharan Africa.) Other estimates put the global subsidy figure as high as $1 trillion.[101]

All of which suggests that it is both urgent and affordable for the world to shift to non-fossil-fuel power sources. And the UN conference was not alone in believing that renewable energy had a major role to play, if not ultimately meeting all our energy needs.

Even where science and technology lacks the huge official backing enjoyed by fossil fuels and nuclear power, it is discovering extraordinary potential. The American scientists Mark Jacobson and Mark Delucchi devised a global plan in which wind, water and solar energy technologies provide 100 per cent of humanity's energy needs, cutting out all fossil fuels. In their scenario, the world moves to a zero-carbon energy system by 2030. Globally, it employs 3.8 million large wind turbines, wind being twenty-five times more carbon-efficient than nuclear power, ninety thousand solar plants and a combination of geothermal, tidal and rooftop solar-photovoltaic installations.

They also discounted both nuclear power and coal plants with carbon capture and storage, either because they relied on non-renewable resources (in the case of existing nuclear plants), or because the technology was insufficiently proven at scale (in the case of carbon capture). A full life-cycle analysis of these technologies revealed them to be either much less carbon-efficient, or beset with security, waste or other pollution problems.

The authors address the various practical challenges of taking renewable energy technologies to such a scale. As in the wartime examples we saw earlier, major tasks that emerge include how to redirect the world's productive capacity to build all the turbines, solar plants and cells, geothermal plants and related infrastructure that will be needed. It is plainly a vast undertaking, but then the stakes too are very, very high.

But Jacobson and Delucchi point out that the world already produces seventy-three million cars and light trucks every year and that factories could be retooled through a latter-day version of swords into ploughshares (Fords into wind farms, perhaps). For comparison, they point out that starting in 1956 the US Interstate Highway System managed to build forty-seven thousand miles of highway in just over three decades, 'changing commerce and society'.[102]

However, focused effort would also be needed, they conclude, to solve the scarcity of some mineral resources used in manufacture, such as the neodymium used in turbine gearboxes, indium and tellurium for thin film solar cells, lithium for batteries and platinum for fuel cells for electric vehicles.

The Sustainable Development Commission (SDC) was an official body set up by the Labour government in 2000. It acted as principal adviser and watchdog on government policy towards sustainable development, and was disbanded in 2011 by the subsequent incoming Coalition administration. The SDC investigated the UK's energy options in response to a UK government review of energy policy in 2006. In particular it looked at whether nuclear power was essential to meeting the UK's energy needs. To do so it analysed a range of alternative strategies for reducing carbon emissions and commissioned additional research on the economics of nuclear power from the Science and Technology Policy Research Unit at the University of Sussex, looking into the availability of uranium resources and several other aspects such as waste disposal.

They found that the 'UK's "practical" wind power resource is around half our current electricity consumption', even before accounting for future technological advances. In addition there are 'huge tidal, wave, biomass and solar resources', and the ability to reduce household CO_2 emissions by 60 per cent using currently available technology, especially energy efficiency. Micro-generation alone could provide 30–40 per cent of the UK's electricity generating needs by 2050, and much quicker with the kind of backing and incentives already enjoyed by fossil fuels and nuclear power.[103]

In summary, the SDC concluded, having examined a broad range of studies that offer different scenarios of our energy future: 'it is clear that there is more than enough renewable resource in the UK to provide a diverse, low carbon electricity supply. All the scenario results suggest that it is possible to meet our energy needs in a carbon constrained economy without nuclear power.'[104]

This future would need 'an aggressive expansion of energy efficiency and renewables', but that would mean that 'the UK would become a leader in low-carbon technologies'.[105]

Other studies have come to the same conclusion. The Centre for Alternative Technology (CAT), based in North Wales and a world-leading centre for research and development in renewable energy, has published two reports on the theme of Zero Carbon Britain. The second of them, *Zero Carbon Britain 2030*, I was involved with. As the title suggests, it concludes that Britain could achieve a zero-carbon energy system by 2030, sooner than some other strategies that focus on the year 2050, and again without recourse to nuclear power. It does so through schemes for a 90 per cent reduction in emissions, and using 'carbon capture' equivalent to the residual 10 per cent. The plan is radical in the sense that it is not just about substituting one technology for another, but in keeping with many of the issues discussed earlier foresees lifestyle changes, different diets, changes to town planning, land use and transport systems. It is a bold re-imagining of a whole economy.

Such a prospect, some might find intimidating, but we can also view it as an opportunity. And from what we know, business as usual is not an option, because climate change and the peak and decline of oil production will in any case force other changes upon us. This is an attempt to manage change, rather than find ourselves managed by it.

For example, current austerity measures mean that the government is already acutely concerned about our balance of trade. The CAT report estimates that with an oil price of just $78 a barrel (it is around $120 at the time of writing), replacing our own North Sea oil and gas with like-for-like imports will add £53 billion to the trade deficit.

At this point the opportunity cost of different courses of action, or rather of continuing as we are compared with making positive changes, becomes very interesting. The Green New Deal group in the UK (for transparency, which I helped to found and am a member of) estimated the cost of a comprehensive low-carbon shift in the UK to be in the range of £50–70 billion per year. Others produced lower figures. The Sustainable Development Commission, before it was disbanded, said that the government should commit £30 billion per year for three years, whereas the Stern Review on the economics of climate change arrived at a figure of around £11 billion per year. Given that inaction is not an option due to the future of the oil market, and the need for action on climate change, all these estimates would seem to represent excellent value on all grounds.

Separately, the international environmental group WWF commissioned the energy consultants Ecofys to explore the same question, whether or not the world could shift to a system based entirely or almost completely on renewables.[106] It argues that dependence on fossil fuels could be reduced by 70 per cent by 2040, and that everyone in the world could have their energy needs met 95 per cent from renewable sources by 2050, reducing greenhouse gas emissions by 80 per cent, which allows for emissions that will come from the production of crops for bioenergy. Their model suggests that actual energy demand in 2050 can be lowered to 15 per cent beneath what it was in 2005, even allowing for population growth, increased economic output and transport. It does this with increased efficiency, recycling, higher building standards and different transport norms. A shift to electric power from renewable sources rather than solid and liquid fuels predominates, and smart electricity grids help to store and deliver power much more efficiently. Biofuels are a 'last resort' for ships, trucks, aeroplanes and industrial processes needing high temperatures. Redesign, radical efficiency gains and lower fuel costs also save €4 trillion annually. Nuclear power was again left out of their model.

The campaign group Greenpeace UK (also for transparency, of whose board I was a member at the time) looked at the contribution that a more decentralised energy system could make to bringing such a revolution about. In *Decentralising Power*, they point out that '67 per cent of primary energy input gets wasted in the current global centralised model of power generation', and that one fifth of the UK's CO_2 emissions also results from energy wasted in centralised fossil fuel power generation.[107]

In each of these examples of re-imagining our use of energy in such a way as to avert catastrophic climate change and to meet humanity's need for power, nuclear energy is unnecessary. It could be argued that this is the result of a more general philosophical or political orientation of the groups and bodies involved. Nevertheless, this might simply be the consequence of their own analysis of the broad costs and benefits of the technology, and the particular 'DNA for society' that it carries – namely, centralised, capital-intensive systems requiring high levels of militarised security, etc. And, equally, the point about the influence of a certain ideological worldview can just as easily be made about those who confidently assert the absolute necessity of nuclear power. But in this light, it is interesting to look at a cool assessment of the potential of nuclear power by those who are fundamentally in favour of the technology.

Even convinced advocates, it seems, can be more cautious than some more recent green converts. Scientists at the world-leading Massachusetts Institute of Technology conducted the assessment because of their 'belief that this technology is an important option for the United States and the world to meet future energy needs without emitting carbon dioxide and other atmospheric pollutants', and assembled an interdisciplinary team to do so. Having set out to discover the maximum potential contribution that nuclear power could make to the global energy mix, they published a first report, *The Future of Nuclear Power*, in 2003, and updated it in 2009.

They looked at a number of scenarios from modest to ambitious. In the most ambitious scenario, which would involve an unprecedented expansion of the industry in both speed and scale, they envisaged a near-trebling of nuclear capacity by 2050. This would mean building between 1000 and 1500 large nuclear power plants. If successful this, the boldest of the approaches, would increase nuclear power's share of electricity generation (electricity only, note, not overall energy, something often missed or confused) from 17 per cent to 19 per cent – an increase of just 2 per cent. But the cold shower wasn't finished. They arrived at several other conclusions to dampen expectations.

In deregulated energy markets, they found that nuclear power is not competitive with other energy options, and they noted that between their first and second reports, costs had risen at the rate of 15 per cent per year. On safety they cautioned that little was known, beyond the operation of the reactors themselves, about the safety of the overall fuel cycle. On the perennial, unsolved problem of nuclear waste disposal, they concluded that while geological disposal (the bury-and-forget approach) is technically feasible, 'execution is yet to be demonstrated or certain'. And that: 'A convincing case has not been made that the long-term waste management benefits of advanced, closed fuel cycles involving reprocessing of spent fuel are outweighed by the short-term risks and costs.'

On the dangers of nuclear proliferation, highlighted more recently by heightened international political tensions over the potential acquisition by Iran of nuclear power, and dangers of terrorists making 'dirty bombs', the MIT group found, disturbingly, that:

> The current international safeguards regime is inadequate to meet the security challenges of the expanded nuclear deployment contemplated in the global growth scenario. The reprocessing system now used in Europe, Japan, and Russia that involves

separation and recycling of plutonium presents unwarranted proliferation risks.

Given the high demands and relatively low gains of their 'ambitious' scenario, and the rate at which reactors would need to be built,
in the 2009 update they noted that: 'After five years, no new plants
are under construction in the United States and insufficient progress
has been made on waste management.'

Still others highlight a range of opportunity costs to building new
nuclear power capacity. As well as distracting funds and interest away
from lower-carbon, more secure and quicker to install renewable
technologies, nuclear power relies on a different kind of infrastructure
that is unfriendly to renewables. As Walt Patterson, an Associate
Fellow of the energy programme at the Chatham House think tank,
put it: 'Nuclear power needs climate change more than climate
change needs nuclear power.'

One of the obstacles frequently raised in the case of renewable
energy is the issue of so-called 'intermittency'. This is the observation
that wind does not blow constantly, nor the sun shine day and night,
but vary during the day and seasonally. The criticism is that this makes
energy planning difficult and limits the share of the energy mix that
renewables can provide: the more you have, it is said, the more conventional energy is needed for 'backup' when nature fails to deliver.

Jacobson and Delucchi looked at this in their global energy model.
First, they make the point that conventional power generation has its
own issues with 'intermittency'. A typical coal plant in the US, for
example, is 'offline' for the equivalent of six and a half weeks per year
for a mix of scheduled and unplanned maintenance. By comparison,
they say, modern wind turbines have a downtime for maintenance of
less than a week on land and around two and a half weeks at sea. Also,
when single wind turbines are down, this affects just a small proportion of overall energy production, whereas significant amounts are lost
if a coal, nuclear or gas power plant has to cease generating. Over one
fifth of the 132 nuclear plants built in the US to date were shut down
early and for good due to operational or cost problems. A quarter more
were closed for at least a year.[108]

The answer for renewables, they say, is how you blend the technologies. For predictable 'base' supply, tidal and geothermal energy

are good. Wind, contrary to myth, is actually reliable over time. Seasonally, and in the cycle of day and night and between land and sea, it is a largely known quantity. The same goes for solar, and both are aided by good forecasting. Equally, the wind will tend to blow on stormy days, and the sun shine in good weather. Hydroelectric power, due to its also good predictability, contributes well to base supply. Smart grids also help to even out variability, and interconnecting wind farms that are displaced at distances of one hundred to two hundred miles apart means that a drop in output from any single farm can be buffered by others. Improvements in energy storage, coupled with grid systems made more resilient by intelligently combining micro, medium, large and 'super grids', all point to a more stable, lower waste energy infrastructure.

The energy analyst David Milborrow backs this analysis in the case of the UK. 'A large pool of backup generation capacity called "short term reserve" is used to step in when coal, gas and nuclear power stations stop generating at short notice,' he writes. 'They can and do "trip" without warning, leading to the instantaneous loss of large chunks of UK generation – as occurred on 27 May 2008, with the Sizewell B nuclear power station.' Outages from big power stations like this create a real risk of so-called 'through tripping', when an overburdened system experiences a failure like a domino-effect. But, according to Milborrow, 'it is extremely unlikely that the equivalent amount of wind will disappear instantaneously'. In January 2009 there was a significant spell of weather that was both cold and still. People wanted power but the output from wind was low. Yet existing backup arrangements were more than sufficient to cope, even though by coincidence around half of the UK's nuclear output was also not available at the time. The energy system is already designed in such a way as to be able to manage the kind of variable output that might come from wind energy.

The notion that nuclear power is reliably never off is an enduring myth. If any place constitutes the spiritual home of nuclear power, it is France. A former French government minister was once asked how France had managed to avoid the kind of popular resistance to nuclear power seen in many other European countries. His candid response, which only gains in translation, was that: 'When you're draining the marsh, you don't tell the frogs.'

In July 2009 temperatures in many parts of France rose above 30°C. There was a huge demand for power to keep cool. Air conditioning across the country came into its own. Only there was a problem. The nuclear reactors of the national energy company EDF were generating their lowest output for six years. It seems they didn't like the hot weather either. Out of nineteen reactors, fourteen are based inland and rely on river water for cooling. Rising temperatures force reactors to shut down to prevent overheating. Reportedly, around one third of total capacity was out of service, causing France to import energy from Britain.[109] Many other nuclear power stations are coastal, and threatened by rising sea levels due to global warming. If the reactors inland prove increasingly vulnerable to heat waves, it merely raises another question over their role in the energy mix.

Another ironic backflip on the standard story of nuclear being dependable and renewables needing a helping hand came in the winter of 2012. During a cold spell, a lack of capacity in France meant rising energy imports from Germany. But where exactly was that helping hand coming from? A spokesperson for the 'transit grid operator' Amprion said at the time that solar 'photovoltaics in southern Germany is currently helping us a lot'.[110]

Great excitement has been generated around the prospects of using a different kind of fuel, thorium, for nuclear power. Yet its development faces many of the same problems experienced by reactors using uranium and plutonium: high costs of development, build and operation, security, pollution and proliferation hazards and long lead-time for introduction. Key drawbacks are:

- the very high costs of technology development, construction and operation;
- marginal benefits for a thorium fuel cycle over the currently utilised uranium / plutonium fuel cycles;
- serious nuclear weapons proliferation hazards: the molten salt reactor (MSR) technology promoted for thorium could be used to produce fissile uranium and plutonium at very high purities well above ordinary 'weapons grade';
- the danger of both routine and accidental releases of radiation, mainly from continuous 'live' fuel reprocessing in MSRs;

- the very long lead time for significant deployment of MSRs of the order of half a century – rendering it irrelevant in terms of addressing current or medium-term energy supply needs.

Let's recap briefly on the scale of the challenge, and finish with a few questions to ask when choosing between different energy technologies.

Allowing for population and economic growth, the UN specialist body on trade and development, UNCTAD, looked at the degree to which carbon has been successfully removed from the economy in the past, and then compared that with what would be necessary to hold global warming below 2°C.[111] At the global level they calculate that in 1980, for every dollar of output 1 kg of carbon was used. By 2008 that had fallen to 770 g. For each dollar of economic activity, that represents an improvement of 0.7 per cent per year. Of course, however, as overall output outstripped greater carbon efficiency, total carbon emissions rose substantially.

Now assume, as many believe will be the case, that the world population rises to around 9 billion by the middle of the century. Assume too that the economy continues to grow at a moderate 2 per cent, and that developing countries are allowed to catch up to European income levels. In this case, UNCTAD calculates, in order to keep below the 2°C climate threshold, the carbon intensity of each dollar's worth of output would have to fall from 770 g to just 6 g, 'almost 130 times lower than it is today (requiring an average annual fall in carbon intensity of 11 per cent)'. It should be said that in writing this report the author formed a sceptical view of the notion that economic growth can ever, in a true sense, be 'green'.

Nevertheless, such figures underline the importance of reducing carbon in the energy mix as fast and efficiently as possible, whilst meeting a broad range of other social and economic needs. So what are the criteria that it would be rational to use?

Cost is an unavoidable one. How much does it cost per unit of energy generated? You also need to ask: What is the cost of the carbon saving and how quickly can it be saved, i.e., at what rate and scale can the technology be introduced? Then how efficient is the technology in terms of how much energy you get back for the amount of energy you put in? All power generation is a form of 'wetting the wick', some just need more wetting than others. This is called 'energy return on energy invested', or just 'energy return on investment'. Many different estimates exist to answer these questions, all of which are highly sensitive to how the technologies are assessed and which parameters are used. For example, in arriving at the full financial and carbon costs of nuclear power there are many hidden subsidies to contend with (such as officially capped insurance liabilities in the event of a major accident), and few (and often incomparable) attempts have been made to produce a full nuclear life-cycle assessment of its carbon and energy required, cradle to grave, from mining and construction to in-perpetuity management of nuclear waste.

Then there are all the other questions that relate to the way the technologies you choose are not neutral in the effect they have on the wider economy, and the type of DNA they carry for politics and society, like the security implications of the nuclear sector. Evaluations of this sort are complex, as we've seen elsewhere, but they matter because they lead to some things happening and others not.

In a government review of energy policy in 2002, nuclear power was, in effect, shelved, only to make a comeback shortly after, driven by assiduous lobbying. The need to tackle climate change was invoked. The nuclear industry made reasonable-sounding calls for a 'balanced-energy' system. This, though, was just code for advocating a full reboot, not just replacing existing, ageing nuclear capacity, but adding to it as well. Whilst they talked up what nuclear power could offer, other voices, like Bernard Ingham's above, talked down the renewable alternatives.

Yet although, for over half a century, the nuclear sector enjoyed large and incalculable government support, it languishes still with many unsolved problems. The renewable sector, on the other hand, has been the very poor relation. A report from the Science and Technology Committee of the House of Lords noted that while 'the sources of renewable energy, such as the sun, wind and tides, are inexhaustible, indigenous and abundant, and their exploitation, properly managed, has the potential to enhance the long-term security of the United Kingdom's energy supplies and to help us cut carbon dioxide emissions', action to tap that potential had been lamentable. 'We deplore the minimal amounts that the Government have committed

to renewable energy related R&D,' they stated.[112] Effective government, we are often reminded, is all about prioritisation. Public
spending choices tend, in practice, to a zero sum game. Money
subsidising nuclear power, in whatever form, is money not invested in
renewables. In energy policy priorities need reviewing. Under the
Labour government, which became pro-nuclear, its own Performance
and Innovation Unit warned that: 'A sustained programme of investment in currently proposed nuclear power plants could adversely
affect the development of smaller scale technologies.'[113]

It's not the purpose of this chapter to burden the reader with a
deluge of comparative technological evaluations. That is not the
point. For the record, there are assessments that, using the sort of
criteria above, compare a range of renewable technologies with
nuclear power and other conventional sources. Estimates vary
depending on assumptions, but all renewables compare favourably in
terms of job creation. A range of energy efficiency, wind, hydro, biofuels and non-renewable Combined Heat and Power (CHP) show up
as already cheaper at reducing carbon emissions, as well as – in a
projection for the year 2020 – being cheaper where generation is concerned.

A Stanford University study found that coal, even with carbon
sequestration fitted, still emits '60 to 110 times more carbon and air
pollution than wind energy'. Nuclear was found to emit up to
twenty-five times more, similarly, than wind energy. To 'improve
energy security, mitigate global warming and reduce the number of
deaths caused by air pollution' it ranked the desirability and effec-
tiveness of energy options as follows: 1, wind power; 2, concentrated
solar power; 3, geothermal power; 4, tidal power; 5, solar photovoltaics (PV); 6, wave power; 7, hydroelectric power; 8, a tie between
nuclear power and coal with carbon capture and sequestration
(CCS).[114]

By shifting assumptions, some variation may be found, but I think
there are two key points. It is theoretically and technically possible,
if not easy, to solve our energy problems relying wholly on renewable
energy. Some may still want to choose nuclear power for particular
reasons. But the assertion, almost moral blackmail, that we must
accept it unquestioningly because of global warming is wrong. Not
only is it not a 'shoo-in', it is a technology with many unsolved prob-

lems that carries in its wake a host of costly challenges around security
and waste, not to mention a range of practical ones to do with slow
speed and high cost of implementation.

It is the point made earlier by Professor Andy Stirling, namely that
a range of different energy futures are possible, reflecting a range of
energy systems. And to repeat his well-chosen words, 'the crucial
issues include contending social values, political interests and future
visions. To deny this and seek instead to assert ostensibly definitive
technical answers is undermining equally of science and democracy.'[115] We can argue about the details of the different options, but
that is the point: we can and should argue the details and the kinds of
society, convivial or otherwise, that different technological choices
lend themselves to.

Personally, where nuclear power is concerned, I believe that
there are good grounds to believe that its further uptake will make
tackling climate change more, not less, difficult. This will happen
because it will absorb limited resources, crowding out alternatives
that are quicker to install and also therefore quicker at cutting
carbon. The alternatives are cleaner, more flexible, bring broader
economic benefits, are open to community-scale ownership and
management, safer both directly in their operation and in the sense
of not presenting a security risk, and altogether less problematic.
Paradoxically, it seems to me that somehow the idea of nuclear
power as synonymous with science, with trustworthy lab-coated

solutions, itself provokes an irrational and quite unscientific fervour of support. It is merely one technology. There are others, with fewer problems, which are equally to do with the appliance of science.

Yet, while the options are there, if they are not embraced the recipe for apocalypse stays on the table. With an unchanged global energy mix, the OECD warns in its outlook on the environment up to the middle of the century that instead of the necessary carbon cuts, fossil fuels 'will supply about 85 per cent of energy demand in 2050, implying a 50 per cent increase in greenhouse gas emissions and worsening urban air pollution'. This in turn will drive temperature rises to the point where warming feeds off itself, in an uncontrollable upward spiral.

Of course, even before any of this, we can all help by conducting our own mini-energy review. Homes account for nearly one third of UK greenhouse gas emissions. In the four decades between 1970 and 2009 the number of consumer electronic gadgets in a typical UK household increased by eleven times.[116] While some individual items used energy more efficiently, the sheer volume increased their energy consumption over the period by 600 per cent. Particular product choices can increase energy consumption too. Take the fashion for flatscreen TVs: replacing traditional cathode ray tube sets with plasma screens typically increased electricity use fourfold. From 1990 to 2009 the number of all household electrical appliances increased three and half times.

Each Christmas the media play a game to guess what is going to be 'the' gadget to get. In one year, 2007, it was meant to be the Nintendo Wii games console. Using its recommended stand-by facility and played for, say, fourteen hours a week, this single household device would be responsible in a year for the equivalent in carbon emissions of the entire lifestyle of an individual living in an African country like Burundi or Chad. Buying electronic gadgets as gifts for Christmas could well be a big mistake regardless. In a book called *Scroogenomics*, the economist Joel Waldfogel demonstrates that, even in conventional economic terms, most typical gift-buying at Christmas destroys economic value. This is because, unless you know someone incredibly well, and know exactly what they want, your gift will be worth less to them than what you paid for it. At best the exchange might break even.

Kurt Vonnegut, whose curious vision of the future began this section, also had a pithy view of humanity in the present:

> Can I tell you the truth? I mean this isn't like TV news, is it? Here's what I think the truth is: We are all addicts of fossil fuels in a state of denial, about to face cold turkey. And like so many addicts about to face cold turkey, our leaders are now committing violent crimes to get what little is left of what we're hooked on.[117]

Now we know we have the mechanisms to break that addiction, and in the next chapter we'll look at how the manacles of the mind get forged, and how we might break those chains too.

9

The Message

Junk highs and the Big Sell – what advertising has to answer for

Advertising at its best is making people feel that without their product, you're a loser.

Nancy Shalek

The function of this new industry would be to recruit the best creative talent of the society and to create a culture in which desire and identity would be fused with commodities to make the dead world of things come alive.

Professor Sut Jhally,
'Advertising at the Edge of the Apocalypse'

It will be those peoples who can keep alive, and cultivate into a fuller perfection, the art of life itself and do not sell themselves for the means of life, who will be able to enjoy the abundance when it comes.

John Maynard Keynes

According to Rory Sutherland, when President of the Institute of Practitioners in Advertising,

The truth is that marketing raises enormous ethical questions every day – at least it does if you're doing it right. If this were not the case, the only possible explanations are either that you believe marketers are too ineffectual to make any difference, or you believe that marketing activities only affect people at the level of conscious argument. Neither of these possibilities appeals to me. I would rather be thought of as evil than useless.[1]

Such a turn of phrase, his last remark delivered with a throwaway insouciance, marked Sutherland as a worthy figurehead of his industry. *Think of Me As Evil?* was instantly taken up as the title of a groundbreaking charity report calling for an ethical debate on the future of advertising. It was long overdue.

The advertising industry is huge. Global spending on advertising in a single year, 2012, was estimated at $540 billion.[2] That is equal to the basic military budget (excluding war spending and nuclear weapons) of the world's last great fighting superpower, the United States.[3]

The previous year, a mere $506 billion was spent. This, so the industry commented, with a slightly disappointed sigh and little sense of irony, was less than expected due to 'natural disasters and political turmoil'. The advertising company that made the observation, WPP, was itself extraordinarily large, spanning the globe with over 150,000 staff and 2400 offices in 107 countries.

Money spent annually on persuading people to buy cars alone is in the region of $40 billion[4] – by coincidence, the same amount estimated by the UN Environment Programme which, if invested globally in forest conservation, could 'halve deforestation, generate millions of jobs and combat climate change'.[5]

As Sutherland remarks, it is hard to imagine so much money being spent, without advertising having significant influence over our behaviour. In obviously controversial areas such as the advertising of tobacco and drink, the industry often deploys the argument that adverts do not persuade people to actually do something that they wouldn't otherwise do, but simply enable the efficient functioning of choice within a pre-existing market. That is to say adverts are meant to help inform people about their range of choices, once they have already made a decision to purchase something.

Several other claims are made in favour of advertising. From an economic perspective it is meant to stimulate competition, help new businesses establish themselves, lead to lower and more stable prices by making price comparison easier, and raise consumption. Although claimed as a benefit, from the point of view of societies already hooked into unsustainable and unsatisfying overconsumption the latter point can, of course, be viewed as the problem.

The industry's own research suggests that it does far more than help you and me to choose between raspberry jam brand A and brand B. In countries that spend more on advertising as a percentage of their national income, levels of consumption at the household level likewise as a share of national income are also higher. Surrounded by more advertising, people are more likely to spend and consume than to save. Hence, countries at the top of the advertising spending league, like the United States, United Kingdom and Australia, are also at the top in terms of households' propensity to spend. This should not surprise us. As we've seen elsewhere, people are anything but the rational, free agents of mainstream economic theory. We are enormously influenced by our surroundings.

Take, for example, what psychologists call 'stereotype activation'. In one groundbreaking study a group of people were subtly primed with words relating to the stereotype of being elderly. Their behaviour was then compared with a separate control group that had undergone no such influence. The group exposed to connotations of ageing and being old then started to change. They began to exhibit stereotypical behaviour for old age. They walked more slowly and actually became more forgetful.[6]

What might be the environmental influence of advertising? I did some primary research during one normal weekday in London. Over twenty-four hours I counted two things. First I added up every advert that I saw (at least those that I noticed; advertising in the urban environment is so pervasive that it is entirely possible that I missed examples, say, of branding and sponsorship). These were visual and aural messages exhorting me to buy goods and services, to be a materialist and consumer. Second, I recorded every public information message I encountered that addressed me and my behaviour more as a public-spirited citizen, messages that promoted civic engagement and responsibility, as someone who, for example, might take action on climate change.

By the end of the day I found I had been exposed to 454 adverts that addressed me as a private consumer and just three messages concerning my role in the public sphere. The latter were so few that I could remember them all. One was a police notice requesting witnesses to a murder, one a train company message asking me, politely, please not to attack their staff, and finally there was one asking drivers to avoid running over cyclists.

Allowing for reading more papers and watching more television at the weekend, it suggests that in a single year, potentially I may be exposed to over 180,000 adverts, prompts to consume and to define myself first and foremost as a consumer. Compare that with seeing perhaps just 1000 prompts to be a good citizen. Put another way, on this small but fairly typical sample you could say that the 'stereotype activation' in my culture is loaded in favour of consumerism and against citizenship at a ratio of 180:1. A numbers game of this imbalance leaves little surprise to a consumer society so often blind to the planet it depends on. After all, we largely make choices from the range of options put in front of us. The consequence seems inexorable if the dice are loaded by the disproportionate number of choices available for private, largely passive consumption, and against active public engagement and production.

Guy Shrubsole of the Public Interest Research Centre (PIRC) thought to use the powerful Google tool Ngram to compare changing occurrences of the terms 'citizen' and 'consumer' in its huge database of publicly available published works. If you reproduce the exercise from the dawn of the consumer age, around when Thorsten Veblen published *The Theory of the Leisure Class*, which introduced the term 'conspicuous consumption', the result is startling. The lines on the graph cross like a

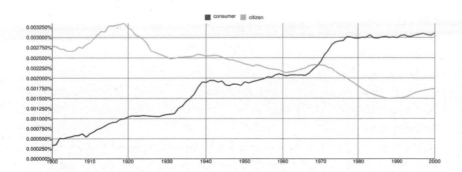

huge X, like a vote in an election for how to live in which only one side had a campaign budget. The graph on page 285 is for the years 1900–2000 (Shrubsole chose a longer time frame but with similar results).

The 'weight-of-numbers' case also undermines some of the other arguments advanced by the industry in its defence. Very much in the same way that candidates in American presidential primaries can simply outspend their rivals, winning by drowning their rivals in aggressive newspaper, radio and television 'attack' adverts, far from helping new small firms in the economy, massively unequal advertising spending has the ability to entrench already large and dominant companies who can outspend upstart market entrants. This can be true not only of competition between firms, but also of competition between corporate profits and the public interest.

Credos is a think tank linked to and serving the advertising industry. The name is interestingly chosen from the word meaning 'a belief or set of beliefs'. (In the dictionary, it is immediately followed by 'credulity' – the 'disposition to believe on insufficient evidence'.) On its blog Credos lamented a reported rise in drink-driving among young people. It also decried the fall in government spending on advertising campaigns to combat drink-driving from £1.1 million in 2009 to £50,000 in 2010. Fair enough, you might think – perhaps a little self-serving, but in a good cause. The short article finished echoing the question of a BBC *Panorama* documentary asking what was driving people to drink and whether the government was doing enough to prevent it.

If Credos read the British Medical Association's (BMA) report *Under the Influence*, they would find a clue to the answer. Although hampered in their research because considerations of commercial confidentiality are used to draw a veil over spending on much drink advertising, a Cabinet Office report from a few years earlier, 2003, provided figures for an interesting comparison. It estimated that the industry at the time spent £200 million annually on direct mass media advertising, a figure that grew to £800 million when all 'marketing communications' were taken into account. The BMA points out that this is five times more than the Central Office of Information's (COI) entire advertising turnover for 2002–03, which covers all the issues that government must communicate on, including the adverse health impact of alcohol consumption. In profiting both from the amount spent on promoting alcohol and the much smaller amount spent warning of its dangers when combined with driving, the advertising industry appears a little bit like the arms-dealer villain of folklore, selling weapons to both sides of the conflict, only much bigger guns to the bad guys.

Spending by the end of the decade would almost certainly have risen but, being very generous even with these numbers, the ratio of spending on advertising to promote alcohol, compared with that on anti-drink-driving campaigns, would have been around 700:1 in 2009 and 16,000:1 in 2010. Without doubt there are other important factors that influence alcohol consumption, but with those figures in mind, and Rory Sutherland's observation, reiterate Credos's question about what drives people to drink and whether there is sufficient government action to prevent it.

Both the advertising industry and the drinks industry have a track record of lobbying hard against regulatory restraint. For example, based on research the medical profession argued strongly to introduce a minimum unit price for alcohol. In favour were the former chief medical officer Sir Liam Donaldson, the National Institute for Health and Clinical Excellence, the British Medical Association and the Royal College of Physicians. Alcohol industry lobbying defeated their efforts in 2011. When a commitment to minimum unit pricing was removed from proposed legislation, opposition MPs reportedly were sent a free case of beer from the brewer SAB Miller.[7]

An article published in the medical journal the *Lancet* by three experts in alcohol-related death and disease calculated that the failure to take a tougher regulatory approach might cause up to 250,000 additional premature deaths over the course of two decades.[8] 'Tougher action' in their view meant steps like the minimum price per unit and the sort of restrictions on alcohol advertising and sponsorship used in France. But the advertising industry dislikes mandatory controls just as much as the drink industry does. The trade body the Advertising Association is linked with Credos and describes its own role like this: 'We inform policy decisions and contribute research papers in order to ensure the benefits and value of advertising and the efficacy of *self-regulation* are taken into account.' (The italics are my emphasis.) The Association makes clear that its relationship with Credos is to ensure that its advocacy is backed with 'high quality research', which sounds suspiciously like an approach of policy-based evidence.

Conflicts of interest like this, and other ethical concerns, are just some of the problematic aspects of the industry. There are other serious economic questions raised. For example, in the context of making the positive case for advertising mentioned above, Dr Maximilien Nayaradou concedes a range of negative economic consequences of advertising.[9] And his major argument in favour, that it fuels growth and consumption, is perhaps its biggest problem. But more orthodox concerns include that the cost of advertising drives up the prices of the goods advertised; that advertising gives further unfair competitive advantage to companies that are already large, dominant and can afford it; that advertising encourages 'superfluous' investments over real and productive ones; and that it 'promotes a proliferation of falsely differentiated goods', in other words that it encourages wasteful duplication of essentially identical products differing only in how they are marketed and possibly appear.[10] British businesses spent £18 billion on advertising in one year, 2009, money not in itself productively invested, as say in improving product quality or development and innovation.

The flaw is that while it might make sense for companies individually to spend large amounts on advertising, when a whole economy and society does it, the spending becomes what economists call 'deadweight'. It's the term used in economics to denote, for example, when an action entails a cost in either monetary or other terms in one place that is not balanced by a commensurate gain elsewhere. Road congestion is a typical example, whereby the cost of one person being stuck in traffic does not have an offsetting benefit for someone elsewhere. And, on the contrary, it is more likely to pollute their air space.

Each year around 1.7 billion items of direct or 'junk' mail, just one tool in the advertiser's box, get delivered to UK homes. It is uninvited, frequently never opened, and creates a mountain of waste that often goes straight into landfill rubbish sites. One county council alone, Cornwall, estimates that it disposes of 4000 tonnes of direct mail every year – 500 dustcarts' worth, costing them around £700,000.[11] Also, rather than assisting the 'efficient market hypothesis', it may be doing exactly the opposite. Such markets depend on transparency and clear information, and even if such a thing as the rational consumer existed, it would be very hard to argue that advertising conveys the kind of information about the price or nature of any one product that enables its balanced assessment against any other. The proliferation and marketing of complex price tariffs in everything from mobile phones to banking and household energy supplies make straightforward comparisons almost impossible. This prevents the so-called 'price discovery' – finding the right price for a product – needed for a market to function optimally.

The Independent Commission on Banking, set up by the UK government after the financial crash of 2008 to recommend financial reforms, found that the marketing of 'opaque' charging structures on people's current accounts made it hard for people to work out which would be most cost-effective, preventing real competition. Ofgem, the regulator for gas and electricity, came to exactly the same conclusion for energy customers.[12] Its chief executive, Alistair Buchanan, accused the big six UK companies of failing to 'play it straight with consumers'.[13] The consumer organisation Which? complains similarly about phone pricing.[14] The practice is so common that it even has its own term, which has entered the English lexicon. 'Confusion marketing' is defined by the Cambridge Dictionary as 'selling products or services together in a way that makes it very difficult to decide which company's products or services are cheapest'. In marketing circles it is known as the strategy of 'deliberately confusing the customer'.

If advertising simply conveys information about what a product does and how much it costs, there is an economic defence that it aids the efficient working of a market. It can help people to find and compare products. But as information increasingly is superseded by persuasion, mood and techniques of subtle emotional and psychological manipulation, it calls in question whether any useful economic purpose remains. Whatever its problematic economic function, the seemless web of advertising, marketing and public relations certainly serves several other purposes.

Burson Marsteller is the public relations subsidiary of the giant WPP group mentioned above. Also global, they have clients ranging from big oil – they represented Exxon over the *Exxon Valdez* tanker disaster – to big chemicals – they managed communications for the Union Carbide company, responsible for the Bhopal disaster that resulted in thousands of deaths and injuries, as well as for Dow Chemicals, who took over Union Carbide. Burson Marsteller has also had clients ranging from big tobacco to companies selling military and nuclear hardware and fossil fuels. I use the past tense here, purely because Burson Marsteller no longer make public their current client list, so it is not possible to positively identify exactly who they might work for today. It did emerge recently, however, that they acted covertly on behalf of Facebook in a campaign against its internet social networking rivals Google.

The company was founded by Harold Burson in 1953, in the relatively early days of the industry. Interviewed in 2006 by the German current affairs magazine *Der Spiegel*, he praised a man called Edward Bernays, known as the 'father of spin', or 'public relations', or even 'misrepresentation', as *Der Spiegel*'s article put it. During the First World War Bernays worked for the Committee on Public Information under Woodrow Wilson's administration. Later he was to write: 'Those who manipulate the unseen mechanism of society constitute an invisible government which is the true ruling power. We are governed, our minds moulded, our tastes formed, our ideas suggested largely by men we have never heard of.' Bernays understood that his job was essentially propaganda, but thought that the term was sullied by the way that Germany had practised the art during the war. So, like a true marketing professional, he rebranded propaganda, coming up with the new term 'public relations', or just 'PR'. Looking back over the last century, one author, Stewart Ewen, concluded: 'The history of PR is . . . a history of a battle for what is reality and how people will see and understand reality.'[15]

And, true to the lineage, Harold Burson alluded to an even more impressive term for his craft. Asked by the magazine to define exactly what PR was, he replied: 'It also has a lot to do with perception. Perception can be controlled through PR, attitudes can be changed.' This is what has come to be known as 'perception management' – yet another new term to thank the industry for, and which has entered the lexicon. Asked whether, indeed, that didn't sound rather like propaganda, Burson responded: 'Propaganda is a form of PR.' For Burson, Bernays was a man who wrote the rule book. 'His methodology, of course, was fundamental,' he says. 'Most of the things we do today were identified by Bernays eighty years ago. He had brilliant ideas.'

Among those ideas was Bernays's insight that 'In almost every act of our lives, whether in the sphere of politics or business, in our social conduct or our ethical thinking, we are dominated by the relatively small number of persons . . . who pull the wires that control the public mind.' While that might sound Machiavellian in the extreme, Burson Marsteller has a code of conduct that staff are required to adhere to. It specifies that the company will 'respect national laws and any other laws with an international reach . . . where relevant', and that it is 'committed to acting ethically in all aspects of our business and to maintaining the highest standards of honesty and integrity'.

Over the years Burson Marsteller has had the opportunity to test its ethics in the application of Bernays techniques in a wide range of situations that go far beyond glossing the reputations of challenging corporate clients. The company represented the Nigerian government when it was complicit in the Biafran famine, and counted the Romanian Communist dictator Nicolae Ceauşescu on its books. They also worked on behalf of the Argentinian military Junta whose campaign of extra-judicial killings against its own people and opponents to the regime still causes protests today. It has had the controversial private military contractor Blackwater, active during the war in Iraq, as a client too.

At the top right-hand corner of Burson Marsteller's website there are two options to contact them. One is a simple 'contact us', the other 'global crisis contacts'. No problem, it would seem, is too hot to handle. There is now, though, one concession according to the company's ethics code: it no longer handles the accounts of tobacco firms. But, asked by *Der Spiegel* about working for the Argentinian Junta, Burson said it was 'not a problem', explaining that when the Junta took power 'many saw it as a liberation'. The article caused something of a stir. It was, perhaps understandably, critical of the industry. But, far from understanding the criticisms and promising to look into any of the issues it raised – which itself would have been a smart crisis-management technique, if not even lesson number one in the crisis-management rule book – leading figures leapt aggressively to Burson's defence.

Richard Edelman is head of another world-leading public relations company that carries his name, Edelman. Writing on his company's website he denounced the *Der Spiegel* article as 'a conflation of cinema-induced fantasy, anti-Americanism, anti President Bush, anti-capitalism, and fear of propaganda'. Given that public relations as an industry was born out of wartime public information campaigns, or 'propaganda',[16] turns of events like this should not, perhaps, surprise.

The term 'perception management' finds its way into the US Department of Defense's *Dictionary of Military and Associated Terms*. Here it is defined as:

> Actions to convey and/or deny selected information and indicators to foreign audiences to influence their emotions, motives, and objective reasoning as well as to intelligence systems and leaders at all to influence official estimates, ultimately resulting in foreign behaviors and official actions favorable to the originator's objectives. In various ways, perception management combines truth projection, operations security, cover and deception, and psychological operations.[17]

Economic issues, a range of ethical issues, and an influence over how we see ourselves, the degree to which our identities are formed as passive consumers or active citizens – here is an industry so pervasive that it can also be oddly invisible. But, as much as all of these concerns, perhaps most important of all is the way in which the multiple disciplines that go to make up 'perception management' are about projecting the version of truth useful to those who can afford to pay for it. Inevitably this results in suppressing or distracting from vital aspects of the real world that are inconvenient to the 'truth projectors'. An ultimately one-sided practice becomes, therefore, as Ewen puts it: 'a battle for what is reality'. In turn this shapes the awareness of problems, and whether and how they are addressed. In this case, mindful citizenship requires a level of vigilance that in normally busy lives is virtually impossible to maintain. Only perhaps when you are lucky enough to be armed with a certain amount of prior knowledge, and the issues themselves are acutely balanced, can action more easily ensue.

When is it right to say no? For the last couple of decades the language of 'positive engagement' with big corporations has dominated environmentalism. Several of the green movement's leading figures gave themselves over to it entirely, some even setting up new organisations solely dedicated to the purpose. The PR agency Edelman, mentioned above, specialises in helping controversial corporate clients to manage relationships with campaign groups who might be critical of them by the use of positive engagement. Saying no is frowned upon as being 'unpragmatic', if not churlish. We are meant to assume that all overtures are made in good faith. To decline amounts to resisting progress. But is that always true? For example, I was invited to speak at an event on the future of the energy system organised by a national newspaper. Initially I accepted. Then it transpired that the event was sponsored by the oil company Shell. Personally, I have always believed that not whether, but how, we engage in debates is important. After careful consideration I decided to withdraw. Others might have done differently, but these were the reasons that I explained to my colleagues and the organisers.

In my experience Shell, a one-time client of both Burson Marsteller and Edelman, has played a particularly cynical role in the discussion of energy futures. On the one hand, it wishes to be seen in public as open, engaged in environmental debate, for example through sponsorship of the conference I was invited to, and even appearing to encourage the expansion of renewable energy and a more balanced energy system. But on the other, the company turned its back on renewables, and has at least twice been reprimanded by the Advertising Standards Authority (ASA) for making misleading environmental claims. Shell ran an advert with the headline 'Don't Throw Anything Away, There Is No Away', in which it made the claim: 'We use our waste CO_2 to grow flowers.' It then transpired that only 0.325 per cent of their emissions were used in this way. Another complaint, also upheld, concerned a claim that investment in Canadian tar sands was part of Shell's strategy for sustainable energy.

Then in 2009 Shell's head of gas and power said in a *Wall Street Journal* (*WSJ*) article: 'We are businessmen, and we put the money we have available for investment into the opportunities that give us the best returns for the shareholders. If those were in renewables today, we'd be putting money there . . . It's just not the case.' The article continued: 'Shell says it will make no significant new investments in wind or solar power in the future,' and that it was maintaining steady investment in oil and gas exploration. According to the *WSJ* only 1.5 per cent of total investment by Shell went to renewables and 'their daily output of renewable energy is less than one-tenth of 1 per cent of their oil and gas production'.

Given all of this, I could not escape the conclusion that Shell's desire to be associated with a progressive debate about energy futures was a clear example of 'perception management', a self-interested manipulation of reality such as to distract from their true purpose, therefore making it easier for them to pursue. As such, it seemed wholly cynical, and driven by a desire to manage its public image, minimising criticism for its single-minded pursuit of profit from fossil fuels. It seemed to wish to create an appearance of openness and plurality, when in fact it's true, rather than projected, course was quite clearly different. This was a course with coordinates set upon an energy system that fuels climatic upheaval. The website Spinwatch has an archive of around fifty articles relating to Shell, and WikiLeaks also published documents revealing that oil companies had agendas in Nigeria, for example, quite different to their public pronouncements.

For those reasons, I explained, I could not in good conscience endorse their strategy by being a part of it. I suspect that, in the long run, such soft marketing approaches (this is how the industry themselves would describe them), like sponsoring high-profile events with national media partners, even where it creates space for debate, can do more harm than good. This is because it normalises their public image and creates the appearance of full, well-meaning engagement, whilst in the process stalling the pressure, likelihood and momentum for any real change. Shell's actual behaviour, as opposed to their public communications, seems to undermine any pretension to be engaging in debate in good faith.

The research and campaign group Cornerhouse showed, using leaked documents from public relations companies, how controversial multinational corporations in fear of the real influence of some campaign groups use highly complex engagement strategies to divide and dilute their critics, in order to allow their usual business to continue unimpeded. Typically this involves engaging selectively with large, more establishment-oriented pressure groups, whilst marginalising smaller, more radical groups.

Nicholas Hildyard of Cornerhouse highlighted the 'divide-and-conquer' strategy used by the US public relations firm Mongoven, Biscoe and Duchin.[18] It separates environmental groups, for example, into four categories: 'radicals', 'opportunists', 'idealists' and 'realists'. Opportunists are self-interested careerists who can be won over 'with at least the perception of a partial victory' in a campaign. Idealists, although a term sometimes used pejoratively, are a tough prospect for the PR industry, as the strategy points out: 'Because of their intrinsic altruism and because they have nothing perceptible to be gained by holding their position, they are easily believed by both the media and the public and sometimes even politicians.' The tactic employed, once pointed out by Hildyard, can be easily discerned in countless public debates. 'Idealists' are undermined by convincing them 'that their position is causing harm to others and cannot therefore be ethically justified'. They are then 'educated into a more "realistic" position'.

Wonderfully, 'realists', says Hildyard, are considered the easiest opponents because they accept industry's claim to be 'the only show in town', and that the best method of 'damage control' is to live with 'trade-offs' rather than push for radical change. He cites Don Naish of the Audubon Society in the US, who explained his choice to approve drilling by the oil company Mobil under an Audubon bird sanctuary in Michigan by saying that 'conservationists have just got to learn to work with industry'. So-called realists are considered the best for 'positive engagement' and, the strategy concludes: 'it is the solution agreed upon by the realists which becomes the accepted solution.' Most disliked, and difficult to deal with by the PR professionals are the 'radicals', who are the least technocratic, most interested in tackling causes rather than symptoms and, as such, concerned with social justice and local empowerment. This, then, is the PR strategy played out again and again in the interest of corporate divide and rule according to Hildyard.

You 'isolate the "radicals", cultivate and educate the "idealists" into becoming "realists", then co-opt the "realists" into agreeing with industry'. Hildyard showed me just such a practical map leaked to him that was produced by the agency for a particular campaign. There, with chilling efficiency, were several familiar organisations plotted against axes for whether they should be co-opted, educated or isolated by their clients. Hildyard's own group, Cornerhouse, was there, labelled 'radical', sectioned off in its own quadrant away from a few household-name green groups marked 'realist'.

It is tempting, almost politically fashionable, to deny or even ridicule notions of conspiracy. 'Cock-up' is the favoured, more comfortable conclusion to explain how the world works. But here was a clear, codified and commercialised example of the dark arts, the advice, thinking and practice that goes into countless issues of concern when public and private interests encounter each other. It is a reality that any attempts to 'cancel the apocalypse' must deal with.

One clever technique that brought this increasingly everyday yet covert political campaigning to attention mimics, or rather synthesises, the community-organising approach of the 'hard to handle' radicals. 'Astroturfing', synthetically green, is the name given to the corporate creation, usually via PR firms, of apparently real community and individual activism, whose purpose is to support the commercial activity of the client or to criticise its opponents. This may take the form of a new, apparently grass roots community organisation appearing to campaign on an issue, or seemingly self-motivated individuals leaving comments on relevant websites and in discussion forums. In this way genuine opposition appears diluted and support broader-based. The reality, however, is one of professional corporate lobbying adopting another, more fluid form.

Researchers and journalists like the environmentalists Andy Rowell, Jonathan Mathews and George Monbiot exposed several astroturfing campaigns. One such concerned a pro-GM food campaign coordinated by the PR firm Bivings Group. Comments from apparently independent individuals were also traced back to the Monsanto company, which has large investments in food biotechnology. The irony, pointed out by Monbiot, is that Monsanto hold a patent for actual AstroTurf – 'real fake grass'. Perhaps ill-advisedly, the urge to crow about the cleverness of their own techniques overcame Bivings, who explained their approach in an article on their own website like this:

> there are some campaigns where it would be undesirable or even disastrous to let the audience know that your organisation is directly involved ... Message boards, chat rooms, and list-serves are a great way to anonymously monitor what is being said. Once you are plugged into this world, it is possible to make postings to these outlets that present your position as an uninvolved third party.

Once its audacity was publicly pointed out, the article was removed, rewritten and re-posted. But not before others had safely kept a record.[19]

It is not only companies that employ campaign techniques like this. Aspects of the conservative Tea Party movement in the US have strayed under their influence, and governments use them too. Campaigns in support of Vladimir Putin in Russia have been revealed, and in China a government department pays a small cash reward for each internet post defending the government or criticising opposition voices.

At Burson Marsteller this toolkit is called, similarly, 'grassrooting'. Harold Burson defended it to *Der Spiegel* as 'fundamental to the democratic process', explaining why like this: 'People believe in things that happen in their neighbourhood, things that they can follow. If they hear a story on a localised level, its credibility increases. This is why we are so enthusiastic about it. Our spin-off company "Direct Impact" specialises in placing such stories.' Sometimes an assumption of engaging in 'good faith' can merely reveal strategic naivety. It may be a subtle difference, but had the event I was invited to only had Shell representatives participating, rather than sponsoring it, I would have been happy to take part. Its purpose would have been unambiguous. But on that occasion, I decided that the best way to 'engage' was by politely saying no.

One response to all these concerns could be that the techniques described are themselves neutral, and could be placed in the service of any cause or issue. The problem with that argument is obvious: not all causes and issues are equally able to afford 'perception management'. It means that the control of the appearance of reality accrues to the already most powerful and wealthy interests, who can then advance their own self-reinforcing worldview. The advertising budgets of charities, even the large ones collected together, are tiny compared with the corporate sector. The state is the only agent capable of paid-for public interest campaigns at scale, that can balance the flow of information advancing private interests. But, as we saw above in the case of alcohol, even here the field is tilted perilously one way. The 'Big Society' was a core idea when Conservatives and Liberal Democrats formed a coalition government in the UK in 2010. It imagined forms of civic engagement to compensate for the shortcomings of both the state and the private sector.

Within a year of coming to power, the government cut its whole marketing budget to £100 million (about half of 1 per cent of what UK

businesses spent on advertising). Putting both the Big Society and the
sector's corporate social responsibility to the test, the Cabinet Office
under Francis Maude, backed by Downing Street, asked the advertising industry to provide pro bono work on important social issues, such
as health campaigns. A new body was proposed following the example
of the Ad Council in the US. Around since the 1940s, it specialises in
public service campaigns and benefits from around $2 billion (£1.2
billion) worth of donated advertising space as well as the work of
advertising copy writers and artists. The Ad Council was, for example,
behind some of the most iconic wartime information campaigns.

The UK trade's Advertising Association, however, had different
ideas. They considered the Big Society notion to be risky and 'not the
most effective approach'.[20] Seemingly, they preferred to be paid for
their work. Providing their services pro bono via a new public-interest
Ad Council would, they argued: 'limit real collaboration between
government and industry on the development of . . . effective two-
way communication with the public'. Join all the dots of the industry
together and what are we left with? A dense, distorting cultural lens
through which, due to its sheer size, we have little choice but to look.
And through it we have managed our perception of reality in a fashion
that is anything but neutral.

'Advertisements may be individually innocent,' wrote the academic Justin Lewis, but 'collectively they are the propaganda wing of
a consumerist ideology. The moral of the thousands of different stories they tell is that the only way to secure pleasure, popularity,
security, happiness or fulfilment is through buying more; more consumption.'[21] The power of advertising has become a broad-spectrum
threat, an assault on our human well-being, the environment and the
urgent need to imagine different economic models. If you want
greater well-being, take a walk, meet friends for a drink, or do a good
turn for someone. Research shows repeatedly that all these beat retail
therapy. The insidiousness of advertising is its relentless misdirection
of our desire for a good life. It draws us away from things that can cost
nothing, yet make us happier, and towards lives in which we prioritise
income over time, in order to buy expensive consumer goods that
never really satisfy.

As a vehicle for consumerism and growth, advertising contributes
to environmentally destructive overconsumption. And by dominating

public discourse, it drowns out other ways of thinking, presenting a huge obstacle to imagining and experimenting with alternative ways to organise the economy and our livelihoods. It obscures adjacent possibilities. In this way, it is a block also to the effective functioning of democracy, a market for ideas that, like any other, relies on equal and open access for a wide range of voices and views in order to function well. The next chapter will look at the restless struggle, however much against the odds, to do just that.

But what to do about the 'perception management' industry? In the same way that governments shrug powerlessly before the influence of financial markets, it would be easy to lean back thinking that the current state of affairs is merely 'how things are'. That would be mistaken. Both historically and in different jurisdictions globally, there is today a wide range of ways in which 'rebalancing' is done.

Parameters change according to shifts in the balance of opinion and the influence of different lobbies. There are always rules. Sometimes they favour public over private interests, but at least as much they work the other way. Finance, for example, was regulated in the run-up to the 2007–8 crisis, but its rules were written to allow the banks to engage in damaging and risky behaviour. At any point, we have to ask what parameters are needed and optimal.

To defend democracy during election campaigns in the UK, for example, there is the Representation of the People Act. Among many other things, it puts into law the right of all candidates in an election to the free delivery of an election mailing setting out their beliefs and policies. The amount of money that can be spent on campaigns is also strictly capped for all candidates. Under the Broadcasting Act a system of broadly equitable allocation based on demonstrable support also controls access to party political broadcasts on radio and television.

Imperfect and endlessly amended as it tends to be, legislation like this recognises that for democracy to function, the exercise of power over information needs to be controlled. Yet the implication for a world living in an 'information age' is much more profound. The notion that dice may be loaded politically only in the brief period of time between an election being called and votes being cast appears increasingly innocent, if not naïve. If the shape of debates, our perception of reality itself, is being moulded in the ways demonstrated above, doesn't this demand a more far-reaching and imaginative response if we are to create and sustain a vibrant, meaningful democracy?

If so, it seems to me that we have a range of options. The creation of new public media, which will allow for a greater diversity of voice and opinion, could take principles used during election times and apply them creatively and much more broadly. Secondly, and a concern raised increasingly in both the US and the UK, there could be far more restraint on lobbying activities that distort existing political procedures. The third major area is reform to the checks and balances on the advertising industry, in recognition of its massive growth, often unacknowledged influence, and ever-deeper reach into everyday life and our souls.

Dan Hind, a former commissioning editor for a publishing house turned author, concluded that commissioning in general in the media needed revolutionising. In *The Return of the Public*, he argues for rethinking how the media operate: 'The media have some explaining to do in Britain and elsewhere . . . Taken as a whole they keep seeing things that aren't there, like weapons of mass destruction in Iraq. And they keep overlooking things that are there, like the shadow banking system.'[22] If the system that 'provides most people with most of their information about the world beyond their immediate experience' can throw up world-changing mirages on the one hand, and miss real economic minefields on the other, that is a problem in need of a solution.

Hind's answer is to carry to the heart of the media the condition that allows it notional freedom to operate, namely democracy. He believes that this could begin with minor reforms: 'not a revolution or a utopia so much as a process'. But his desired destination is a shift in the centre of gravity for the decisions that determine what we get to hear about and how. The key proposal is a kind of informed, democratic, crowd-sourced system of public commissioning that would allocate resources to researchers and investigative journalists, diluting the control of the current small, powerful group of editors who act as gatekeepers to our perception and awareness of what is going on in the world. The benefits would be threefold according to Hind:

> First, it would widen the realm of civic equality, in which market relations are suspended or heavily qualified, and allow individuals otherwise silenced or excluded to address others on

matters of common concern as fellow citizens . . . Second, civic action in conditions of equality – the process of securing greater popular control over the climate of popular opinion – will make further participation seem less daunting or pointless . . . Third, and most importantly, by giving the general population the means to inquire into the nature of social arrangements, public commissioning could provide the facts, and the publicity for the facts, that constitute the only sure basis for political change.

A system of public commissioning – in which a share of programming and investigative journalism would be determined democratically by public interest – would not remove traditional media, but it would complement it with a genuinely civic alternative. It would be the equivalent of the public town square as opposed to the private, gated, shopping mall or state department store, the commons to stroll on instead of the themed leisure park. A glimmer of something similar can be seen in the UK government's e-petitions initiative. If public suggestions gather at least 100,000 signatures, they are considered for debate in the House of Commons. To prevent trivialisation, open-access media commissioning could be made to conform to a public interest test. Hind is fully aware of the likely resistance (not to say horror) of existing commissioning editors, but equally convinced of the logic and necessity of change:

> Having tried all other options, perhaps we can finally consider democracy as a method for generating information in what is, in some senses at least, a democracy. The notion that the citizen body should have some independent power to shape the content of its own beliefs strikes many professional journalists and liberal reformers as anathema. But the existing arrangements are indefensible and we have the means now to create a movement for substantive media reform.

Reform of political lobbying is already a major issue at least in the UK and United States, two of the more aggressive neoliberal economies. But resistance to change is strong. If anything in the US, where reform of campaign finance is a major electoral issue, movement has been in the opposite direction, with controls over third-party political funding and lobbying weakened. Since 2010 Super Political Action Committees (Super PACS) have been allowed to raise unlimited funds from corporations to spend on campaigning for or against candidates in elections.

Yet the corruption that stalks the purchase of political influence is ultimately destructive of the system it seeks to co-opt, delegitimising the very regulatory structures it hopes to benefit from. The need for a latter-day Reformation Act – in this case the separation of corporation and state – is implicitly acknowledged in the various but weak pieces of legislation that circumscribe the declaration of interests, conflicts of interest by elected and public officials, and the rules surrounding the movement of former politicians and civil servants into the corporate sector where they may profit from their previous offices.

Corrosive corruption of this kind, which is not always even subtle, abhors daylight. When secret filming for a documentary on lobbying for Channel 4 television revealed three former Labour Party government ministers offering their services for a price to the corporate sector, all three – Stephen Byers, Patricia Hewitt and Geoff Hoon – were suspended from the Parliamentary Party.

Stephen Byers, formerly a Cabinet member with the brief for trade and industry and, appropriately, transport, described himself as a 'cab for hire' at £5000 per day in a secretly filmed conversation. The former defence secretary Geoff Hoon was a little cheaper, seeking extra-parliamentary work in the private sector at just £3000 per day. The Parliamentary Standards and Privileges Committee judged that Hoon's recorded comments, in which he implied he 'had, or could access confidential information from the MoD for the benefit of business clients who might be seeking contracts', was a 'particularly serious' breach. His punishment was to apologise and to lose his parliamentary pass for five years.[23] This, however, as a deterrent was probably limited in effect. The conversations were made public in 2010, when an election was due soon, and Hoon had already announced that he would not be standing again for election.

At the time of writing, lobbying reform in the UK remains a hugely contentious issue. Even modest suggestions, such as for a statutory register of lobbyists, which was a measure promised in the agreement signed between Liberal Democrats and Conservatives as part of their platform to create a coalition government, have not been implemented. While that was sidelined, close collusion between private-sector interests and new legislation to further marketise the National Health Service were revealed. On the very morning of writing, secret filming by the *Sunday Times* newspaper exposed the Conservative Party's joint treasurer, Peter Cruddas, for saying that a donation of £250,000 would give 'premier league' access to party leaders. This could include private dinners with the prime minister and the chancellor, and a promise that any concerns about policy issues would be tabled for discussion in committees at Downing Street. Regulation to ensure transparency, limit the influence of corporate donors – for example by public funding of political parties – and stop the revolving door between government office and the corporate boardroom are prerequisites for change.

Checks and balances on the impact and influence of advertising can take three basic forms. There are controls over what things get advertised, and how. For example, the laws relating to advertising tobacco have shifted continually over the last few decades. Doctors endorsing cigarettes as good for your health were common in the 1940s and 1950s. Cigarette advertising was ubiquitous in the 1960s. I recall iconic print and television adverts exhorting that 'Happiness is a cigar called Hamlet.' Now some cigarette adverts carry compulsory full-colour photographs of internal organs rotting as a result of smoking. Similarly alcohol advertising is circumscribed. Companies are not supposed to juxtapose scenes of drinking with swimming or driving, for example, although only very recently I noticed very visible whisky sponsorship on television coverage of Formula 1 motor racing. There are many loopholes. Things change in the face of evidence and shifting norms about the ethics of promoting individual behaviour that imposes broader costs on society. This is an area needing vigilance.

Two more approaches are taxes that would recognise and compensate for the damage and costs resulting from the promotion of certain goods, and the creation of certain domains as advertising-free zones. These might be domains in the sense of spans of our lives, like childhood, or physical locations like schools, parks or the streets where we live, when the absence of advertising might improve our quality of life and the environment. It might be seen as a sort of visual pollution control, or consumerism's equivalent of demilitarised zones.

There is a conventional economic case to be made for taxing advertising. A tax would help to correct for the way in which, on the one hand, advertising represents unproductive expenditure, and on the other it contributes to 'market failure' by distorting the 'perfect information' and rationality that markets are said to rely on to operate efficiently. The other case for taxation is to raise the cost of an activity that can have negative social and environmental consequences – as is the case with smoking and drinking – and which, as discussed, undermines human well-being (quite deliberately so in many cases, creating dissatisfaction in order to sell products as solutions).

Taxes on advertising are common internationally. The Public Interest Research Centre records that in France and Sweden portions of the money raised from taxing adverts goes towards helping fund other forms of media, such as regional daily newspapers. Austria, Spain, Italy, the Netherlands and Canada all have various taxes on advertising, while the US goes the other way and makes advertising tax-deductible. In Britain, Hugh Dalton, who was president of the Board of Trade during the Second World War, and responsible for engineering the changes in consumer behaviour described in chapter 7, attempted to introduce an advertising tax when chancellor after the war. A breach of parliamentary protocol forced him from office and the proposal morphed into a voluntary agreement between business and government that companies would limit the amount they spent on advertising. This lasted until 1949, although tensions obviously remained, as Britain continued to live with rationing for several more years. In the 1960s, the Labour prime minister Harold Wilson and other members of his party condemned advertising for being both wasteful and distorting. They organised committees, issued reports and made broadcasts to air their criticism. It's a curious historical reflection on the decade during which consumerism really took off. In the 1970s again there were several more calls for a tax. Shirley Williams as the Labour minister of Prices and Consumer Protection accused the industry of fuelling inflation.[24]

There's a scene in the film of Anthony Burgess's novel *A Clockwork Orange* in which the offending youth, or 'droog', is being reformed by extreme compulsion in the form of a kind of invasive behavioural aversion therapy. This was the film-maker Stanley Kubrick's critique of the theories of B. F. Skinner, which were fashionable at the time. Skinner devised and advocated a school of 'radical behaviourism' in which technologies of control could overcome thought, perception and emotion to determine people's behaviour. In the scene the droog has his eyelids fixed open and is shown images. Bad images receive negative feedback (he is wired to a chair), and good ones positive. Whatever else he may think or do, he cannot look away.

It may be less extreme in any given moment, but that is what advertising often feels like. I go to my home page on my email account, and there's an advert for life insurance. Glum-looking human faces spin with a jolting movement as on a fruit machine, implying that your number could be up at any moment, and not in a good way. It's mildly terrifying, although the faces are probably meant to look like ordinary family members that you should be caring for by buying the product. Similarly, open a magazine, go to the cinema, into a train station, walk down the street – adverts, adverts, everywhere. It's like being beaten into submission by an Argos shopping catalogue until you agree to buy something, as opposed to quitting crime and antisocial behaviour as the droog had to do.

Which is partly why I find the notion of advertising-free zones so appealing. These too are already a small-scale reality in various parts of the world and in certain circumstances. Before becoming American vice-president in 1920, and president himself in 1923 on the death of Warren Harding, Calvin Coolidge was the governor of Massachusetts from 1918 to 1920. In spite of being a Republican, part of his legacy as governor was socially progressive. Public employees enjoyed his support for a cost-of-living pay rise, and women and children had their working week limited to forty-eight hours. Notably, and largely lost in history, he also put limits on outdoor advertising.[25] Leap forward nearly a century and there are bans on billboard advertising in four American states, Maine, Vermont, Hawaii and Alaska. In the two years after Vermont had its last billboard removed, revenue from tourism rose by 50 per cent. Cause and effect are hard to prove, but removal clearly did no harm to Vermont's attraction to visitors. Two further states, Rhode Island and Oregon, have put bans on new billboards being built.

Further controls are promoted by a campaign called Scenic America, which explains its motivation like this: 'Visual pollution. Sky Trash. Litter on a stick. The junk mail of the American highway. Nothing destroys the distinctive character of our communities and the natural beauty of our countryside more rapidly than uncontrolled signs and billboards.' At the local level, Scenic America cites over seven hundred communities prohibiting the erection of new billboards on the grounds that 'billboard control improves community character and quality of life – both of which directly impact local economies'.[26] The before-and-after effects of regulations limiting billboards were studied in the towns of Williamsburg in Virginia, Houston in Texas, and Raleigh in North Carolina. In each case, after stricter billboard controls were introduced, local businesses saw their trade increase. The suggestion is that the aesthetic appeal of the areas had improved, making them more attractive tourist destinations.[27]

Brazil has something of a reputation for being a good-time country. London has a large Brazilian community, and from experience, they are usually the last to leave a party. Brazilians are not a killjoy people. It's striking, then, that one of the most radical removals of advertising from public space occurred in 2007 in the country's biggest city, São Paulo, and that the scheme was the work of the city's conservative mayor, Gilberto Kassab.[28] He explained the initiative like this: 'The Clean City Law came from a necessity to combat pollution . . . pollution of water, sound, air, and the visual. We decided that we should start combating pollution with the most conspicuous sector: visual pollution.' The problem wasn't advertising per se, he explained, but too much of it. The result was a near-total ban effecting billboards, digital signs and advertising on buses. From behind the city's history, distinctiveness and architectural heritage re-emerged.

In Paris, new rules are being introduced to reduce advertising on the city's streets by 30 per cent, as well as setting new maximum allowable sizes for hoardings.[29] No adverts will be allowed within 50 metres of school gates. The new rules came from a working group that found a majority of Paris residents wanted less invasive advertising.

The Paris initiative touches on two issues: location-based restrictions on visual pollution and, with the reference to schools, psychological pollution of children. The *Think of Me As Evil?* report mentioned above explains the growing consensus on why this matters:

'A recent UNICEF study found that materialism isn't just detrimental to children's well-being: materialism appears to be problematic for UK adults as well as children.' It suggests that 'in the UK parents and children seemed to be locked into a compulsive consumption cycle'.

Sweden has strong rules on consumer protection, especially for vulnerable groups. In 1991 it introduced a ban on television advertising aimed at children under twelve years old, establishing the principle that childhood should be a largely advertising-free zone. This was the result of several studies which established that children cannot distinguish between advertising and general television programming and do not understand properly the purpose and intent of advertising. It follows that children deserve 'zones' where they can be free from the pressure of commercial influences.

There is meant to be a ban in Britain on the direct advertising of junk food in children's programmes, in operation since 2007. This seems to have done little, though, to stop the smiling faces of sporting celebrities promoting crisps and other junk food. Nor did it protect a television extravaganza like the Olympics, watched by millions of children, from having as sponsors Coca-Cola and McDonald's. During its presidency of the European Union in 2001, Sweden tried and failed to inaugurate a Europe-wide ban on television advertising to children. Norway, however, also has a Swedish-style ban, and Denmark, Greece and Belgium partial bans.

These different approaches of taxation and the creation of advertising-free zones are not mutually exclusive. There is a Chinese proverb (another Chinese export) that runs: If you are thinking one year ahead, plant a crop, if you are thinking ten years ahead, plant a tree, but if you are thinking one hundred years ahead, educate your people. If only on the basis of the immediate, negative effect advertising has on the well-being of children, encouraging extrinsic values and materialism while undermining intrinsic motivations, concentrated play and social skills such as forming friendships, let alone other concerns, of all the possibilities explored here, the most urgent and beneficial appears to be setting childhood as free as can be done from advertisements.

And in the spaces left by the missing ads, it will be fascinating to see what new thinking, expression and experiences can emerge. Of course, many people are not waiting for that invitation. In all directions the culture of passive consumerism is being challenged, pulled apart, and more satisfying ways of living being created. The next section explores this colourful, enterprising and changing landscape.

Strangelujah! – from passive consumers to active producers

Don't be shy, testify.

Reverend Billy

The gospel choir's green silk swayed down the aisle like high summer grass. Behind them stalked the preacher in a tooth-shine white suit, his steps staccato, hair unnaturally still, quite convinced of his own possession. Mouths in the congregation hung open. It could have been awe or joyous disbelief. One by one the choir took to the stage, preparing the preacher's ascent, readying the faithful for rapture. Words of wisdom in foot-high letters sat in a crest above the stage. Sweaty evangelical fervour was all around, but the words weren't biblical, they weren't from the First Epistle to the Thessalonians, warning of the End Times. They said simply: 'To Thine Own Self be True', the advice given by Polonius to his son Laertes in Shakespeare's *Hamlet*. Good secular words of advice to address the audience in a building where appeals are made more often to humanism than to the divine.

And, contrary to appearances, tonight is business as usual. Because the singers are the Stop Shopping Gospel Choir and the man in the white dog collar with ice-cream moulded hair is the Reverend Billy. They are in London's Conway Hall for one night only on their *Earthalujah* tour. Last time Rev Billy was in town he took his choir to exorcise the vast, shiny new Westfield Shopping Centre (a cathedral to consumerism, it is the size of thirty football pitches and has ninety-six escalators). The day after his Conway Hall sermon he had another exorcism due, this time at one of Britain's biggest public art galleries, the Tate Modern. The bad spirit to be cast out was the gallery's sponsor, the giant oil company BP.

His antics may have had a specific, very worldly purpose (as, of course, did many of Christ's reported actions, helping the poor and marginalised, challenging power and vested interests, that sort of thing), but it would be a mistake to think that Rev Billy was not about the spirit and soul. He was just focused on a particular kind of redemption, concerned about saving the planet we depend on, and breathing life into the neighbourhoods where we make our homes. In the course of doing so, he railed against those who threaten those precious things, the banks and corporations (a little like the money-lenders in the temple) who put profit ahead of everything.

'Don't be shy, testify,' he starts a cry quickly taken up by the choir. 'I want to hear about how you are getting in touch with nature, because the Earth itself is giving us the design.' He turns now to the importance of diversity and cooperation, and talks about how vibrant neighbourhoods operate like an ecosystem.

At this point Billy is in good company. There's been a burst of establishment interest in searching for insights from nature to explain the deep operation of economies. As we saw in chapter 6, the Executive Director for Financial Stability at the Bank of England, Andrew Haldane, teamed up with the former government chief scientific adviser, Robert May, to see what ecological theory can teach us about systemic risk in banking systems.[30] In essence, they found the same flaw that J. K. Galbraith highlighted in his exposé of the Great Crash of 1929: lots of people pursuing self-interest with little or no regard for the viability of the system upon which they all depended.

The modern working world, Rev Billy went on (unknowingly backed, at least on some points, by these pillars of the establishment), deliberately encourages us to be selfish in the misguided belief that, when the combined effects of all that self-interested energy are gathered together, it will lead to better outcomes for everyone. This is the 'astounding belief' about capitalism, ridiculed by John Maynard Keynes.

But, thought the Rev, narrow definitions of efficiency and economic success wrapped up into a package often called 'development' are destroying community and fellowship, and impoverishing our working lives. Then when we are at our weakest we are offered the baubles of consumerism as compensation. Apocalypse is inevitable if destruction is profitable. Yet the potential for salvation he saw everywhere.

The day before they were in Liverpool. On Granby Street they came across five grandmothers of mixed race holding out against plans for demolition and development. The grandmothers stood for a very different kind of economy to one based on property price inflation. They ran a gift-and-share economy enriched by storytelling and mutual aid. They helped each other out and had a different idea of value. It was the opposite of the developer's dream where we sit isolated in overpriced new flats and houses, chained to soulless jobs by mortgages that drag across generations, and engage in solitary, passive consumption.

Again the Rev found himself well supported by academic research. Grandparents played a crucial role in human evolution according to Professor Rachel Caspari of Central Michigan University. As people started living longer, becoming grandparents, there were great leaps forward in terms of 'artistic expression, food production and the creation of complex tools'.[31] Professor Chris Stringer, based at London's Natural History Museum, takes the idea further. Knowledge accumulated by the older generation increases the resilience and survival chances of a community. They know what food is safe and what is poisonous, where to find water and how to make and mend things. They are living webs of relationships and so can help in negotiating over problems and conflicts. Obviously they provide additional child care too, freeing up time to grow and forage for food. 'Older people would have been vital to survival,' says Stringer.[32]

'We are not just social animals,' cried the Rev. 'If we are antisocial, we pour poison into the gaps between us.' Loneliness and insecurity fuel consumerism and environmental destruction. In a perfect pastiche of what even the Rev Billy described as a 'bigoted, homophobic, right-wing, hypocritical, reactionary, tele-evangelist preacher', the tables are turned on the stereotype, just as Jesus turned the tables in the temple. His peroration sweeps us along. It urges us to face down the demonisation that happens when people 'stop buying stuff' and to 'destroy the economic equations that make destruction profitable'.

It is gloriously camp, and strangely moving. 'Strangelujah!', in fact, as someone called out from the audience.

Then, without warning, the Rev strode from the stage, followed by the Stop Shopping Gospel Choir, out into the Sunday-evening air of Red Lion Square. They gathered again among the trees of the public park and sang, their joyful, undulating choruses echoing back from the surrounding Victorian houses and modern offices, some of them lit up, and with the odd out-of-hours worker staring curiously down.

I left the square, hopeful and rejuvenated, wondering (in an atheistic sort of way) if a blessing from the Rev upon the nation's drinking-water supply might perform some kind of anti-materialist miracle. But it seems there is work still to be done, and work of a very different sort to the normal 9-to-5 of the service economy.

'Eight disgusting flavours of environmentalist'

If it's new it must be good. I'm simplifying, but that's modernism: easily put and immensely powerful. Dare to find fault with the latest offerings of technology, as we saw earlier in discussions on options for the global food and energy systems, or with consumer culture, and opponents will claim that you want to live in a cave, not to mention forcing everyone else to build your fire.

Stand against whatever throughout history carries the mantle of modernity – motorways, high-rise tower blocks, hypermarkets, industrial farming, the airport or shopping mall – and you become an enemy of progress.

There is even a book (and a website) called *The Enemies of Progress*, which talks about the 'dangers of sustainability' and divides the enemy up into 'eight disgusting flavours of environmentalist'. Beware of those wreckers who campaigned to deny children the right to breathe in lead from petrol exhaust fumes, and by saving the ozone layer denied humanity as a whole its chance to be fried in the sun's high-frequency ultraviolet radiation. Those people are damned variously as 'limit setters', 'indoctrinators' and 'pessimists'.

But the dismissal of environmentalism has, in the past, been almost as strong on the left, who have seen the unwelcome identification of environmental limits as an obstacle at best, and a middle-class plot at worst, to deny working people their material aspirations. Derek Hatton, the former deputy leader of Liverpool City Council, often referred to as a Trotskyist and militant, exemplified a kind of champagne socialism that set a universal entitlement to own and drive a Mercedes at least on a par with access to decent public transport. In this world socialism and materialism happily conspire. Paradoxically the incomes and ambitions of the poor become, like everyone else's, legitimate fodder for the consumer capitalism that keeps them in their place.

But the 'anti-progress' accusation is repeated so often that environmentalists end up censoring themselves, worried about appearing to stand for a world drained of indulgence and material comfort. The case for living simply, and phrases such as 'less is more', fell out of fashion in fear that the whiff of austerity might ruin the consumer party.

Scared of its own shadow, the green in-crowd took to preaching green consumerism. It became okay still to campaign, but only with a bit of bling. On a march? That's fine, but wear the latest designer sandals to make it aspirational. Some in the environmental movement say that tolerating business as usual is not enough: it must go further and be 'comfortable with capitalism' and all which that entails in terms of endless growth, profits first and wasteful competition.

Yet, by internalising the criticism of their opponents, did environmentalists concede too much, too quickly? Was confidence lost to the point where we grew blind to the real, deep, human benefits of living differently?

When it comes to consumer issues, the green agenda has for decades already been quite distilled. Instead of a throwaway society (in every sense of the word), we know we should *repair, reduce, reuse* and *recycle*.

Herman Daly puts it rather more eloquently. The economy of the future, he writes, needs to be: 'A subtle and complex economics of maintenance, qualitative improvements, sharing, frugality, and adaptation to natural limits. It is an economics of better, not bigger.'[33]

Unambiguously this describes a shift from a consumer society to more of a producer society. It looks more to the respect for skill of the half-forgotten craft guilds than to the mountains of waste from the modern shopping mall. It suggests a world in which we roll back the gradual deskilling of society, the reduction of community to a collection of flats and houses unconnected to each other, mere repositories of consumption, and the impoverishment of work. Something is wrong when it takes a celebrity chef to remind us how to boil an egg, a television makeover programme to show how to paint a wall, and when fifty households living inches apart feel the need to own fifty lawnmowers, fifty identical power drills and assorted gadgets.

A producer or consumer to be?

Erich Fromm wrote in *To Have Or to Be*: 'Everything one owned was [once] cherished, taken care of, and used to the very limits of its utility. Buying was "keep-it" buying.' To extend the life of an object, the owner would know how to polish, adjust, oil and repair it. With the advent of disposability, built-in obsolescence and the introduction of constant upgrades (very similar to obsolescence), orchestrated by mass advertising, the market learned to earn more money by persuading people to throw things away. It came between the individual and the household and their need and ability to maintain and repair goods.

Reskilling, on the other hand, not only equips us for a world in transition, it helps us connect to it. By understanding how to work with materials, from textiles to metal, wood and words, old-style consumer materialism, based on fleeting engagement, rapid boredom, dissatisfaction and quick disposal, makes way for a different kind of materialism.

Using skills to make, do and mend brings engagement, allows expression and growth through learning. It extends and helps both the doer and the thing done to endure.

In his book *The Craftsman*, Richard Sennett quotes the American sociologist Charles Wright Mills, who wrote during the birth of modern consumerism and at the height of industrial mechanisation built on the division of labour. Mills saw both the value of skilled 'craft' work and the broader implications of losing it:

> The labourer with a sense of craft becomes engaged in the work in and for itself; the satisfactions of working are their own reward; the details of daily labour are connected in the worker's mind to the end product; the worker can control his or her own actions at work; skill develops within the work process; work is

connected to the freedom to experiment; finally, family, community and politics are measured by the standards of inner satisfaction, coherence and experiment in craft labour.

Sennett himself comments: 'The slowness of craft time serves as a source of satisfaction; practice beds in, making the skill one's own. Slow craft time also enables the work of reflection and imagination – which the push for quick results cannot. Mature means long; one takes lasting ownership of the skill.' Active, skill-based production trumps the short-lived and ultimately disappointing sugar high of passive consumption.

Brian Perkins renovates old bicycles. He specialises in Moultons, small-wheeled revolutions in cycling that began in the 1960s (one revolution from that tumultuous decade, at least, that endured). Its designer, Alex Moulton, was an engineer who designed the suspension system on the Mini. Moulton himself was a self-confessed 'petrolhead'. He loved big thirsty cars, the sort like the discontinued Alvis marque that look like country houses on wheels. But when the Sucz crisis struck he glimpsed a petrol-dry future and used his skills to reinvent the bicycle with small wheels and built-in suspension. Something clever about the physics of small wheels means they accelerate fast from traffic lights, leaving the bigger, more macho bikes indignantly behind. Several cycling speed records were set on Moultons. Bicycle sales had been falling for years, but the launch of the Moulton was a turning point. Sales edged up ever after.

With skill, greased fingers and patience, Brian keeps the older models on the road. He's not like a museum restorer, cautiously and precisely recreating originals. He brilliantly remakes them, not pedantically but true to the spirit. I have one of his works. It's duck-egg and midnight-blue and has a unique hub gear once adapted by Jack (Jacob) Lauterwasser, a former cycling engineer and 1928 Olympic medal-winning cyclist. He cycled from London to Amsterdam to take part, and somehow managed to take home both the bronze and the silver medal for the same event. Some people think the Moulton is a shopping bike until you float past them, effortlessly. Then they look confused. To perform his craft Brian has collected spare parts, lots of them, over two decades. 'Have you ever watched candy floss being made?' he asks. 'The spun sugar winds up in a mass on the stick, seemingly from nowhere, until it becomes enormous. At first you're delighted – until you try to deal with it. Old bike parts are a lot like that.'

Sometimes Brian sounds like a barefoot doctor running a field clinic for those who cannot afford to pay, in a country where the health service has been starved of cash and equipment. It's a fairly accurate description of the state of the green economy:

Bicycles don't usually reject a transplant, so I feel compelled to save things for future use. And old bikes are cheap, because they are generally unwanted. For compact storage, collected machines are always reduced to their discrete components and gobbled up by the collection of cardboard boxes, margarine tubs, sauce jars and biscuit tins. It all comes in useful sooner or later. When you enjoy tinkering with old bikes, the value that even small things have makes you lavish disproportionate care and attention upon them.

At other times, the act of renovation comes across as his navigating a path through appreciative musing on the tangible world, wide-eyed curiosity and meditation: 'I knew there was a biscuit tin somewhere with a good selection of beautifully made clamps that could be polished to a sparkling finish. Or were they in an ice-cream tub? That rang a bell. Or perhaps it contained bells? I just wasn't sure.'

This absorption, almost reverie, for materials is not unusual among people who devote their lives to making things. It inverts conventional materialism and its associations with glib disposability, and suggests a new, better meaning for the term – a new materialism focused on a deeper enjoyment of, and respect for the physical world.

The potter and ceramicist Marianne de Trey, reflecting on her long career, described her work like this:

The satisfaction comes through the use of every part of oneself, hand and eye, brain and intuition, and through being always in contact with natural materials and the power of earth, air, fire and water. It makes one aware also of worldwide traditions and artifacts, of their similarities and differences. It is, in fact, a voyage of discovery into the very heart of things. How lucky we are.[34]

One thing is sure, if the great transition to a low-carbon, high-well-being future is to happen, it will arrive riding a bicycle. As H. G. Wells wrote: 'When I see an adult on a bicycle, I do not despair for the future of the human race.' The former Catholic priest and critical observer of industrial society Ivan Illich wrote extensively in the 1970s about how the choice of technology either undermines or encourages conviviality. Then, as now, Latin America and the Caribbean were scenes of both radical social experiment and authoritarianism. Illich quotes José Antonio Viera-Gallo, assistant secretary of justice in Chile before Augusto Pinochet's military coup against Salvador Allende's democratically elected government. Viera survived, unlike Allende, ending up in exile in Italy. Pinochet triumphed, backed by big foreign industrial interests. Perhaps that's what led Viera-Gallo to comment that salvation 'can only arrive by bicycle'. Illich thought that deskilling and the division of labour taken to extremes in consumer societies were destructive of both individual well-being and community:

> Society can be destroyed when further growth of mass production . . . extinguishes the free use of the natural abilities of society's members, when it isolates people from each other and locks them into a man-made shell, when it undermines the texture of community by promoting extreme social polarisation and splintering specialisation.[35]

It is by accident rather than anyone's design that modern-day Cuba has some of the best mechanics in the world. An economic embargo lasting more than half a century demonstrates how physical constraints can release ingenuity, creativity and innovation. Lacking new vehicles or even spare parts for old ones, somehow Cuba's miracle mechanics have kept cars on the road for decades past their intended 'scrap-by' date. Creating parts from beaten waste metal and discarded plastic medicine bottles, Cuba's accidental museum motor fleet has become internationally iconic, a tourist attraction in its own right. Even though born out of adversity, it alone is proof that our low expectation of durability, of inevitable disposability, replacement and upgrade, is not a natural nor inevitable condition, but a deliberate artefact of one very wasteful, ultimately impoverishing system. Other lessons to emerge from Cuba's volatile recent history were high-lighted earlier in chapter 7.

Yet a world in which we all hold a wider range of practical skills leaves us less at the mercy of disposable goods and built-in obsoles-cence, and more in a position to shape and fashion our surroundings in satisfying ways. We learn about practical problem-solving and are compelled, in accord with the philosophy of ages, to be wholly pre-sent in the moment and place, when and where we practise the skill.

The attractiveness of a 'great reskilling' has been taken up by the Transition Town movement. Having 'lost many of the basic skills taken for granted by every previous generation – to grow, gather, pre-serve and cook local and seasonal food; to repair clothes and household goods; to make and mend rather than throw away; to work with local materials such as wood and clay for items of function as well as beauty', they think that: 'We need to relearn these skills to prepare for an energy scarce and relocalised future.' Courses on offer range from how to make your own radio programme to building your own house.

Such approaches offer obvious environmental benefits, but they also suggest a different way of being in the world. And it is here, per-haps, that the environmental movement has been too shy of what it has to offer. Because the evidence suggests that doing more, and pas-sively consuming less, is the difference between a shoddy, brief, encounter with pornography, and having a satisfying sex life.

The first UK study of well-being estimated that only 14 per cent of the population had a high level of well-being, described as 'flour-ishing'. This was mirrored by the same amount, another 14 per cent, who had a very low level of well-being (composed of people with diagnosed mental disorders).[36] Well-being is determined by a range of factors, but what we actually do in life, and the attitude we bring to it, has a very significant impact.[37]

Wealthy societies have generally replaced sitting in old-fashioned factories (no sad farewells) with sitting in modern air-conditioned offices (no glad arrival). Romance for the lost world of manufacturing in vast factories is tempered by the knowledge that we did not go easy onto those dread production lines. 'So great was labor's distaste,' wrote Keith Sward on the legend of Henry Ford's great innovation, that 'toward the close of 1913 every time the company wanted to add 100 men to its factory personnel, it was necessary to hire 963 because so many walked away appalled at the dehumanizing nature of the work.'[38]

But the problem is that what we do in the clean, modern workplace is not very much. That is, we do very little in terms of asserting the full range of our practical, creative, human potential, even if the air is cleaner and the noise level lower.

A Universal Job Description for life in the service economy could simplify many anguished application procedures. Essential skills – candidate must be able to:

- Sit at desk
- Write emails
- Answer phone
- Make tea and/or coffee
- Go to meetings
- Fiddle with spreadsheets
- Eat lunch

Office life has become subject to a kind of 'digital Taylorism', says the economics writer Aditya Chakraborti, quoting the labour market academic Phil Brown.[39] It's a world in which only a tiny minority have 'permission to think'. The rest are technologically corralled and carefully monitored through their working days, like water tricked into concrete channels and directed towards dams and sluice gates.

In 1974 E. F. Schumacher published an article in *The Times* about the curse of 'insane work'. Replace 'factory' with 'office' and the quote still works:

> Dante, when composing his vision of hell, might well have included the mindless, repetitive boredom of working on a factory assembly line. It destroys initiative and rots brains, yet millions of British workers are committed to it for most of their lives.

According to the OECD, a body that operates like a pro-market think tank for rich countries, the UK is the only country in Europe that has seen the length of the working week grow since the mid-1980s.[40] The *Daily Mail* called this phenomenon 'Thatcher's legacy'.

The United States, that other home of the Anglo-Saxon economic model, was one of the very few other countries in which the poorest were also working longer hours.

Long hours coupled with regimented and sedentary work – typical office and factory work for millions – paints a poor picture. The American Cancer Society found that people are more likely to die if their work involves sitting for long periods, and studies of Alzheimer's disease show that more active people build a natural defence system of 'neural reserves' that, for example, reduces memory loss. 'As for F. W. Taylor, the godfather of "scientific management", it is enough to know that his thinking influenced both Stalin and the Harvard Business School,' writes Ruth Potts. 'The sociologist Robert Jackall, who spent years inhabiting the world of corporate managers, describes Taylor's legacy – the worker: "constantly vulnerable and anxious, acutely aware of the likelihood at any time of an organisational upheaval which could overturn their plans and possibly damage their careers fatally".'[41]

One of the simplest yet most profound exit routes from this hellish vision is to work less in formal employment. Easy to say, hard to do in practice when many are reversing the historical trend to shorter working hours and toiling longer just to stand still. Exactly how we might shift to the norm of a shorter week in the office or at the call centre I'll come back to in the last chapter. But first let's look at how our time could be used if it was liberated, if only we stepped off the treadmill of working ever longer hours to earn the money to buy the convenience we need because we have no time to do anything for ourselves, because we spend so much time working to earn the money . . .

From making clothes to food growing, preparation and preserving, from building skills and the use and repair of everyday household goods to even the making of music and art, simple skills that were taken for granted by countless generations have withered. The subtle knife of the market severed individuals, families and communities from their abilities to do things for themselves.

A wide range of activities, goods and services were incorporated into the market as it expanded like a cuckoo in society's nest, displacing other ways of organising life. They were then commodified and sold back to the people they were taken from. Why pick an apple from a tree growing on common land and eat it for free, when you can buy one plastic-wrapped and cut into segments from the shop in a petrol station?

Almost by definition, the market's expansion forecloses on the possibility of exchange based on reciprocity, mutual aid and present-giving – all of which, when left to flourish, strengthen the fabric of community.

When supermarkets began it probably wasn't their direct intention to breed a nation of deskilled consumers who don't know how to cook. But it was the dawn of domestic deskilling, the nemesis of general home food preparation, and the rise of processed food. A meaningful backlash has finally begun. A great reskilling is already under way. In the process communities are pulling together, economic self-education is spreading and the narrow world-view of the so-called 'free market' is being rolled back. This is already happening with food.

From baking your own bread to growing your own food and keeping your own chickens, there is a striking trend in the UK for people to do much more for themselves. In 2008 there was a huge growth in the sale of breadmakers and chicken coops. So-called 'guerrilla gardeners' are applying their gardening skills to transform some of the bleakest parts of the urban landscape.

In the London borough of Hackney, an urban social enterprise called Growing Communities runs an organic food box scheme, a farmers' market, and helps people to 'make, bake, grow or pick good food' throughout the year (the fashion for food foraging is on the rise again more generally). It celebrates the annual harvest period with the Good Food Swap, when people exchange recipes, tips and food.

The Transition Town Brixton initiative have a fruit and nut map and organise food walks round local council estates. The walks are often rounded off by home-made Brixton apple and walnut marmalade. In East Dulwich, South London, a woman planted geraniums in upturned police hats at the police station.

In Sheffield, the Abundance project brings together a team of volunteers who map and harvest seasonal local fruit like apples, pears and plums. They redistribute the surplus to community cafés, nurseries and individuals. Tonnes of fruit get juiced and made into jams, pickles and preserves. Lessons are given to local schoolchildren. They also run seasonal planting and pruning workshops, and have published a guide to urban food harvesting.

In 2009 more than a quarter of us were growing our own fruit and vegetables, while a further one in ten considered that this will be the year they start. Sales of flowers declined, as sales of vegetable seeds rose by 128 per cent in a year and ready-to-plant vegetables by 40 per cent. Sales of greenhouses rose by 157 per cent. Some local food cooperatives and growers are adapting to changing growing conditions by trialling new and heritage crops, and actively relocalising food production.

The National Trust recently announced plans to use plots of its land for public allotments. In some areas, waiting lists can stretch to over ten years and local papers are reporting record levels of interest as people turn to home growing. There are now more than one hundred thousand people waiting to grab a small plot of land and try their hand at growing food for themselves. People are also able to get a taste of farming on a virtual farm designed by the Trust.

It is a very modern version of the allotment tradition, which although it can be traced back to medieval commons, owes much to the more recent nineteenth-century campaigning Liberal MP Jesse Collings. In David Boyle's short history of allotments, he recalls what inspired Collings's attachment to the land, that led him to believe that all should be able to have access to 'three acres and a cow', the rallying cry of his campaign. Collings grew up surrounded by the urban privations of a brutally industrialising country, and access to a plot of productive land left a strong impression in his childhood memories: 'On these four acres we grew wheat, barley, potatoes, and other vegetables. We kept a number of pigs and a large number of fowls. For myself I had a fancy for rabbits, guinea pigs, hedgehogs, and ferrets. We grew each year sufficient wheat to supply the family with bread.'[42]

His activism eventually saw an Act passed in 1882 that resulted in 394,517 smallholdings of under four acres and 272,000 'garden allotments'. The mere fact of creating the allotments increased awareness of threats to other commons land, multiplying other local campaigns, and linking land reform in Britain to both urban and rural poverty.

On the international side, according to the Cuban permaculture expert Roberto Perez, before Cuba experienced the shock of losing access to the cheap Soviet oil that fuelled its agriculture, many of the nation's food-growing skills were disappearing. The fact that people relearned together, he believes, was a key factor in Cuba's successful transition to food self-sufficiency, particularly the skill-sharing between the old and the young.

But the rise of reskilling reaches much further than food. Although a tool of the market, the internet has also liberated many people, providing ways of circumventing over-powerful retailers like the supermarkets, and in several cases avoiding the market altogether. Today people can sell their own houses and organise their own holidays more easily and, in the latter case, sometimes without money changing hands. But we can also often get tools, other essentials and fancies for free as people offer up things they no longer need.

Skillswap, for example, is a website – www.swapaskill.com – that does exactly what it appears to do. Instructables.com is a thriving online community where members exchange instructions on how to produce home-made alternatives to consumer goods. The site has instructions on making everything from chairs, to soap, to solar-heating panels.

The freecycle phenomenon is a network made up of around five thousand groups with 8.6 million members globally – a number sure to grow by the time this book is published. Freecycle describes its goal as keeping 'usable items out of landfills. By using what we already have on this earth, we reduce consumerism, manufacture fewer goods, and lessen the impact on the earth. Another benefit of using Freecycle is that it encourages us to get rid of junk that we no longer need and promote community involvement in the process.'

It also has an online 'café' for people to share information, ideas and requests for help. When I looked posts included a search for ideas for a good party venue, a seamstress and transport. The Furniture Re-Use Network comprises four hundred organisations, who save around two million items per year from landfill sites and pass them on for reuse to low-income families. That includes around about forty-five thousand fridges alone.[43] This is just one of a large and growing community of 'sharing platforms' that range from the US-based portal Shareable.net to favabank in the UK.

Elsewhere there are people car sharing and couch surfing. A share economy is on the move. Some are 'unschooling' – an open, unconventional approach to education which declares that 'birds fly, fish swim, and children learn'. There is even 'free-birthing', an initiative to promote giving birth at home.

Taken together, ironically, most of these things represent a backlash against a consumerism promoted with the rhetoric of choice, but which offered ultimately only one throwaway lifestyle. The backlash aims to give real choice – not just between brands but about approaches to how we get things and do things.

Less challengingly, more people are making and mending their own clothes, and the sale of sewing machines quintupled in the aftermath of the 2008 financial crash. Haberdashery sales from the cooperatively owned John Lewis store also rose by 30 per cent. The list of knitting clubs is getting longer and there is a vast and active network of guilds and societies.

The Nottingham Craft Mafia is a network of amateur craftspeople who meet up to exchange skills and support. The group offers classes, social events and even a regular knitting circle. It's open to craftspeople at all levels. The Craft Mafia network started in Austin, Texas, and there are groups in the UK from Manchester to Glasgow.

Not the mafia, but a gentle, wise matriarch of sorts, my own mother, June Simms, retrained as a textile artist after raising three children and when her career as a theatre nurse, hospital ward sister and midwife came to an end. The way that she developed a unique multimedia style, rooted in but greatly evolved from traditional embroidery techniques, demonstrates how it is possible to grow at any age through the creative expression allowed by the mastery of a craft. As she gave a class at the School of Life, a venue in London that teaches, literally, lessons in the art of living, an audience of women less than half her age sat rapt. There were seemingly infinite possibilities for combining thread, silk, paint and even cast-off industrial materials used to waterproof buildings that, treated properly, lend extraordinary properties to textile art.

'The greatness of a craft,' wrote Antoine de Saint-Exupéry, 'consists firstly in how it brings comradeship to men.' Again, such an intuitive insight from a writer appears to be well supported by science. One of the many revelations from the rapidly growing field of neuroscience is that mutual cooperation is associated with enhanced neuronal responses in reward areas of the brain. This tends to suggest that social cooperation is intrinsically rewarding.[44]

For his book *Together*, Henry Hemmings carried out a nationwide survey of small groups many of which were craft-based. He came across ones ranging from Knitting Hill and the Hadleigh Bobbin Lace-Making Class, to allotment associations all over the country and the East London Advanced Motorcyclists. It's easy to underestimate even something as seemingly prosaic as motorcycle maintenance. The University of Chicago academic Matthew Crawford found it so fulfilling that he wrote a whole book about it with the glorious title *The Case for Working with Your Hands: Or Why Office Work is Bad for Us and Fixing Things Feels Good*. Not only did he find intrinsic personal satisfaction from his work, he found that his mechanical craft gave him membership of an appreciative community: 'I try to be a good motorcycle mechanic. This effort connects me to others, in particular to those who exemplify good motorcycling, because it is they who can best judge how well I have realised the functional goods I am aiming at.'

Passing on knowledge directly evokes the relationship between the skilled and the apprentice, teacher and student, what Crawford calls 'a kind of philosophical friendship, the sort that is natural between teacher and student: a community of those who desire to know'. Lifelong learning – the natural complement to a society relying more on mutual aid – also has multiple benefits: enhancing an individual's self-esteem, encouraging social interaction and a more active life.[45]

Everywhere, it seems, people are beginning to make and do and get involved. In short, a human response to the failure of markets appears to be producing the opposite of the depressing phenomena described by Robert Putnam in *Bowling Alone*, which described the atomisation of family and community life and the withering of communal groups.

From the rebirth of street parties like the 'big lunch', a celebration of local, seasonal food, to new ways of making music and making music compilations for friends, when it comes to signs of a cultural renaissance involving reskilling, people are busy here too.

New home audio technology has opened up music creation to many more people. Mobile clubbing is increasingly popular – where you descend en masse to a spot (usually a station or monument such as St Paul's Cathedral) to dance. There are no expensive nightclub fees or surly bouncers (until the police come) and you can take your own home-made refreshments. More mildly the popularity of pic-nicking in a local park or the country is growing, as an alternative to expensive days out at Alton Towers or Legoland.

People are also making their own exercise, rather than buying it: by cycling, walking, and 'wild' outdoor swimming, rather than going to expensive gyms. Brighton Lesbian and Gay Sports Society is a growing network of people who find others interested in the same sports and organise activities among themselves. At the last count the group had around six hundred members and was growing each year.

Combining healthy outdoor activity with positive environmental action, senior citizens in the United States are leading the way. 'Gray is Green' is an initiative set up by the retired academic Robert Lane, president of the National Senior Citizens Corps. In 2007 the Green Council of Whitney Center was set up with a mission to learn about conservation and do something about it. Whitney Center went fluo-rescent, sorted recyclables more efficiently, did some carpooling to save petrol, and 'preached thrift to their profligate neighbors'. With the help of Al Gore and a Yale colleague, Arthur Galston (the biologist who fought Agent Orange), they learned why and how humans were making their beloved habitat unliveable. Now they also help others set up Green Teams in retirement communities.

The much broader social potential for the arts is often overlooked, especially where managing conflict and transition are concerned. Encounters is a group of artists which does just that, using their abili-ties to work with communities on a wide range of problems, projects and periods of change. They hosted 'Combatants for Peace', a group of former Palestinian and Israeli combatants now committed to conflict resolution and lauded by Amnesty International. In contrast they worked with the learning community of the Dartington Arts Trust over how to handle the closure of its art school and its local impact.

Storytelling, too, is on the rise. From twenty-five countries around Europe storytellers met in Switzerland in 2009 to initiate formally a Federation for European Storytelling. Donald Smith, the director of the Scottish Storytelling Centre, was there. 'Storytelling is millennia old, but now it is bursting out all over Europe,' he said.[46] The revived popularity of history societies, and local history groups in particular, is a telling indication of a kind of re-engagement. Memory, both national, communal and individual, is an important facet of resilience – we build on what we know, and innovate from there.

Taken together, and given that its borders are ill-defined, this proliferation of DIY productive culture has earned itself a moniker. While all of these might not fit easily within it, the term 'collaborative consumption' has entered the language. It has its own website, book and strapline, 'What's yours is mine', and describes itself as a 'rapid explosion in swapping, sharing, bartering, trading and renting being reinvented through the latest technologies and peer-to-peer marketplaces in ways and on a scale never possible before'.

Even so, the accusation can be levelled that all these different individual initiatives do not add up to a comprehensive alternative to old-fashioned, passive consumerism. They can appear as ad hoc, disconnected actions, patchwork and piecemeal, good copy fodder for Sunday newspapers but not a new dawn for how to thrive in a finite world with greater conviviality.

In the campaigning community known as Occupy LSX (short for London Stock Exchange) that organised itself outside St Paul's Cathedral for several months over the winter of 2011/2012, a self-education centre that called itself Tent City University was set up. Some London academics saw the list of lectures on offer and thought that their own formal college courses looked lacklustre by comparison. It had its downside: if you happened to be speaking when a prolonged peal from the cathedral bells was due (as happened to me), there were two choices, shut up or bellow (I chose the latter option). One talk was given by Conor Gearty of the London School of Economics. He said something about social movements that caught the imagination of many, including two of the moving forces of Occupy LSX, Naomi Colvin and George Barda.[47] It was that: 'Minds are not changed by singular actions, however singular. They are changed when society comes to regard these singular actions as the rule rather than the exception, when common sense shifts on to the side of the erstwhile heretic.' Something that may help the shift from the exception to the rule is the opportunity opened up by the financial crisis to re-imagine both the places where we live, specifically our embattled high streets, and the days that we live in, meaning how much time we 'spend at the office' as opposed to doing other things. These two issues I'll look at in the last chapter.

The other thing that changes minds is whether the type of myriad initiatives described actually work. And the evidence is that not only do they work, but they succeed in very important and difficult circumstances when business as usual has utterly failed. It is one thing for the profusion of share- and DIY-based projects to blossom in the voluntary soil of people dissatisfied with consumerism, quite another in situations of desperation where a negative view of human nature might expect a dog-eat-dog Hobbesian nightmare in which only the strongest survive. (This is sometimes called Hobbes's 'state of nature', which we will also see in the last chapter is an erroneous notion.)

Greece has been subjected to an official, self-fulfilling rhetoric that 'there is no alternative' to a hard-line, socially divisive, austerity-driven return to neoliberal economic normality. It's a policy in which: 'It's the rich who get the pleasure and the poor who get the blame.' In this case, however, the poor include the vast majority of Greek society.

In the chapter on banking reform, we saw that the Euro policymakers' mantra of 'no alternative' is simply not true where the money system is concerned. Local currencies can restart the engines of local economies when mainstream finance has caused them to seize. There are also alternatives concerning defaulting on debt, which was the long-term successful route taken by Argentina after its banking collapse in 2000, and the introduction of capital controls, which proved successful in South America and many countries in Asia during several financial crises, including the most recent.

Greek suffering, although terrible for the Greeks, not only lays bare the failure of orthodox economics but positively highlights the benefits of doing things differently. Ironically it is in the gaps of a broken system that the shoots of a different, new economy get a chance to grow. This is the progressive opposite to Naomi Klein's chilling account of neoliberal economics' exploitation of disasters, *The Shock Doctrine*. Nowhere in daily coverage of worsening conditions in the Eurozone in 2011 and 2012 was the full irony effectively exposed of a system's advocates using its very failure to further promote it.

But while disaster reveals a society's economic and social weaknesses, it also shows up where true resilience and real value can be found – and that is in the ability of people to cooperate at the local level to meet a community's needs.

Decades of work on humanitarian disasters show that in the first key hours that follow them, how well a community responds depends on the strength, quality and capacity of the social networks it already has. These, obviously, are set by how the community and economy have been organised until then. Small island states, referred to in chapters 3 and 7, used to being on their own, tend to develop more cooperative systems and be more resilient when disasters strike. Local people are first on the scene, and usually best understand who needs what kind of help. It was local businesses, for example, not big corporations, who first showed up to rebuild after the flood disaster in New Orleans.

Elsewhere, in the wastelands created by recession and industrial decline in Detroit in the United States, unemployed people turned to urban farming to grow their own food and reclaim abandoned plots of land. Detroit had been as famous for music as for manufacturing automobiles, so the new movement was dubbed 'From Mo-Town to Gro-Town'. The new urban farmers became part of a movement with an international mission to 'create an abundance of food for people in need' by growing 'an economically sustainable system to uplift communities around the globe'. Across Detroit thousands have engaged in planting, growing and harvesting their own food. A single apiary at Green Toe Gardens yields around about 3000 lb of honey which is traded through local markets.

The rebirth is exemplified by the Georgia Street Community Garden, which – amazingly in a city left otherwise desolate by the wrecking ball of economic globalisation – does not get vandalised. Detroit's urban food enterprise has emerged 'not just as a hobby or a sideline but as part of a model for a wholesale revitalisation of a major city'.[48] In doing so it completes a cycle of history that may stand for something much broader than just the city's own experience. For the last century Detroit was all about big, energy-intensive industry. Now it is re-imagining how it was before the factories were built: a trading settlement with fields and farms around it. Urban farming is not a sop here to pampered middle classes, it is working for the poorest and the unemployed, and making some of the most shattered neighbourhoods liveable again. The same has happened in some of the poorest parts of New York City and the potential for further development is significant. In the most densely populated city in the US, a study by Columbia University found an astonishing five thousand acres of land

In the First World War Bryant Park, by the New York Public Library in Manhattan, was turned into a victory garden to grow food. But modern-day New York has over five thousand acres, not including parks like this, that could be turned to urban farming.

suitable for urban farming. A further one thousand acres were identi-fied in housing projects and under-used land.[49] There were also 'many other potentially suitable sites and properties that are not included in these designations that would greatly expand the total amount of land available for agricultural production'. This would not feed the whole city, but the study found it would 'significantly contribute to food security', especially in poorer neighbourhoods.

Similarly, after the financial crisis that wrecked Argentina's economy at the turn of the millennium, *huertas comunitarias*, community gardens, sprang up everywhere, such as in the La Boca district of Buenos Aires. Alongside them, community kitchens were also established. But things went much further in Argentina, as whole arms of government ceased to function properly. El Movimiento de Trabajadores Desocupados, the Movement of Unemployed Workers, assembled groups to do eve-rything from making food to building shelters, creating markets for people to sell their products, schooling and also demonstrating.[50] They created, in effect, a parallel economy. *Panaderia*, *bloquera* and *ropero* – bakeries, block making, and clothes making and selling – were a particular focus, the very basics of a livelihood: food, shelter and cloth-ing. One such group, CTDAV, had fifteen thousand members and paid out nine thousand unemployment benefits per month in 2002.

Japan has a large, dynamic and radical consumer cooperative

movement, which grew from the wreckage of the Second World War. Today it has some twenty-two million members, meaning that around one person in six is a member of one of over six hundred consumer co-ops. Post-war occupation forces encouraged Japanese citizens to set up political organisations, including radical ones. The hope was of changing a culture overly deferential to imperial power. New rights of citizenship were eagerly embraced. Activists, farmers and small businesses aligned against big corporations and the profiteers who prospered in spite of war's damage to the economy. Cooperatives emerged that re-imagined the consumer as an active citizen, a member of a dynamic civil society and the national body politic.

Today, the Seikatsu Club Consumers Cooperative Union is one of the largest, with nearly a third of a million members, and well known. In one sense, the circumstances of its birth echo the beginnings of the cooperative movement in Rochdale, England, during the Industrial Revolution. Workers were being exploited with poor-quality, overpriced food and clubbed together to do better providing for themselves. In the process they changed the relationship between producers and consumers, and gave themselves an economic education. Similarly, the Seikatsu Club began in 1965, when householders took a stand against poor-quality, overpriced milk, and got together to purchase milk themselves collectively through their consumer co-op. A club member will, on average, buy about a third of their food through the cooperative, with some buying a much higher share. The Shinto belief system, which focuses on continuity between generations, the immediate world around you, and the essential goodness of people, is a backcloth to the club. In rejecting 'cheapness' for its own sake, and focusing on quality, values and environmental concerns, the Japanese groups are perhaps better described as anti-consumerist co-ops. Other co-ops include the Zen-Noh Security System (the National Federation of Agricultural Cooperative Associations), and Oisix e-commerce.

This suggests that a community's own capacity and resilience are the foundations of economic life, while the bright lights and shiny trappings of international financial services that so spellbind politicians is more a froth, merely the 'cappuccino economy', as Richard Murphy puts it in his book *The Courageous State*. It's a simple insight for some extreme circumstances, but has more general application. In

Yorkshire, the more genteel towns of Hebden Bridge and Todmorden are part of what has been called a 'sharing revolution'. The local community took over a cinema, theatre, the town hall, and is trying to take over a local pub, all to put them to good use. Communal initiatives focused on food growing and sharing proliferated, then came the bolder moves to convert abandoned or under-used buildings and shops into assets for the communities. A national newspaper described it as 'neither hippy nor New Age', but 'made up of ordinary people, old and young, from both affluent homes and social housing'.[51] Depending on where you live, the recession has either invited people to think more deeply about what is important to them, or forced them to innovate because the system failed them.

In October 2011, the *New York Times* reported that, just as elsewhere when times get hard, in Greece people were turning their backs on a failed mainstream to grow their own parallel economy.[52] In the Greek port city of Volos, the paper reported, Theodoros Mavridis bought eggs, milk and jam at market using a new informal barter currency, a Local Alternative Unit, or TEM as it is known locally. 'I felt liberated, I felt free for the first time,' he said. The system combines an element of barter with an alternative currency, and similar systems are emerging around Greece and are being used for basics like food as well as business and services. The Volos network had eight hundred members.

Initiatives like this regularly emerge in times of crisis, and from Buenos Aires to Detroit and Volos, they have enormous benefits. People who get involved feel happier, healthier, and as if they have more control over their lives. They build community and more resilient local economies. The question is, why wait for disasters to strike – economic or environmental – before taking the initiative to do things differently?

In normal times the dominant financial system creates a disempowering dependency culture of passive consumerism. When this happens, community erodes, we become deskilled, our lives less healthy and economies more vulnerable to shocks. On the basis that prevention is better than cure, what happened in Greece and elsewhere is an opportunity to learn from what we do in times of disaster and redesign the mainstream economy to prioritise well-being and resilience.

Examples of a richer, lighter livelihood are all around us. They may be unsupported, ignored and sometimes derided, yet they work and they thrive, a testimony to their vigour. The future is already here, if we have eyes to see it.

Wendell Berry, the American writer, farmer and cultural critic, put it like this: 'My wish simply is to live my life as fully as I can. In both our work and our leisure, I think, we should be so employed. And in our time this means that we must save ourselves from the products that we are asked to buy, ultimately, to replace ourselves.'[53]

Berry was influenced in turn by another American writer, activist and man of the soil, Edward Abbey. Abbey was controversial because his writing was said to have inspired a generation of radical environmental activists – his book *The Monkey Wrench Gang* reportedly led to the creation of the direct-action group Earth First!. Berry defended him, perhaps seeing personified in Abbey the uncontained, vibrant life force that he so admired in nature. Abbey died fairly young, at sixty-two, but he had the presence of mind to pass on some advice before he himself passed on. I don't fish or hunt, but this passage from a speech he gave titled 'Joy, Shipmates, Joy!' is one of my favourites in the English language. It seems suitable here:

One final paragraph of advice: do not burn yourselves out. Be as I am – a reluctant enthusiast . . . a part-time crusader, a half-hearted fanatic. Save the other half of yourselves and your lives for pleasure and adventure. It is not enough to fight for the land; it is even more important to enjoy it. While you can. While it's still here. So get out there and hunt and fish and mess around with your friends, ramble out yonder and explore the forests, climb the mountains, bag the peaks, run the rivers, breathe deep of that yet sweet and lucid air, sit quietly for a while and contemplate the precious stillness, the lovely, mysterious, and awesome space. Enjoy yourselves, keep your brain in your head and your head firmly attached to the body, the body active and alive, and I promise you this much; I promise you this one sweet victory over our enemies, over those desk-bound men and women with their hearts in a safe deposit box, and their eyes hypnotized by desk calculators. I promise you this; You will outlive the bastards.

10

Mutual interest

The future is already here – it's just not evenly distributed.

William Gibson

Many theories . . . begin with the idea that inequality is somehow a beneficial cultural trait that imparts efficiencies, motivates innovation and increases the likelihood of survival. But . . . rather than imparting advantages to the group, unequal access to resources is inherently destabilising and greatly raises the chance of group extinction.

Deborah Rogers, *New Scientist*, 30 July 2012

The great divergence – growing larger and further apart

'Gourmet restaurants, world-class nightclubs, favorable tax breaks – not to mention proximity to the world's financial centers. These are some of the attributes that make a city particularly attractive to billionaires,' declared *Forbes* magazine. Beating Tokyo, Los Angeles, San Francisco and Dallas, in 2011 Mumbai made it on to *Forbes*'s list of the world's top ten cities for billionaires. Mumbai is the biggest, richest city in India, itself the world's largest democracy, with the second-biggest population. With twenty-one billionaires, Mumbai was in joint sixth place. Their combined wealth equalled $106.6 billion, greater than the total average per capita income of thirty-five million Indians. One Mumbai-based billionaire, the energy tycoon Mukesh Ambani, lives in a twenty-seven-storey skyscraper, thought to be the world's most expensive home at a cost of $1 billion. When he turns on his taps it is fair to assume that water flows on demand. Water is a big part of life in Mumbai, surrounding the city and flowing through it. When the rains come, it is often as a deluge.

Coastal megacities like Mumbai are on the front line of climate change. Temperature and sea-level rise will touch everyone and everything somehow. About one quarter of Mumbai is low-lying and parts are built on land reclaimed from the sea. The future holds more flooding, heatwaves and heavier summer monsoons. Diseases that thrive in these conditions – diarrhoea, malaria, leptospirosis – are expected to worsen.[1] Finding water to drink, however, the stuff of life, should not be a problem in this vast, fabulously wealthy city. But for millions, it can be. Mumbai is a jewel of economic globalisation, a bridge between developing and developed countries, and a proud monument to the transformational power of finance. It is meant to show the promise of development and point to a future in which the great urban centres of the global South escape poverty. But the water flowing beneath that bridge tells a different story.

The day begins unpredictably when water first starts gurgling through taps. Residents leave them open overnight so as not to miss any of the few precious hours of available supply. Exactly when the water comes appears to be at the whim of some invisible power. Millions living in the poor neighbourhoods of Mumbai have a rhythm of life dictated by liquid feudalism.

The river bed, banks and intermittently operational plumbing of the city's troubled waters are made of the cracks of history and a toxic cocktail of economic doctrine, social division and power politics. It is partly a postcolonial legacy, and partly an interweaving of rapid urban growth, authoritarianism, and the strong, distorting influence of 'middle-class interests within a denuded public realm', according to Professor Matthew Gandy of University College London.[2] This is not, however, another sad, simple and overfamiliar tale of the poor denied access to essential services, and of the health impact of inadequate clean drinking-water supplies.

Water in India is about more than meeting the physical needs of life. As the Indian anthropologist Arjun Appadurai explains, it carries other powerful cultural meanings to do with spiritual cleansing and purification.[3] In a society still dominated by caste differences, says

Gandy, it also plays a role in social differentiation. As a direct result, a lack of equal access to water among castes can entrench and deepen existing divisions. Something as prosaic as plumbing therefore dictates the relative cohesion or disorder of a whole urban society.

Inspired by Tate Modern's exhibition *Century City*, Gandy saw in the flow of water around Mumbai something much larger, and made contact with the Indian-based group PUKAR (Partners for Urban Knowledge and Research) and the Mumbai-based film-makers Savitri Medhatul and Amala Popuri to see what a closer analysis would reveal and to capture it on film. When the crew gathered in Mumbai, the city still stood in the shadow of over 450 deaths during the previous year's record monsoon. Dangerous floods were made yet more lethal by drains that were absent or blocked. Water that had nowhere else to escape flowed into people's houses and makeshift dwellings. Over the following months of 2007 and early 2008 they saw, in the way that glaciers once carved out valleys, the role of water in creating the urban landscape.

When a water system supplies eighteen million people, and there are high levels of official caution about terrorist threats, not anyone is allowed into one of its vital treatment complexes, but with a local, Hindi-speaking assistant producer, Medhatul and Popuri were able to gain access to key parts of the city's water infrastructure that the general public never would. Dreams of radically modern, 'Haussmann-esque' urban planning survive, anachronistically, in the neglected air of Mumbai's municipal water authorities and alongside the daily slog of ensuring that enough potable water reaches the city's millions of inhabitants. A map of Paris's water supply hung on a wall in the water authorities offices in Mumbai, but the scale of conflict between this memory of urban modernity, and the ambition it fed, is stark. Western models of the orderly and universal provision of services across relatively coherent urban areas will not work in the modern megacities of the developing world, Gandy concluded. That is because they are blind to the realities of extreme social polarisation and geographical fragmentation experienced by cities like Mumbai.

Monsoon is a time of irony for the slum dwellers of Mumbai. 'There is water everywhere,' people say, 'except in the taps.' One of the reasons stretches back to the interwoven histories of Britain and India. The British colonial government had a policy towards its overseas territories which was not to invest in internal improvements unless they stood to generate a profit. It left poorer communities badly served as cities grew. Hence there was overcrowding in the city and an inadequate infrastructure before independence.

At independence in 1948, when the population stood at two million, there were still significant shortages and highly variable access to water. A 'technocratic honeymoon' of investment and development, which began with a surge of national self-confidence, ended by the mid-1960s. The growing complexity of city-wide water management led to the creation in 1971 of the Water Supply and Sewage Department, but left out at the time was joint and coherent responsibility for storm-water drainage and regional resource management.

Now, perhaps half of the city's eighteen million inhabitants live in the poorly served slums, known as *zopadpatti*, that stretch along rivers, ditches and railway lines. The politics of access to water ranges from the dilapidation of the city's infrastructural networks to political manipulation of slum communities in need of basic services.

Facilities like the Bhandup Water Treatment works ensure that water is well cleaned at source, but it can easily become contaminated in pipes and overhead storage tanks in transit, in poorly maintained housing stock, some of which may not have been cleaned for decades, and in the process of illegal tapping.

By 2015 Mumbai's population is expected to reach twenty-two million. Once, the pattern of the monsoon was largely predictable, allowing people to prepare for and work around it. But the floods of 2005 were seen locally as a change in that pattern. Climatic instability linked to global warming adds further pressure and urgency to the task of reforming the management of the city's water system. Plans to upgrade to meet these challenges – the so-called Mumbai IV project – are beset by financial and technical problems. One concern, given the likely future of energy prices, is that they include energy-hungry, powered rather than gravity-fed distribution systems.

The city's water infrastructure, far from being a one-dimensional, purely functional utility, has itself, and unintentionally, created aspects of a new urban landscape. Slums of the sort seen in the film *Slumdog Millionaire*, with some of the worst access to clean drinking water, are traversed by giant water pipes that local people have turned into precarious elevated walkways.

*The pipes that carry water over and past poor neighbourhoods
in Mumbai find a use as local walkways.*

Spaces between the pipes have formed what Gandy called 'ribbons
of extreme deprivation' connecting some of the poorest communities
in the city. An infrastructure that is failing the poorest in its intended
purpose has nevertheless been co-opted for another function by the
otherwise disappointed communities. What the anthropologist Appadurai calls 'spectral housing' dominates much of Mumbai, characterised
by low investment due to a combination of rent controls and 'shadowy
networks of ownership'. Altogether the conditions of many of the poorest communities have been termed 'landscapes of disaster'.

Now, change is being driven in an aggressive, top-down fashion by
well-organised corporate interests under the umbrella of groups like
the coalition Bombay First. The city's elite are pushing for Mumbai to
follow in the Asian footsteps of cities like Shanghai and Singapore. But
to achieve their vision, a kind of Faustian development is being pursued, the brutal architectural revisionism of a latter-day Haussmann.
It risks marginalising the majority of the population, as well as repeating and more deeply entrenching the legacy of unequal access to
essential services left by nineteenth-century colonial water engineers.
For the majority, access to basic necessities like water is being brutally
circumscribed.

A polluted river divides the city. In places it darts through pipes
and concrete waterways. One day while filming Gandy and his film
crew saw figures by a culvert along Mahim Creek, huddled in stark

humanity like the subjects of a Sebastião Salgado photograph. To interview them the crew had to climb down to the ledge where they were sitting. When they did, instead of the poor or homeless people they had expected, they found a group of dedicated junior water engineers. They were on a four-day-long shift monitoring the performance of the system.

'If someone comes to our house, we would offer them a glass of water,' explained one of the engineers. 'We do this work in the same spirit.' They were motivated by public service, not financial reward or ambition for advancement. Another engineer commented: 'We do this work as a good deed.' There is a pervasive rhetoric of state failure that surrounds the management and operation of basic utilities like water. Yet, on the ground, reality belies the mantra. Underfunded departments function only because dedicated public servants struggle, often far beyond their terms and conditions of employment, to keep things working.

A hidden cost of privatising such utilities is the loss of senior water engineers whose decades of experience constitutes a unique and irreplaceable institutional memory of problems and solutions. But in Mumbai, French water companies circle like vultures waiting to take over.

The Mumbai municipal authority has been hollowed out in stages over the last three decades. Most recently, dramatically rising land prices led to a new authoritarianism and increasingly violent local politics in which hundreds of thousands are being made homeless in the wake of slum demolitions. But not without resistance.

When a pilot study was done on the prospect for water privatisation in Mumbai, the chosen ward was a rich one. 'At least they should have chosen an "average" [income] ward,' says Nirupa Bhangar, a local activist. The impacts, she adds, should properly be judged by the effect that privatisation will have on the poorest. Deindustrialisation and encroaching free-market economics have led to a vast growth of the informal economy and the spread of poverty to communities that were previously prosperous. A particular brand of 'saffron capitalism' has been promoted through a tactical alliance of the Hindu nationalist party Shiv Sena (Army of Shiv) and large corporations.

Corruption is real, but it is also far more nuanced than the pieties of, often hypocritical, Western politicians and financial institutions allow for, ranging from the payment of 'speed money' at the household level to accelerate the installation of services, to price-fixing cartels higher up, and full-blown political corruption higher still. More recently, claims Gandy, access to water has been 'increasingly linked with criminalised networks as part of an intensification of political corruption in Mumbai associated with Shiv Sena control of public institutions'.

Other daily manipulations heighten the atmosphere of 'liquid feudalism'. For example, hotels and wealthy apartment blocks employ illegal booster pumps that suck more water out of the system, worsening inequality in access at the local level. Farming and tribal communities in districts like Thane have had more and more of their water diverted to new, middle-class urban developments. Elsewhere, rural water resources get exploited by companies like Coca-Cola, who sell Kinley-brand 'packaged drinking water' in the city. The company's water-extraction activities at Wada, in the context of weak or absent regulation, divert water that is much needed by local farms and villages.

In a clear example of William Rees's findings on the ecological footprint of cities, Mumbai is extending its ecological catchment area deeper into the surrounding mountains of Maharashtra state through its demand for potable water. The often callous disregard, close to contempt, with which middle-class elites regard the poor is ironic. Without its army of underground workers, the city would cease to function. To Gandy it is 'a microcosm of larger global patterns, of how we all rely on (disregarded) cheap labour'. The wealth divide in the city widens as more people live in slums, while Mumbai's premium property prices can be higher than in London or Manhattan.

Some divisive consequences are subtle, but damaging and long-lasting. The timing of water supplies, for example, to certain poorer districts means the children in families are left behind to collect the water, so they in turn miss school, and deepen the poverty trap. The city gets richer as its public health deteriorates and people trapped in poverty come to be seen by an intolerant middle class as 'impostors' here. Elsewhere things can be even worse. It's often said that, in spite of frequently terrible conditions, nobody actually starves in Mumbai, but beyond the city there are farmers committing suicide over debts of just £30, and a political class that appears intent on eliminating the peasant class.

A new kind of bourgeois environmentalism, focused on urban pret-
tification, also has a dark side in its assault on informal settlements.
Often led by middle-class interest groups in partnership with the state
or international agencies, it can result in failed urban infrastructure
being disguised rather than corrected. To compensate there has been
a grass roots revival of traditional approaches to water management.
But even here, the benefits from relearning, for example, techniques
of rainwater harvesting tend to get cancelled out by more profligate
water use among the city's middle classes in new luxury leisure complexes.

Nevertheless, there are local campaigns spreading to improve
municipal services, for example by listening more to local engineers
who understand best the problems on the ground. An alternative to
privatisation and self-seeking private finance would be for Indian
cities to issue municipal bonds instead, in much the same way that
both European and North American cities did in their past to finance
vital infrastructure. Nurturing a vibrant secular public sphere will also
help avoid city life growing more fractured and violent. These precise
dynamics may be particular to Mumbai, but they exemplify tensions
and choices being made in megacities the world over.

But if problems are solved by communities working together (with
general benefits identified at least as far back as the sixteenth-century
French philosopher Michel de Montaigne) who in the process rebuild
the public sphere, resolving the difficulties of 'liquid feudalism' in a
city like Mumbai could be a catalyst and example for much broader
progressive change. The greater vulnerability of Mumbai's urban
poor to a changing climate and the struggle to improve their condition, whilst muddied by the distractions of the city's super-rich, is a
microcosm of a global challenge.

Managing water in a warming world is a test of our ability to coexist
in a human-stressed biosphere. Get it right and we all could benefit;
mistakes weaken the fabric of society. Water privatisation has already
caused rioting and protest from Bolivia to Africa and Asia, where it
worsens the effects of inequality and puts profit before people. Of
course, inequality, both of the kind seen in modern Mumbai and
between countries, doesn't just appear of itself. When a charity campaign called 'Make Poverty History' was at its height, it was given a
twist by a UK activist who produced T-shirts with the slightly altered

slogan 'History Makes Poverty'. Inequality is rooted in our past history, and in political and economic developments going back centuries.

We should move forward

Visiting Dar es Salaam in Tanzania on a tour of Africa in 2005, the UK chancellor of the Exchequer, Gordon Brown, said: 'The days of Britain having to apologise for its colonial history are over. We should move forward.' He added: 'We should celebrate much of our past rather than apologise for it.'[4] Perhaps Brown felt confident because it was the French who were major players in the slave trade from Tanzania, or because a campaign grew up from the grass roots in Britain against an establishment that fiercely defended the trade. Either way, the shadow of empire, and its worst excesses in the slave trade, still shape the global economic map. But slavery also provides another note from history on the possibility of rescuing the human condition from apocalyptic circumstances in which we find ourselves trapped by daunting economic obstacles.

When Thomas Clarkson arrived in Bristol, the same city that gave birth to Samuel Plimsoll and his life-saving low-water burden line, it was the first stop in his long campaign to abolish slavery, and he described his feelings:

> The bells of some of the churches were then ringing . . . It filled me, almost directly, with a melancholy for which I could not account. I began now to tremble, for the first time, at the arduous task I had undertaken of attempting to subvert one of the branches of the commerce of the great place which was then before me . . . and I questioned whether I should even get out of it alive.[5]

But he chose the city well. In just twenty years up to 1770, 393 slave ships sailed from Bristol to Africa, and on to the Caribbean and America. At its height, the Bristol slave trade saw these floating human tombs embark every week. In addition to the slavers, in the same period 852 ships sailed directly to the West Indies to collect the fruits of the slaves' labour, typically sugar. Four hundred more sailed to the mainland American colonies collecting their cotton and tobacco.[6] To the city's merchants, of course, slavery wasn't an end in itself, but a means for enrichment.

In terms of wealth, the countries of the world were relatively equal up to the mid-eighteenth century. The average standard of living was probably lower in Europe than in the rest of the world. Labourers in South India, for example, earned more than their British equivalents. Two centuries of colonial economic re-engineering would change all that, leaving a permanent legacy of poverty, conflict and large and rising inequality. There were other economic spin-offs too. Bristol exported firearms and gunpowder to slavers along the African coast. In 1750 Bristol's first bank was set up on the profits of slavery.

The sheer weight of international trade was evident even then, although, unlike today, it concentrated largely on things that could not be produced domestically. In the middle of the eighteenth century, Bristol had 261 Bristol sugar importers. In one year alone, 1773, the city imported 20,896 hogsheads of sugar from the West Indies. (A hogshead is one of many rich, lost and obscure metrics that measure the world, it is a weight of 600 lb. Others include the 'cat', the lethal dose of a substance per kilogram of cat, the 'cran', 37.5 gallons of herring, and the 'open window,' a measure of sound – but I digress.)[7]

John Wesley, on one of his frequent visits, preached on 'the chief besetting sins' of Bristol, namely 'a love of money and love of ease'.[8] Every cup of sweetened tea drunk in local salons, and every rub of tobacco smoked by the waterside, not only made the city and nation richer, but was stained with the sweat and blood of human bondage.

During the horror of the infamous middle passage, the transatlantic trade quite literally submerged humanity beneath the sea of commerce and the commerce of the sea. In 1729 the Bristol ship *Greyhound* left the West African coast with 339 human souls manacled on board. When it arrived in Barbados only 214 were still alive. Such figures were typical. The trade continued legally from 1698 to 1807, and surreptitiously for decades more. Why did it go on so long?

Economic fashion and short-term vested interests blinded people to injustice and what now seems a murderous and indefensible exploitation. Edward Colston, described as Bristol's 'greatest benefactor', whose legacy stands in the walls of Colston Hall on Colston Street, still a popular concert venue, was a sugar merchant who 'built his fortune on the back of the African slave trade'.[9] John Cary was the Bristol sugar merchant we heard from earlier who thought slavery the 'best Traffick', and was a major influence on British economic policy. In fairness, the city produced great abolitionists as well as slavers, such as the socialite turned campaigner Hannah More, who became an integral figure in the movement. She wrote an epic poem, better politics than literature, that included the lines: *Shall Britain, where the soul of freedom reigns; Forge chains for others she herself disdains?* This may have overlooked the lack of universal suffrage in Britain at the time, but the point was well made.

Gordon Brown's words were too glib. The legacy of slavery lives still all around us. As too do other colonial abuses ranging from Britain's drug-pushing opium wars involving India and China, and the destruction of India's textile industry, to the lasting upheaval and murderous brutality of King Leopold II's rubber trade in the Congo, from which the region has never recovered. But from slavery alone we can trace a direct line of descent to the criminalisation and imprisonment of America's poor, and social division in its great cities. However tedious and uncomfortable the unshakeable bonds of history, overlay a map of the slave trade's victims and profiteers with one of poverty and inequality in the modern world, and they will not greatly differ.

In modern-day Benin, in West Africa, to describe someone that you do not trust, the phrase 'He will sell you and enjoy it' is still in common use. From the African countries where people were stolen into slavery, and the plantation lands like Haiti in the Caribbean where they were taken as bonded labour, the long-term negative economic and social consequences still glisten with injustice. I once travelled to investigate conditions on contemporary, corporate-controlled plantations on the border between the Dominican Republic and Haiti. It was like being in a time machine to pass through villages in the middle of the sugar plantations, as if an eighteenth-century etching had come to life. This is of course only possible if, since the days of slavery, the global economy has either neglected to redress such asymmetric development, or further contributed to it. In the last half-century or so, the fashion and doctrine in policies for economic development has come and gone. They are dealt with at great length elsewhere, but a brief recap is useful to understand our current context and how things have shifted.

In East Asia, for example, the so-called 'miracle' economies emerged from the 1960s onwards. These were the four 'tigers' or 'dragons' of Singapore, South Korea, Taiwan and Hong Kong (while still British-administered). They grew quickly through a combination of rapid industrialisation, being emerging financial centres, manufacturing and the early uptake and development of information technology. Their successful formula was not taken from the playbook of Western financial institutions like the World Bank and IMF, however. On the contrary, they embraced active government intervention, supporting particular sectors and companies with explicit industrial policies, and focused on selling goods to already industrialised nations. Korea's success, for example, was built on the foundations of land reform, extensive public provision of social services and policies to promote progressive income distribution.

These countries did all the things that the neoliberal cookbook frowns on. As well as exporting, they developed their own manufacturing capacity to make the things their own people and businesses wanted rather than importing them. They used a wide range of capital, investment and trade controls to engage with the world on their own terms, rather than those of a free-market borderless fantasy. Why? Perhaps because they understood what J. K. Galbraith pointed out, that throughout history free trade has benefited most those who are already powerful: 'Free trade was for the first arrival, whereas in Britain, it was, indeed, an attractive design for confining the later contenders to their earlier stages of development.'

From the end of the eighteenth century, whenever a non-Western nation attempted rapid development, or to control the terms on which it integrated in the global economy, one of the major Western powers used either military or economic sanctions to stop it. Before preaching free trade to the world, both Britain and the United States used protectionism extensively to develop and establish economic dominance. Their effective tariff rates on imported goods edged down only gradually from upwards of around 50 per cent in the early part of the nineteenth century to the middle of the twentieth according to the UK-based Korean economist Ha-Joon Chang.[10]

Learning from history, the tigers used state-owned banks to support domestic industry, had high public and private savings rates, and

invested heavily in education. They were, however, also often author-
itarian, undemocratic and anti-union.

Following the 'tigers' came the so-called 'tiger cubs' – Indonesia,
Malaysia, Thailand, Philippines – named ironically, given their much
greater populations. They too successfully ignored the neoliberal
mantra, using industrial policy and import substitution backed by
tariffs to achieve export-led growth. The 'cubs' also invested heavily
in public goods like education, from primary school to university
level. In 1997, when Asia was hit with a financial crash, countries like
Malaysia and Thailand were also sufficiently confident to ignore the
advice of the International Monetary Fund and used capital controls
to protect their economies from the caprices of footloose international
finance. Overall, these two waves of nations in Asia expanded their
economies whilst avoiding very sharp divisions between rich and
poor – their experience has been dubbed 'growth with equity'.
Environmental questions are another story.

Latin America's experience was quite different. The region's big
economic powers of Brazil, Argentina and Mexico became synonymous up to the 1980s with the policy of 'import-substituting
industrialisation', which history has judged unkindly. Their motivation was clear and understandable, built on a similar awareness of
history. They sought to insulate themselves from external economic
shocks by building strong, more self-sufficient domestic markets and
to generate employment. Instead of being trapped as producers of
low-value primary commodities, they wanted to do what successful
industrialised countries had done, and make things that added value
and could be sold at a higher price.

This was the strategy of escaping the so-called 'resource curse' in
which several African countries such as the Congo, Angola, Nigeria
and others have long been trapped. Great natural assets, poorly managed, can leave in their wake more conflict and division than wealth
and development. Latin America wanted greater sufficiency and less
dependency. They too used a targeted industrial policy, nationalising
some enterprises and providing targeted support to key areas such as
manufacturing, agriculture and energy. They used tax policy, trade
protection and controls on investment to support it. Why was it less
successful? Partly it worked less well because their strategies of substituting imports and promoting exports were not as well connected.

Some sectors – the 'infant industries' – were not as well chosen: for example, there wasn't a large and wealthy enough middle class to buy all the white goods produced domestically, and the same goods didn't compete with what American and European manufacturers were making. Economists argued that Latin American currencies were overvalued too, making their exports too expensive and deterring foreign buyers.

This is too simple, however. There was a political edge to dismissing what happened in Latin America. The interpretation of what happened in America's back yard needs to be seen in the light of Cold War politics. Too much self-sufficiency and independence was a threat, and there was a new neoliberal orthodoxy emerging which hated the scale of state intervention in the economy, even though it had proved so successful in Asia, not to mention America's own past.

Some initiatives were successful, not only on their own terms, but now stand as examples to the likes of Britain and the US. One colonial legacy Brazil cleverly turned to its own advantage. Portuguese colonists established vast sugar-cane plantations and oversaw the kidnap, trafficking and enslavement of millions of Africans to work on them. Brazil is another country whose modern economic and social geography was shaped by slavery. However, the plantations provided foundations for a big national shift to the biofuel ethanol in the 1970s, growing from earlier experiments dating back to the late 1920s.

The first OPEC oil-shock of 1973 dramatically accelerated the uptake of ethanol. Oil became expensive, sugar cane was cheap, and Brazil's distillery industry had spare capacity. The phase-out of cars manufactured to run on petrol became government policy. Results were dramatic. In 1979 only 0.5 per cent of cars made ran on ethanol. Just seven years later, by 1986, the figure was over 70 per cent and remains so today.

Volatile price changes for both oil and sugar in the years that followed created an uncertain economic environment for ethanol-fuelled vehicles, but after a dip in the late 1990s and early part of the new millennium, several concerns, from energy security to the environment and advantageous tax arrangements, saw a triumphant return. Energy security had been the primary motive for developing ethanol, but there were environmental benefits too. While lead was still

common in petrol, there was none in ethanol, which also lacked petrol's sulphur content and other pollutants. There were lower carbon
emissions across ethanol's overall fuel cycle, even though this isn't
the case universally for biofuels. In general their environmental benefits are very sensitive to the type of land used, how it is managed and
what grew there before. More recently, of course, liquid biofuels have
become embroiled in controversy to do with the competition for land
between growing food for people and growing feedstocks to make
fuel for vehicles.

I remember watching news footage as a child of the toylike
Brazilian Volkswagen Beetles that ran on sugar. No car is made in
Brazil now that runs only on petrol. With a concerted national effort
and ambition, investment and legislation, it demonstrates the potential for re-engineering systems at speed and scale, and rethinking
transport is one of our prime challenges.

And then there is Africa, and especially sub-Saharan Africa, on
most economic and social development measures the greatest losers
in the global game. Their weakness and the immediate aftermath of
the post-colonial period after the Second World War left them more
vulnerable to foreign policymakers. It is a simplification, but one that
is extensively substantiated, to note one overriding error made by
Western policymakers in regard to much of Africa, as the influence of
institutions like the World Bank and IMF grew. Africa was expected
to repeat the successes seen in Asia, but without any of the policies
to create 'developmental states' that worked there. An economic tide
turned in the 1980s in response to two major dynamics. First there
was enormous fall-out from a debt crisis rooted in the oil crises.
Second there was the rise of the so-called Washington Consensus – a
package of neoliberal economic policies applied with little discrimination across many countries with some entirely predictable and
negative consequences.

By restricting supply, the oil producers had hiked the price of oil
and their profits. As a result, vast sums in petrodollars from the 1980s
were sitting in banks. The banks lent the money out (loan-pushing is
an appropriate term for what went on) very cheaply, often to finance
hastily and badly chosen large infrastructure projects that frequently
failed or never paid for themselves, but which profited the construction companies – typically Western in origin – that built them, and

left corruption in their wake. Money was a product in search of a market, and the lenders cared little which country or dictator they lent it to, assuming that countries could not go broke. Then a global recession hit and the prices of goods sold by African countries plummeted, so when the time to repay the loans came, they couldn't afford it. This pushed them into the ideological hands of the financial institutions. In return for economic support countries had to agree to so-called 'structural adjustment programmes' mostly written by technocrats in Washington. About the only thing these programmes shared with the Asian experience was a focus on export-led development. Beyond that it was all different.

Instead of higher-value-added goods that helped build domestic industries, Africa was to focus on what it had done before, the export of primary commodities. The drawback was that many African countries exported similar things – oil, unprocessed agricultural products, wood and unprocessed minerals dug from the ground. When they all followed the same advice, it led to something called the fallacy of composition. Demand for these goods didn't vary much, so when supply increased it reinforced a long-term downward pressure on prices. Economically speaking, Africa was being bled of its natural resources, and running faster just to stand still, and in some cases fall further behind. Commodity dependence proved very expensive. In just over a decade between 1980 and 1992 declining terms of trade delivered a bill of around $350 billion, only to worsen thereafter, more than Africa's total external debt that was the justification for structural adjustment.[11]

In 1999 the UN body on trade and development, UNCTAD, noted: 'After more than a decade of liberal reforms in developing countries, their payments disorders . . . remain as acute as ever, and their economies depend even more on external financial resources.'[12] Representatives from Africa felt that the Washington Consensus had locked them into tight macroeconomic policies that favoured 'capital against labour, finance against industry . . . speculation against human development'. The new economic doctrine had 'limited the policy options that are available to the late developers . . . Today, many of the policy measures that were applied so successfully in the transformation of the South and South East Asian region are no longer possible.' Trade and adjustment policies were negative, they argued, for both 'stability and development'.[13]

Africa was expected to tie itself to the export of primary commodities, and open its markets while both Europe and the United States continued to apply extensive domestic protection to their own. At the same time, under structural adjustment it was to cut spending and privatise public services. The state was to withdraw from the economy, sell off state-owned enterprises, and reduce support for key sectors. Currencies were to be devalued. Measures to manage trade and the flow of investment for domestic benefit were to be removed. Whatever the merit of any individual proposal – perhaps an economy might benefit from devaluing its currency – the combined effect was disastrous. Even the economically orthodox newspaper the *Financial Times* concluded that the IMF through promoting adjustment programmes under the Washington Consensus 'probably ruined as many economies as they have saved'. The economist James Tobin thought: 'Their [the World Bank's and IMF's] standard remedies, fiscal stringency and punitive interest rates, are devastating to economic life.'

Eventually, a damning critique of this system emerged from the heart of the very institutions themselves. We have already encountered Joseph Stiglitz. He is the former chief economist at the World Bank who resigned after being pressured to stop publicly criticising its policies. Of its sister organisation the IMF, he stated: 'In theory, the fund supports democratic institutions in the nations it assists. In practice, it undermines the democratic process by imposing policies.' More telling still was his appreciation of exactly how the system worked, with teams of technocrats visiting countries in Africa like late-medieval nuncios sent to police doctrine across the Catholic world on behalf of papal authority. In Stiglitz's words:

When the IMF decides to assist a country, it dispatches a 'mission' of economists. These economists frequently lack extensive experience in the country; they are more likely to have firsthand knowledge of its five-star hotels than of the villages that dot its countryside. I heard stories of one unfortunate incident when team members copied large parts of the text for one country's report and transferred them wholesale to another. They might have gotten away with it, except the 'search and replace' function on the word processor didn't work properly, leaving the original country's name in a few places. Oops.[14]

Reports were also written in haste, often relying on flawed mathematical models.

What kind of world did all these economic ebbs and flows, nudges and shoves, create? As we saw much earlier, it left a massively expanded global economy in which people are ever more interconnected, and yet paradoxically further apart. Neoliberal Washington Consensus policies still rule, in spite of the catastrophic failure of financial markets in 2008, which saw the finance sector in whose interest many of the policies are framed, bailed out by the reviled public sector.

The success of the policy package ultimately depended on the assumption that we all stand to gain from a world made 'attractive to billionaires'. It is our old friend, 'trickle-down' economic theory. And yet, in the world, just as in the city of Mumbai, once more attention goes to 'world-class nightclubs and favourable tax breaks', then when the poor turn on their taps (supposing that they have one), invariably they hear only the hollow moan of failed plumbing. The water neither flows nor trickles. Resources have gushed up from the poorest to the rich, not vice versa.

During the 1980s, which was a bad decade for Africa, where many of the world's poorest people live, if you took a notional $100 worth of global economic growth, a share of $2.20 found its way to those in the world who subsist on $1 a day, the World Bank's rough definition of 'absolute poverty'. During the following decade, the 1990s, which saw the implementation of structural adjustment combined with a series of new global commitments to poverty reduction under the heading of the Millennium Development goals, the share of the absolute poor in the benefits of that notional $100 of growth shrank from $2.20 to 60 cents. This meant that to generate a single dollar of poverty reduction below the $1-a-day line would need $166 of additional global production and consumption, with all its associated environmental impacts. Here is the paradox of relying on the efficiency of growth to reduce poverty: it requires ever more overconsumption by the already rich to deliver shrinking micro-shifts in poverty reduction.

According to World Bank data the number of people beneath the extreme poverty line did fall between 1980 and 2008, from 1.9 billion to 1.3 billion. We'll examine below in more detail the extraordinary fact that this fall stems almost wholly from one country, China, the reliability of whose statistics is frequently questioned, but the point is that the gains at the bottom of the global income stretch were far, far weaker than those at the top. This, too, left nearly half of the world's population – 43 per cent – living on less than $2 a day, practically unchanged over the same period. What does it mean to live on that kind of income?

Compare someone at the bottom of the pay scale in the UK with someone living on $2 a day. Imagine a person in the UK working forty hours a week on the adult minimum wage, who is unable to borrow and has no savings. Assume that they get no other benefits or free goods or services of any kind from any source. And now imagine that they are also supporting at least eighteen other family dependants. That is what it would be like to be living around the $2-a-day line.[15] Given that the strong link between life expectancy and income only begins to loosen at an income level of between $3 and $4 per day, and the paradox under the current system of the rich needing to consume a lot more to generate small amounts of poverty reduction, what would be the natural resource footprint of getting the whole world onto an income of just $3 a day? The answer in a very rough, conservative estimate is around fifteen planets' worth. And the inevitable result of pursuing human development under the current model: environmental collapse.

As often as not, seductive metaphors guide economic policy as much as analysis. In the old order a rising tide – growth – is meant to float all boats. But this overlooks the fact that millions don't own boats, and many others are not seaworthy. Ironically, too, growth now fuels climate change and sea-level rise, and we can't all live on boats. The waves of inequality also lap dangerously onto our own shores, in the wealthier world. They are part of the same economic ocean and the man-made tidal system we have created for ourselves. London is just as driven to be billionaire-friendly as Mumbai, to which there are also consequences.

A year after he retired, becoming a professor emeritus, the social epidemiologist Richard Wilkinson published a book with his fellow academic Kate Pickett called *The Spirit Level*. It caused a sensation. Towards the end of his formal career he noticed something: he saw patterns. It was already well established that beyond the level of wealth achieved by industrialised countries like the UK, Europe and

North America, inequality (relative rather than absolute poverty) has a very strong impact on health, but he noticed that it was bad for very many other things too:

> Inequality causes shorter, unhealthier and unhappier lives; it increases the rate of teenage pregnancy, violence, obesity, imprisonment and addiction. It corrodes the social fabric and the quality of social relationships throughout society but, by increasing status competition it functions as a driver of the consumerism which stands between us and sustainability.[16]

Decades of research backed Wilkinson's conclusions, but the implication was hugely provocative to the economic orthodoxy: namely that the redistribution of wealth to create greater equality was far more efficient than the pursuit of more wealth and growth to improve the human condition and make better societies.

From an environmental perspective Wilkinson would go on to add that indeed, given that further overall economic growth cannot be sustained, redistribution is the only viable solution. After they published *The Spirit Level*, Wilkinson and Pickett engaged in lengthy, detailed debates with their critics. Each challenge and answer can be found on the website of the organisation they founded to communicate their work, The Equality Trust. There is not space here to duplicate their findings and analysis, but they are readily accessible. The relationships they describe between inequality and the incidence of a wide range of social problems have yet to be disproved, likewise the outcomes they found under the reverse conditions.

More equal societies suffer less abuse of illegal drugs, their children do better at school and have higher levels of well-being, according to measures used by Unicef. Levels of trust, an important determinant of subjective well-being, are higher where equality is greater and society less harsh and punitive, with lower homicide rates, less experience of violence among children and a smaller proportion of offenders imprisoned. Positive self-reinforcing feedbacks seem to correlate with greater equality, and the opposite appears true for higher inequality.

What connects these themes to the politics and economics of long-term austerity, itself the fallout from the 2008 financial crash, is the way that executive self-raising pay became a lightning conductor for protest and political debate. 'It is hard to escape the conclusion that the high levels of inequality in our societies reflect the concentrations of power in our economic institutions,' conclude Wilkinson and Pickett; 'the institutions in which we are employed are, after all, the main source of income inequality.'[17] Our places of work provide us with many things: the means to keep a roof over our heads and food in the fridge, a social life and an environment in which we pass much of our lives. It is less usual to think of the workplace specifically as the active source of inequality that generates huge costs for society, and rather than being a reflection of some innate social order, to view it as something that can be challenged and changed. Yet, especially in countries like the UK and the US – billionaire-friendly economies – this has become a prime feature of corporate life.

The pay gap in Fortune 500 companies grew by a factor of ten between 1980 and 2007, just as the recession driven by the banking collapse was beginning.[18] Before the financial crisis, boardroom pay among the FTSE 100 index companies rose each year consistently far ahead of average wage rises and way above inflation, at 16 per cent, 13 per cent, 28 per cent and 37 per cent in the year before things fell apart by dint of multiple economic misjudgements. This happened even though there was little if any evidence to support the existence of a causal relationship between executive high pay and company performance. High pay was, if anything, more a reflection of the 'dominant bargaining position' that executives found themselves in.[19] In the US the twenty top-paid executives from listed companies paid themselves forty times more than their non-profit counterparts and two hundred times more than the highest-paid government employees.[20]

Even these figures may turn out to mask much higher levels of actual inequality. In recent years the amount of wealth held offshore in tax havens and beyond the reach of normal national accounts has risen dramatically. It was estimated in 2012 that private banks, most of which had enjoyed substantial public support, helped channel at least £13 trillion of assets into secretive tax jurisdictions up to 2010, a sum equal to the incomes of Japan and America combined. The actual figure could be half as much again or more. Not only does this mean that actual levels of inequality are being substantially underreported, it suggests that a sum of public tax income is probably being lost each year which is greater than the global aid budget.[21]

In the UK the widening gap in workplace pay coincided with the privatisation of many industries and public utilities and the demutualisation of many financial service providers, such as the building societies, previously run for the benefit of their member-owners. Significantly, the 'disproportionate influence' of the financial sector is thought, over many years, to have driven the huge increases in executive pay. The example of soaring pay in banking appears to have exerted a tidal pull on the higher business levels of pay overall. It also played a significant role in house-price inflation by pumping up prices at the top of the market.

Many things created the circumstances in which executive pay rose to previously unimaginable levels: the rising power of finance, the loosening and loss of mutual models that distributed benefits more equally, and the closed, self-reinforcing world of the globe-trotting CEO. Perhaps most powerful of all, though, is the seemingly unchallengeable notion that you get what you pay for: if you pay more, you will get more from top bosses. A problem with this dogma in business management is that it seems to be completely wrong.

In his book *Drive: The Surprising Truth About What Motivates Us*, Daniel Pink highlights research summarising the findings from 128 separate experiments on work and incentives. The consistent conclusion was that 'tangible rewards tend to have a substantially negative effect on intrinsic motivation'. Not only did the promise of greater material reward fail to improve performance, it did the opposite. The psychologist Alfie Kohn specialised in the study of rewards, performance and motivation and came to a conclusion that contradicted all received wisdom and most business practice on the matter. It was a counter-intuitive finding roughly approximating to the realisation that the Sun didn't, after all, orbit the Earth:

Not a single controlled study has ever found that the use of rewards produces a long-term improvement in the quality of work. Rewards usually improve performance only at extremely simple – indeed, mindless – tasks, and even then they improve only quantitative performance.[22]

A now famous experiment backed Kohn's conclusion. A group of economists from the Massachusetts Institute of Technology, the University of Chicago and Carnegie Mellon were funded by the Federal Reserve Bank of Boston to observe the influence of financial incentives. What they found astonished many. Rewards worked well only in very limited circumstances, when the tasks in question were simple and mechanical. The moment that any other cognitive skills were demanded, even rudimentary ones, the influence of a financial reward not only failed to incentivise better performance, it made things worse. 'In eight of the nine tasks we examined across the three experiments,' observed the researchers, 'higher incentives led to worse performance.' Their findings were corroborated by separate research at the London School of Economics, which found that 'financial incentives can result in a negative impact on overall performance'.[23]

From MIT to the Federal Reserve system and the LSE, here was 'the establishment of the establishment', as Pink put it, coming up with findings to contradict their core philosophy. Using pay to reward and motivate senior executives, often disproportionately so compared with the contributions of other staff, was found not only to be divisive, and socially damaging, with real costs attached for the wider community, it was also economically useless and actively damaging for the (un)lucky individual on the receiving end of the remuneration committee's largesse. Somehow, experimental results on the downside of high pay, reported in the literature for decades, have yet to make a mark on mainstream business practice. Yet if they did, it is hard to resist the conclusion that it would benefit both shareholders and society at large.

A report by the High Pay Commission, which became the High Pay Centre, puts this into perspective.[24] Trends towards ever-widening pay gaps continue. Over the decade that Labour was in government, income at the top grew by 64.2 per cent, while an average earner saw a 7.2 per cent rise. The chief executives of the top FTSE 100 companies earned an average of £4.2 million in 2009–10, or 145 times the average wage. Even though ratios are much higher in the private as opposed to public and voluntary sectors, extreme private-sector disparities exert a copy-cat influence. The financial sector accounts for one third of the 0.1 per cent at the very top of the pay scale. Unless remuneration habits change, by 2020 their pay will have reached a level 214 times greater than the average. Should this trend continue unabated, the Commission found that by 2030 the UK will have returned to Victorian levels of inequality. Overall take-home pay fell during 2010 in the UK for the first time in thirty years, but boardroom pay rose by an estimated 55 per cent in the FTSE 100 and 45 per cent in the larger FTSE 350. Average wages rose just 2 per cent, below the rate of inflation.

Financial incentives to top executives fail to relate even to the most basic measures of corporate success. While the FTSE 100 rose by 14.5 per cent in 2010, executive bonuses rose by over a third, their share option gains by over 90 per cent, and long-term investment plans by over 70 per cent. 'It seems the days of earnings restraint by FTSE-350 directors were short-lived. It is as though the recession never happened,' said Steve Tatton, editor of the *Income Data Services Directors Pay Report*. 'It stands in stark contrast to the coalition Government's concerns about pay fairness and calls for senior executives in the public sector to accept pay cuts.'[25]

In a country scarred by high and rising inequality, large-scale unemployment and low pay sit uneasily beside high and rising executive remuneration. The Annual Survey of Hours and Earnings for 2010, from the Office for National Statistics, revealed 271,000 jobs with pay less than the national minimum wage, a rise of 33,000 on the previous year. Alongside that, several chief executives are enjoying pay levels of over one thousand times the median national wage, among them Frank Chapman, chief executive of British Gas, at 1081 times the median national wage; Mick Davies, chief executive of mining company Xstrata, at 1042 times; and Bob Diamond, former chief executive of Barclays, the same at 1042 times.[26]

The idea that any individual's intrinsic worth or economic contribution could be measured by such widely diverging financial rewards does not appear to be supported by any rational evidence base, regardless of whether it could be challenged morally. With great contemporary irony, a century ago J. P. Morgan, founder of one of the world's biggest commercial banks, argued that a ratio between highest- and lowest-paid of no more than 20:1 was needed to motivate a workforce. That appears to be a lesson lost on the modern JP Morgan Chase & Co. Still in the shadow of the crash, chief executive Jamie Dimon received $20.8 million in 2010. Given that a teller in the same bank could be earning $11 per hour, or around $19k per year, possibly less, that would put the ratio at 1095:1.[27]

It's also possible to make global comparisons of people engaged in similar tasks and who yet receive vastly different remuneration. The economist Ha-Joon Chang uses the example of two bus drivers, one based on the safe streets of Stockholm, the other navigating the chaotic traffic of New Delhi, or Mumbai. The former is paid perhaps fifty times more, for an easier job requiring fewer driving skills, and however gifted, it is hard to imagine the Swedish driver being fifty times better. In this case Chang argues that only the artificial obstacle of border controls, like economic fortress walls protecting lordly wealth, sustains the difference in reward. But, going further still, when different metrics are applied that attempt to capture the social benefits of the contributions made to society by different professions, some startling inversions of current practice can emerge.

Applying the tool called Social Return on Investment that we came across in chapter 4, it is possible to make some observations about the differences between how an economy rewards different professions in relation to the social and environmental value of the work they do. In an ideal world there would be a strong correlation between the two. In the real world we expect some deviation, but even so the outcomes cause surprise.

To make calculations of this sort, certain parameters need drawing and assumptions making. It would be wrong, for example, to attribute the same responsibility for the financial crash to a bank cashier as to someone who devises and trades in complex derivatives and debt instruments. So, in this case, the damage to the economy resulting from the bank crisis was attributed only to those City bankers earning over £1 million in bonuses. Economic losses to the economy resulting for the crisis were then calculated on the basis of the IMF's pre-crisis expectations, the real events that happened, and the damage to the public finances that resulted. A figure of £2.7 trillion was arrived at, which is in the lower half of the Bank of England's assessment mentioned earlier on (and for methodological simplicity leaves out a number of other costs that are hard to estimate). The damage caused was then compared with the economic contribution of one of these highly paid finance workers over a twenty-year indicative career in terms of 'UK economic activity, taxes paid, and jobs supported'.[28] This was done using the Office for National Statistics figures for 'gross value added' from the sector, and other sources for tax paid and jobs created. When the two were compared it showed that the highest-paid bankers destroyed more economic value than they created: £7 of value destroyed for every £1 of value created.

For comparison, other professions were looked at too, including some of the lowest-paid in the economy such as hospital cleaners. Here, the baseline for an assessment of their value was the avoidance of hospital-acquired infections, as assessed by a cost-benefit analysis published in the *British Medical Journal*. In this case, for every pound spent on wages more than £10 of social value were created. Following similar logic, of the professions surveyed, the impact of tax account-ants was most negative, largely explained by the fact that their key function is to minimise (legally) tax contributions to the public purse. They destroyed £47 in value for every £1 created. The most positive contribution came from recycling workers: although this calculation is sensitive to the price put on waste and carbon emissions saved, for every pound in pay they generated £12 of value for society.

Rather than asking if a city is billionaire-friendly, it seems we should be asking if billionaires are society-friendly. Not only, then, does there appear to be an urgent need to reverse the widening pay gap, but also to produce a more rational basis upon which to decide who gets what. Public attitudes are shifting decisively in favour of action. In evidence to the High Pay Commission, Liane Hoogland from the University of Sheffield cites a ComRes survey for the BBC showing strong support for lower incomes to be higher, and higher ones to be lower. A more recent survey commissioned by the Institute for Public Policy Research found 82 per cent in favour of government intervention to close the pay gap.[29]

An intuitive grasp of the general benefits of greater equality seems to go deeper than that. Dan Ariely did a survey based on a classic thought experiment by the political philosopher John Rawls. In it, you are asked to imagine that you are to be placed in society at a random point on the income scale, but before you know where you will end up you are given the power to arrange the distribution of wealth across society. Ariely carried out a version of this for the US. Respondents were broken down according to voter persuasion, Republicans and Democrats, men and women, and high-, medium- and low-paid. First people were asked to estimate how wealth was actually distributed in the US. All groups, with very little variation among them, substantially overestimated how equal their society was. By a thin margin women, Republicans and the lowest-paid overestimated equality the most.

When asked the question about what would be the ideal distribution of wealth for a society in which they might end up in any income group – richest, poorest or somewhere in the middle – all the groups opted to shift in the same direction, towards a very substantially more equal distribution. This time there was more variation of outcome, but only within this large shift. The poorest, women and Democrat voters opted for the most equal society; the richest, men and Republicans varied only by degree, not by an order of magnitude, in opting for greater equality.[30]

Because, from birth, we are inserted into a pre-set income bracket, that of our families, this is obviously more than just a thought experiment. The challenge is how to translate such a strong common denominator into policies that yield a more equal society. Denmark is the great example of a country that has used its tax system, and investment in education and equal opportunities, to create a much more equal society. Denmark is also the country with the highest life-satisfaction rating among the rich countries of the OECD.[31] Reality, as we saw earlier, is doing just the opposite: chief executive pay in the US rose threefold between 1990 and 2005, while production workers' pay *fell* by 4.3 per cent and the minimum wage by 9.3 per cent.

Resistance to change is deeply entrenched. In the aftermath of the bank crisis, John Varley, then Barclays' chief executive, reacted in horror to the suggestion by a BBC Radio interviewer that some parameters should be put around pay and bonuses awarded to bank staff. It would 'interfere with the market', he said. Yet, had the banking market not been interfered with to the tune of hundreds of billions in public bailouts and support, it would not have survived in its current form. The market, meanwhile, doesn't think twice about interfering with anything else.

Digby Jones said that his move from the private sector to become head of the Confederation of British Industry, a big-business trade association, led to a move from a comfortable salary to one that was 'appallingly' lower. What constituted an appalling level of pay, asked a member of the public audience he was addressing? Hard times, for Jones, meant going from £600k per year, to just £250k. Realising he'd made a potentially damaging gaffe with unemployment high and thousands of public sector jobs being cut, Jones apologised profusely. But he'd revealed the level of expectation and sense of entitlement in the higher echelons of business.

Millionaires in London and Mumbai can visit each other by stepping onto any one of the eighteen different airlines that offered scheduled flights between the two cities on a randomly selected day. They stay in the same kind of luxury hotels, read and watch the same newspapers and television programmes, and their political influence, tax affairs and investment decisions create the world in which the poorest do or do not have water flowing from their taps.

The eminent Indian academic M. S. Swaminatham once wrote that instead of World Bank and IMF-style economic programmes that are all about the balance sheet, 'what we really need is adjustment to sustainable life styles [that] the Bank would not recommend. Because their structural adjustment is in money terms, not value. But if developing countries have to undergo such an adjustment in terms of financial problems . . . industrialised countries will also have to go through a structural adjustment process.'[32]

At the turn of the millennium Juan Somavia was the first head of the UN's International Labour Organization to come from a developing country and understood that the global economy has not the result of unquestionable forces of nature. On the contrary, the rules of the game had 'been made by policymakers and they can be changed by policymakers in order to expand the benefits of globalisation'. Warning against measures that rode on the backs of the weakest members of society, in a way that is as relevant to the global North now, as it was to the global South then, he asked:

> Is that the only way we can balance a budget? . . . Inequality continues to widen. The needs of ordinary people for security, for identity and for decent work somehow do not flow from economic objectives . . . But the institutions of the international community do not operate in a way which reflects this basic truth . . . the multilateral system . . . is under-performing.[33]

Relieved of the constraints of office, even the International Monetary Fund's former managing director, Michel Camdessus, who both presided over and promoted the financial deregulation that fuelled inequality, commented on retirement in 2000 that both poverty and inequality 'are morally outrageous, economically wasteful and potentially socially explosive', adding: 'Poverty will undermine the fabric of societies through confrontation, violence and civil disorder.' Little, fundamentally, had changed in this regard by 2012 when Min Zhu, the deputy managing director of the IMF, said: 'The increase in inequality is the most serious challenge for the world.'[34]

Camdessus's words may carry a deeper truth than even he was aware of. Inequality is often defended on the grounds that it creates the conditions to motivate innovation and efficiency, and merely demonstrates the reality of the survival of the fittest. The same argument suggests that creating greater equality introduces weakness to a society, threatening survival instincts by confounding Darwinian natural selection. But studies in demography suggest that exactly the opposite appears to be true, that 'unequal access to resources is inherently destabilising and greatly raises the chance of group extinction'. The strong suspicion being tested in research is that natural selection will pick different characteristics under more or less equal societies. At the group level, equality looks likely to encourage selection for behaviour that adds to stability and resilience, like cooperation, altruism and reproductive behaviour conducive to more stable populations. Inequality is likely to do the opposite at the individual level, selecting for 'high fertility, competition, aggression, social climbing and other selfish traits'.[35]

Interdependence Day

When we try to pick out anything by itself, we find it hitched to everything else in the Universe.

John Muir

Compared to the carbon emissions that someone in Tanzania will generate over a whole year, a typical American will have produced the same amount by early morning on 2nd January, and a UK citizen by the evening of 4th January.

The UK Interdependence Report

In the weeks before Christmas 2006 a Danish-built cargo ship called the *Emma Maersk*, the longest in the world at four hundred metres, made its maiden voyage from Shenzen and Hong Kong in China to Felixstowe in Suffolk, England. It was built to carry 11,000 to 14,000 standard shipping containers, which if taken by rail would require a train seventy-one kilometres long. If stuffed with bananas, someone calculated that it could transport over five hundred million of them, more than enough for one each for the entire populations of Europe or North America. Its anchor alone was equal in weight to five adult African elephants. The ship can carry 45,000 tonnes of stuff. And this is what it does, month in, month out, shuttling from China to Europe via the Suez Canal.

The year that the *Emma Maersk* set sail, the UK imported nearly half a million tonnes' worth of children's toys and indoor games from China, costing £1.25 billion. Among all the cargo were 50,000 tonnes of Christmas decorations; seven out of ten of which we import are made in China.

Alongside the toys and Christmas baubles, the UK imported another £14 billion worth of goods from China to fill our homes and offices, ranging from sports and electrical goods to IT and telecommunications equipment, clothes, shoes, plastics and furniture. The sheer scale of this trade is one of the reasons that when people present statistical pictures of the world comparing groups of countries at different stages of development, the figures are often shown both with and without China. It's a country so big in every way that it can't help but distort any graph it appears on.

Especially extraordinary is China's role in reducing the number of people living in extreme poverty over almost three decades from 1980. Because, according to the World Bank, without China there would have been no reduction at all in the total number of people living below that threshold. Take China out of the equation and in developing countries there were the same number in 2008 as there were in 1981.[36] And, even here, a loud note of caution needs to be sounded, as the reliability of Chinese official data as free from political manipulation is severely doubted in international circles.[37] But, taken at face value, the overall fall from 1.9 billion to 1.3 billion is entirely accounted for by China, although 173 million people there still live on less than $1.25 a day – more than the combined population of the UK, France and Canada.

The questions then follow: What is China doing as a developing country, and why can't others copy their example? First is the obvious point that the country is an oppressive one-party state, and many would not want to emulate that aspect of its ability to plan and implement policies without a free press and democratic checks and balances.

Secondly, China is a superpower. No other developing country wields so much power internationally, in either diplomatic or economic circles. For example, China's massive trade surplus has allowed it to become one of the principal creditors of the United States, while at the same time getting American consumers hooked on its endless supply of cheap consumer goods. To be clear, China has also achieved this by ignoring almost entirely the economic policy paradigm of the Washington Consensus. The government is heavily interventionist, and carefully manages foreign investment in its industries, as well as the movement of goods and finance across its borders.

In the process, China has created a new prospect for Western policymakers and trade theorists. In 2007 China's Foreign Ministry spokesman Qin Gang summarised what many were realising: 'China is now the factory of the world. Developed countries have transferred a lot of manufacturing to China. What many Western consumers wear, live in, even eat is made in China.' Other emerging developing countries made great leaps before, but China is somehow different.

It doesn't merely enjoy 'comparative advantage' in certain areas – the basic theory lying behind the notion that everyone should ultimately benefit from economic globalisation as each country works out what it can do best given its particular circumstances. China seems to have potentially *absolute advantage* in all economic areas. Harvard economist Richard B. Freeman observed: 'What is stunning about China is that for the first time we have a huge, poor country that can compete both with very low wages and in hi tech. Combine the two, and America has a problem.'[38] Janez Potočnik, the EU Science and Research Commissioner in 2005, said: 'If we think that the competition from emerging economies such as China and India is simply about low wages and manufacturing, then we are kidding ourselves. These countries are also competing with us in hi-tech, high-skilled sectors because they are investing more and more in research and innovation.'[39] An OECD study found fifteen at-risk job categories in the EU representing '19 per cent of total employment in the pre-enlargement EU'.[40]

Then there is the pact that China has made with the planet to get to this point. Before looking at some of those issues, I want to say that I think that China has, in some important ways to do with climate change, become a Western scapegoat. Too often Western politicians deflect what they can achieve by pointing to China's rising emissions. This is disingenuous. China is a big country with a lot of people, yet, per person, their carbon emissions remain substantially less than those of any developed country.

Estimates vary about when it happened, perhaps in 2006, but the Chinese government admitted in November 2010 that the country had become in total the world's biggest emitter of carbon.[41] However, per person, emissions in China are less than one third of those in the United States (although more than three times those of India). Historically, too, they are responsible for far fewer emissions per person. As recently as 1990, for example, a single American had the same emissions as nearly ten Chinese people and comparable British emissions were nearly five times the Chinese equivalent.

China may have been a net importer of oil since 1993, and is now the world's fasting-growing importer. And it may be building coal-fired power stations at a phenomenal rate (it is also probably the world's largest manufacturer of small-scale renewable energy technologies), but around one third of total Chinese carbon emissions result from making goods for export to places like Europe and the US – they explain fully half of China's rise in emissions in the middle of the last decade.

Accounting for carbon in this way – when the responsibility for emissions is attributed to the consumer who demands and consumes the product, rather than the producer – fundamentally alters the picture of how well a country is doing in tackling greenhouse gases. Where the UK is concerned, for example, the government's own research showed that instead of falling, as normal official figures indicate, between 1990, the baseline year for reductions called for at the Earth summit, and 2009, the nation's carbon footprint actually increased by 20 per cent. Change the accounting mechanism and the outcome is as different as up from down. Including such imported 'consumption-based' greenhouse gases puts total UK emissions far higher.[42]

China feels quite understandably that it has a right to do what the British and Americans, for example, have done for centuries, and that is to grow their economies without fundamental environmental constraints. And yet China's model does sit heavily on the Earth and, as relatively successful as it has been, what chance is there that other developing countries can follow their example, even if they had similar political and strategic strength? And if even China's strategy won't work for others, what will?

For such a large country, China is relatively resource-poor. Per person, its levels of fresh water, cultivated land, forest and grassland are well below the global average,[43] as are domestic reserves of key mineral resources needed for manufacturing. Yet China managed to grow phenomenally as a trading nation – to decorate our Christmas trees and provide just about everything else we fill our lives with. China's exports increased at an annual rate of 17 per cent from 1980 to 2001, rising in value from $18.6 billion to $266 billion. Then, up to 2006, in the years before the global economic crisis, exports increased at a rate of around 30 per cent a year by value.[44]

But China has already overshot its domestic biocapacity. Since the early 1970s it has needed more natural resources than the ecosystems and land within its borders can provide. China's ecological footprint per person is more than twice what its fields, forests and fisheries can provide. To feed that huge volume of output and consumption, the country needs more resources, and has become adept at scouring the world to secure them. The competition between developing countries, rather than between the rich and poor, is one of the less well understood and most under-reported characteristics of economic globalisation – as is the competition within developing countries by different social groups.

China's power and reach are such that the world has become both its supermarket for resources and its export market. Oilfields, land for crops, mines for minerals, forests for trees – China is now a big player in the global market for all of them, and their targets are as likely to be rich as poor countries. A survey of recent known global land-grabbing, whereby public or private agents of one country gain control of parcels of the productive land of another, sees China as a major player alongside rich and middle-income countries and wealthy but resource-poor Middle Eastern countries. A list of China's gains alone since 2006 reads like an alphabetic tour of nations. Through various arms of its government and corporations, acquisitions already completed or under way include:

- A 1500-hectare pilot rice farm in Angola
- 80,000 h of farmland for dairy and 30,000 h for wool in Australia and various other smaller deals
- In Benin 10,000 h for palm oil and 4800 h cassava and sugar cane
- 12,500 h for maize and soya bean in Bolivia
- 400,000 h of Brazil for soya bean and cotton
- In Bulgaria, 2000 h for alfalfa, maize and sunflowers
- 10,000 h of Cameroon, for cassava, maize and rice
- A proposed deal for 400,000 h of Colombia to grow cereals
- 100,000 h of land to grow palm oil in the Democratic Republic of Congo
- 25,000 h of sugar cane in Ethiopia
- 18,000 h of sugar cane in Jamaica
- 50,000 h of cassava in Laos
- 10,000 h of sugar cane in Madagascar
- 20,000 h sugar cane in Mali
- 1000 h of Mozambique for an unspecified purpose
- A very specific 8615-h plot of New Zealand for dairy farming
- 6000 h growing cassava in Nigeria
- 4000 h growing fruit in Pakistan
- A massive deal for China to acquire 1,280,000 h of the Philippines was suspended after popular protest and is now under review
- A deal for a substantial 426,667 h of Russia to grow crops
- 100,000 h of Senegal to grow peanuts and 60,000 h for sesame
- 8100 h of Sierra Leone to grow cassava and sugar cane and 30,000 h for rice (the idea of Sierra Leone exporting rice to China must be the modern global economy's version of sending coal to Newcastle)
- 10,000 h growing oil seed in Sudan
- A tiny plot of just 110 h in Tajikistan to do with cotton and rice
- Another small plot of just 300 h in Tanzania focused on a research centre developing rice seeds
- And 4500 h of Uganda for various crops

These figures are the result of work by a small, diligent, Spanish-based organisation called Grain, which conducts research and analysis in support of small-scale farmers in Africa, Asia and Latin America. Looking just at large-scale land-grabs for growing food crops, Grain counted over four hundred deals in the five years from the end of 2006 that were led by foreign investors. The total land acquired by all purchasing countries runs to nearly thirty-five million hectares across sixty-six nations.[45]

China's second-largest category of exports to the UK has been furniture, but to make it China has been implicated in the large-scale illegal import and export of wood and the products made from it. Because of the nature of the trade, finding figures is difficult, but in one year, 2005, nearly three million cubic metres of illegal timber were estimated to have entered the UK, worth around £500 million. Nearly half of that amount by value was thought to come from China.[46]

Burma has the second-largest area of natural forest in South East Asia after Indonesia, an estimated 34 million hectares, which is under threat of illegal logging driven by demand from China. The international environmental watchdog group Global Witness reported wide-scale deforestation in Burma's northern Kachin state, which has one of the world's forests with the richest biodiversity. Nor is it just beyond China's own borders that the footprint of its development is felt. A World Bank report suggested in 2007 that within them, pollution kills around half a million people per year. Bad enough, but then the *Financial Times* revealed that political pressure led to the real number being downplayed. Before publication, the original estimate had been half as much again, suggesting that 750,000 people annually died prematurely each year in China, largely due to air and water pollution.[47]

I enjoy reading the *Financial Times*, for many reasons. Its journalism is high quality, its coverage of international issues good, and it can be surprisingly critical of its core audience, the business elite. But what I relish most is the unintentional humour that springs from its occasional complete blind spots on issues like the environment, and pure unawareness that quite other worldviews exist. In 2009 it ran a headline that to me blistered with irony, but to the *FT* had none. The story appeared beneath the heading: 'China predicts rare earths shortage'. I was conscious of the nature of China's growth and the ecological footprint of its hunger for resources, and of course that the Earth itself is indeed rare in our solar system as home to an advanced civilisation. The whole thing put a big, ironic smile on my face. The story, however, was completely straight.

In becoming the factory for the world, and in its domestic race to emulate Western-style consumerism, China has come to dominate the global market in the exotic minerals known as rare earths. They are vital ingredients in everything from the manufacture of wind turbines to, more ubiquitously, our disposable, endlessly upgraded mobile phones and media players like the iPod.

These are often mined in conditions of human exploitation and environmental degradation in countries like the Democratic Republic of Congo, where violent intimidation of local communities controls areas around some of the mines that export to China. It has been dubbed part of the new 'scramble for Africa', and exploitative just like the last one. Now, global commodity traders, immune to irony, have created a market for, and now a shortage in, 'rare earths'. It might have been even too obvious and literal as the product of Jonathan Swift's satirical imagination, but the Chinese Society of Rare Earths really did complain that 'rare earths have been sold too cheaply'.

Rounding off a full serving of news irony, on the very same page of the *FT*, immediately underneath the story about rare earths, was another about the booming insurance market for 'catastrophe bonds'. Apparently they had 'only really taken off in the aftermath of Hurricane Katrina'. They dipped a bit with the recession, but now, reassuringly, they were on the up and up again.[48] In summary, there are numerous factors that make China's development trajectory impossible for most other countries in the global South to copy, and the poorest African countries especially so, as it is the very growth of China that is sucking the wealth of their own natural resource base away.

Striking in the data concerning land-grabs is targeting by wealthier, more stable countries of land in weaker, conflict and post-conflict African states. Much of the list reads like a roll-call of post-colonial war-shattered states: Angola, Congo-Brazzaville, Democratic Republic of Congo, Ethiopia, Liberia, Mozambique, Sierra Leone, South Sudan, Sudan. China may be a major player in extracting economic benefits from these countries in asymmetric deals, but it is very far from being the only one.

In Sudan alone, the United Arab Emirates has a stake of 1.5 million hectares of farmland, South Korea 690,000 h, Egypt 400,000, and United States interests have taken at least 1 million hectares in South Sudan.

Land-grabs can appear initially to offer mutual benefits to host country and investor. Money changes hands and some jobs and infrastructure may follow investment. Investors too have become more adept at addressing potential concerns, such as local competition for water. But ceding sovereignty over the land that feeds your people is hugely sensitive, can lead to protests and led, at least in one instance, to the fall of a government in Madagascar. According to the US-based Oakland Institute, one UK company, Sun Biofuels, that promised not to compromise water sources surrounding its jatropha plantation in Tanzania, went ahead regardless, leaving local residents either having to walk much further to get water, or having 'to creep onto the Sun Biofuels plantation to access their old water sources and "steal" the water, or buy it at inflated prices'.[49]

The UK, which in terms of its annual domestic environmental budget starts living beyond its own means around April, thereafter in effect depending on the rest of the world, has not been shy in bringing land overseas under its own influence. Since 2006, deals with various UK interests have included the acquisition of: 100,000 h in Ghana to grow rice, 106,000 h of Guinea for maize and soya beans, 169,000 h of Liberia for palm oil, 200,000 h of Madagascar for beef, 20,000 h of Malawi for rice, 37,000 h of Mali for sugar cane and 10,000 h more for other crops, 16,700 h of Mozambique for cattle and another 150,000 h for animal ranching, plant-based oils and various other crops, 300,000 h of Nigeria for rice, around 90,000 h of Sierra Leone for palm oil, and 20,000 h of Zambia for a range of crops.

For some, developments like this are not a threat to Africa, but an opportunity. It fits the export-led development model promoted by Western aid donors and the Washington-based financial institutions. It's an example of the private sector (public also in the case of China) contributing to poverty reduction whilst making a profit for shareholders too. But that is to ignore an awful lot of factors that can tip the balance of cost and benefits. The deals are struck between unequal partners, and often with the elites of weak states that have questionable records in defending the interests of their populations.

Secondly, as Mark Twain famously quipped whilst offering investment advice: 'Buy land, they're not making it anymore.' The capture of productive farmland is ultimately a zero-sum game. Wherever you live in the world, having a secure livelihood starts with ensuring you have enough to eat, what in the development jargon is called 'food security'. It's all very well for a government to give long-term land leases to foreign interests in return for cash, but if doing so makes it harder for local people to grow their own food it creates a much more circuitous and unreliable route to guarantee someone's livelihood. Farm-to-plate, when it is your own farm, is the surest way to get food on your table. And land-grabs mean crops for export, not for local markets.

Bad enough that poor countries with high malnutrition rates should lose prime farming land to foreign interests, but the impact isn't limited to the land alone. Crops need water, and many export crops, such as luxury horticulture and rice, are very thirsty. Climate change threatens to damage already stressed water sources in Africa, with more severe droughts in some areas and flooding in others. But the water demand for crops to be grown on 'land-grabs' stands to create a burden of another order. Research by the Oakland and Polaris institutes estimated that if all the land acquired in 2009 were to come under cultivation, the irrigation needs would be 'approximately twice the volume of water that was used for agriculture in all of Africa in 2005'. If land acquisitions continue at the same rate, they find that 'demand for fresh water from new land investments *alone* will overtake the existing supply of renewable fresh water on the continent by 2019'.[50]

If the purpose of the food system is primarily to feed people rather than to make a profit, as I assume it should be, we've already seen that there's a host of ways to greatly enhance the resilience and productivity of small-scale farming, which can also bring greater direct security to the millions who depend on it. Conversely, water extraction for large-scale agribusiness in Ethiopia, for example, threatens access to water for communities downstream in Sudan and Egypt, which is both a problem in itself and a source of current tension and potential future conflict.

If all these approaches to economic development are so flawed, what can be done instead? When hurtling headlong in the wrong direction, first you stop and think. That's what David Woodward did, a development economist with impeccable establishment credentials. Formerly an economic adviser in the UK Foreign and Commonwealth Office, he had spells as technical assistant to the UK Executive Director to the IMF and the World Bank, and was a development economist in the Strategy Unit of the World Health Organization. Restlessly inquisitive about solving problems, in 1992 he wrote one of the first comprehensive critiques of structural adjustment policies that he could see were having powerful negative effects. Health and education services to some of the world's poorest communities were suffering and the core economic problems were not being solved. When David first saw projections for world oil reserves and future supply in the *BP Statistical Review of World Energy* (imperfect but the nearest thing to an industry standard text) he was shocked to recognise the scale and imminence of the problem. Other economists remained in denial for decades.

Unsurprisingly, he also turned his mind to the challenge of rethinking the basic template with which we try to solve John Maynard Keynes's famous 'economic problem': how to meet basic human needs and escape the struggle for subsistence.

Woodward begins by restating basic objectives and then seeing how best they might be achieved given real-world economic and environmental constraints. The objectives, he sees as fulfilling basic needs, increasing quality of life, and sustaining these achievements over the long term.

Many of the environmental constraints we've already seen, and the economic obstacles to relying on the export of primary commodities include weak prices, which are further worsened by everyone doing the same thing, thus flooding markets, and the threat to farming in Africa from climate change.

However, within these parameters Woodward sees a clear outline of a new, flexible development model that can both eradicate poverty and address climate change and resource scarcity. Its first steps look much like a global 'Green New Deal'.

First, there's a strong link between carbon emissions in poor countries and rising urbanisation that suggests the need to focus on revitalised rural economies as drivers of development. This would slow migration to urban areas, reducing the strain on infrastructure, and would do better to reduce poverty, which tends to be worse in rural areas. But the problems with agriculture mentioned above call for a more nuanced approach than merely giving more support to farmers.

Woodward proposes a twin approach: diversify rural economies away from agriculture; and shift the emphasis of farming so that it aims first and foremost at meeting local needs, and only after that at export markets. Such a strategy would increase the need for energy in rural areas, where its absence has been one of the great limiting factors in social and economic development. Here is an opportunity to create a virtuous circle of poverty reduction.

Small-scale decentralised renewable-energy technologies are ideally suited to rural areas that are frequently 'off-grid'. Manufacturing, installing and maintaining a range of solar, wind, hydro and biogas technologies is a potentially huge growth area capable of creating jobs, income and energy. 'Creating a large-scale market in the South,' writes Woodward, 'it would be possible simultaneously to incentivise technological development more suited to conditions in rural areas in the developing world, and to drive costs down considerably through economies of scale and learning effects.'[51]

The energy so generated can power further diversification into making goods that go to meet the basic needs of the people in rural areas. The energy content of increased consumption by the poorest tends to be much lower than that of wealthier people.

When poor households buy more things, according to Woodward, especially in rural areas, it tends to be 'goods which are (or can be) locally produced using relatively limited energy inputs', such as higher-value foods, clothing and basic household goods.

As an overall economic strategy, he argues, this points to measures that focus directly on raising 'the incomes of poor households rather than on increasing economic growth and relying on the benefits trickling down to the poor'. Hence the familiar conclusion: that economic growth is only 'good to the extent that it promotes the fulfilment of basic needs and/or increases quality of life, and bad to the extent that it undermines them immediately, or in the long term; for example, through adverse environmental effects'. Simple as it may seem (as

indeed is the failing neoliberal policy mantra), an alternative economic model emerges from this that:

> Revolves primarily around a revitalisation of rural economies,
> taking advantage of the synergies arising from consumption pat-
> terns at low-income levels (raising demand, production and
> consumption of basic goods, of and by low-income communities
> in a virtuous cycle). It also looks at the potential for widespread
> application of micro-renewable energy technologies in rural areas,
> exploiting the potential for considerable cost reductions and tech-
> nological improvements from the creation of a mass market.

If that forms a successful foundation for lifting people above the
poverty line, both effectively and in an environmentally friendly way,
Woodward's other work in progress, as yet unpublished, offers the
tantalising promise of dealing with overconsumption at the other end
of the global income stream. Until the work is made public, it suffices
to know that he intends to 'propose and test the hypothesis that there
is a "plenty line", beyond which further increases in income cease to
increase well-being significantly'. When complete, and if a successful
course of inquiry, a 'plenty line' would set a target for countries on the
Happy Planet Index described earlier. Woodward states: 'This might
be seen as a counterpart to the poverty line, of increasing importance
in a carbon-constrained global economy, highlighting the problem of
over-consumption and placing it on the global political agenda in the
same way that the "dollar-a-day" poverty line (for all its problems) has
for under-consumption.'[52]

'Before you finish eating breakfast this morning,' famously observed
Martin Luther King, 'you've depended on more than half the world.'
The global economy has been with us for a very long time and is not
going to be uninvented. Admittedly, for much of human history trade
was for luxuries, while the vast bulk of our material needs were met
close to home.

For a similarly long period, the notion that an all-out competitive
struggle for individual gain was either desirable or a sensible way for
a whole society to move ahead would have been considered laugh-
able. Insights on the broad advantages of cooperation, well understood
intuitively and seen in organisational forms that emerge and thrive in

adversity, like the nineteenth-century cooperative movement, are deeply rooted in our cultural, religious and economic life. New advances in biology and psychology are revealing how we are wired to cooperate and happier when we do.

We live, in all senses, in an interdependent world. Yet it is possible for very different messages to be communicated along those lines of interdependence. There is the abusive dependence of kidnapper and kidnapped, the so-called 'Stockholm syndrome', the creative dependence of musicians in an orchestra, the nurturing of teacher and pupil, and the practical dependence on each other's skills and assistance of a community raising a barn, no one individual of which can hold, lift, angle and place the beams. There are, of course, to take Charles Darwin's words only slightly out of context, 'endless forms most beautiful and most wonderful' in which interdependence exists in nature – it is, after all, an interdependent system.

Woodward's vision above has echoes for me of the Swadeshi movement in India, part of an economic struggle to free itself of British domination and enhance the nation's self-sufficiency. Colonial designs brutally re-engineered India – literally, in terms of its transport networks – as a land for the extraction of wealth. The Swadeshi movement used tactics that would be familiar to modern campaigners for fair trade. They boycotted British goods and sought to revive industries that the British had oppressed, such as textiles. When Gandhi joined the independence struggle, one of the abiding images of that period is of him demonstrating home spinning. It became a symbol of the independence campaign, Gandhi's 'home-spun revolution', in which Indians were exhorted to wear khadi (homespun cloth) and this became an act of honour and national self-respect. In present-day Mumbai the notion might seem impossibly dated and quaint, yet Gandhi was no small-town reactionary wanting to turn his back on the modern world. 'I do not want my house to be walled in or my windows blocked. I want the cultures of all lands to be blown about the house as freely as possible,' he said, with one important caveat. 'But also I refuse to be blown off my feet by any.'

A progressive, even celebratory interdependence was what he sought, not the exploitative relationships of empire. Gandhi also suspected, rightly as it would turn out, that British lifestyles and material aspirations would be unrealistic for the world as a whole. After his decades-long struggle, on the eve of independence, he was asked if India should now copy Britain's industrial model. 'It took Britain half the resources of this planet to achieve its prosperity,' he replied. 'How many planets will India require for development?'

And yet, since Indian independence, the world in general has not followed Gandhi's vision. For over half a century, the winds of trade have blown hard, its share of the global economy, exemplified by the leviathan *Emma Maersk*, has got bigger and bigger. Now the interaction of the 'economic problem' with the environmental problem invites a rethink.

But suppose that the big ship turned around, and the emphasis shifted from further globalisation to more localised economies. Bear in mind that this does not mean attempting to meet all your needs in your neighbourhood, but a relative relocalisation in which the default position becomes one of producing, trading and consuming the stuff of life at the most appropriate local level. Hence, bread would be baked in every community, but there would probably not be a factory producing the ovens in which the bread is baked in every neighbourhood.

Where would a change like this, in which the world's poorer countries meet their own needs first, leave a country like the UK, which can only get by on its own resources for around one third of the year? Trade as a share of the UK's GDP rose consistently since the mid-1970s, and we are increasingly reliant on both energy and food imports. The UK has a large negative trade balance, it imports much more than it exports. But European countries like Germany, France and the Netherlands, along with the United States, make up our major trading partners. Not forgetting China, which as of January 2012 was our second-largest source of imports, after Germany and before the US, and the seventh-biggest export market.

Quite apart from whether we actually need to co-opt Africa's productive farmland and trade the fruits of its soil for profit, there's a lot more trade happening on our doorstep that raises questions about common sense, and economic and environmental efficiency. Because we do not pay the full environmental price of trade, there is little to dissuade ships, lorries and planes carrying virtually identical goods back and forth needlessly, passing each other day and night on

Europe's superhighways. Over the years I've collected a long list of goods caught up in what I like to call boomerang trade (bottled water shipped back and forth between the UK and Australia was low in volume and high in illogic). A few choice examples from a single year's trade data are sufficient to make the point.

I grew up in Chelmsford, Essex. Each summer an ice-cream van from Rossi's of Southend-on-Sea would visit, musically jangling its arrival on the road outside my house. I loved Rossi's ice cream (and still do), it was so much better than the soft Mr Whippy piped ice cream that was partly former prime minister Margaret Thatcher's gift to the world, when a junior commercial research chemist. I'm sure we could have made ice cream in Chelmsford (it was more famous for ball-bearings, soft drinks and military communication technology), but Southend was only twenty miles away, and thinking of it you imagined the sea, summer, and hence ice cream. Reputation and image obviously matter where products are concerned.

When looking at the UK's trade data,[53] I could just about reason why we would want to import 4400 tonnes of ice cream from Italy, even though I knew from personal experience that we were perfectly capable of making a very good version on the Essex coast. What I found less explicable was that in the same year we also exported 4200 tonnes in the opposite direction, back to Italy. In case you conclude this is the result of a peculiar, unreported friendship exchange scheme, in a previous year's data it lists 2297 tonnes of ice cream exported from the UK to Sweden (even stranger) and 2257 imported straight back. Not dissimilar volumes were sent back and forth between the UK and Portugal, Germany and Switzerland. Once again, in case you think I stumbled across a case of carousel fraud in frozen goods, these are anything but isolated edible examples.

In the same year that ice cream was yo-yoing in roughly equal volume between Italy and the UK, 4000 tonnes of toilet roll were on their way from the UK to Germany, and 5000 tonnes of the same were headed straight back. Neither is this limited to trade within the European Community. In the same year 27,000 tonnes of potatoes were exported from the UK to Egypt and 22,000 tonnes traded back the other way. To show how arcane this phenomenon can be, ten tonnes of 'gums and jelly' confectionery ping-ponged between the UK and Thailand. Commenting on a similar example many years ago concerning practically identical biscuits travelling between the North of England and mainland Europe, the former World Bank economist Herman Daly asked whether it wouldn't have been easier to fax the recipe (that's how long ago it was).

Waste and duplication has become a commonplace part of the overall global economy in a way that would never be tolerated in an efficiently run individual company. As all the unnecessary emissions further overburden the atmosphere's ability safely to absorb them, more heavily loading the dice of global warming, the subsidiary economy threatens to bankrupt the parent company, our benign biosphere.

As a thought exercise (it was only nearly a necessity when Britain found itself almost isolated in the Second World War), could Britain do without all that food trade? Could Britain feed itself if it needed to? If the reality is that it could do so even substantially more than now, that would make room for manoeuvre, and at the very least remove any residual justification for grabbing the fertile farmland of much poorer countries where, for complex economic, social and environmental reasons, populations struggle far harder to feed themselves.

Colin Tudge organises the Oxford Real Farming Conference. It runs as an alternative and counter to a regular large, agri-industrial event held in Oxford. In 'Can Britain Feed Itself? Should Britain Feed Itself?', which grew out of the Real Farming conference, Tudge explores the possibility and desirability of rethinking global food trade and arrives at some striking conclusions. The answer he draws to the first question is, yes, 'Easily!' Allowing for a generous calorie allocation of 3000 per day (most people need far fewer) and a population of 70 million, he calculates that these could be provided with 'almost exactly the amount of land which, in practice, Britain now devotes to arable farming', around 3 million hectares. To allow additionally for our essential fats and micronutrient needs (minerals and vitamins), from horticulture, oilseeds and livestock, there is more than enough agricultural land left for that.

'Two wondrous serendipities' help us.[54] The first is that the most energy-efficient and ecologically sound form of farming is perfectly aligned with healthy eating: it captures 'the essence of nutritional theory of the past thirty years'. This is farming based on 'plenty of plants, not much meat, and maximum variety'. The second bit of luck comes as reassurance for those who fear that doing the right thing is hard-wired to austerity and miserabilism. Why? Because this formula also 'captures the essence of all the great cuisines of the world'. Tudge, something of a bon viveur himself and a man of Falstaffian conviviality, speaks from extensive personal experience when he goes through gourmet delights ranging from Italian to Anatolian and Indian cooking, all of which express themselves deliciously from the formula above. 'In short,' he writes, 'farming that is designed primarily to provide *enough*, sustainably, also provides us with excellent nutrition and the best possible cooking. So we would eat much better than we do now if only we farmed as if we really wanted to feed people.' The latter is his reference to having a world food system that leaves as many people overweight as undernourished, and which relies on unsustainable inputs of energy, fertiliser and pesticides.

Even allowing for radical swings to organic cultivation, a positive shift in this direction does seem possible. Because the ability of the rest of the world to provide has been taken for granted for so long, few studies have been done. But in a world stressed by rising and volatile energy prices, and where crop failures are linked to greater extremes of climate that in turn trigger the withdrawal of major commodity producers from the global markets, such reassessments are pragmatic and overdue. Self-reliance in this model is not about complete self-sufficiency. The food trade will always be important. Tea, coffee and bananas it makes sense to import into Britain, but for Europe to import soya grown on cleared Amazon rainforest with little benefit reaching local people, only to be fed to pigs and cattle, is 'highly undesirable', says Tudge.

A still more radical vision can be found in the film *A Farm for the Future*, made by Rebecca Hosking and focused on her own family's farm in Britain's West Country. Hosking grew up on the farm and understood what made it tick, but as an environmental film-maker by trade, she became aware of how compromised the conventional agricultural model was becoming. Peak oil and climate change called for farming's reinvention. Her film, which is available to view online, ends by presenting a vision in which the UK converts to a kind of highly diverse forest gardening, which requires much less tilling of the soil, much less farm machinery and lower chemical inputs. It would change our diets, she says, and might need fewer hours of toil.

However far-off is such imagination and experimentation from the mainstream, more shocking is that so little official effort gets invested in even sensible contingency planning for an uncertain future, by exploring the potential of such opportunities. With the exception of work by individuals like Tudge, Hosking and Simon Fairlie, who produces a magazine called *The Land*, and by those engaged in transition initiatives, little else on alternative basic frameworks is done, certainly at the official level. The most detailed assessment, still yet to be bettered, says Tudge, was Sir Kenneth Mellanby's book *Can Britain Feed Itself?*, written nearly forty years ago in 1975. It would be ironic if Britain ploughed on regardless, as developing countries began to seek different futures.

'The presumptions and aspirations of what constitutes a civilised life will have to be modified,' writes Jayati Ghosh, professor of economics at Jawaharlal Nehru University, New Delhi, and the executive secretary of International Development Economics Associates. 'The model popularised by "the American Dream" is perhaps the most dangerous in this context, with its emphasis on suburban residential communities far from places of work, market and entertainment and linked only through private motorised transport.'

India is a country with per capita incomes far below Europe and the US, and yet Ghosh rejects orthodox development, and imagines a very different economic path:

To start with, a much greater emphasis on creating communities that do not require major and continuous movement of individuals on a daily basis – by bringing together home, work and leisure locations as far as possible – is important. Second, a major impetus must be given to affordable, efficient and fast public transport networks. Third, there must be incentives to reduce unnecessary mobility, for example by using the possibilities created by newer information and communication technology.[55]

If Jayati Ghosh is prepared to embrace such a bold re-imagining of India's future, what immediate steps can we take in countries like the UK to embark on a similarly imaginative, different journey? The final chapter looks at some of these.

II

The Momentum

A hymn to things whose time has gone and what will come instead

Traveller, there is no path,
The path is made by walking.

Antonio Machado, 'Traveller, There Is No Path'

Old truths have been relearned; untruths have been unlearned. We have always known that heedless self-interest was bad morals; we now know that it is bad economics . . . This new understanding undermines the old admiration of worldly success as such. We are beginning to abandon our tolerance of the abuse of power by those who betray for profit the elementary decencies of life.

Franklin D. Roosevelt

In court

How shall we cancel the apocalypse? On the preceding pages several ways have been suggested. One not yet mentioned is going to court. A retired American radiation safety officer and a Spanish science writer decided to give it a try. Their case put the European Centre for Nuclear Research, better known by its acronym, CERN, in the dock. The jurisdiction they chose was Hawaii, which first considered but then ultimately declined the case. Whatever its public excuse, the court's refusal may have had something to do with its basic nature, rather than technical, legal and procedural matters. The plaintiffs' 'allegation of an injury', it concluded, was arguably 'conjectural and hypothetical'.[1]

CERN is the Geneva home of one of the biggest, possibly *the* biggest, scientific experiments ever conducted – a particle accelerator known as the Large Hadron Collider. The tunnel in which it sits is 27 km in circumference. In forcing the collision of subatomic particles its designers hope to understand more about the fundamental nature of matter, and the creation and history of the universe. But the plaintiffs had a concern. They thought it could lead to the *ultimate* apocalypse. There was a theoretical possibility that one or more black holes would be created by the experiment. If that happened, they argued, and things went badly, the Earth and everyone on it would be gone in a twinkle (or rather the opposite of a twinkle, as not even light escapes a black hole, hence the darkness). The legal action was an attempt to stop it. They failed. The experiment went ahead. We didn't disappear into a singularity, the unimaginably dense centre of a black hole, and are still here to make the best of things.

To cherish and enjoy the full sensory materiality of the world that is still with us, we might begin by attending to the quality and vitality of the places where we live, and the time we spend here. By doing so, we can take the next steps of the living experiment in adapting an economy that cannot infinitely grow in scale. Changing how we think about ourselves in the world turns out to be as important as introducing any new technology.

Re-imagining places

What we are seeing here is a triple 'decentring.' Big cities are defined firstly by their capacity to import and export people, products images and messages . . . In the dwellings themselves, houses or apartments, the television and computer now stand in for the hearth of antiquity . . . The individual, finally, is decentred in a sense from himself. He has the instruments that place him in constant contact with the remotest parts of the world [and] . . . can thus live rather oddly in an intellectual, musical or visual environment that is wholly independent of his immediate physical surroundings.

Marc Augé, *Non-Places*

A paradoxical achievement of sophisticated modern living is to have stumbled into a world in which we are permanently somehow distanced from the places where we actually are, distracted, locked out even. It's as if endless, restless transit and the need to be in constant contact with other places, people and events, which are not in the same room as us, have hidden the keys that allow us to enter and truly inhabit our own cities, homes and selves.

Technology has enabled and exaggerated a tendency identified by Blaise Pascal in the seventeenth century, namely that: 'The sole cause of man's unhappiness is that he does not know how to stay quietly in his room.' Today the danger is that our default setting is to be absent from where we are.

Decentring, as Augé calls it, or displacement, is a key dynamic of 'supermodernity'. It can lead to extreme ambitions. On the radio, I heard a woman, once a voice on the far left of British politics and now drifted to the slightly random right, speculate wistfully on how digital technology might free us altogether from our inconvenient earthly bonds and slave-like relationship to the natural world. We could, she imagined, find liberation as digital ciphers of ourselves in a parallel reality, untroubled by the weather, pollution, scarce resources and other worldly cares.

As a variant of technological utopia, it might appear to be a logical next stop. It has some superficial attractions, and not a few practical problems (all that energy still needs to come from somewhere, and is anyone left to dust and fix the roof if the rain gets in above the server centre?). Hollywood and writers like William Gibson allow us to imagine such worlds, making them seem tantalisingly close. More crude actual innovations like *Second Life* provide intimations of possibility.

And yet, rather like the febrile and still fruitless search through our galaxy to find another planet to support life, in case we mess up finally and fatally on Earth, this striving feels less like exhilarating exploration and more like running away, a masked preparation for admitting defeat. Such dreams seem to float, like TV monitors in a departure lounge, or weightless astronauts, drained of full sensory engagement.

They reject nature, and in rejecting nature become expressions of self-loathing because, as we are part of nature, it means we are rejecting ourselves.

It is unsurprising, however, that such views percolate into the mainstream. So many of the global elite, international businessmen, bureaucrats and decision-makers, presiding over what is allowed to happen and what is not, spend so much time in the non-places of supermodernity. Listless, and with only each other for reassurance that they are doing the right thing, arid visions get born of disconnected souls in decentred worlds fed by sensory deprivation. And they are spun to be modern and compelling. Welcome to our hell, it is the best and only reality we can imagine, we're sure you will like it too. Out of such impoverishment only short, limited horizons are visible.

With all the invasive hostile technologies that seek to dominate and control the biosphere, rather than working with its grain, we appear to be a civilisation in conflict with the world we depend on, which means, as E. F. Schumacher noted, that even if we win, we lose.

Fuelled by anxieties of the apocalypse, we find ourselves gripped by a modern version of the ancient fear of the woods. Rather than learn to fruitfully coexist, it seems easier to reach for the nearest technological axe, nuclear power or GM crops, and start cutting. In doing so, instead of conquering our fears we become more insecure, even paranoid (what if terrorists get hold of nuclear materials, or create superpests – both possible), and instead of finding lasting solutions to our problems, we opt for short-term fixes that entrench different, deeper problems and displace longer-term and more enduring answers.

Writing from the perspective of a culture that has been subjected to decades of obsessive individualism, materialism and multiple 'decentring', I believe that the way ahead – and I am fully aware that this involves inviting the scorn of that same culture – is to fall back in love with the world, and each other. In other words, we need to reconnect. To find a spell of re-enchantment with the physical world, the soil, forests, oceans and fields that sustain us, and re-enchantment with the potential of collective endeavour, of communities engaged in tasks of important common purpose.

That sounds rather high-falutin, but it can take on some of the many practical other ways of organising our livelihoods discussed in the previous chapters. It can, for example, change the shape of your high street, or main street if you live in America.

Over several years, and in a series of studies and a book called

Tescopoly, I charted a twin dynamic at the heart of communities in Britain. It was the emergence of 'ghost towns' on the one hand – high streets and town centres killed off by giant out-of-town supermarkets and the profit-enhancing choices made by banks and others to close local branches – a mass-extinction event in business terms to rival what is happening to plant and animal species in the natural world; and on the other hand, the rise of the 'clone towns', where money still flows, but mostly through the tills of desultory, characterless chain stores, leaving high streets homogenised across the country. The work underpinned a successful campaign to pass a law, the Sustainable Communities Act, which although insufficiently used, gives communities greater say over the direction of local developments if local authorities opt in.

Both trends impoverish local life. Ghost towns are monuments to wasted enterprise, lost endeavour and potential, self-fulfilling spirals of decline in which local resources, money and hope leave an area to find another home. Clone towns, with their null sense of place, suffer chain-store business models. These function like efficient but ultimately disinterested vacuum cleaners, sucking wealth and distinctiveness out of an area to satisfy the expectations of remote fund managers. These so-called investors are, as we've seen, really rather ineffectual gamblers, more likely to destroy value than create it. They neither know nor care that a Tesco store or other major chain has used its financial muscle to outbid a local business for a high-street premises, or what that means for the vibrancy, resilience and conviviality of a community.

Complex interactions can occur between ghost and clone towns. A high street efficiently killed off may later make cheap pickings for chain stores. Whilst an independently owned local store may fight harder to stay open during a recession than a fair-weather chain store with remotely set targets and demographics to meet, sole traders lack the ability to cross-subsidise their operations and can find it harder to bounce back. The worst can be when the giant chains use anti-competitive practices, lobbying and political influence to kill off local competition, and then, when the economy hits hard times, themselves close and move on, leaving nothing.

Basically, a local economy comprising a good mix of small to medium-sized businesses and independent stores, and whose high street is more than just estate agents, phone shops and other chain stores, will create more jobs, keep more wealth circulating and expanding, create and strengthen the relationships upon which strong community depends, and have a stronger identity, all helping create overall benefits for our well-being. This happens because big, remotely owned retailers have business models that rely on reducing costs by employing fewer people, pound for pound of turnover. In spite of their spin to the contrary, a large supermarket opening will destroy more jobs in the retail sector than it creates, and research in the US shows that people shopping in giant stores like WalMart (owners of Asda in the UK) will have fewer conversations with other people, and that the appearance of such stores so erodes local life that as well as negative effects on wage levels, even voter turnout for elections declines.[2]

It is the future as foreseen in 1927 by G. K. Chesterton when he warned in *The Outline of Sanity*: 'There is nothing in front but a flat wilderness of standardisation either by Bolshevism or Big Business.' And yet nature abhors a vacuum.

In Britain, from the disappearance or retreat of household names like the general store Woolworths, the confectioner Thorntons and the homeware retailer Habitat, the recession following the 2008 crash further changed the shape of the high street. Three decades of retail and banking consolidation had already had the effects described above. Now we were told that it was our patriotic duty to shop for the recovery.

But, even if we wanted to, the opportunities were becoming fewer with one in seven high street premises standing empty. The tone of advice from certain voices also changed in surprising ways, such as from the Bank for International Settlements (BIS), mentioned in chapter 2, a sort of trade body for central banks, whose guidelines for commercial banks failed so utterly to prevent the crisis. Chastened, the BIS seemed finally to realise that spending money we don't have on things we don't really need isn't such a good idea after all. In their 2011 Annual Report they concluded: 'The sooner advanced economies abandon the leverage-led growth that precipitated the Great Recession, the sooner they will shed the destabilising debt accumulated during the last decade.'[3] It was, in effect, a direct challenge to official government policy in Britain, whose economic strategy depended on restoring pre-recessionary habits of consumption. 'Expansionary Fiscal Contraction', the notion that big cuts in public spending would trigger a private-sector, consumer-led recovery, was (is) their policy.

Regardless of other problems associated with such an approach that this book has explored (for example, the impact of overconsumption on the biosphere and the failure of materialism to deliver human well-being), even on its own terms this exotic economic policy is a long leap of faith. It relies on the logic that people will start spending again, because their confidence will be restored, because they understand that tax cuts in the future (not now) will give them more to spend . . . in the future. I can't even say that this is mainstream economics achieving a level of self-parody, because it is not really mainstream. It is a quirky idea, plucked from obscure journal articles and used because it seems to serve a particular ideological mindset. Such floundering presents the opportunity for a much bigger rethink on the shape of the local economy that can meet multiple economic and environmental challenges, as well as crises of community, purpose, meaning and identity.

In looking to how to rebuild the economy, fundamentals need rethinking, and that includes the high street. Speaking at the annual congress of the Cooperative movement, which includes large, fairly orthodox businesses, even if their ownership structure is different, I found surprising and welcome heretical thoughts percolating up through the membership. 'How should we change our model, so that we are not just selling more stuff and promoting consumption for its own sake?' asked one. 'How can the cooperative movement engage with Transition Towns?' asked another.

Behind the questioning was a big thought. Can high streets become more than places where we go to shop, and can shops become places where we do more than simply buy things? For example, what if the shop of the future had only some of its space given over to shifting goods, and the rest of the space reserved for trading the skills and knowledge to make, maintain, repair, share, reuse and recycle things? Tiny gesture as it might be, Fiona Reynolds, head of the National Trust at the time, pointed out that the DIY store B&Q was already looking into leasing rather than just selling tools.

The degradation of the high street in the face of the recession and of unfair competition from the big supermarkets has the economic and social costs described above. But a vibrant local economy can be the place where community gets built. When denuded, the opposite happens. But why can't we rebuild and re-imagine the high street so that it is better than before, and make it a place where we not only shop, but learn, do, share and interact? Skills and activities of this sort are fundamental to a low-carbon, green economy.

Planning laws and compulsory purchase orders can already be used to compel absentee landlords to bring empty properties back into use. Innovations like a local economy 'Good Use Order' could be used to bring some of those one in seven empty premises on Britain's high streets back into use.

All necessary safeguards and caveats could be applied to reassure owners. In economically shattered Detroit, local people set a precedent with their 'Mo-Town to Gro-Town' initiative by taking unused land and using it for community groups to grow food. It gave people work, brought communities together, lowered crime, and people had to drive less and had healthier diets. Empty high-street properties could become bases for a wide range of community, cooperative and social enterprise-led centres. This book has explored new approaches to banking and money, rethinking approaches to the food chain and energy system, innovations based on the economics of shared use of goods rather than just purchase, passive consumption and disposal, as well as a cultural revival in which we also shift the balance from being passive consumers to more engaged, active producers.

I can imagine, in a myriad different incarnations, high streets becoming places where there are: 'food hubs', for trading, sharing and learning about how to grow, cook and preserve food that we may have grown ourselves or in community allotments; 'energy hubs', which could be comprehensive centres supporting a local, low-carbon energy transition, and a possible base for transition-town initiatives; 'local money hubs' as centres for the vision of taking back the banking system explored earlier; and 'arts hubs', where we can pursue Keynes's 'art of living', and flourish in other ways. There is already a self-motivated 'empty shops network' in which artists are attempting to do just this. *The Times* newspaper said it was 'Helping local individuals and groups to work with councils in converting less glamorous spaces to good use'. The leading broadcaster on the arts Alan Yentob called it 'An ingenious way of bringing art to the people'.

In 2011, the government Department for Business Innovation and Skills commissioned an independent review of the high street, led by the retailer and broadcaster Mary Portas. Its objective was 'to identify what the Government, local authorities, businesses and others can do together to promote the development of new models of prosperous and diverse high streets'.

At its launch the prime minister, David Cameron, declared: 'The High Street should be at the very heart of every community, bringing people together, providing essential services and creating jobs and investment; so it is vital that we do all that we can to ensure they thrive.' His deputy, the Liberal Democrat leader Nick Clegg, added: 'Empty high streets are a blight on the local economy. Vacant shops are also a wasted opportunity with far-reaching consequences. When goods and services start to disappear our sense of community can be weakened and undermined.' The inquiry took evidence from me and my colleagues based on our years of work on the issues. A large number of the report's subsequent recommendations were to do with getting empty properties back into use.

Landlords should be pressured not to leave units vacant, and negligent ones be served with new 'Empty Shop Management Orders'. Banks that own such empty property should have to put them into use or be required to sell them. Local authorities should use compulsory purchase orders proactively, or otherwise encourage redevelopment of high-street retail spaces. There were also imaginative proposals to give local communities a much stronger say in what happens, among them to 'run a high-profile campaign to get people involved in Neighbourhood Plans, promote the inclusion of the High Street in Neighbourhood Plans', to see that developers 'make a financial contribution to ensure that the local community has a strong voice in the planning system', and perhaps best of all, to 'support imaginative community use of empty properties through Community Right to Buy, Meanwhile Use and a new Community Right to Try'.

The review also called for pilot studies to test the proposals in real places. In response, the government announced a modest budget to allow for some, but declined to act on some of the issues to do with rebalancing the overweening power of big retailers. Portas herself said she would have 'liked greater central intervention' to deal with out-of-town developments and planning laws that can see useful diversity on high streets replaced by rows of estate agents and mobile phone stores. And the danger of independent reviews commissioned by governments is that they create the appearance of action without anyone actually having to do anything. But the need for, and logic of, these kind of measures is now accepted.

Why don't we now go further, and create places at the heart of our local communities where micro- and small producers can sell and exchange, where people can swap knowledge, learn more about energy saving, mending, making your own entertainment, growing food, how to cook and conserve it, and tool- and transport-sharing schemes? It would bring back vibrant local life. At a stroke it would revitalise local economies and help reskill Britain for the challenges of the modern world. It would, in other words, help cancel the apocalypse.

Why is the resurgence of localism so interesting? In Augé's conception, the local sits outside the system, providing an implicit challenge. In some places it has been co-opted, incorporated into global markets and homogenised, for example in the way that supermarkets try to promote their small stores as local, and Tesco used a definition of 'local' so loose that milk sold 150 miles away from where it was produced was still called local. But where it still has meaning, the idea of local sits outside the networks and chains of control represented by economic and technological globalisation. It is distinctive, empowering, and it reconnects. It says: 'No thank you, we would prefer to do things our own way,' aiding the re-enchantment with the world that enables it to flourish rather than collapse.

Re-imagining our time

The mass of the people can hardly conceive of a time when the Saturday half-holiday did not exist . . . Latterly, controversy over hours of work has resolved itself into the question: to work or not to work on Saturday morning.

E. S. Turner, *Roads to Ruin*

If society was organised so that you could get by working the equivalent of only three days' paid work a week, with the rest of your time available for family, friends, making music, making anything, learning, walking, playing sport, joining clubs, reading, gardening, or anything else, would you do it? To achieve the better, not bigger, economy I've described, time is the resource required as much as money, or anything else. At the turn of the 1900s there was a progressive social campaign in the US to establish a shorter, eight-hour working day. It was vehemently opposed by the American National Association of Manufacturers (NAM) as potentially ruinous to the economy. If that argument sounds familiar it is because it is much the same case used to oppose the abolition of slavery, the introduction of the maximum load line in shipping, and most other progressive reforms throughout history. In the 1920s NAM also lobbied against a shorter, five-day working week. In the 1930s, however, the very same lobby group paid for a billboard advertising campaign boasting that the US now had the 'world's shortest working hours', underlining the point with 'there's no way like the American way'. Nothing succeeds like success or, indeed, the gymnastic contortions of those who find themselves on the wrong side of history.[4]

Today, the UK has the third-longest working hours in Europe, behind Austria and Greece, according to the Office for National Statistics. The UK Trade Union Council calculates that a rising number of people are doing unpaid overtime in their jobs. Over 5 million are estimated to be providing the equivalent of a whole day's worth of free work to their employers every week, worth £29.2 billion to the economy in 2011.

Yet the momentum towards a shorter working week is long-established and not new. The 'struggle for Saturday afternoon' was just another step in a 150-year campaign for shorter hours of work. Giving workers a half-day's holiday on a Saturday, it was said, would lead to 'immorality'.

The pressure for the shorter week flowed directly from agitation to abolish child labour in the nineteenth century. The Industrial Revolution had robbed men, women and children of the privileges that they had once enjoyed even under feudal lords. Calculations of the number of weeks worked in some medieval periods suggest that annual hours of labour were shorter than in the modern age, and in Barbara Ehrenreich's *Dancing in the Streets: A History of Collective Joy*, she describes the embarrassment of riches there could be in terms of time off. In fifteenth-century France one in every four days was an official holiday. In the Industrial Revolution it was only in 1825 that child labour was limited to twelve hours on a weekday and nine hours on Saturday. Each reduction in hours was fought 'tooth and nail' by economic interests. A reduction to ten hours, it was argued in familiar fashion, would be 'utterly ruinous'.

The French have a saying: 'The English kill themselves to live.' But this is not innate. 'We English certainly do not like working for work's sake,' wrote J. B. Priestley in the *New Statesman* in 1949. 'There is nothing inside us that cries to be set going at an early hour and kept at it until a late hour. We have no private passion for being industrious.' And John Maynard Keynes famously imagined that by now, with the logic of economic, social and technological development, we would have just a fifteen-hour week, with the rest of our time devoted to the art of living. It didn't happen and, contrarily, in an economic system that generates both high levels of overwork (often unpaid) and unemployment (which is demonised), in the puritan tradition, working a full long week is still held to retain some kind of moral superiority.

It may have lost some of its campaigns, but through its lobbying and publishing against the shorter working week in the 1930s, the NAM did, however, bequeath the lasting notion of the 'lump of labour fallacy', an idea which ever since has been used against proponents of shorter work time. But we will see that the 'lump of labour fallacy' is itself a fallacy. What does it mean? Critics of shorter work time assume that its advocates believe there to be only a fixed amount of work available in the economy, and therefore that the way to tackle overwork and unemployment is to share better the amount of work that is there. They say that this is simply not true, and that an expanding economy can create more work. Yet the whole argument is just a deeply rooted misunderstanding.

This could be a genuine misinterpretation, or a tactical argument in the service of a more political agenda opposed, for whatever reason, to shorter working weeks. I do not know. A writer on economic history, Tom Walker, points out that even within orthodox, classical economic thought the case is made for restraints on the length of the working week. In 1909 Sir Sydney Chapman made a presidential address to the Section on Economic Science and Statistics of the British Association for the Advancement of Science. 'Alfred Marshall, Lionel Robbins, John Hicks and Arthur Pigou all referred to Professor Chapman's theory as authoritative,' writes Walker. 'Hicks called it the "classical statement of the theory of 'hours' in a free market".'

The case made was that 'competitive pressures would tend to set the working day at a longer than optimal length', and it cited a body of empirical evidence that productivity improved after shorter working hours were introduced. Walker argues, in consequence, that 'if current hours of work exceed the optimum . . . the reduction of working time could result in simultaneous increases in wages, productivity and employment. That result has nothing to do with a "fixed amount of work".'[5]

In any case, the mere fact that the amount of work in an economy is not fixed does not mean that it cannot also be better distributed. Further, from my perspective as discussed earlier, I believe that in a green economy there will be much more work for people to do. Low-carbon economies need people for all the repairing, reusing and recycling demanded in a closed-loop system. But, if work is better shared out *as well* between those who are overworked and unemployed, or underemployed, we can also solve a raft of other problems. To explain this argument more fully, together with my colleagues Anna Coote and Jane Franklin we produced a report called *21 Hours: Why a shorter working week can help us all to flourish in the 21st century*.

Our argument was that a radical redistribution of paid and unpaid time can help to tackle three serious problems that we face in the twenty-first century. It would not be compulsory, or introduced overnight in the form of shock therapy, and several other simultaneous reforms would be needed, such as ways of making housing more affordable and a rise in the minimum wage. But the main benefits would be threefold.

First, economic – as mentioned, it would help to resolve the paradox of overwork and unemployment, and how the credit-induced collapse of the global financial systems led to the deep, intractable recession and rising unemployment that followed. It would also help to shift the balance of the global economy to serve the needs of society and the environment, rather than depending on overconsumption.

Second, social – the redistribution of paid and unpaid work would address widening inequalities, and the fact that working and earning more beyond a certain point doesn't make us happier. It would give more people more time to be better parents, carers, friends, neighbours and citizens, and everyone a chance to earn a living. We'd save money by being able to do more things for ourselves, and with more people around to care for and help each other out it would take the pressure off public services, and reduce the stress of retirement.

Third, environmental – it would help us escape the consumer treadmill in which we work ever longer hours to earn money to buy things we don't really need, which don't make us happy and which the planet cannot afford. And, intriguingly, it seems that neither do we have the space in our homes to keep them. Yellow Box, the company that provides units for household storage, is expanding by 40 per cent a year in the UK. In the few economic models that have been designed with the purpose of working out how to live within our environmental means, the length of the working week (along with the issues to do with productivity discussed in the chapter on measures) is one of the few variables that give us room to manoeuvre.

Creating a new social norm of a shorter working week could turn negative, prevailing economic circumstances from a problem into an opportunity. It would also be the next step on a long historical path that, designed well, could ensure that everyone benefits, especially those who are currently unemployed and poor. So-called 'time affluence', or reduced working hours, relates positively to improved well-being.

Glimpses of possibility are already emerging. The Netherlands has for some time embraced a four-day working week. In reaction to the Europe-wide recession in the 1980s, the Dutch government hired new workers at 80 per cent of the old, full working week. It proved popular. Employment contracts across sectors allow for a four-day week, and it even became the norm in the banking sector.

When the state of Utah in the US introduced a four-day week for state employees as a cost-saving measure in response to the recession in 2008, they had the presence of mind to monitor the results. It was not an exact parallel because it was done without reducing the total number of hours worked, but by giving everyone a three-day weekend. Nevertheless the results were striking. More than half said they were more productive and three-quarters said they preferred the new arrangements with a longer weekend. Workers were clearly happier, as absentee rates went down. The state saved $4.1 million as a result of fewer staff being off work and through overtime savings. Nor did the benefits end there. It also saved $1.4 million through less travel in state-owned vehicles; and carbon emissions went down by 4546 metric tons or 14 per cent, above even the ambitious annual target that climate science tells us is necessary, other greenhouse gases fell by 8000 tons and petrol consumption by 744,000 gallons. Over eight out of ten employees wanted the year-long experiment to carry on.

The former Harvard economist and professor of sociology Juliet B. Schor says of the rising interest in a shorter working week: 'The sustainability movement motivated it, the internet facilitated it, and the economic downturn mainstreamed it, as cash got scarce and time got more abundant.'

If the idea of a twenty-one-hour working week becoming the norm in economies like Britain's sounds strange and radical, it's worth noting that twenty-one hours is close to the average number of hours actually worked by all those of working age in the UK: 19.6 hours in paid employment and 20.4 hours in unpaid housework and childcare. And that productivity does not diminish in line with shorter hours was shown by the three-day week in 1974, when production fell by only 6 per cent. The French experiment with a statutory thirty-five-hour week, abolished by President Sarkozy, is often used to demonstrate the failure of shorter hours. In fact, in spite of the law change, most workplaces left their arrangements as they were.

Following Utah's experience, with fewer days in the office, happier, more productive workers and less pollution, it would appear to be an experiment worth repeating. To begin, employers could offer all new members of staff the option of working a four-day week. I've suggested such a scheme be called 'National Gardening Leave'. You wouldn't have to garden on the fifth day, but it is one of the best things you can do for your health and well-being, with many other potential benefits.

The climax economy: re-imagining how we get on

You are narrowly self-interested, perfectly informed, rational and infinite – you are economic man. The markets within which you exist are axiomatic. Most disciplines create models, make assumptions and simplify in order to understand and interrogate the world. In economics, however, there's a sense that maybe they went too far. If the object of investigation is a cat, and you begin by assuming that all cats bark and love to swim underwater, you will struggle to match the results of your study with reality. Mainstream economics makes similar assumptions. At its heart lies a colossal misreading of human nature. It is an erroneous simplification and a partial self-fulfilling prophecy, with mutually destructive tendencies.

Dr Marc Arvan is an assistant professor of philosophy at the University of Tampa in the US. Given the tone and practice of economics in America he rather bravely conducted an experiment that looked into the relationship between 'moral judgments and three "dark" personality traits: Machiavellianism (i.e., tendencies to deceit), narcissism (over-inflated sense of self-worth), and psychopathy (lack of guilt and remorse)'. To do so he looked at people's beliefs concerning several issues. These included attitudes to the death penalty and neoconservative views on detaining suspected terrorists without trial and waging war without the explicit authority of UN resolutions. But he also looked at 'economic libertarianism' – the notion that the role of the state in relation to the market should be minimal, only intervening to prevent or punish the breaking of the law.

This, in effect, is the ideal habitat in which economic man – that is all of us, because we are all meant to behave as 'economic men' – is supposed to prosper. But Arvan found that this view 'correlated significantly . . . with all three dark personality traits'.[6] In other words, the projection of an economic system built on foundations of self-interest, individualism and self-regulation, which is supposed to be good for everyone, in fact describes the comfort zone for a dark triad of personality dysfunctions including psychopathy, Machiavellianism and narcissism. Rather than finding ways to ameliorate and lighten these aspects of human darkness, it seems that the response of economic libertarianism is to suggest that we should all switch out the lights and let the darkness flourish. It is a system quite methodical in pursuing these aims. One might almost say that the darkness has been institutionalised.

Frustration with the teaching of economics is reaching new heights. The grip of neoliberalism in university departments has been tight to the point of exclusive, leading to accusations of preaching doctrine rather than teaching economics. It has provoked a backlash. French students formed a breakaway initiative called the 'post-autistic-economics' network to celebrate the heterogeneous study of the subject. It quickly spread to other countries like the UK. In America, frustrated students at Harvard University walked out of a lecture in protest at the 'relentless idiocy of neoliberalism' that was being taught there. The lecturer in question was Gregory Mankiw, who had been chairman of the Council of Economic Advisers under President George W. Bush and is the author of a leading economics textbook. Condemning his 'biased instruction matter', they left his 'Econ 101' class in November 2011 at the height of the 'Occupy' protests, which Mankiw unsurprisingly had not supported.

The author and *Financial Times* journalist Tim Harford writes of a 'niche in the economics literature, exploring the question: does studying economics make you a bad person?'[7] Professor Robert H. Frank was one of the early occupants of that niche, based at Cornell University in Ithaca, New York. He'd been struck by the insistence in the economics literature on the essential selfishness of human nature. He cites the economist Gordon Tullock's assertion that 'the average human being is about 95 per cent selfish, in the narrow sense of the term'.[8] In response, Frank and his colleagues thought to investigate whether the 'self-interest' model of the economy was a reflection of how people in essence were, or whether it was an artificially constructed model that attracted an unrepresentative, more selfish sample of society to its cause, and in so doing was actually making people selfish. The conclusion he began to arrive at, and which has troubled economists ever since, is that the appeal, study and internalisation of neoliberal economic models did select an unrepresentative, more selfish slice of society.

An even earlier study at the dawn of the Reagan–Thatcher economic revolution noted that economics undergraduates were more likely to behave selfishly, and 'free-ride' off the more public-spirited behaviour of others. An experiment was devised in which people were given money and had the choice of sharing different proportions of it between their own private account and a public pot. Money put into the public pot would be multiplied and then shared out equally later. The experiment was designed such that the optimum outcome for everyone would be if everyone put their money into the public pot. While the other players gave nearly half – 49 per cent – of their money to the public share, first-year graduate economics students gave only 20 per cent in this way. They knew that they would in any case benefit from the sharing of the public pot, but chose to contribute less, 'free riding' on others' good will.

This work has been developed more recently by Yoram Bauman, an environmental economist at the University of Washington. Altogether it reveals how the 'public goods' conundrum gives the lie to mainstream economics' belief that aggregating private, self-interested behaviour brings about optimal results for society as a whole.[9] Acting selfishly might make sense in the short term for an individual, writes Bauman, 'but as more and more people choose to act selfishly, the good disappears and everyone loses'. Adam Smith's 'invisible hand' first picks everyone else's pocket, and then ends up picking the pocket of its own host body, and throwing the wealth away. Bauman's study confirmed much of the earlier work showing that students of economics were less altruistic than the social norm, but added a twist. He looked at the effect of exposure to the teaching of economics on students not majoring in the subject. These were people studying a range of other subjects who decided to dip their toes into mainstream economics as taught in universities. For this group, people who started out as part of the more generous majority, as opposed to full-time students of economics, became more selfish as a result of exposure to studying the 'dismal science'.

The doctrine of neoliberalism, it seems, pushes you towards becoming the kind of human being that it relies on. Rather chillingly, the study of this branch of economics seems to behave like an intellectual version of *Invasion of the Body Snatchers*, turning the host mind to its own preset purpose. It is a kind of reality-by-assertion, and many other sciences are calling its ideological bluff. Because, when this branch of economics opines that 'you have to live in the real world', they tend to mean the opposite. They mean you have no choice but to live in an economic system that is doomed precisely because it can neither account for, nor accommodate, the parameters of the real, real world and its biosphere.

In recent years there has been a minor deluge of findings published from evolutionary biology, anthropology, psychology, ecology and neuroscience that contradict the reduction of humanity to competitive vessels of short-term, self-interested individualism.

First of all, for those fond of analogies with nature, there are powerful arguments within biology that the emergence on Earth of life itself owes as much to processes of symbiosis and association as to competition. This appears to be the case with early-evolving bacteria, engaged in a kind of giant social networking exercise in which microbiological forms evolved the tricks that still lie at the heart of life.

Further still, what seems to make humanity unique, or at least special, in the animal kingdom is our prodigious and skilful capacity for empathy and cooperation. In this other, broader, view we are in fact 'super-cooperators' who are living in an 'age of empathy'. Representative of this large and growing literature are Frans de Waal and Martin Nowak.

For Nowak, author of *Supercooperators: the Mathematics of Evolution, Altruism and Human Behaviour*, contrary to the pseudo-Darwinian caricature of animals caught in a death struggle for individual dominance where might is right and competition is all, we are creatures riddled with the mechanisms of cooperation. These include 'direct reciprocity', common in the animal kingdom from colourful fish on coral reefs who offer delicate 'cleaning services' to 'generous vampire bats that share blood meals'. Nowak quotes David Hume to demonstrate this long-established thread in human philosophy: 'I learn to do service to another, without bearing him any real kindness, because I foresee, that he will return my service, in expectation of another of the same kind . . . ' There is also 'indirect reciprocity', in which reputations help develop cooperative behaviour when there are 'repeated encounters within a group of players'. Cooperators do well in evolution, according to Nowak, by forming 'networks and clusters in which they help each other'.

Group success due to effective cooperation was noted by Darwin: 'There can be no doubt that a tribe including many members who . . . were always ready to give aid to each other and to sacrifice themselves for the common good, would be victorious over other tribes; and this would be natural selection.'

The powerful bonds of family need less explanation. Nowak is acutely aware that the conclusions he draws, based on scientific observation, experiment and quantitative study, nevertheless share an awful lot with the truths stumbled on by the world's great religions. From Krishna to Jesus they call for unselfish action: 'they have come to the conclusion that love, hope and forgiveness are essential components of what is needed to solve the biggest problems.' Nowak, a professor of biology and mathematics at Harvard University, writes that he is 'struck – perhaps awestruck – by the extent to which humans cooperate . . . no animal species can draw on the mechanisms (of cooperation) to the same extent as seen in human society'.

For Frans de Waal, a world-leading biologist and primatologist, the under-recognised human quality is empathy, but he makes a similar case. The fact that we are 'hard-wired' for altruism, the expression of our ability for empathy, has kept society as a whole from falling apart. In the animal kingdom quite broadly he catalogues how, from the herding instinct to conflict resolution and dolphins saving their own kind (and sometimes people) from drowning, 'feeling' for each other, in such a way that it shapes mutually supportive, rather than competitive behaviour, is designed in.

Alongside competition in nature you will find evolutionary victories for symbiosis, for example in the bacteria that fix nitrogen in plant roots and which consequently makes life continuingly possible. Or for collaboration, as was the case with primeval slime mould which got life going. There is also the co-evolution that gave us the pollinating honey bee responsible for those one in three mouthfuls of the food we eat. Reason is another advantage for problem-solving animals like elephants, dogs, cats, rats, sperm whales and, sometimes, humans. In a world witnessing the unhealthy concentration of economic power into ever fewer corporate hands, optimal diversity too is a key condition, nature's insurance policy against disaster.

Yet we regulate the economy in favour of one-sided competition, which allows the spread of monocultures and clone towns that are increasingly vulnerable to that wide range of external shocks. An interesting story of the recent recession is the way in which companies with more progressive governance structures, cooperatives like John Lewis and the Cooperative Bank, and mutuals like the Nationwide, proved more resilient and economically successful than those dominated by the single bottom line of profit.

De Waal sees amusing contradictions in the highly selective co-option by mainstream economics of evolutionary theory. Just as a rejection of real Darwinism, or refusal to endorse it, washes over the religious, conservative branch of the Republican movement, the very same people promote Social Darwinism that depicts 'life as a struggle in which those who make it shouldn't be dragged down by those who don't'. Hence, neo-conservatives draw invisibly on early misinterpretations of Darwin's theories and their application to the world of business. It was the philosopher Herbert Spencer, for example, in the nineteenth century who coined the phrase 'survival of the fittest'. He thought equality was a bad idea, and that it was counterproductive 'for the "fit" to feel any obligation toward the "unfit"'. Yet, as we saw earlier, quite the opposite is true in practice. Not only is inequality associated with economic disasters, it also raises costs to society as a whole across the board. Equality, on the other hand, is very productive indeed. Calling on our inborn capacity for empathy, writes De Waal, 'can only be to any society's advantage'.

But, as practised and taught, mainstream economics marginalises and minimises our natural tendencies to cooperate and live by empathy. Robert Frank concluded in his 1993 study that: 'In an ever more interdependent world, social cooperation has become increasingly important – and yet increasingly fragile. With an eye toward both the social good and the well-being of their own students, economists may wish to stress a broader view of human motivation in their teaching.' That, I think, is to put it mildly. Rather, I think it is time for a paradigm shift in which the colossally erroneous notion of 'economic man' is removed from the centre of our theoretical solar system, much as the Earth once had to be replaced by the Sun to correct a similarly mistaken belief.

Biology gives us the rather attractive notion of the 'climax ecosystem', defined as the last stage in ecological succession, an ecosystem in which all populations (plant and animal) are in balance with each other and the factors of their non-living environment.

A combination of all the issues discussed in this book points towards the need for a new concept of 'climax economics'. An economy in which we optimise how we live, rather than maximise what we consume, would allow us to find an enduring balance with the biosphere that we depend on. In this way, I think that we are more than capable of cancelling the apocalypse far into the foreseeable future. To save you, the reader, the inconvenience of having to leaf back to the front of the book, I'll summarise again, why I think that is the case.

It is because we have: *the motive* – to ensure a world in which we, our loved ones and the other life upon which we depend may continue to flourish; *the model* – to replace the visibly flawed economy that we have with one that can work in dynamic equilibrium with the biosphere; *the measures* – we already have, and can constantly improve, the compasses to point us in the right direction; *the myth* – there is wisdom and power in the deep cultural stories we have to guide this and future generations; *meaning and imagination* – a better understanding of human well-being than that offered by passive consumerism is already filtering through in society, and we are already demonstrating the imagination to lead fuller lives; *the money* – the aura of mystery and superiority long and carefully cultivated around the finance sector evaporated under the midday heat of the banking crisis; we now know that we can make money, and make it work for us to produce the things we really need; *the memories* – both our deep and our recent past has lessons to help us avoid mistakes and learn to do better; it reminds us too that great transitions can be quickly achieved; *the mechanisms* – in just the examples of food and energy alone, it is clear that we can both feed and power the world without having to make Faustian pacts with technology; *the message* – the marketing and advertising industries may have created a world in which we exist apparently primarily as passive consumers, but to our joy and satisfaction, many are finding life more satisfying when they do and create things for themselves; *mutual interest* – solving problems of all scales becomes much easier in a more equal world, and it is entirely within our collective power to produce one; *the momentum* – with the eyes to see it, a great transition has already begun, and there are opportunities everywhere for virtuous cycles of change.

These are big, thematic observations. There is another group of threads to twist together. Our growth-addicted economy creates enormous inertia. To overcome it, we have to be able to imagine living without growth. Can we begin to do that? Throughout this book there is evidence, I believe, that we can, and in several cases already have. For example, at the aggregate, global level, relying on wealth trickling down from growth to reduce poverty reveals itself as inefficient, unreliable and potentially counterproductive. Better distribution of wealth is a quicker, simpler and more reliable way to achieve that goal. The indicator for growth, too, handcuffs the political imagination. But now we have metrics that can tell us about the quality, rather than the mere volume, of economic activity. Knowing whether social and environmental value are rising, and targeting policy at that goal, should weaken the simple obsession with growth. Rethinking money – who creates it, for what, and under what terms – whether, for example, to inflate property prices or build important new infrastructure – allows us to imagine other ways than relying on growth, to afford the things a society needs and considers important.

Many find it difficult to see how public services will be affordable in the absence of growth, but social innovations, such as building in reciprocity, or give-and-take, as we saw earlier, has the potential not just to lower the cost of, and pressure on, services, but also to make them more effective.

Then comes the fear about security in old age. Without growth, what will happen to pensions? Firstly, recent years showed that a system geared to growth is no guarantor of a reliable pension. Quite the opposite, as it turned out for millions. Value in savings was destroyed by the instability of a finance-led growth system. It is, in any case, not growth per se that people want, but the presumed security in old age that we've been told it will pay for. Here, a well-designed transition economy that helps reweave local social fabrics could be a much less scary place in which to grow old. As we get older we may find that what once we feared we could not afford becomes available without the need to depend entirely on the ability to pay. Care, help and household items can more easily be found in a society with a shorter working week, more sharing and recycling schemes, and innovations in which people give their time to others through time banks and having 'give-and-take' relationships with their local services. Also, a shorter working week as the social norm could soften the line between work and retirement, and the fear of dependence on an inadequate pension. We might work less, but be able to participate and contribute for longer, getting the best of both worlds. In that way old age is less likely to be a dismal ghetto of casual exclusion, isolation and dependence.

Better awareness of where our life satisfaction stems from could reduce the futile search for it in places where typically it cannot be found, such as wealth accumulation and consumption beyond what is sufficient for a good life. This, too, would help defuse the growth dynamic. Related is the 'better not bigger' economy in which value is maximised in a well-plumbed material economy. Goods being repaired, recycled and reused implies a big shift towards the substantial growth of employment in maintenance and services – a dynamic economy, but one in which the absolute throughput of materials is reduced – an ecological 'plugging the leaks'.

How can we circumvent the pressure for growth that results from the expectations of shareholders for high returns on their investment in firms? The power of an investment bank like JP Morgan, which expects a 20 per cent return on its money, is like having a giant financial whip cracking over the head of the economy, telling it to grow. An obvious forward step is to shift the balance of corporate ownership and governance away from the domination of the shareholder model. It is easier to balance social and environmental concerns against the normally disproportionate privilege given to finance when business models embrace broader objectives. Mutuals, cooperatives and social enterprises are, well, more mutual, cooperative and socially interested, as well as better insulated from pressure to grow for its own sake. We can, then, readily begin to imagine living without growth.

Following waves of cynicism and controversy in the build-up to the London 2012 Olympics, its opening ceremony surprised and confounded millions. It transpired after that the person in charge, the film director Danny Boyle, had asked himself a simple question: what is good about this nation, the United Kingdom? His answer led to a performance celebrating the establishment of universal primary health care, the creation of the open, public domain of the World Wide Web, children's literature, music and comedy. It lauded bold industrial transformation (while noting its costs) and applauded the struggle for justice and universal suffrage. A single Suffragettes' banner held aloft seemed to capture the tone of the whole show: 'Be Just, And Fear Not'. It was a witty song of praise to the triumph of bold, creative and collective endeavour. As a reminder of what is achieved oblivious of modern financial markets, it seemed to many a turning point. Reflecting on the Games, the poet laureate Carol Ann Duffy finished with these words: 'We sense new weather. We are on our marks. We are all in this together.'

Hope and walking

But here we have to sound a note of caution. No inevitability attaches to the replacement of a flawed and failing economic model with a better one. I do not think it will recognise its own mistakes and retire to be replaced. There is every chance that, like the financial markets, it will follow its nose short-sightedly over a cliff and drag the rest of us along behind it, all the while blaming everyone else for the rush of passing air and fast-approaching rocky valley floor. All of the enormous potential listed above will only come to pass if we choose to act. Many already are. However, there needs to be a majority, or at least a critical mass. I am hopeful.

I think no one has expressed this better than Rebecca Solnit, writing in *Hope in the Dark: the Untold History of People Power*:

> To hope is to gamble. It's to bet on the future, on your desires, on the possibility that an open heart and uncertainty is better than gloom and safety. To hope is dangerous, and yet it is the opposite of fear, for to live is to risk. I say all this because hope is not like a lottery ticket you can sit on the sofa and clutch, feeling lucky. I say it because hope is an ax you break down doors with in an emergency; because hope should shove you out the door, because it will take everything you have to steer the future away from endless war, from the annihilation of the earth's treasures and the grinding down of the poor and marginal. Hope just means another world might be possible, not promised, not guaranteed. Hope calls for action; action is impossible without hope. At the beginning of his massive 1930s treatise on hope, the German philosopher Ernst Bloch wrote, 'The work of this emotion requires people to throw themselves actively into becoming, to which they themselves belong'. To hope is to give yourself to the future, and that commitment to the future makes the present inhabitable. Anything could happen, and whether we act or not has everything to do with it.

Two steps forward would be to re-imagine the places where we live and how we spend our days. Sometimes I feel as if I have won the lottery of time and place. Expressed as odds to do with where and in what state matter finds itself, it is so unlikely merely to be alive in the universe, as to make it a virtual impossibility to be here at all. Given around 3.8 billion years of life on the planet, and the fact that an ounce of soil might contain as many micro-organisms as there are people on Earth – many with little more than a split-second lifespan – what is the chance of you getting your chance to be you, as opposed to being inert, bacteria, or a nematode?

Thinking about this makes me a little nauseous, not with repulsion but vertigo. I asked the best mathematicians and physicists I know to calculate the odds that any one of us might be alive right now, let alone being lucky enough to be born into a relatively well-off society, as I have been. Impossible to do, they said, but, on balance you are, in effect, impossible. The odds are much, much too remote. And yet, here I am, living in a period of history and part of the world that enjoys unparalleled abundance. Others have strived, ceaselessly, even in the direst circumstances.

On a cold dark night when in prison during the apocalyptic upheaval of Europe in 1917, the writer and radical Rosa Luxemburg found her spirits lifted, despite her perilous situation, by an awareness of the strangeness and beauty of the force of life. Through 'layers of darkness, boredom, bondage, winter', she found that her heart nevertheless 'beats with an inconceivable, unknown inner joy'. Then she smiles at life, as if she knew 'some magic secret which gives the lie to all that is evil and sad and transforms it into sheer radiance and happiness'. The secret, she decides, is 'nothing but life itself, the deep nocturnal darkness is as beautiful and soft as velvet', and even in the sound of sentries' heels grinding in gravel outside, 'there is the small, lovely song of life – if one knows how to hear it'.[10]

I ask myself what I should do with the astonishing opportunity of life, of now. When we agonise over the meaning of existence, sometimes I wonder if we undervalue the act of merely observing it. Unlikely, maybe, but what if we are the only way that the universe has created to know itself, if only we have the consciousness to knowingly bear witness? That is, potentially, a vast responsibility which could just as easily crush as elevate you.

But there is more to it. That's why we engage with the world, why we're here and restless, curious and annoyed that we don't seem able to organise things better. That we have allowed a world to evolve in which nearly half of humanity exists on under $2 per day – remember, that's the equivalent of someone in the UK on the minimum wage, with no other means of support, having to feed and keep a family of at least eighteen other people. While the global economy has grown enormously in scale, it has diverged massively and quite recently between richest and poorest.

How, knowing the unnecessary suffering that economic doctrine, among other things, creates, should we use our front-row seats in the show of life, the universe and everything?

Another like Mark Augé who analyses the rootlessness of modern life is the sociologist Zygmunt Bauman. His term for it is 'liquid modernity'. He believes that the good society is the society that does not think it is good enough. Utopia cannot be achieved, because to be utopian is precisely to engage with the world in a state of hope that it can be better. Gardeners he calls 'obsessive compulsive utopians', because their job is never done. This echoes the Latin American chronicler Eduardo Galleano, who describes how, as quickly as he walks towards utopia, it recedes from him. 'What then,' he asks, 'is the purpose of utopia?' To walk, he concludes, and to advance.

We are both closer together and further apart, but the potential for a progressive, cooperative, positively interdependent world is there. We can combine our impressive resources to tackle the wide range of systemic threats from financial collapse to the floodwaters and droughts of climatic upheaval. Not long ago I saw for the first time at dusk a field of fireflies. As night fell, their light grew brighter. They were all around me for as far as I could see, pulsing, drifting, lighting up the darkening landscape. I thought of the song of life Rosa Luxemburg heard in the night through her prison window, and of the millions of people around the world who don't accept the world as it is, but use their life's pulsing energy to improve it.

That inequality worsens and we seemingly accelerate towards potentially irreversible, destructive environmental change, is significantly a fault of mainstream economics. Its model of the world, a mental landscape in which all people are islands – isolated and self-interested agents – is not just damaging, but wrong on all counts.

It is a few years since I wrote about them, but I am still fascinated by supermarkets, both as modern consumer temples, one of the main places where our livelihoods interact with the rest of the world, and for the distorted map of our island planet that they offer. It's a map of a flat, unchanging Earth, a place without seasons or reasons to question how the world does business, and where an already overconsuming population is encouraged to purchase ever more, in such a way that we end up discarding, wasting, one third of the precious food we buy. The pictures on packaging of smiling people and happily grazing animals bear as much relation to reality as did the joyous workers and natural abundance of Stalin-era paintings of socialist realism.

It's a world of consumption largely detached from consequences, and the processes of production that fill the regimented aisles. It is also a world in which meaningful human contact is incrementally designed out, weakening the bonds upon which achieving a positive interdependence, both local and global, rely. Could it be more symbolic, than that we are now invited to 'self-checkout'? I wonder what is ultimately being checked out – the goods, or us. Would the last person leaving the planet please check themselves out . . .

Yet bad things abhor daylight. Child labour, the worst practices of supermarkets, oil companies working hard in remote places ultimately to guarantee the loss of the climate in which human civilisation emerged – these things struggle to survive exposure.

And, closer together, we now have great potential to shed light on exploitative and unjust relationships both among people and between people and the biosphere. With new maps, compasses and social media, not only can we find things that hide in shadow, we can redraw those relationships. I mentioned that I understand, and yet find odd, the obsession with space exploration (there is so much of fascination, still requiring exploration and understanding, much closer to hand). There may be anything from ten to thirty or more planets in our galaxy, the Milky Way, for every person alive, but what would you do with them all, and how would you get there?

There is a wonderful thing called the Drake Equation, devised by the astrophysicist Frank Drake, to estimate the likely number of advanced civilisations in our galaxy at any one time. The question of whether or not there is any other life 'out there' gets asked frequently and portentously (are we too not also and already 'out there'?), but the average number of civilisations arrived at through the Drake Equation is around ten thousand. Tantalising, and yet the distances separating them are so great as to make contact extremely unlikely. But, it seems likely that out there are civilisations coming and going like soil micro-organisms, if on a different timescale.

Perhaps the greatest gift of space exploration remains that it enabled us to see ourselves as an island planet, where the greatest wonder is to be found around us, between us and even within ourselves. In Milan Kundera's *The Book of Laughter and Forgetting* there is a scene involving Kundera and his father who, recently having suffered a stroke, has difficulty speaking. The father had, for years, been studying and writing about Beethoven's sonatas and their magical variations. His barely coherent remarks trigger in Kundera an understanding that the greatest journey is not into the infinity of the external universe, but to 'that other infinity, into the infinite diversity of the interior world lying hidden in all things'. To explore *that* is more than a lifetime's rich work. Right now, the challenge is to offer an irresistible invitation to look differently and afresh at the world, and imagine how we can do things better.

One of the most extraordinary things to strike me, almost certainly not original but something I hadn't encountered elsewhere, is the realisation that everything alive today must, by definition, be part of an unbroken chain of life dating back upwards of three billion years to the first splutterings of slime mould. Not only is everything alive literally, not just metaphorically, related to everything else, but we're all over three billion years old. That feels both special and, again, vertiginous. Having got this far, it is easy to feel a little self-conscious about whatever next step we might take. 'Permissive path' is a term used to describe when people create an unofficial trail simply by walking, regardless of who owns the land beneath their feet, and it then becomes an accepted route.

How should we set about creating a grand, permissive path to a better future? I found my answer listening to the radio late at night in 2010, and I'd like to share what I heard. On a BBC Radio 4 programme called *Something Understood*, there was an interview with a man called Mark Hennessy. 'Walking is how the body measures itself against the earth,' and how we align our mind and body with the world, wrote Rebecca Solnit.[11] But Hennessy couldn't measure or align himself after he suffered a serious brain injury, and he had to learn to walk all over again. This is how he described what he went through after the injury:

Since I have learnt all about what makes up the component parts of learning to walk through quite a few trials and a few errors, I feel duty bound to tell you that what you take as ordinary, is anything but. Now the first, and I would say most important, component is one that is so automatic, that if one had to draw up a list of components, it wouldn't even feature. And that component is confidence. Without it you are doomed. I've had to painstakingly re-learn walking. I've discovered that you first place your heel down and then transfer your weight onto the ball of your foot as you move your pelvis forward. Then, as you hover momentarily on the toes of your back foot, you bring the other foot over and down to become the next forward step. The trick is to immediately repeat the process. Thus creating the second component part of walking, momentum. Momentum prevents you from falling over. It is the driving force. Try standing on one leg and you will see how important momentum is.[12]

Learning how to walk. Trial and error. There is no path, paths are made by walking. Confidence and momentum, confidence and momentum, confidence and momentum. What should we do now? Now is always the time to hazard a step, and then another, and then . . .

Notes

I. The Motive

1   Chris Nelson examined an enormous range of works – more than thirty in total – including Richard Abanes, *End-Time Visions* (New York: Four Walls Eight Windows, 1998), Jeane Dixon, *The Call to Glory* (New York: Bantam, 1971), Leon Festinger, Henry Rieken and Stanley Schachter, *When Prophecy Fails* (New York: Harper-Torchbooks, 1956), Stephen Jay Gould, *Questioning the Millennium* (New York: Harmony, 1997), Richard Kyle, *The Last Days are Here Again* (Grand Rapids: Baker, 1998), B. J. Oropeza, *99 Reasons Why No One Knows When Christ Will Return* (Downers Grove: IVP, 1996) and Hillel Schwartz, *Century's End: An Orientation Manual Towards the Year 2000* (New York: Doubleday, 1996).

2   Chris Nelson, 'A Brief History of the Apocalypse: The early days: 2800 BC–1700 AD', <http://www.abhota.info/end1.htm>.

3   Felix Just, 'Links to Revelation, Apocalyptic and Millennial Websites and Materials', <http://catholic-resources.org/Bible/Apocalyptic_Links.htm>.

4   Quoted in Elizabeth Kolbert's 2006 essay, 'The Darkening Sea: What carbon emissions are doing to the oceans'. Reproduced in McKibben (ed.), *The Global Warming Reader*.

5   Lomborg, *The Skeptical Environmentalist*.

6   Debora MacKenzie, 'Calculations may have overestimated extinction rates', *New Scientist*, 18 May 2011.

7   The Earth Institute at Columbia University, 'Ocean acidification rate may be unprecedented, study says', <http://crocodoc.com/ChGFVkw>.

8   Hansen et al., 'Target atmospheric CO_2'.

9   Brendan O'Neill, 'Green predictions of End Times are just as demented as Christian ones – so why are they treated more seriously?', *Daily Telegraph*, 19 May 2011.

2. The Model

1   A male hamster roughly doubles its weight each week until it reaches puberty at six to eight weeks old. Assuming a birth weight of 2g, after six weeks the hamster reaches 128g (within the range of the average hamster weight of 85–140 g). If, however, this rate of growth continued for an additional forty-six weeks the hamster would reach a weight of 9,007,199,255 tonnes. Given that a hamster consumes roughly 1g of food

for every 10g of body weight, based on this ratio the daily food requirement at one year would be 900,719,925 tonnes. According to the International Grains Council, in 2007–8 global maize production was just over 795,000,000 tonnes.

2 Daly, *Steady-State Economics*.

3 See, for example, Murray Patterson, 'Selecting headline indicators for tracking progress to sustainability in a nation state', in Philip Lawn (ed.), *Sustainable Development Indicators in Ecological Economics* (Cheltenham: Edward Elgar, 2006).

4 Nicholas Georgescu-Roegen, *The Entropy Law and the Economic Process* (Cambridge, MA: Harvard University Press, 1971).

5 Herman E. Daly, 'On Nicholas Georgescu-Roegen's contributions to economics: an obituary essay', *Ecological Economics*, 13:3 (1995).

6 Corinne Le Quéré, Michael R. Raupach, Josep G. Candell, et al., 'Trends in the sources and sinks of carbon dioxide', *Nature Geoscience*, 2 (2009).

7 Shilong Piao, Philippe Ciais, Pierre Friedlingstien, et al., 'Net carbon dioxide losses of northern ecosystems in response to autumn warming', *Nature*, 451 (3 January 2008).

8 Global Footprint Network, 'Global Footprint Accounts, 2009 Edition' (revised 2012).

9 Colin Challen, 'We must think the unthinkable, and take voters with us', *Independent*, 28 March 2006.

10 UNDP, *Human Development Report 1996*.

11 See OECD Secretariat, 'Growth, Employment and Inequality in Brazil, China, India and South Africa: An overview' (2008).

12 Bernard Porter, 'Other People's Mail', *London Review of Books*, 31:22 (19 November 2009).

13 Hilary Osborne, Jessica Shepherd and Press Association, 'Wonga withdraws student loans information', *Guardian*, 12 January 2012.

14 Mill, *Principles of Political Economy*, Book IV, Chapter VI.

15 Ibid.

16 Ruskin, 'Ad Valorem'.

17 Frederick Soddy, *Cartesian Economics: The Bearing of Physical Science upon State Stewardship* (London: Hendersons, 1922).

18 Quoted in Herman E. Daly, 'The economic thought of Frederick Soddy', *History of Political Economy*, 12:4 (Winter 1980).

19 Ibid.

20 Ibid.

21 Quoted on the jacket of Donella Meadows, Jorgen Randers and Dennis Meadows, *Limits to Growth: The 30-Year Update* (London: Earthscan, 2004).

22 Turner, 'A comparison of *The Limits to Growth* with 30 years of reality'.

23 Debora MacKenzie, 'Doomsday book', *New Scientist*, 7 January 2012.

24 'Budget 2009: Alistair Darling's speech, *Daily Telegraph*, 22 April 2009.

25 Professor Roderick Smith, 'Carpe diem: The dangers of risk aversion', The 2007 Lloyd's Register Educational Trust Lecture, 29 May 2007, Royal Academy of Engineering, London.

26 For an elaboration of the Jevons effect, see: Andrew Simms, Victoria Johnson and Peter Chowla, *Growth Isn't Possible* (London: nef, 2010); Len Brookes, 'The greenhouse effect: The fallacies in the energy efficiency solution', *Energy Policy*, 18 (1990); George Henderson, Dan Staniaszek, Brian Anderson and Mark Phillipson, 'Energy savings from insulation improvements in electrically heated dwellings in the UK', ECEEE Summer Study Proceedings (2003); Steven Sorrell, 'The rebound effect: an assessment of the evidence for economy-wide energy savings from improved energy efficiency' (London: UKERC, 2007); Mathias Binswanger, 'Technological progress and sustainable development: what about the rebound effect?', *Ecological Economics*, 36:1 (2001); Lee Schipper and Michael Grubb, 'On the rebound? Feedback between energy intensities and energy uses in IEA countries', *Energy Policy*, 28:6 (2000); Harry D. Saunders, 'The Khazzoom-Brookes postulate and neoclassical growth', *Energy Journal*, 13:4 (1992).

27 *Stern Review: The Economics of Climate Change* (2006), <http://webarchive. nationalarchives.gov.uk/+/http:/www.hm-treasury.gov.uk/sternreview_ index.htm>.

28 Kevin Anderson and Alice Bows, Anderson, 'Reframing Climate Change: What does the latest science & emissions tell us about mitigation, adaptation & equity?', talk at Tyndall Centre for Climate Change Research, University of Manchester, November 2009; Kevin Anderson, 'Is avoiding dangerous climate change compatible with economic growth?', presentation at the Tyndall Assembly, Manchester, 2009; and Kevin Anderson and Alice Bows, 'Reframing the climate change challenge in light of post-2000 emission trends', *Philosophical Transactions of the Royal Society A*, 366:1882 (13 November 2008).

29 UNFCCC media release, 'Island nations oppose dismissal of 1.5 degree C concerns'.

30 Anderson and Bows (2008), op. cit.

31 Smith, op. cit.

32 Robert F. Kennedy, Address at the University of Kansas, 18 March 1968. Transcript at <http://www.jfklibrary.org/Research/Ready-Reference/ RFK-Speeches/Remarks-of-Robert-F-Kennedy-at-the-University-of-Kansas-March-18-1968.aspx>.

33 ACLU Ohio, *Prisons for Profit: A Look at Prison Privatization* (2011).

34 See Vicky Peláez, 'The prison industry in the United States: big business or a new form of slavery?' (2008), <http://www.globalresearch.ca/ index.php? context=va&aid=8289>.

35 'Prime Minister's speech on economic growth', 6 January 2011, <http:// www.number10.gov.uk/news/speeches-and-transcripts/2011/01/prime-ministers-speech-on-economic-growth-58486>.

36 Steve Johnson, 'Fund industry "overpaid by $1,300bn"', *Financial Times*, 3 April 2011.

37 Bank for International Settlements, *BIS Annual Report 2010/11*.

3. The Measures

1 NASA Mars Exploration Program media release, 'Mars climate orbiter team finds likely cause of loss', 30 September 1999.

2 NASA History Program Office, 'Project Apollo: A Retrospective Analysis', <http://www.hq.nasa.gov/office/pao/History/Apollomon/Apollo.html>.

3 Jones, *The Plimsoll Sensation*.

4 Quoted in ibid.

5 James Hansen, 'Coal-fired power stations are death factories. Close them', *Observer*, 15 February 2009.

6 Turner, *Roads to Ruin*.

7 Quoted in James A. Rawley with Stephen D. Behrendt, *The Transatlantic Slave Trade: A History* (Lincoln: University of Nebraska Press, 2005).

8 Internal memo by Lawrence H. Summers, Chief Economist of the World Bank, 12 December 1991. See <http://www.whirledbank.org/ourwords/summers.html>.

9 Frances Gibb, 'Trafigura's £30m payout approved after "slops" dumped in Ivory Coast', *The Times*, 24 September 2009.

10 Jones, op. cit.

11 Meinshausen et al., 'Greenhouse-gas emission targets for limiting global warming to 2°C'.

12 Catherine Brahic, 'Humanity's carbon budget set at one trillion tonnes', *New Scientist*, 29 April 2009.

13 Quoted in 'UK pension funds at particular risk of fossil fuel reassessment – analyst', Environmental Finance, 14 April 2011.

14 Mark Campanale, 'Some IPOS should be too hot to handle', 5 October 2010, <http://www.carbontracker.org/news/some-ipos-should-be-too-hot- to-handle>.

15 The campaign for a currency transaction tax is decades old, motivated both as a means to raise additional finance for public expenditure and to stabilise volatile capital markets. In 2001 I co-authored *The Robin Hood Tax*, a report for nef and the development agency War on Want, advocating the tax for both purposes. Years later a campaign of the same name was launched, promoted by groups such as Oxfam and Comic Relief.

16 William D. Nordhaus and James Tobin, 'Is Growth Obsolete?', *Economic Research: Retrospect and Prospect*, vol. 5: Economic Growth, 1972.

17 Longyearbyen, 'Breathing difficulties. A market in need of a miracle', *The Economist*, 3 March 2012.

18 Richard Clarkson and Kathryn Deyes, Government Economic Service Working Paper 140: 'Estimating the Social Cost of Carbon Emissions' (January 2002), <http://www.hm-treasury.gov.uk/d/SCC.pdf>.

19 Richard Price, Simeon Thornton and Stephen Nelson, 'The Social Cost of Carbon and the Shadow Price of Carbon: What they are, and how to use them in economic appraisal in the UK' (December 2007), <http://archive.defra.gov.uk/evidence/series/documents/shadowpriceofcarbon-dec-0712.pdf>.

20 See 'The Economics of Ecosystems and Biodiversity', <http://ec.europa.
eu/environment/nature/biodiversity/economics/index_en.htm>.

21 See table, 'Humanity's Ecological Footprint and Biocapacity Through
Time', <http://www.footprintnetwork.org/images/uploads/2010_NFA_
data_tables.xls>.

22 Rockström et al., 'A safe operating space for humanity'.

23 Andy Coghlan, 'Fishing fleets squander half their catches', *New Scientist*,
15 April 2009.

24 Quoted in Mark Buchanan, 'Prophets of doom: The secret of soothsay-
ing', *New Scientist*, 2 February 2011.

25 Tim Jackson and Peter Victor, 'Productivity: re-thinking productivity
for a steady-state economy', paper for the New Economics Conference:
Laying the Foundations for the New Economic Model, 2010.

26 Office for National Statistics, 'Initial investigation into Subjective Well-
being from the Opinons Survey' (December 2011).

27 Saamah Abdallah, Juliet Michaelson, Sagar Shah, Laura Stoll and Nic
Marks, *Happy Planet Index: 2012 Report – A global index of sustainable well-
being* (London: nef, 2012).

28 Chambers and Chambers, *Unity of Heart*.

29 The International Union for Conservation and Nature Red List identified 5488 species in 2008.

30 Pawlyn, *Biomimicry in Architecture*.

4. The Myth (and reality)

1 Armstrong, *A Short History of Myth*.

2 Ibid.

3 Ibid.

4 Ibid.

5 Interviewed for *High Flyers: How Britain Took to the Air*, documentary
made by Diarmuid Lavery, Leona Coulter and Brian Henry Martin and
broadcast on BBC 4 in 2011.

6 See 'Airline Industry Overview', <http://web.mit.edu/airlines/analysis/
analysis_airline_industry.html>.

7 Agnes Teh,'The Fabulous lives of air miles millionaires', CNN, 21
January 2010.

8 Quoted in Simms and Smith (ed.), *Do Good Lives Have to Cost the Earth?*.

9 See Olsthoorn, 'Carbon dioxide emissions from international aviation:
1950–2050'.

10 Victoria Johnson and Martin Cottingham, *Plane Truths: Do the Economic
Arguments for Aviation Growth Fly?* (London: nef, 2008).

11 Kersely, Lawlor and Cheshire, *Grounded*.

12 See Alice Bows, Paul Upham and Kevin Anderson, *Growth Scenarios for
EU & UK Aviation: Contradictions with Climate Policy*, report for Friends
of the Earth Trust Ltd.

13 See Kevin Anderson and Alice Bows, 'The UK's 2°C Commitment,
Aviation Emissions and the EU', presentation to the Royal Society,
2008.

14 Kevin Anderson, 'Offsetting (& CDM): a guarantee for 100 years or just a clever scam? . . . from a climate change perspective, is offsetting worse than doing nothing?', memorandum, March 2012, Tyndall Centre for Climate Change Research, University of Manchester.

15 'Myths about tourism, air travel and poor people exploded', 30 September 2010, <http://www.aef.org.uk/?p=1116>.

16 Civil Aviation Authority, *UK Business Air Travel: Traffic Trends and Characteristics* (May 2009).

17 Civil Aviation Authority, *Flying on Business – A Study of the UK Business Air Travel Market* (November 2011).

18 Press Association, 'Business jet flights on the rise', 16 October 2011; and Reuters, 'Business flights, budgets seen growing in 2011', 11 March 2011.

19 Kersley, Lawlor and Cheshire, op. cit.

20 Ibid.

21 Buehler and Pucher, 'Sustainable transport in Freiburg'.

22 'Case study summary: City of Ghent, Belgium', <http://www.ashden.org/files/Ghent%20full%20winner.pdf>.

5. Meaning and imagination

1 Rory Cellan-Jones, '#getmehome: Social media and stranded travellers', BBC online, 18 April 2010.

2 Alain de Botton, 'A World without Planes', *Today* programme, BBC Radio 4, 17 April 2010.

3 Sam Jones, 'Iceland volcano: Tales from travellers stranded around the world', *Guardian*, 18 April 2010.

4 Samantha Bomkamp, 'Impact of volcanic ash surfacing for US businesses', Associated Press, 17 April 2010.

5 Ibid.

6 Thomas Homer-Dixon interviewed by Debora MacKenzie, 'Why the demise of civilisation may be inevitable', *New Scientist*, 2 April 2008.

7 Kasser, *The High Price of Materialism*.

8 Kasser and Ahuvia, 'Materialistic values and well-being in business students'.

9 Delhey, 'From materialist to postmaterialist happiness?'.

10 Jody Aked, Nic Marks, Corrina Cordon, Sam Thompson, *Five Ways to Well-being: The Evidence* (London: nef and The Foresight Programme, 2008).

11 Tim Jackson, 'An Economic Reality Check', TED talk July 2010. Transcript at <http://dotsub.com/view/e7a15613-f014-4658-8885-d39da2154fdc/view Transcript/eng>.

6. The Money

1 Schumpeter, *Capitalism, Socialism and Democracy*.

2 Marshall Berman, *All That Is Solid Melts into Air: The Experience of Modernity* (New York: Verso, 1983).

3 Jonathan McCarthy and Richard W. Peach, 'Are home prices the next "bubble"?, *Economic Policy Review*, 10:3 (December 2004).

4 Transcript of UK Budget statement 2007, 21 March 2007, <http://www.direct.gov.uk/en/Nl1/Newsroom/DG_067074>.

5 Jim McTague, 'Looking at Greenspan's Long-Lost Thesis', *Barron's* online, 28 April 2008.

6 Haldane, 'Control rights (and wrongs)'.

7 Sarah Anderson, John Cavanagh, Chuck Collins, Mike Lapham and Sam Pizzigati, 'Executive Excess 2008: How average taxpayers subsidize runaway pay', 25 April 2008, <http://www.ips-dc.org/reports/executive_excess_2008_how_average_taxpayers_subsidize_runaway_pay>.

8 UNCTAD, *World Investment Report 2011: Non-equity Modes of International Production and Development* (New York: United Nations, 2011).

9 Mervyn King, 'Banking: From Bagehot to Basel, and back again', Second Bagehot Lecture, Buttonwood Gathering, New York City, 25 October 2010. Transcript at <http://www.bankofengland.co.uk/publications/speeches/2010/speech455.pdf>.

10 Keynes, 'National Self-Sufficiency'.

11 Galbraith, *Money*.

12 Ben S. Bernanke, 'Deflation: Making Sure "It" Doesn't Happen Here', speech to National Economists Club, Washington, DC, 21 November 2002.

13 See Professor Jacqueline Barnes, Mog Ball, Pamela Meadows, Professor Jay Belsky and the FNP Implementation Research Team, *Nurse-Family Partnership Programme. Second Year Pilot Sites – The Infancy Period*, Department for Children, Schools and Families research report (DCSF-RR166, 2009), <http://www.iscfsi.bbk.ac.uk/projects/files/Second_year.pdf>.

14 Richard Douthwaite, *The Ecology of Money* (Dartington: Green Books, 1999).

15 Haldane and May, 'Systemic risk in banking ecosystems'.

16 See James Ball, 'Bureau publishes comprehensive civil service hospitality database', 17 June 2010, <http://www.thebureauinvestigates.com/2010/06/17/bureau-publishes-comprehensive-civil-service-hospitality-database/>.

17 See 'Minutes of meeting on Goldman Sach settlement', *Guardian*, 11 October 2011, <http://www.guardian.co.uk/business/interactive/2011/oct/11/minutes-meeting-goldman-sachs>; and Andrew Goodall, 'Hartnett denies misleading MPs and says sorry for interest "mistake"', *Tax Journal*, 13 October 2011.

18 Rajeev Syal, 'Goldman Sachs whistleblower threatened with the sack', *Guardian*, 8 December 2011.

19 Mervyn King, op. cit.

20 Reported in the Treasury Select Committee verbatim record: <http://www.publications.parliament.uk/pa/cm201011/cmselect/cmtreasy/uc612-vi/uc61201.htm>. See also Sharlene Goff and George Parker, 'Diamond says time for remorse is over', *Financial Times*, 11 January 2011; and Tim Shipman and Lucy Farndon, Barclay's boss says banks

should no longer be sorry for crisis (24 hours after his '£9m' bonus is revealed), *Daily Mail*, 12 January 2011.

21 Mervyn King, speech to Scottish business organisations, Edinburgh, 20 October 2009. Transcript at <http://www.bankofengland.co.uk/publications/speeches/2009/speech406.pdf>.

22 Andrew G. Haldane, 'The $100 billion question', comments given at the Institute of Regulation and Risk, Hong Kong, 30 March 2010. Transcript at <http://www.bankofengland.co.uk/publications/speeches/2010/speech433.pdf>.

23 Adair Turner, speech at the City Banquet, Mansion House, London, 22 September 2009. Transcript at <http://www.fsa.gov.uk/library/communication/ speeches/2009/0922_at.shtml>.

24 Adair Turner, 'What do banks do, what should they do and what public policies are needed to ensure best results for the real economy?', speech at Cass Business School, 17 March 2010. Transcript at <http://www.fsa.gov.uk/pubs/speeches/at_17mar10.pdf>.

25 Andrew Simms and Tony Greenham, *Where Did Our Money Go? Building a Banking System Fit for Purpose*, October 2010, <http://neweconomics.org/sites/neweconomics.org/files/Where_did_our_money_go.pdf>.

26 More detail can be found in the wealth of submissions to the Independent Commission on Banking readily available on the internet (except that the majority of submissions from the major banks whose contributions are held to be largely confidential), or visit the finance section of the nef website

27 Derek French, *Branch Network Reduction Report 2010* (London: Campaign for Community Banking, 2009)

28 Ministry of Justice, Mortgage and landlord possession statistics, <http://www.justice.gov.uk/publications/statistics-and-data/civil-justice/mortgage-possession.htm>.

29 Tim Lezard, 'Workers today earning less than counterparts 30 years ago', *Union News*, 30 January 2012.

30 Post Bank Coalition, *The Case for a Post Bank* (2011).

31 Guy Rubin, Polly Raymond and John Taylor, *The Last Post: The Social and Economic Impact of Changes to the Postal Service in Manchester* (London: nef, 2006).

32 Suggested by Nick Silver in *Towards a Royal Bank of Sustainability: Protecting Taxpayers' Interests; Cutting Carbon Risk* (RBS report, 2009).

33 Meeker-Lowry, *Invested in the Common Good*.

7. The Memories

1 'Background Note: Nauru', 13 March 2012, <http://www.state.gov/r/pa/ei/bgn/ 16447.htm>.

2 Quoted in McDaniel and Gowdy, *Paradise for Sale*.

3 Interview for *Channel 4 News*, 27 January 2002.

4 McDaniel and Gowdy, op. cit.

5 Diamond, *Collapse*.

6 McGuire, *Waking the Giant*.

7 Tainter, *The Collapse of Complex Societies*.
8 Ibid.
9 Goldsworthy, *The Fall of the West*.
10 Tainter, op. cit.
11 Ibid.
12 Ibid.
13 Johan Rockström, Will Steffen, Kevin Noone, et al., 'Planetary boundaries: Exploring the safe operating space for humanity', *Ecology and Society* 14:2 (2009).
14 Quoted in Walton and Seddon, *Free Markets and Food Riots*.
15 E. P. Thompson, 'The Moral Economy of the English Crowd in the Eighteenth Century', *Past and Present* 50:1 (1971), 78–186.
16 Quoted in Walton and Seddon, op. cit.
17 Ibid.
18 Theodore Roosevelt, letter to Winthrop Murray Crane (Governor of Massachusetts), 22 October 1902, in Morrison (ed.), *The Letters of Theodore Roosevelt*, vol. 3.
19 Theodore Roosevelt, letter to Seth Low, 3 October 1902, in Morrison (ed.), op. cit.
20 Draft and final copy of opening address to 3 October 1902 Conference, Theodore Roosevelt Papers (TRP); Theodore Roosevelt, letter to Mrs W. S. Cowles, 16 October 1902, TRP; Theodore Roosevelt, letter to Winthrop Murray Crane, op. cit.
21 See Griffiths and Brock, 'Twentieth century mortality trends in England and Wales'.
22 *On the State of the Public Health During Six Years of War: Report of the Chief Medical Officer of the Ministry of Health, 1939–45*, (London: HMSO 1946).
23 A full history can be found in Stallibrass, *Being Me and Also Us*.
24 *Hansard*, House of Commons, 12 November 1936.
25 Sayers, *Financial Policy 1939–45*.
26 Quoted in ibid.
27 Longmate, *How We Lived Then*.
28 Hancock and Gowing, *The Lessons of the British War Economy*.
29 Addison, *The Road to 1945*.
30 Foreword to Felton, *Civilian Supplies In Wartime Britain*.
31 Roodhouse, 'Rationing returns'.
32 Ibid.
33 Bernard Porter, 'We're Not Jittery', *London Review of Books*, 32:13 (8 July 2010).
34 Addison and Crang (ed.), *Listening to Britain*.
35 Ibid.
36 Porter, op. cit.
37 Mike Davis 'Home-front ecology: What our grandparents can teach us about saving the world', *Sierra* (June/July 2007).
38 Ibid.
39 Ibid.
40 United States Code, Title 15 – Commerce and Trade, Chapter 16B:

Federal Energy Administration, Subchapter I, Section 761, Congressional Declaration of Purpose.

41 Quoted in Davis, op. cit.

42 Quoted in ibid.

43 Mario Alberto Arrastía Avila with Laurie Guevara-Stone, 'Teaching Cuba's Energy Revolution', *Solar Today* (January/February 2009).

44 For an in-depth exploration of the Cuban transition to a more sustainable and largely self-sufficient food system, see Julia Wright, 'Falta Petroleo!: Perspectives on the Emergence of a more Ecological Farming and Food System in Post-crisis Cuba' (2005), unpublished doctoral thesis, Wageningen University.

45 Mario Gonzalez Novo and Catherine Murphy, 'Urban agriculture in the city of Havana: a popular response to a crisis' in N. Bakker, M. Dubbeling, S. Guendel, U. Sabel Koschella and H. de Zeeuw (eds), *Growing Cities, Growing Food: Urban Agriculture on the Policy Agenda: A Reader on Urban Agriculture* (Feldafing: DSE, 2000).

46 Franco et al., 'Impact of energy intake, physical activity, and population-wide weight loss on cardiovascular disease and diabetes mortality in Cuba, 1980–2005'.

47 Riley, 'An Ethnography of "Community Development" in a Neighbourhood of Havana, Cuba'.

48 See Derrick Nunnally, 'Recalling the suburban gas riots of 1979', *Philadelphia Inquirer*, 29 May 2008.

49 United States Code, op. cit.

50 Richard Heinberg, 'Peak Denial', 2 July 2012, <http://www.postcarbon.org/blog-post/985668-peak-denia>.

51 Iverson et al., *Response of Washington State Residents to Higher Transportation Costs and Energy Shortages*.

52 Defence Analytical Services and Advice figures quoted by Dr Stuart Parkinson in 'Arms Conversion for a Secure and Sustainable Society', presentation at Desmond Tutu Centre for War and Peace Studies, Liverpool Hope University, 31 March 2011, <http://www.sgr.org.uk/sites/sgr.org.uk/files/Arms_Conversion_Liverpool_Mar11.pdf>.

53 Ministry of Defence report, quoted in *Sunday Times*, 23 August 2009.

54 Quoted in Parkinson, op. cit.

55 Linda J. Bilmes and Joseph E. Stiglitz, 'The Iraq War Will Cost Us $3 Trillion, and Much More', *Washington Post*, 9 March 2008.

56 Andrei Shleifer, 'Seven things I learned about transition from communism', 5 February 2012, <http://www.voxeu.org/index.php?q=node/ 7593>.

57 Colten and Sumpter, 'Social memory and resilience in New Orleans'.

58 See Barthel et al., 'Social–ecological memory in urban gardens – retaining the capacity for management of ecosystem services'.

8. The Mechanisms

1 'Impact of September 2000 fuel price protests on UK critical infrastructure', Public Safety Canada Incident Analysis: IA05-001, 25 January 2005, <http://www.publicsafety.gc.ca/prg/em/ccirc/2005/ia05-001-eng.aspx>

2 The NHS serves more than 300 million meals per year. The Strategy Unit, *Food Matters: Towards a Strategy for the 21st Century* (London: Cabinet Office, 2008).

3 Nick Robinson, 'Fuel protests: governing the ungovernable?', *Parliamentary Affairs*, 56:3 (2003), 423–40.

4 United States Department of Agriculture, Agricultural Research Service, 'Honey bees colony collapse disorder (CCD)', <http://www.ars.usda.gov/News/ docs.htm?docid=15572>, and 'Colony Collapse Disorder: A complex buzz' (May 2008) , <http://www.ars.usda.gov/is/AR/archive/may08/colony0508.htm>.

5 See Cox-Foster and vanEngelsdorp, 'Solving the mystery of the vanishing bees', *Scientific American*, March 2009.

6 Ibid.

7 James Smith, 'Colony collapse disorder and the human bee', 4 November 2010, <http://www.conspirazzi.com/colony-collapse-disorder-and-the-human-bee/>.

8 'Diseases could wipe out honeybees by 2018', *Daily Telegraph*, 10 March 2008.

9 'Hunger on the rise: soaring prices add 75 million people to global hunger rolls', UN FAO Newsroom, 18 September 2008. The estimated number of undernourished people worldwide rose to 923 million people in 2007.

10 See 'Countries in Crisis Requiring External Assistance', *Crop Prospects and Food Situation*, 2 (April 2008), <http://www.fao.org/docrep/010/ai465e/ai465e02.htm>.

11 Tony C. Dreibus, 'Wheat Surges to Record as U.S. Supply May Drop to 60-Year Low', Bloomberg, 8 February 2008.

12 David Bennett, 'Growers and economists push for strategic grain reserves', Delta Farm Press, 4 August 2008, <http://deltafarmpress.com/corn/grain-forum-0804/>; Sue Kirchhoff, 'Surplus US food supplies dry up', *USA Today*, 2 May 2008.

13 Isabel Oakeshott, 'Government asks stores to stockpile food to overcome hauliers strike', *Sunday Times*, 6 July 2008.

14 See Defra, *Agriculture in the United Kingdom 2006* (Norwich: The Stationery Office, 2007).

15 Robin Maynard (15 September 2008), 'Response from the Soil Association to Defra discussion paper, Ensuring the UK's Food Security in a Changing World', Soil Association.

16 Katja Gloger, 'George Soros: "We are in the midst of the worst financial crisis in 30 years', *Stern*, 3 July 2008.

17 Kenneth Schortgen Jr, 'George Soros making a move to control food and grain production', *Examiner*, 30 March 2011.

18 Javier Blas, 'Glencore and Xstrata deal could reshape industry', *Financial Times*, 7 February 2012.

19 Brett Scott, *Barclays Plc & Agricultural Commodity Derivatives*, World Development Movement (2011).

20 Ian Sample, 'Oil: The final warning', *New Scientist*, 25 June 2008.

21 See <www.peakoil.net>.

22 International Energy Agency Medium Term Oil Report, 'Despite slow-ing oil demand, IEA sees continued market tightness over the medium term', 1 July 2008.

23 John Vidal, 'WikiLeaks cables: Saudi Arabia cannot pump enough oil to keep a lid on prices', *Guardian*, 8 February 2011.

24 Neil King Jr, 'Saudi industrial drive strains oil export role', *Wall Street Journal*, 12 December 2007.

25 See Andrew Simms and Victoria Johnson, *Chinadependence: The Second UK Interdependence Report* (London: nef, 2007) and Andrew Simms, Victoria Johnson and Joe Smith, *The Consumption Explosion: The Third UK Interdependence Report* (London: nef, Open University and Geographical Association, 2009)

26 Jeremy Leggett, 'Dawn of an energy famine', *Guardian*, 2 May 2008.

27 Sample, op. cit.

28 Simms, *Tescopoly*; Norman Baker, MP, *How Green Is Your Supermarket? A Guide for Best Practice* (March 2004).

29 Anthony J. McMichael, John W. Powles, Colin D. Butler and Ricardo Uauy, 'Food, livestock production, energy, climate change, and health', *Lancet*, 370:9594 (2007).

30 Henning Steinfeld, Pierre Gerber, Tom Wassenaar, Vincent Castel, Mauricio Rosales and Cees de Haan, *Livestock's Long Shadow: Environ-mental Issues and Options* (Rome: FAO, 2006). The figure is around 18 per cent, measured in CO_2e, including transportation of livestock and production of feed. Increasingly meat based diets stand to worsen this problem.

31 Mario Giampietro and David Pimentel, 'The tightening conflict: popu-lation, energy use, and the ecology of agriculture' (1994), <http://www.dieoff.com/page69.htm>.

32 Pimentel and Pimentel, 'Sustainability of meat-based and plant-based diets and the environment'.

33 Cornell University press release, 'US could feed 800 million people with grain that livestock eat, Cornell ecologist advises animal scientists', 7 August 1997.

34 Steinfeld et al., op. cit.

35 Compassion in World Farming, *Global Warning: Climate Change and Farm Animal Welfare* (Godalming: Compassion in World Farming, 2008).

36 Defra, *Agriculture in the UK* (2004),

37 See Defra, 'Energy use in organic farming systems', 2000, Defra report OFO182, 2000, and Adrian Williams, 'Developing and delivering envi-ronmental Life-Cycle Assessment (LCA) of agricultural systems', Defra project ISO222.

38 Soil Association press release, 'Soaring prices and climate change expose fertilisers as economically and environmentally unsustainable', 12 June 2008.

39 WHO facts, http://www.who.int/dietphysicalactivity/publications/facts/obesity/en/

40 Phil Edwards and Ian Roberts, 'Transport policy is food policy', *Lancet*, 37:9639 (2008).

41 Ian Roberts, 'How the obesity epidemic is aggravating global warming', *New Scientist*, 27 June 2007.

42 Walpole et al., 'The weight of nations'.

43 John Lipsky, First Deputy Managing Director, IMF, speaking at the Council on Foreign Relations, 8 May 2008. Transcript at <http://www.imf.org/external/np/speeches/2008/050808.htm>.

44 FAO Director-General, Jacques Diouf, speaking at the Rome summit, 3 June 2008. See <http://www.fao.org/newsroom/en/news/2008/1000853/index.html>.

45 Oakland Institute press release, 'WTO Doha round will not solve the global food crisis: civil society calls for real solutions', 3 June 2008.

46 Food and Ethics Council, June 2008. The IMF has commented that increasing demand for biofuels explains '20 to 30 per cent' of recent food price increases. This is corroborated by the International Food Policy Research Institute (IFPRI), which puts the contribution of biofuels to the crisis at 30 per cent. The Commission's conservative estimate that the EU 10 per cent target will lead to a 3–6 per cent price increase in cereals could result in up to 100 million extra people in hunger by 2020.

47 Lobell and Field, 'Global scale climate–crop yield relationships and the impacts of recent warming'.

48 Burke et al., 'Modeling the recent evolution of global drought and projections for the twenty-first century with the Hadley Centre climate model'.

49 'Climate squeeze could wipe out vital crops', *New Scientist*, 8 June 2011.

50 Quoted in Susanna Rustin, 'Has the green movement lost its way?', *Guardian*, 2 July 2011.

51 Professor Andy Stirling, 'No definitive answers in the nuclear debate', letter to the editor, *Guardian*, 6 April 2011.

52 These questions were first suggested by Professor Jules Pretty.

53 UN Department for Economic and Social Affairs, *World Population Prospects: The 2010 Revision, Highlights and Advance Tables* (New York: United Nations, 2011).

54 Foresight, *The Future of Food and Farming* (London: The Government Office for Science, 2011).

55 Ibid.

56 Mark W. Rosegrant, Siwa Msangui, Timothy Sulser and Claudia Ringler, 'Future scenarios for agriculture: plausible futures to 2030 and key trends in agricultural growth', background paper prepared for the *World Development Report 2008*.

57 J. P. W. Rivers, J. F. J. Holt, J. A. Seaman and M. R. Bowden, 'Lessons for Epidemiology from the Ethiopian famines', *Annales de la Société belge de medécine tropicale*, 56 (1976).

58 International Labour Organization, *Global Employment Trends for Youth: 2011 Update* (Geneva: ILO Publications, 2011).

59 Oksana Nagayets, 'Small Farms: Current Status and Key Trends', brief prepared for the International Food Policy Research Institute Future of Small Farms Research Workshop, Wye College, 26–29 June 2005.

60 J. P. Reganold, L. F. Elliott and Y. L. Unger, 'Long-term effects of organic and conventional farming on soil erosion', *Nature*, 330 (1987).

61 Jelle Bruinsma (ed.), *World Agriculture: Towards 2015/2030 – An FAO Perspective* (Rome: FAO, 2002).

62 Pretty and Koohafkan, *Land and Agriculture*.

63 UNEP-UNCTAD Capacity-building Task Force on Trade, Environment and Development, *Organic Agriculture and Food Security in Africa* (Geneva and New York: United Nations, 2008).

64 Kevan Bundell, *Securing Future Food: Towards Ecological Food Provision* (London: UK Food Group, 2010).

65 C. Reij, G. Tappan and A. Belemvire, 'Changing land management practices and vegetation on the Central Plateau of Burkina Faso (1968–2002)', *Journal of Arid Environments*, 63:2 (2005).

66 Erika Styger, Goumar Aboubacrine, Malick Ag Attaher and Norman Uphoff, 'The system of rice intensification as a sustainable agricultural innovation: Introducing, adapting and scaling up a system of rice intensification practices in the Timbuktu region of Mali', *International Journal of Agricultural Sustainability*, 9:1 (2011).

67 Beeby, J. Doran and J. Jeavons, 'Biologically Intensive Agriculture – Renewing Earth and Its People', 18th World Congress of Soil Science, 2006.

68 Food and Agriculture Organization, 'Small-scale irrigation for arid zones: Principles and options' (1997), <http://www.fao.org/docrep/W3094E/W3094 E00.htm>

69 Speaking at the Intelligence Squared US debate, April 2010. See <http://vimeo.com/10930957>.

70 See profile at <http://www.lobbywatch.org/profile1.asp?PrId=73>.

71 Interviews and transcripts at: *Breakfast With Frost*, 19 August 2001 <http://news.bbc.co.uk/1/hi/programmes/breakfast_with_frost/1499148.stm>; BBC News 'Rural recovery chief under fire', 13 August 2001, <http://news.bbc.co.uk/1/hi/uk_politics/1488468.stm>; and Anne Perkins and Patrick Wintour, 'Half of farms "will close by 2020', *Guardian*, 13 August 2001.

72 *Report of the International Conference on Organic Agriculture and Food Security*, Rome, 3–5 May 2007, <ftp://ftp.fao.org/paia/organicag/ofs/OFS report.pdf>.

73 Bundell, op. cit.

74 Tim LaSalle and Paul Hepperly, *Regenerative Organic Farming: A Solution to Global Warming* (Kurtztown: Rodale Institute, 2008).

75 'King throws out challenge over GM crops', *Scotsman*, 21 January 2010.

76 Zia Haq, 'Ministry blames Bt cotton for farmer suicides', *Hindustan Times*, 26 March 2012.

77 Wang et al., 'Bt-cotton and secondary pests'.

78 Yanhui Lu, Kongming Wu, Yuying Jiang, Yuyuan Guo and Nicolas Desneux, 'Widespread adoption of Bt cotton and insecticide decrease promotes biocontrol services', *Nature*, 19:487 (2012).

79 Jack Kaskey, 'Monsanto corn injured by early rootworm feeding in Illinois', Bloomberg, 15 June 2012.

80 Suzie Horne, 'Cereals 2012: GM corn – not a "panacea"', *Farmers Weekly*, 14 June 2012.

81 Navdanya International, *The GMO Emperor Has No Clothes: A Global Citzens Report on the State of GMOs – False Promises, Failed Technologies* (2012). Available at <http://permaculturenews.org/2012/08/20/the-gmo-emperor-has-no-clothes/>.

82 Charles M. Benbrook, 'Impacts of genetically engineered crops on pesticide use in the US – the first sixteen years', *Environmental Sciences Europe*, 24:24 (2012).

83 Andrew Simms, Julian Oram and Petra Kjell, *The Price of Power: Poverty, Climate Change, the Coming Energy Crisis and the Renewable Revolution* (London: nef, 2004).

84 'Maldives maps its renewable energy potential', 15 December 2010, <http://www.renewableenergyfocus.com/view/14696/maldives-maps-its-renewable-energy-potential/>.

85 'Case study summary: Isle of Eigg Heritage Trust, Scotland', <http://www.ashden.org/files/reports/Isle%20of%20Eigg%20case%20study.pdf>.

86 'Head-to-head: Nuclear power', BBC Radio 4, 29 November 2005. Transcript at <http://news.bbc.co.uk/1/hi/uk_politics/4481380.stm>.

87 John Vidal, 'An ill wind?', *Guardian*, 7 May 2004.

88 The Offshore Valuation Group, *The Offshore Valuation: A Valuation of the UK's Offshore Renewable Energy Resource* (Machynlleth: Public Interest Research Centre, 2010).

89 Andrew Simms, Petra Kjell and David Woodward, *Mirage and Oasis: Energy Choices in an Age of Global Warming: The Trouble with Nuclear Power and the Potential of Renewable Energy* (London: nef, 2005).

90 Thomas B. Johansson, Kes McCormick, Lena Neij and Wim Turkenburg, 'The Potentials of Renewable Energy', Thematic Background Paper, International Conference for Renewable Energies, Bonn, January 2004.

91 Simms, Kjell and Woodward, op. cit.

92 Sorrell et al., *Global Oil Depletion*.

93 Murray and King, 'Oil's tipping point has passed'.

94 Christopher Helman, 'CERAWeek: Total's upstream chief says peak oil is around the corner', *Forbes*, 6 March 2012.

95 Kate Mackenzie, 'Marginal oil production costs are heading towards $100/barrel', *Financial Times*, 2 May 2012.

96 'Some Transition reflections on George Monbiot's announcement that "we were wrong on peak oil"', Transition Culture, 4 July 2012, <http://transition culture.org/2012/07/04/transition-reflections-on-george-monbiots-announcement-that-we-were-wrong-on-peak-oil/>.

97 Jaromir Benes, Marcelle Chauvet, Ondra Kamenik, Michael Kumhof, Douglas Laxton, Susanna Mursula and Jack Selody, *The Future of Oil: Geology versus Technology*, IMF Working Paper WP/12/109, 2012.

98 Presentations of forenoon of day two (Thursday), 10th Annual ASPO Conference, Vienna, 30 May–1 June 2012. Available at <http://www.aspo2012.at/conference-presentations/day2part1/>.

99 Sylvia Pfeifer, 'Rising oil price threatens fragile recovery', *Financial Times*, 4 January 2011.

100 Joint report by IEA, OPEC, OECD and World Bank on fossil-fuel and other energy subsidies: An update of the G20 Pittsburgh and Toronto Commitments: Prepared for the G20 Meeting of Finance Ministers and Central Bank Governors (Paris, 14–15 October 2011) and the G20 Summit (Cannes, 3–4 November 2011).

101 Oil Change International, 'No time to waste: The urgent need for transparency in fossil fuel subsidies' (2012), <http://priceofoil.org/wp-content/uploads/ 2012/05/1TFSFIN.pdf>.

102 Jacobson and Delucchi, 'A Path to Sustainable Energy by 2030'.

103 Sustainable Development Commission, *The Role of Nuclear Power in a Low Carbon Economy: Paper 2: Reducing CO2 Emissions – Nuclear and the Alternatives* (2006).

104 Sustainable Development Commission, *The Role of Nuclear Power in a Low Carbon Economy* (2006).

105 Sustainable Development Commission press release, 'Nuclear power won't fix it', 5 March 2006.

106 WWF, Ecofys and OMA, *The Energy Report*.

107 Greenpeace UK, *Decentralising Power*.

108 Amory B. Lovins, Imran Sheikh and Alex Markevich, *Nuclear Power: Climate Fix or Folly?* (Snowmass: Rocky Mountain Institute, 2008, revised edn).

109 Joe Romm, 'France imports UK electricity as summer heatwave puts a third of its nukes out of action', *Thinkprogress*, 6 July 2009.

110 'German power exports to France increasing', *Renewables International*, 6 February 2012.

111 Hoffmann, *Some Reflections on Climate Change, Green Growth Illusions and Development Space*.

112 House of Lords Science and Technology Committee, *Renewable Energy*.

113 Cabinet Office, *The Energy Review*.

114 Jacobson, 'Review of solutions to global warming, air pollution, and energy security'.

115 Stirling, op. cit.

116 Energy Saving Trust, *The Elephant in the Living Room: How Our Appliances and Gadgets Are Trampling the Green Dream – An Update to The Rise of the Machines* (London: Energy Saving Trust, 2011).

117 Kurt Vonnegut, 'Cold Turkey', *In These Times*, 10 May 2004.

9. The Message

1 R. Sutherland, 'We can't run away from the ethical debates in marketing', *Market Leader*, Q1, 2010.

2 WPP press release, 'GroupM forecasts 2011 global ad spending to increase 4.8%', 6 July 2011.

3 Eli Clifton, 'FPI hides massive military spending growth by framing DoD budget as a percentage of GDP and total federal spending', *Thinkprogress*, 28 July 2011.

4 'Big shift to online ad spend in $40b global audo ad market by 2011', *MarketingCharts*, 14 December 2007.

5 UNEP press release, 'UNEP report spotlights economic benefits of boosting funding for forests', 5 June 2011.

6 Bargh and Chartrand, 'The unbearable automacity of being'.

7 Sarah Boseley and Rajeev Syal, 'Alcohol pricing loses out as super strength drinks lobby triumphs', *Guardian*, 16 February 2011.

8 Nick Sheron, Chris Hawkey and Ian Gilmore, 'Projections of alcohol deaths – a wake-up call', *Lancet*, 377:9774 (16 April 2011).

9 Maximilien Nayaradou, *Advertising and economic growth*, doctoral thesis (2006).

10 See Albert and Reid, *The Contribution of the Advertising Industry to the UK Economy*.

11 Tom Heap, 'Royal Mail delivering "human tragedy" of scam mail', *BBC Panorama* online, 4 July 2011, <http://news.bbc.co.uk/panorama/hi/front_page/newsid_9525000/9525992.stm>.

12 Ofgem, 'Simpler energy tariffs', factsheet 107, 14 October 2011.

13 Sylvia Pfeifer, 'Ofgen accuses Big Six over complex tariffs', *Financial Times*, 21 March 2011.

14 Catherine West, '0845 call charges still too complex', *Which?*, 17 December 2010.

15 Interview with Stuart Ewen, author of *PR! A Social History of Spin*, quoted at Corporate Watch UK, 'Public relations and lobbying industry: An Overview' (2003), <http://www.corporatewatch.org/?lid=1570>.

16 Richard Edelman, 'Hit me with your best shot, again and again', 7 August 2006, <http://www.edelman.com/p/6-a-m/hit-me-with-your-best-shot-again-and-again/>.

17 *Department of Defense Dictionary of Military and Associated Terms*, as at 12 April 2001 (amended 17 December 2003). The term has been removed from more recent versions of the dictionary but is still cited widely elsewhere, for example in the glossary of the US *Air Force Intelligence and Security Doctrine*.

18 'MDB's Divide-and-Conquer Strategy to Defeat Activists', *PR Watch* 1:1, 1993, p. 5. PR Watch is published by the Centre for Media and democracy, 3318 Gregory Street, Madison, WI 53711, USA.

19 This is the full source and explanation given by George Monbiot on his website: Andrew Dimock, head of the Bivings Groups Online Marketing and Promotions Division, 'Viral Marketing: How to Infect the World', 1 April 2002. The original article was at <http://www.thebivingsreport.com/search_view_full_article.php?article_id=73> but was removed, with a subsequent note to says it had been 'recently edited for clarification', altering its original meaning and re-posted at <http://www.bivingsreport.com/2002/viral-marketing-how-to-infect-the-world/>. Extracts from the original version are available at <http://www.lobbywatch.org/profile1.asp?PrId=166>.

20 Jim Pickard and Tim Bradshaw, 'Media groups reject Big Society request', *Financial Times*, 1 February 2011.

21 Justin Lewis, 'The power of advertising: a threat to our way of life', openDemocracy, 18 June 2011.

22 Dan Hind, 'The Trouble with Media Reform', New Left Project, 22 August 2011.

23 'Ex-Ministers face Parliament ban over lobbying breach', Channel 4 News, 9 December 2010. Transcript at <http://www.channel4.com/news/ex-ministers-face-parliament-ban-over-lobbying-breach>.

24 'An advertising tax for the UK?', PIRC briefing, December 2011.

25 American President: A Reference Source, Miller Center, University of Virginia.

26 'Billboard control is good for business', Scenic America, <http://www.scenic.org/billboards-a-sign-control/the-truth-about-billboards/100-billboard-control-is-good-for-business>.

27 According to a five-year study of 35 cities conducted by the Mississippi Research and Development Center, quoted at Ibid.

28 David Evan Harris, 'São Paulo: A city without ads', Adbusters, 3 August 2007.

29 Hannah Godfrey, 'Paris to cut amount of advertising on streets by 30%', *Guardian*, 22 June 2011.

30 Haldane and May, 'Systemic risk in banking ecosystems'.

31 Robin McKie, 'Wisdom of grandparents helped rise of prehistoric man', *Observer*, 24 July 2011.

32 Ibid.

33 Herman E. Daly, 'From adjustment to sustainable development: The obstacle of free trade', in Ralph Nader (ed.), *The Case Against 'Free Trade': GATT, NAFTA, and the Globalization of Corporate Power* (Berkeley: North Atlantic Books, 1993).

34 David Whiting and Marianne de Trey, *Marianne de Trey* (Shepton Beauchamp: Richard Dennis, 2007).

35 Illich, *Tools for Conviviality*.

36 Professor Felicia A. Huppert, *Psychological Wellbeing: Evidence Regarding its Causes and Consequences*, Foresight Project State-of-Science Review: SR-X2, <http://www.bis.gov.uk/assets/foresight/docs/mental-capital/sr-x2_mcwv2.pdf>.

37 Ibid.

38 Keith Sward, *The Legend of Henry Ford* (New York: Rinehart, 1948).

39 Adyita Chakrabortty, 'Why our jobs are getting worse', *Guardian*, 31 August 2010.

40 OECD Forum, *Growing Income Inequality in OECD Countries: What Drives It and How Can Policy Tackle It?* (2011).

41 Ruth Potts, 'Reconnecting work with the art of living', *Guardian*, 1 September 2010.

42 Jesse Collings and Sir John L. Green, *Life of the Rt Hon Jesse Collings* (London: Longmans, Green, 1920).

43 See FRN: Furniture Re-Use Network: <http://www.frn.org.uk/about-frn.html>.

44 James K. Rilling, Andrea L. Glenn, Meeta R. Jairam, Giuseppe Pagnoni, David R. Goldsmith, Hanie A. Elfenbein and Scott O. Lilienfeld, 'Neural correlates of social cooperation and non-cooperation as a function of psychopathy', *Biological Psychiatry*, 61 (2007).

45 T. Kirkwood, J. Bond, C. May, I. McKeith, and M. Teh, *Mental Capital through Life: Future Challenges* (London: Foresight Mental Capital and Wellbeing Project, 2008).

46 Ben Hoyle, 'Revival of ancient tradition of storytelling draws in the crowds', *The Times*, 11 August 2009.

47 Naomi Colvin and George Barda, 'The fight for democratic change can't be left to Occupy', *Guardian*, 28 February 2012.

48 Paul Harris, 'Detroit gets growing', *Observer*, 11 July 2010.

49 Ackerman, *The Potential for Urban Agriculture in New York City*.

50 Gordon and Chatterton, *Taking Back Control*.

51 Tracy McVeigh, 'Free food, caring and sharing: new spirit of community in Yorkshire', *Observer*, 6 May 2012.

52 Rachel Donadio, 'Battered by economic crisis, Greeks turn to barter networks', *New York Times*, 1 October 2011.

53 Wendell Berry, *What Are People For?: Essays* (Berkeley: Counterpoint, 1990).

54 Quoted in Reed F. Noss and Allen Y. Cooperrider, *Saving Nature's Legacy: Protecting and Restoring Biodiversity* (Washington, DC: Island Press, 1994)

10 Mutual interest

1 Rakesh Kumar, Parag Jawale, Shalini Tandon, 'Economic impact of climate change on Mumbai, India', *Regional Health Forum* 12:1 (2008).

2 Interview with Professor Matthew Gandy. See also Gandy, 'Landscapes of disaster'.

3 Interviewed in *Mumbai: Liquid City – water, landscape and social formation in twenty-first century Mumbai*, film by Dr Matthew Gandy, Department of Geography, UCL, and the Arts and Humanities Research Council.

4 Benedict Brogan, 'It's time to celebrate Empire, says Brown', *Daily Mail*, 15 January 2005.

5 Peter Aughton, *Bristol: A People's History* (Lancaster: Carnegie, 2003).

6 Morgan, 'Shipping patterns and the Atlantic trade of Bristol, 1749–1770'.

7 Boyle, *The Tyranny of Numbers*.

8 Entry for 15 September 1786 in *The Journal of the Rev. John Wesley* (ed. Nehemiah Curnock), vol. 7 (London: R. Culley, 1909–16, 8 vols).

9 Aughton, op. cit.

10 Chang, *Kicking Away the Ladder*.

11 Alfred Maizels, *UNCTAD X: High-Level Round Table on Trade and Development Directions for the Twenty-First Century, Bangkok 12 February 2000: Economic Dependence on Commodities* (Geneva: UNCTAD, 2000).

12 UNCTAD, *Trade and Development Report 1999* (Geneva: UNCTAD, 1999).

13 Ambassador Vijay S. Makhan, Assistant Secretary General OAU/AEC, statement at UNCTAD X, Bangkok, 12–19 February 2000.

14 Joseph Stiglitz, 'What I learned at the World Economic Crisis', *New Republic*, 17 April 2000.

15 This calculation was prepared for the 2006 nef report *Growth Isn't Working*, by David Woodward and Andrew Simms, when the adult minimum wage was £5.05.

16 Richard Wilkinson, 'Inequality and the wellbeing of adults and childhood in rich countries', in ECSWE/Alliance for Childhood European Network Group, *Improving the Quality of Childhood in Europe 2011*, vol. 2 (ECSWE: Forest Row, 2011).

17 Pickett and Wilkinson, *The Spirit Level*.

18 Ibid.

19 ILO, *World of Work Report 2008*.

20 See Pickett and Wilkinson, op. cit.

21 James S. Henry, *The Price of Offshore Revisited: New Estimates for 'Missing' Global Private Wealth, Income, Inequality, and Lost Taxes* (2012), <http://www.taxjustice.net/cms/upload/pdf/Price_of_Offshore_Revisited_26072012.pdf>.

22 Kohn, *Punished by Rewards*.

23 Pink, *Drive*.

24 Deborah Hargreaves, foreword to *More for Less: What Has Happened to Pay at the Top and Does It Matter?* Interim report of the High Pay Commission, May 2011.

25 Quoted in Incomes Data Services press release, 'FTSE-100 bosses see earnings rise 55%', 29 October 2010.

26 Emily Dugan, 'Salaries for top executives are rocketing "out of control"', *Independent on Sunday*, 15 May 2011.

27 See salary figures at <http://www.glassdoor.com/Salary/JPMorgan-Chase-Salaries-E145.htm>.

28 Lawlor, Kersley and Steed, *A Bit Rich*.

29 Daniel Boffey, 'Pay gap is too wide, say two-thirds of Britons', *Observer*, 5 June 2011.

30 Norton and Ariely, 'Building a Better America – One Wealth Quintile at a Time'.

31 OECD, *How's Life? Measuring Well-Being* (Paris: OECD, 2011).

32 M. S. Swaminathan, *Caring for the Future: Making the Next Decades Provide a Life worth Living – Report of the Independent Commission on Population and Quality of Life* (Oxford: Oxford University Press, 1996)

33 Juan Somavia, Director General of ILO, to the High Level Round Table with Heads of United Nations Agencies, Programmes and Related Institutions, UNCTAD X, Bangkok, 12 February 2000.

34 Philip Aldrick, 'UK needs rich to get richer, OBR finds', *Telegraph*, 14 July 2011.

35 Rogers, 'Inequality'.

36 World Bank, 'An update to the World Bank's estimates of consumption poverty in the developing world' (2012).

37 OECD, *Governance in China (China in the Global Economy)* (Paris: OECD, 2005).

38 Quoted in *Business Week*, 6 December 2004.

39 David Gow, 'China is targeting hi-tech jobs, EU warns', *Guardian*, 13 October 2005.

40 Richard Ernsberger Jr, with R. M. Schneiderman, Karen Miller Lowry, Ron Moreau and Sudip Mazumdar, 'The Big Squeeze: A "second wave" of off-shoring could threaten middle-income, white-collar and skilled blue-collar jobs', *Newsweek*, 30 May 2005.

41 Chris Buckley, 'China says it is world's top greenhouse gas emitter', Reuters, 23 November 2010.

42 Defra, 'UK's carbon footprint 1990–2009'. See also University of York press release, 'Carbon dioxide emissions associated with UK consumption increase', 2 July 2008.

43 Dennis Pamlin and Long Baijin, *Re-Think: China's outward investment flows* (Gland, WWF International: 2007). The government's sustainability strategy formulated in 1989 estimated that per capita fresh water; cultivated land, forest and grassland in China comprised 28.1 per cent, 32.3 per cent, 14.3 per cent and 32.3 per cent of the world's per capita average respectively, while per capita reserves of key mineral resources that support the growth of the national economy like petroleum, natural gas and coal in China are only 11 per cent, 45 per cent and 79 per cent of the world average.

44 UN Comtrade (UN Commodity Trade Statistics).

45 GRAIN, 'GRAIN releases data set with over 400 global land grabs', 23 February 2012.

46 *The United Kingdom's Imports of Illegal Timber – An Overview*, report prepared for Global Timber. Available at <http://globaltimber.org.uk/ukillegaltimber.doc>.

47 Richard McGregor, '750,000 a year killed by Chinese pollution', *Financial Times*, 2 July 2007.

48 'Cat bonds begin to come back into play', *Financial Times*, 4 September 2009.

49 The Oakland Institute, *Understanding Land Investment Deals in Africa. Country Report: Tanzania* (Oakland: Oakland Institute, 2011).

50 Polaris Institute and Oakland Institute, 'Understanding land investment deals in Africa: Land grabs leave Africa thirsty', December 2011, <http://polarisinstitute.org/files/OI_brief_land_grabs_leave_africa_thirsty_1.pdf>. http://www.grain.org/bulletin_board/entries/4478-land-grabs-leave-africa-thirsty

51 David Woodward, 'More with less: Rethinking poverty reduction in a changing climate', in Andrew Simms, Dr Victoria Johnson and Dr Michael Edwards, *Other Worlds are Possible: Human Progress in an Age of Climate Change* (London: nef and IIED, 2009).

52 Unpublished draft, David Woodward and Saamah Abdallah (2011), 'When Enough is Enough: Incomes, Well-Being and Plenty Lines'.

53 See uktradeinfo.com data for 2008.

54 Tudge, *Can Britain Feed Itself?*.

55 Simms, Johnson and Edwards, *Other Worlds*.

11. The Momentum

1 Gilles Cuniberti, 'Jurisdiction to prevent the end of the world', ConflictofLaws.net, 1 October 2008.

Cancel the Apocalypse

2 See Simms, *Tescopoly* and Boyle and Simms, *The New Economics*.
3 Bank for International Settlements, *BIS Annual Report 2010/11*.
4 TUC press release, 'Surge in older workers doing unpaid overtime', 22 February 2012.
5 Tom Walker, 'The "lump-of-labor" case against work-sharing: Populist fallacy or marginalist throwback?' in Figart and Golden (ed.), *Working Time*.
6 Marcus Arvan, *Bad News for Conservatives? Moral Judgments and the Dark Triad Personality Traits: A Correlational Study* (2011). Available at <http://ssrn.com/abstract=1903914>.
7 Tim Harford, 'Selfish, dishonest, mean . . . who are you calling an economist?', *Financial Times*, 13 February 2010.
8 See Frank et al., 'Does studying economics inhibit cooperation?'.
9 Yoram Bauman, 'The dismal education', *New York Times*, 16 December 2011.
10 Quoted in Peter Vansittart, *Voices from the Great War* (London: Pimlico, 1998).
11 Solnit, *Wanderlust*.
12 Interview with Mark Hennessy, 'Something Understood', BBC Radio 4, 12 December 2010. Author's transcript.

Picture credits

Select bibliography

Ackerman, Kubi, The Potential for Urban Agriculture in New York City: Growing Capacity, Food Security, & Green Infrastructure (New York: Earth Institute and Columbia University, 2011)

Addison, Paul, *The Road to 1945: British Politics and the Second World War* (1975; London: Random House, 1994, revised edn)

Addison, Paul and Jeremy A. Crang (ed.), *Listening to Britain: Home Intelligence Reports on Britain's Finest Hour – May to September 1940* (London: Bodley Head, 2010)

Albert, Alexandra and Benjamin Reid, *The Contribution of the Advertising Industry to the UK Economy A Creative Industries Report* (London: Credos and The Work Foundation, 2011)

Altucher, James and Douglas Sease, *The Wall Street Journal Guide to Investing in the Apocalypse: Make Money by Seeing Opportunity Where Others See Peril* (New York: Harper Business, 2011)

Armstrong, Karen, *A Short History of Myth* (Edinburgh: Canongate, 2005)

Anderson, Kevin and Alice Bows, 'Reframing the climate change challenge in light of post-2000 emission trends', *Philosophical Transactions of the Royal Society A*, 366:1882 (2008)

Augé, Marc (trans. John Howe), *Non-Places: An Introduction to an Anthropology of Supermodernity* (London: Verso, 1995)

Bargh, John and Tanya Chartrand, 'The unbearable automacity of being', *American Psychologist* 54:7 (1999)

Barry, Frank and Michael Devereux, 'Expansionary fiscal contraction: A theoretical exploration', *Journal of Macroeconomics*, 25 (2003)

Barthel, Stephan, Carol Folke and Johan Colding, 'Social–ecological memory in urban gardens: Retaining the capacity for management of ecosystem services', *Global Environmental Change*, 20:2 (2010)

Berman, Marshall, *All That Is Solid Melts into Air: The Experience of Modernity* (London: Verso, 1983)

Berry, Wendell, *What Are People For?: Essays* (Berkeley: Counterpoint, 1990)

Buehler, Ralph and John Pucher, 'Sustainable transport in Freiburg: Lessons from Germany's environmental capital', *International Journal of Sustainable Transportation*, 5 (2011)

Boyle, David, *The Tyranny of Numbers: Why Counting Can't Make Us Happy* (London: HarperCollins, 2000)

—————, *On the Eighth Day, God Created Allotments* (London: Endeavour Press, 2012)

Boyle, David and Andrew Simms, *The New Economics: A Bigger Perspective* (London: Earthscan, 2010)

Burke, Eleanor, Simon J. Brown and Nikolaos Christidis, 'Modelling the recent evolution of global drought and projections for the twenty-first century with the Hadley Centre climate model', *Journal of Hydrometeorology*, 7:5 (2006)

Cabinet Office Performance and Innovation Unit, *The Energy Review* (London: Cabinet Office Performance and Innovation Unit, 2002)

Centre for Alternative Technology et al., *Zero Carbon Britain 2030: A New Energy Strategy – The Second Report of the Zero Carbon Britain project.* (Machynlleth: Centre for Alternative Technology, 2010)

Chambers, Keith and Anne Chambers, *Unity of Heart: Culture and Change in a Polynesian Atoll Society* (Long Island: Waveland Press, 2001)

Chang, Ha-Joon, *Kicking Away the Ladder: Development Strategy in Historical Perspective* (London: Anthem Press, 2002)

Cohen, Harriet L., Katie Meek and Mary Lieberman, 'Memory and resilience', *Journal of Human Behavior in the Social Environment*, 20 (2010)

Craig E. Colten and Amy R. Sumpter, 'Social memory and resilience in New Orleans', *Natural Hazards*, 48:3 (2009)

Crawford, Matthew, *The Case for Working with Your Hands: Or Why Office Work is Bad for Us and Fixing Things Feels Good* (London: Penguin, 2010)

Daly, Herman E., *Beyond Growth: Economics of Sustainable Development* (Boston, Beacon Press, 1996)

——————, *Ecological Economics and Sustainable Development: Selected Essays of Herman Daly* (Cheltenham: Edward Elgar, 2007)

——————, *Steady-State Economics* (Washington, DC: Island Press, 1991)

Davis, Mike, *Late Victorian Holocausts: El Niño Famines and the Making of the Third World* (London: Verso, 2001)

Dawnay, Emma and Hetan Shah, *Behavioural Economics: Seven Principles for Policy-makers* (London: nef, 2005)

Delhey, Jan, 'From materialist to postmaterialist happiness? National affluence and determinants of life satisfaction in cross-national perspective', *World Values Research*, 2:2 (2009)

De Waal, Frans, *The Age of Empathy: Nature's Lessons for a Kinder Society* (London: Souvenir Press, 2011)

Diamond, Jared, *Collapse: How Societies Choose to Fail or Survive* (London: Allen Lane, 2005)

Ehrenreich, Barbara, *Dancing in the Streets: A History of Collective Joy* (London: Granta, 2007)

Felton, Monica, *Civilian Supplies in Wartime Britain* (London: Ministry of Information, 1945; facsimile reproduction by the Imperial War Museum, London, 2003)

Franco, Manuel, Pedro Orduñez, Benjamín Caballero, José A. Tapia Granados, Mariana Lazo, José Luís Bernal, Eliseo Guallar and Richard S. Cooper, 'Impact of energy intake, physical activity, and population-wide weight loss on cardiovascular disease and diabetes mortality in Cuba, 1980–2005', *American Journal of Epidemiology*, 166:12 (2007

Frank, Robert H., Thomas Gilovich and Dennis T. Regan, 'Does studying economics inhibit cooperation?' *Journal of Economic Perspectives*, 7:2 (1993)

Galbraith, J. K., *The Great Crash, 1929* (New York: Houghton Mifflin, 1954)

————, *Money: Whence It Came, Where It Went* (Boston: Houghton Mifflin, 1975)

Gandy, Matthew, 'Landscapes of disaster: water, modernity, and urban fragmentation in Mumbai', *Environment and Planning*, 40 (2008)

Gilbert, Daniel, *Stumbling on Happiness* (London: Harper Press, 2006)

Golden, Lonnie and Deborah M. Figart (ed.), *Working Time: International Trends, Theory and Policy Perspectives* (London: Routledge, 2000)

Goldsworthy, Adrian, *The Fall of the West: The Death of the Roman Superpower* (London: Weidenfeld & Nicolson, 2009)

Gordon, Natasha and Paul Chatterton, *Taking Back Control: A Journey through Argentina's Popular Uprising* (Leeds: University of Leeds, 2004)

Gordon, Robert J., 'Is US Economic Growth Over? Faltering Innovation Confronts the Six Headwinds', National Bureau for Economic Research Working Paper No. 18315 (2012)

The Green New Deal Group, *The Green New Deal* (London: nef, 2008)

Greenpeace UK, *Decentralising Power: An Energy Revolution for the 21st Century* (London: Greenpeace, 2007)

Griffiths, Clare and Anita Brock, 'Twentieth century mortality trends in England and Wales', *Health Statistics Quarterly*, 18 (2003)

Haldane, Andrew and Robert May, 'Systemic Risk in Banking Ecosystems', *Nature*, 469 (2011)

Hancock, William Keith and Margaret Gowing, *The Lessons of the British War Economy* (London: HMSO, 1949)

Hansen, James, *Storms of my Grandchildren: The Truth about the Coming Climate Catastrophe and our Last Chance to Save Humanity* (London: Bloomsbury, 2009)

Hansen, James, Makiko Sato, Pushker Kharecha, David Beerling, Robert Berner, Valerie Masson-Delmotte, Mark Pagani, Maureen Raymo, Dana L. Royer and James C. Zachos, 'Target atmospheric CO_2: Where should humanity aim?', *Open Atmospheric Science Journal*, 2 (2008)

Hoffmann, Ulrich, *Some Reflections on Climate Change, Green Growth Illusions and Development Space* (Geneva: UNCTAD, 2011)

Hylton, Stuart, *The Darkest Hour: The Hidden History of the Home Front 1939 –1945* (Stroud: Sutton, 2001)

Illich, Ivan, *Tools for Conviviality* (New York: Harper and Row, 1973)

Imai, Katsushi, Raghav Gaiha, Samuel Annim and Veena S. Kulkarni, 'Reducing Malnutrition in Rural India', worldpoverty@manchester (University of Manchester and Brooks World Poverty Institute, 2012)

International Labour Organization, *World of Work Report 2008: Income Inequalities in the Age of Financial Globalization* (Geneva: ILO, 2008)

Iverson, Evan, Robert Jacobson and Brian Limotti, *Response of Washington State Residents to Higher Transportation Costs and Energy Shortages* (Olympia: Washington State Transportation Commission, 1981).

Jacobson, Mark Z., 'Review of solutions to global warming, air pollution, and energy security', *Energy & Environmental Science*, 2 (2009)

Jevons, William, *The Coal Question: An Inquiry Concerning the Progress of the Nation, and the Probable Exhaustion of Our Coal-mines* (London: Macmillan, 1865)

Jones, Nicolette, *The Plimsoll Sensation: The Great Campaign to Save Lives at Sea* (London: Little, Brown, 2006)

Jones, Pip, *Satan's Kingdom: Bristol and the Transatlantic Slave Trade* (Bristol: Past & Present Press, 2007)

Kasser, Tim, *The High Price of Materialism* (Cambridge, MA: MIT Press, 2002)

Kasser, Tim and Aaron Ahuvia, 'Materialistic values and well-being in business students', *European Journal of Social Psychology*, 32 (2002)

Kersley, Helen and Eilis Lawlor, *Grounded: A New Approach to Evaluating Runway 3* (London: nef, 2010)

Keynes, John Maynard, *Essays in Persuasion* (1931; New York: Norton, 1963)
—————, *How to Pay for the War: A Radical Plan for the Chancellor of the Exchequer* (London: Macmillan, 1940)
—————, 'National Self-Sufficiency', *Yale Review*, 22:4 (1933)

Klein, Naomi, *The Shock Doctrine: The Rise of Disaster Capitalism* (Toronto: Vintage, 2008)

Kohn, Alfie, *Punished by Rewards: The Trouble with Gold Stars, Incentive Plans, A's, Praise, and Other Bribes* (Boston: Houghton Mifflin, 1999)

Kuhn, Thomas, *The Structure of Scientific Revolutions* (1962; Chicago: University of Chicago Press, 1996)

Lanchester, John, *Whoops! Why Everyone Owes and No One Can Pay* (London: Allen Lane, 2010)

Lane, Robert, *The Loss of Happiness in Market Democracies* (New Haven: Yale University Press, 2000)

LaSalle, Tim J. and Paul Hepperly, *Regenerative Organic Farming: A Solution to Global Warming* (Kutztown: Rodale Institute, 2008)

Lawlor, Eilis, Helen Kersley and Susan Steed, *A Bit Rich: Calculating the real value to society of different professions* (London: nef, 2009)

Lobell, David B. and Christopher B. Field, 'Global scale climate-crop yield relationships and the impacts of recent warming', *Environmental Research Letters*, 02:014002 (2007)

Lomborg, Bjørn, *The Skeptical Environmentalist: Measuring the Real State of the World* (Cambridge: Cambridge University Press, 2001)

Longmate, Norman, *How We Lived Then: A History of Everyday Life during the Second World War* (1971; London: Pimlico, 2002)

Maher, Neil, *Nature's New Deal: The Civilian Conservation Corps and the Roots of the American Environmental Movement* (Oxford: Oxford University Press, 2008)

Margulis, Lynn and Dorian Sagan, *Microcosmos: Four Billion Years of Microbial Evolution* (Berkeley: University of California Press, 1997, revised edn)

Maugeri, Leonardo, *Oil: The Next Revolution: The Unprecedented Upsurge of Oil Production Capacity and What It Means for the World*, Harvard University report (2012)

McDaniel, Carl N. and John M. Gowdy, *Paradise for Sale: A Parable of Nature* (Berkeley: University of California Press, 2000)

McGuire, Bill, *Waking the Giant: How a Changing Climate Triggers Earthquakes, Tsunamis and Volcanoes* (Oxford: Oxford University Press, 2012)

McKibben, Bill (ed.), *The Global Warming Reader* (London: Penguin, 2012)

Meeker-Lowry, Susan, *Invested in the Common Good* (Philadelphia: New Society, 1995)

Meinshausen, Malte, Nicolai Meinshausen, William Hare, Sarah C. B. Raper, Katja Frieler, Reto Knutti, David J. Frame and Myles R. Allen, 'Greenhouse-gas emission targets for limiting global warming to 2°C', *Nature*, 458 (2009)

Metz, David, *The Limits to Travel: How Far Will You Go?* (London: Earthscan, 2008)

MIT, *The Future of Nuclear Power: An Interdisciplinary MIT Study* (2003; Cambridge MA: Massachusetts Institute of Technology, 2009, updated edn)

Mill, John Stuart, *Principles of Political Economy* (1848)

Morgan, Kenneth, 'Shipping patterns and the Atlantic trade of Bristol, 1749–1770', *William and Mary Quarterly*, 46:3 (1989)

Morison, Elting E. (ed.), *The Letters of Theodore Roosevelt*, vol. 3 (Cambridge MA: Harvard University Press, 1951)

Murray, James and David King, 'Oil's tipping point has passed', *Nature*, 481 (2012)

Norton, Michael and Dan Ariely, 'Building a better America – one wealth quintile at a time', *Perspectives on Psychological Science*, 6:9 (2011)

Nowak, Martin, *Supercooperators: The Mathematics of Evolution, Altruism and Human Behaviour* (Edinburgh: Canongate, 2011)

Olsthoorn, Xander, 'Carbon dioxide emissions from international aviation: 1950–2050', *Journal of Air Transport Management*, 7:2 (2001)

Pawlyn, Michael, *Biomimicry in Architecture* (London: RIBA, 2011)

Pearce, Fred, *The Last Generation: How Nature Will Take Her Revenge for Climate Change* (London: Eden Project Books, 2006)

Peters, Glen P., Tom Boden, Josep G. Canadell, Philippe Ciais, Corrine Le Quéré, Gregg Marland, Michael R. Raupach and Charlie Wilson, 'The mitigation challenge to stay below two degrees', *Nature Climate Change*, 1783 (2012)

Pfeiffer, Dale Allen, *Eating Fossil Fuels: Oil, Food and the Coming Crisis in Agriculture* (Gabriola Island: New Society, 2006)

Pickett, Kate and Richard Wilkinson, *The Spirit Level: Why Equality is Better for Everyone* (London, Allen Lane, 2009)

Piketty, Thomas and Emmanuel Saez, 'Income Inequality in the United States, 1913–1998', *Quarterly Journal of Economics*, 118:1 (2003)

Pimentel, David and Marcia Pimentel, 'Sustainability of meat-based and plant-based diets and the environment', *American Journal of Clinical Nutrition*, 78:3 (2003)

Pink, Daniel, *Drive: The Surprising Truth about What Motivates Us* (Edinburgh: Canongate, 2010)

Pomeranz, Kenneth, *The Great Divergence: China, Europe and the Making of the Modern World Economy* (Princeton: Princeton University Press, 2000)

Portas, Mary, *The Portas Review: An Independent Review into the Future of our High Streets* (London: Mary Portas and The Department for Business Innovation and Skills, 2011)

Pretty, Jules and Parviz Koohafkan, Parviz, *Land and Agriculture: From UNCED, Rio de Janeiro 1992 to WSSD, Johannesburg 2002. A Compendium of Recent Sustainable Development Initiatives in the Field of Agriculture and Land Management: Challenges and Perspectives for the World Summit on Sustainable Development Johannesburg 2002* (Rome: FAO, 2002)

Price, Andrew, *Slow-tech: Manifesto for an Over-wound World* (London: Atlantic, 2009)

Reinert, Erik, *How Rich Countries Got Rich . . . and Why Poor Countries Stay Poor* (London: Constable, 2007)

Riley, Kathy, 'An Ethnography of Community Development in a Neighbourhood of Havana, Cuba', unpublished doctoral thesis, University of Sussex (2008)

Rockström, Johan, Will Steffen, Kevin Noone, Åsa Persson, F. Stuart Chapin III, Eric F. Lambin, Timothy M. Lenton, Marten Scheffer, Carl Folke, Hans Joachim Schellnhuber, Björn Nykvist, Cynthia A. de Wit, Terry Hughes, Sander van der Leeuw, Henning Rodhe, Sverker Sörlin, Peter K. Snyder, Robert Costanza, Uno Svedin, Malin Falkenmark, Louise Karlberg, Robert W. Corell, Victoria J. Fabry, James Hansen, Brian Walker, Diana Liverman, Katherine Richardson, Paul Crutzen and Jonathan A. Foley, 'A safe operating space for humanity', *Nature*, 461 (2009)

Rogers, Deborah, 'Inequality: Why egalitarian societies died out', *New Scientist*, 2875 (2012)

Roodhouse, Mark, 'Rationing returns: a solution to global warming?', paper for History and Policy, March 2007

Ruskin, John, *Unto this Last: Four Essays on the First Principles of Political Economy* (1862)

Sayers, R. S, *History of the Second World War: Financial Policy 1939–45* (London: HMSO, 1956)

Schumpeter, Joseph A, *Capitalism, Socialism and Democracy* (1942; New York: Harper, 1975)

Schwarz, Barry, *The Paradox of Choice: Why More is Less* (London: HarperCollins, 2003)

Sennett, Richard, *The Craftsman* (London: Allen Lane, 2008)

Shell, *Signals & Signposts: Shell Energy Scenarios to 2050* (The Hague: Shell, 2011)

Sen, Amartya, *Poverty and Famines: An Essay on Entitlement and Deprivation* (Oxford: Oxford University Press, 1983)

Simms, Andrew, *Ecological Debt: Global Warming and the Wealth of Nations* (London: Pluto, 2009, second edn)

————, *Tescopoly: How One Shop Came Out On Top and Why It Matters* (London: Constable, 2007)

Simms, Andrew and Joe Smith (ed.), *Do Good Lives Have to Cost the Earth?* (London: Constable, 2008)

Solnit, Rebecca, *Hope in the Dark: The Untold History of People Power* (Edinburgh: Canongate, 2005)

————, *Wanderlust: A History of Walking* (London: Allen Lane, 1999)

Sorrell, Steve, Jamie Speirs, R. Bentley, Adam Brandt and R. Miller, *Global Oil Depletion: An Assessment of the Evidence for a Near-term Peak in Global Oil Production*, UKERC report (2009)

Spratt, Stephen, Andrew Simms, Eva Nietzert and Josh Ryan Collins, *The Great Transition: A Tale of How it Turned Out Right* (London: nef, 2010)

Stallibrass, Alison, *Being Me and Also Us: Lessons from the Peckham Experiment* (Edinburgh: Scottish Academic Press, 1989)

Stiglitz, Joseph, *Globalization and its Discontents* (London: Allen Lane, 2002)

Tainter, Joseph A., *The Collapse of Complex Societies* (Cambridge: Cambridge University Press, 1988)

Tudge, Colin, *Can Britain Feed Itself? Should Britain Feed Itself?* (Oxford: LandShare.org, 2009)

Turner, Adair, *Economics after the Crisis: Objectives and Means* (Boston: MIT Press, 2012)

Turner, E. S, *Roads to Ruin: The Shocking History of Social Reform* (1950; London: Penguin, 1966)

Turner, Graham, 'A comparison of "The Limits to Growth" with 30 years of reality', *Global Environmental Change*, 18 (2008)

UNDP, *The Human Development Report 1996: Economic Growth and Human Development* (New York: United Nations, 1996)

UNEP-UNCTAD Capacity-building Task Force on Trade, Environment and Development, *Organic Agriculture and Food Security in Africa* (Geneva and New York: United Nations, 2008)

Walpole, Sarah C., David Prieto-Merino, Phil Edwards, John Cleland, Gretchen Stevens and Ian Roberts, 'The weight of nations: an estimation of adult human biomass', *BMC Public Health*, 12:439 (2012)

Walton, John and David Seddon, *Free Markets and Food Riots: The Politics of Global Adjustment* (Oxford: Blackwell, 1994)

Wang, Shenghui, David R. Just and Per Pinstrup-Andersen, 'Bt-cotton and secondary pests', *International Journal of Biotechnology*, 10:2/3 (2008)

WWF, Ecofys and OMA, *The Energy Report: 100% Renewable Energy by 2050* (Gland: WWF, 2011)

Index

Abbey, Edward, 332

Abundance project in Sheffield, 320–1

accountancy firms, 154, 358

Action for Happiness, 124

Adams, Mary, 201

adaptability and change: biomimicry, 76–8, 150–2, 309; failures from history, 173–5, 176–8, 179, 184–5, 186, 187; food supplies and, 108, 320–2; human ability for, 12, 101–2, 216; inevitability of change, 14–15, 170; initiatives from below, 11–12; innovation and, 12, 44, 101–2, 105–6, 180–2; rapid transformations, 5, 12, 13, 170, 189, 193–5, 198–203, 206–10, 216; renewable energy schemes and, 256–61, 268–70; shift to producer society, 312–13; transport and, 99–102, 105–9; well-being and, 110, 122; *see also* transition, low carbon

Addison, Paul, 200

advertising and marketing, 116, 118, 120, 282–6, 303–7; advertising-free zones, 124, 303, 305–7; aimed at children, 120–1, 303, 306–7; of alcohol, 39–40, 92, 116, 283, 286–7, 303; calls for better regulation of, 39–40, 124, 287, 299–300; checks and balances on, 303–4, 305–7; claims made in favour of, 283–4, 286, 288, 289, 297; conflicts of interest and, 287–8; 'confusion marketing', 288–9; falsely differentiated

goods and, 288; global spending on (2012), 283; happiness and, 110, 116, 298; individuality paradox in, 92; in-flight shopping, 91–2, 109, 123; link with consumption levels, 283, 284, 288, 298; passive consumer and, 13, 285, 292, 309, 401; promotion of disposability, 313; as propaganda wing of consumerist ideology, 105, 298; soft marketing approaches, 293–4; of tobacco, 92, 116, 283, 291, 303; in United States, 298, 304–5; *see also* public relations (PR)

Advertising Association, 287, 298

Advertising Standards Authority (ASA), 293

Aeronautical Research Committee, US, 191

'aerosol loading, atmospheric', 66, 67

Africa: debt crisis caused by oil crises, 347–8; fallacy of composition and, 348, 371; foreign land-grabs in (post-2006), 223, 366, 368–70; land degradation by industrial farming, 246; negative consequences of neoliberal reform, 347–51, 369–71; 'resource curse' and, 165, 345, 368; riots over water privatisation, 340; Sahel region, 247; new 'scramble for Africa', 368; small farms, 233, 244, 245, 247–8, 249, 370; stressed water sources in, 231, 232, 370; sub-Saharan, 74, 244, 249, 347